Literature and Social Practice

Literature and Social Practice

EDITED BY

Philippe Desan, Priscilla Parkhurst Ferguson, and Wendy Griswold

The University of Chicago Press
Chicago and London

Most of the essays in this volume originally appeared in CRITICAL INQUIRY, Spring 1988 (volume 14, number 3).

The University of Chicago Press, Chicago 60637
The University of Chicago Press, Ltd., London
© 1988, 1989 by The University of Chicago
All rights reserved. Published 1989
Printed in the United States of America
95 94 93 92 91 90 89 88   5 4 3 2 1

Library of Congress Cataloging-in-Publication Data

Literature and social practice / edited by Philippe Desan, Priscilla
   Parkhurst Ferguson, and Wendy Griswold.

    p.   cm.
  Includes bibliographical references and index.
  ISBN 0-226-14341-4 (alk. paper): $30.00 (est.).—ISBN
0-226-14342-2 (pbk.: alk. paper): $13.50 (est.)
  1. Criticism.   2. Literature and society.   I. Desan, Philippe.
II. Ferguson, Priscilla Parkhust.   III. Griswold, Wendy.
PN98.S6L58   1989
801'.95'05—dc19

        88-38577
        CIP

The paper used in this publication meets the minimum requirements of the American National Standard for Information Sciences—Permanence of Paper for Printed Library Materials, ANSI Z39.48-1984. ⊚ ™

Contents

On the cover: "Le Souffleur" by Honoré Daumier, Le Charivari, 7 February 1870. Reprinted from Honoré Daumier, Lithographien: 1861–1872 (Munich).

They ran about all over with the mirror.

Editors' Introduction:
Mirrors, Frames, and Demons: Reflections on the Sociology of Literature

Philippe Desan, Priscilla Parkhurst Ferguson, and Wendy Griswold

Paradoxes

The sociology of literature, in the first of many paradoxes, elicits negations before assertions. It is not an established field or academic discipline. The concept as such lacks both intellectual and institutional clarity. Yet none of these limitations affects the vitality and rigor of the larger enterprise. We use the sociology of literature here to refer to the cluster of intellectual ventures that originate in one overriding conviction: the conviction that literature and society necessarily explain each other. Scholars and critics of all kinds congregate under this outsize umbrella only to differ greatly in their sense of what they do and what the sociology of literature does. They subscribe to a wide range of theories and methods. Many would not accept the sociology of literature as an appropriate label for their own work; others would refuse it to their colleagues. Nevertheless, every advocate agrees that a sociological practice is essential to literature. For the sociology of literature does not constitute just one more approach to literature. Because it insists upon a sociology of literary knowledge and literary practice within the study of literature, the sociology of literature raises questions basic to all intellectual inquiry.

The sociology of literature begins in diversity. The way that it combines the ancient traditions of art with the modern practices of social science makes the very term something of an oxymoron. There is not one sociology of literature, there are many sociological practices of literature, each of which operates within a particular intellectual tradition and specific institutional context. These practices cross basic divisions within the contemporary intellectual field, especially within the university. Inherently interdisciplinary, the sociology of literature is subject to constant reformulation as scholars re-evaluate their disciplines. In consequence, disciplinary boundaries seem less rigid, less logical, and, hence, less authoritative than ever before. Even so—and this is another paradox of the sociology of literature—any sociological conception of literature is best situated in terms of an original discipline and its institutional setting. However frequently individual scholars cross over disciplinary lines, the fundamental divisions retain their force.

The most basic boundary line divides literary studies and social science, each of which confronts literature on a separate terrain. The fundamental opposition between the two determines work in the sociology of literature more than might be supposed for such avowedly interdisciplinary work. Conflict extends to every level, from means and ends to theory and method, to the questions each field asks, and to the answers each proposes. Where social scientists use literature to reveal, exemplify, or interpret social process, literary critics regard the literary work as an end in itself. Literary studies focus on the aesthetic, even though few interpreters bother to define what they intend by the concept. Then too, critical judgment in literary studies entails participation in the production, diffusion, and legitimation of literary canons and of the institutions that support and are supported by those canons. This process of evaluation, in turn, encourages a series of distinctive conflations. Social valorization of the art object tends to interact with and confirm the mystique of art. The literary judge—whether critic, teacher, scholar, or creative writer—identifies, often fervently, with the work of literature. No social science instills comparable psychic investment in the literary object.

The very terms by which literary studies and sociology name their objects of study disclose the enormous gulf between the two. Literary critics look at *works, texts, writers,* and *readers.* They speculate about the *creation, reception,* and *interpretation* of literature. Social scientists, on the other hand, discuss *books* and literary *institutions* and dwell upon the *production, distribution,* and *consumption* of cultural *products.* In an American

Philippe Desan is an assistant professor of French at the University of Chicago. The author of *Naissance de la méthode: Machiavel, La Ramée, Bodin, Montaigne, Descartes* (1987), he is completing a book entitled *Les Commerces de Montaigne: l'émergence du discours économique au XVIᵉ siècle.* **Priscilla Parkhurst Ferguson** is professor of French at the University of Illinois at Chicago; she is the author of *Literary France: The Making of a Culture* (1987). **Wendy Griswold,** associate professor of sociology at the University of Chicago, recently published *Renaissance Revivals: City Comedy and Revenge Tragedy in the London Theatre, 1576–1980.*

department of sociology, for example, the sociology of literature generally focuses on organizations and markets, centralized and decentralized publishing, networks of editors and booksellers, copyright laws and censorship norms, strategies of diffusion, and the reading habits of particular social groups. The specific nature of the art object—what makes a text "literature"—is seldom at issue.

A second tension sets theory against empirical work. In some settings this fundamental split coincides with actual divisions between disciplines, but more often it cuts across those divisions. Sociology, at least the American variants thereof, tends toward empirical work primarily because sociologists like to ask questions that are amenable to quantification. At the same time, although the term is rarely employed, the work of many literary historians and critics also qualifies as empirical. Interpretations of texts do not meet the criterion of testability that distinguishes the empirical work of social science, but the groundwork of traditional literary interpretation raises a comparable prospect. Standard critical tasks create verifiable data through biographical investigation, publishing history, textual variants, concordances, and the like. Indeed, the constraint empirical work has exercised on literary studies can be gauged in the reactions of contemporary literary theories, some of which have attacked just this empirical side of the once customary labors of the literary scholar. The whole issue is then complicated by the fact that empirical literary scholarship and contemporary literary theories alike disavow or, at the very least, studiously ignore the social context of literature: both, in fact, challenge the sociology of literature.

The predisposition to theoretical discussion or to empirical analysis is of great moment for the definition of the sociology of literature. Wary of what they disdain as so much theoretical verbiage, American scholars of literature and society, whether social scientists or literary critics, have tended to produce largely empirical studies—case studies of particular literary institutions (publishers, booksellers, academies, journals), discussions of given literary figures and their work ("Social phenomena in the work of X . . . ," "Literature and Society in Z . . . "). In general, an American sociology of literature has deliberately adopted an empirical approach.

In Europe, on the contrary, the sociology of literature encompasses a broader range of humanistic undertakings. This greater resonance in European intellectual circles owes much to the prevailing theoretical climate. In contrast to the American inclination to fix intellectual activity within a specific academic discipline and with respect to a given subject, European scholars are far more likely to seek a theoretical locus for their work. Because it allows, encourages, and requires crossing of disciplinary boundaries, theory facilitates the interdisciplinary perspective that is essential to any sociological view of literature. Or rather, theory subsumes such boundaries and the intellectual divisions they represent. Inevitably, the closer research remains to empirical work, the stronger the influence of any given subject and the more difficult it becomes to see beyond the material at hand. Traditional literary history just like much social science is bound to case studies as predominantly theoretical work can never be. These epistemological differences between American and European intellectual practices reveal the disjunctions and the strains in the many sociological practices of literature on each side of the Atlantic. It is not surprising that the sociology of literature has a greater following in Europe where intellectuals like Michel Foucault, Roland Barthes, and Raymond Williams move easily between disciplines and use their work to address issues of broad intellectual and social significance.

The institutional organization of intellectual life accentuates certain of these predispositions and minimizes others. The preponderant American empiricism promotes what seems to be an innate skepticism about "foreign" theoretical perspectives that seem to remove the critic from literature, whether it is regarded as a text by literary critics or as a social product by social scientists. The evident respect for disciplinary boundaries visible in American universities means that many academics think of "interdisciplinary" as a code word for indiscriminant borrowing and a fundamental disregard for crucial disciplinary distinctions. Perhaps, in some perverse sense, interdisciplinary work needs the partitions erected by departments. In any case, despite the recent proliferation of interdisciplinary committees in American universities, departments mostly prevail. To get ahead in the university, the academic—student or professor—must find a niche. Finding a niche means finding a specialization, and that still, in the United States, means a departmental affiliation.

By contrast, the very different organization of European universities stimulates movement between disciplines. The small number of chairs in any discipline and in most European universities accords the individual professor considerable latitude in defining and redefining a field. Barthes, in effect, institutionalized his particular conception of semiotics by calling the position to which he was elected at the Collège de France a Chair of Semiology. Researchers, and to a lesser degree students, choose a professor (who may well also direct a research center) with as much care as they select a discipline. Here, disciplinary labels often mislead, which is why for European scholars it is imperative to know *whose* brand of history a historian actually practices, *whose* sociology, *whose* sociology of literature.

In both Europe and the United States, though for different reasons, the sociology of literature occupies a marginal position within the academy. That position is likely to remain peripheral. Inevitably, the interdisciplinary nature of the sociology of literature must struggle against the disciplinary organization of universities and the ideological rigidities of schools of thought. The lack of consensus over ends and means, the absence of agreement over central concepts erect an even greater obstacle to institutionalization. Without some elements of common understanding the sociology of literature will never possess significant institutional space—

the space filled by university departments and research centers, by courses, majors, degrees, and appointments within existing departments, or by a professional support network, the journals, colloquia, and associations that assure the exchange of information and ideas essential to any organized intellectual enterprise. To develop as a field in American universities, the sociology of literature would need to follow the path followed by American studies beginning in the 1930s, by comparative literature in the 1950s and 1960s, and by fields as different as semiotics and women's studies in the 1970s and 1980s. In Europe, it would need to find support in chairs within the university system. In both places the sociology of literature would need to define a set of shared problems and methods; it would have to fix a research agenda. But resolutions of its contradictions would entail sacrificing the diversity that makes the sociology of literature so exciting an adventure. The final paradox is that sociologists of literature might not want to pay that price.

Legacies

The sociology of literature owes its current disarray at least in part to the conflicting traditions that are its intellectual heritage. Like sociology itself, the sociology of literature arose in the nineteenth century, a product of its many revolutions. Momentous changes in the intellectual landscape notwithstanding, a sociological perspective on literature faced obstacles that were numerous and significant. On the philosophical front, Kant's separation of aesthetics from metaphysics and ethics removed literature and art to a world apart, beyond the contingencies of the material world. Closer to specifically literary concerns, the insistence of classical aesthetics upon the universality of art similarly removed literary works from the influence of any one milieu. Romanticism rebelled against classical aesthetics on many counts. Yet the romantic conception of genius effectively took the writer out of society by defining him (the stereotype was almost exclusively masculine) in terms of divine inspiration. Much as Kantian aesthetics abstracted art itself, a certain romanticism detached the artist from any relevant social context.

Other aspects of romanticism proved more favorable to a sociological perception of literature. Against the forces that denied the relevance of material factors, certain currents of thought supported a reconceptualization of the relationship between literature and society. Expressly relevant to the sociology of literature were Voltaire's social history (*The Age of Louis XIV*, 1751), Johann Herder's literary nationalism and the Sturm und Drang movement of the 1780s, and Germaine de Staël's assignment of characteristic literary traditions to the vagaries of climate (*On Literature*, 1800). Out of these disparate elements romanticism fashioned a distinctive and inherently sociological perspective on literature which invoked particular cultural traditions to clarify the essential differences between literatures.

In the mid and late nineteenth century the sociology of literature gathered momentum from the combined forces of realism and the novels it inspired, from the positivism of Comte, and from science. The humanitarian and properly political concerns evident in the social novels of the mid nineteenth century and thereafter construed literature as the record, and even more the critique of the emergent bourgeois, capitalist society. The theory of realism on which these novels drew fortified their assumptions and legitimated their practice. With its stress on the particular, the quotidian, and the assumed equivalence of the sign and the referent, the realism identified with these novels offered exemplary grounds for the critical stance adopted by the novel toward this same society. And finally, the positivism bequeathed by Comte and amplified by a pervasive scientism encouraged a belief in progress and in the possibility of discrete analyses of social units. With enough care in definition, positivists maintained, anything could be analyzed—virtue and vice, as Taine once contended in a notorious comparison, as easily as sugar and vitriol. Science acknowledged no bounds; literature came under its dominion as fully and as logically as any material factor.

Romanticism, realism, and positivism each made a signal contribution to the rethinking of literary relations necessary to a truly sociological conception of literature. But the primary impetus to the sociology of literature came not from any of these but rather from Marx and his theory of knowledge and society. Marxian theory and Marxist critiques of society have been the driving force for the sociology of literature from the beginning. The concepts of ideology, alienation, and class consciousness are central to European sociological practices of literature, and those American literary critics who deem their work sociological tend to place themselves within the European theoretical tradition that comes out of Marx. If there is a dominant lineage in the sociology of literature, it derives from latter-day Marxist critics like Georg Lukács, Lucien Goldmann, and Louis Althusser, writers who have heavily influenced European scholarship and who are gradually becoming better known in the United States.

Marxist theory grounded literature not in a vague ethos of *Zeitgeist* or *génie* or in traditions that stretch back to antiquity, but in the social, political, and above all economic and ideological structures of contemporary society. The Marxian division of society into intellectual superstructure and economic base correlated literature and the writer with specific social milieux, with a unique economic system, and with the class relations and the ideologies sustained by that system. Marxism sees literature as it sees all knowledge as a reflection of the economic infrastructure of society. What is the exact nature of the associations between infrastructure and superstructure? Where is causal responsibility? How is influence passed on? Mediated through what individuals or institutions or ideas? Even today these questions bedevil Marxist criticism of literature and the arts, but they remain the questions to ask.

Certainly, the same questions bear upon the sociology of literature today. Because the problems raised by Marxist analyses apply virtually across the board, Marxism can be said to set the agenda even for those who most emphatically reject Marxist theories. The command of Marxism lies much less in its highly problematic and hotly contested theories of literature than in the force of the metaphor from which those theories derive. The mirror—literature as the "reflection" of society—has currency well beyond Marxism. In one way or another the reflection model supports practically all work in the sociology of literature. Indeed, the strenuous efforts of critics to circumvent the mirror attest to the seduction of the metaphor. Mikhail Bakhtin's "adequacy," Lukács' "totality," Goldmann's "homology" and "world vision," Terry Eagleton's "Literary Mode of Production" (LMP), Alain Viala's "prisms," Raymond Williams' attempt to elude the causal relationship between infrastructure and superstructure, and even Pierre Bourdieu's "field"—all attempt to invent a theoretical concept, and a metaphor, adequate to the task of relating literature to society.

The reflection model advanced by Marxist theory spoke all the more forcefully to nineteenth-century literary intellectuals because of its base in nineteenth-century literary practice. Realism relied on the mirror quite as much as Marxism. After all, well before Marx, Stendhal defined the novel as a "mirror carried along a road." Not for the last time a radical social theory went hand in glove with a decidedly conservative theory of literature. As the theory of realism legitimated novelistic practice, so Marxist theory and practice rested upon and ratified the mirror as a model for criticism and as a metaphor for the relationship of literature and society. This shared metaphor does much to clarify the attraction of realist fiction for sociological studies of literature. It was no doubt predictable that Marx and Engels and so many since should have considered the nineteenth-century realist novel the best possible mirror of society: it also mirrored Marxist theory.

Contemporary literary theories pose a radical challenge to this nexus of social theory and literary practice on which the sociology of literature has so long relied. In redefining literature these theories forced a reconceptualization of all literary relations. The disaggregation of the sign effected by linguistic theory subverted the connection between text and referent. Semiotics exacerbated this fragmentation by subjecting the literary work to the same kinds of analyses as any other production of signs. No longer does creative genius have the final word. The promotion of the reader in contemporary criticism displaced the writer from the center of literary study. Interpretations that pay no heed whatsoever to the author undermine the authority of the writer. The literary work, too, forfeited its preeminence, and literature as a collective phenomenon relinquished its mystique.

Logically, the incorporation of literature into a general linguistic or semiotic order should favor the conjunction of literary theory and the sociology of literature. Other facets of contemporary theories, however, effectively block cooperation. The sociology of literature opens literature to society; literary theory turns works back on themselves, enclosing the text within the linguistic order. Reaching outside of that order requires reaching outside of the theory. Exploring the social order, on the other hand, sends research in many different directions at once, and the considerable time such exploration takes may be more than many are willing to spend in the face of vocational pressures to complete a degree, find a job, get tenure. Focusing on the text alone allows greater concentration of effort, and hence more obvious access to intellectual specializations. These strategic advantages certainly play a significant role in the favor enjoyed in past and present American academic circles by a variety of formalist approaches, from New Criticism to deconstructive theory. They join in a collective denial of the social and historical components of any text.

Those scholars who do invest the effort to move beyond the text will discover that the very formulation commonly employed—literature and society—fosters an opposition between texts and institutions, between literary studies and sociological practices—precisely those oppositions that the sociology of literature should surmount. The dichotomies become all the more powerful to the degree that they respect a "logical" division of intellectual labor. The antagonism, as durable as it is simplistic, offers further testimony to the power of the reflection metaphor. Theory and institution betray similar conceptions of social and intellectual organization. By working from the opposition between literature and society, the reflection model justifies disciplinary boundaries that similarly divide up knowledge about the world. These boundaries between literary studies and the social sciences, in return, support the reflection theory and its assumption of an absolute division between material reality and intellectual activity. The reciprocal relationship between theoretical model and institutional setting strengthens each. Although discussions of texts as well as institutions become ever more sophisticated, few studies effectively challenge the principle of division upon which this work depends or the model that it accredits. Although most critics strenuously reject the naive perception of literature and society implied by the reflection model, the mirror endures in practice even as it is denied in theory. If the reflection model has been discredited, it has not been replaced.

Perspectives

A metaphor that cannot be avoided deserves closer attention. If we examine the mirror more closely, we may find that the metaphor actually

the shattered that mirror misreflects

serves the sociology of literature in unexpected ways. The marvelously revealing mirror in Hans Christian Andersen's "The Snow Queen" offers a case in point. In this tale a demon invents a unique mirror: it does not reflect, it systematically misreflects. Andersen's mirror shrinks and distorts every good and beautiful thing, and it magnifies everything evil or ugly. In this glass pleasant landscapes look like boiled spinach, normal people appear hideous, and kind thoughts become wicked grins.

The demon creator appears mildly amused by his invention, but his students, simple reflectionists all, take it very seriously:

> All the pupils in the demon's school—for he kept a school—reported that a miracle had taken place: now for the first time, they said, it was possible to see what the world and mankind were really like. They ran about everywhere with the mirror, till at last there was not a country or a person which had not been seen in this distorting mirror.[1]

Eventually the mirror breaks. Shards of glass fly through the world and lodge in people's eyes and hearts. These shards retain the peculiarities of the mirror, so that everyone sees the world through bent, distorted, and misshapen images.

Like the demon's fantastic mirror, literature presents structured misreflections, which magnify or diminish certain aspects of reality, twist some or leave others out altogether. The sociology of literature challenges these mirrors and their inventors, examines their misreflections, their causes and consequences. It shows how and why a particular text or genre or period or writer reflects in one way and not in another; it specifies the properties of the mirror that determine its (mis)reflections.

The mirror of "The Snow Queen" also boasts an ornate frame and three demons to carry it about the world. That frame and those demons too belong within the purview of the sociology of literature. Critics who focus on the reflections or misreflections of literature usually neglect the frame, that is, the institutional and intellectual context of reflection. Such critics are even less likely to consider the demons, that is, the agents of diffusion and canonization. In sum, the sociology of literature makes a point of what others overlook. It concentrates upon those who hold the mirror. Many studies explore the literary text or literary institutions or writers. A sociology of literature requires the integration of text, institution, and individual—mirror, frame, and demons.

If no intellectual practice exists apart from the subject of investigation or away from the framework within which that investigation is pursued, it is equally significant for the sociology of literature that no inquiry

1. Hans Christian Andersen, *Andersen's Fairy Tales*, trans. E. V. Lucas and H. B. Paull (New York, 1946), pp. 108–9.

occurs independently of the inquirer. These shards in the eye of the perceiver also figure conspicuously in the sociology of literature. By including the individual looking at the mirror, the shards in Andersen's story take the metaphor to its logical and necessary conclusion. A mirror assumes an observer, who assesses the image, evaluates the reflection, and places both in perspective. The sociology of literature must take account of this primal act of interpretation. The singlemindedness of disciplinary training, of intellectual circles frequented and artistic traditions assimilated, of social horizons and, more simply, of hunches, biases, idiosyncracies—these are the shards that limit perception. Just as every mirror misreflects, so too, because of these shards, every observer misperceives. As all literature represents structured misreflections, so all interpretation and analysis build on structured misperceptions. When the reflection model incorporates the onlooker as well as the mirror and the frame, the metaphor becomes richer, more complex, and in the last analysis, absolutely essential to the sociology of literature. The necessary incorporation of the observer into the observation, the confrontation of the critic with the literary mirror, its frame and its demons, opens into a truer sociology of literary practices.

Every sociological practice of literature must determine the place where it stands, the position from which it will agree to interpret the world. The decided advantage of Marxism, an advantage that does much to explain its hold over the sociology of literature, has to do with the strong stand that it takes. Whatever its limitations, Marxism creates an unequivocal perspective for looking at the mirror. In looking beyond those limitations, students of literature and society would do well to remember that only through a clearly defined perspective can we hope to elucidate the inevitable variation in the sociology of literature and the disagreements among its proponents. The essays that follow, diverse, even contradictory, are bound by the simultaneous impossibility and necessity of looking beyond the mirror. This predicament at once defines the sociology of literature and explains the vitality of the enterprise and the commitment of its partisans.

Sociology of Literature in Retrospect

Leo Lowenthal

Translated by Ted R. Weeks

For more than a half century I have primarily concerned myself with the sociology of literature and the problem of mass culture. With financial support from the Institute for Social Research at the University of Frankfurt, I began in 1926 with studies on German writers in the nineteenth century.[1] In these studies one may discern the socially critical spirit which motivated this group of young scholars at the Institute to reject conventional research methods and to seek a new and bolder mode of analyzing material in the social and human sciences—in short, to dare to break through the walls of the academic ivory tower where specialists pursued their professional interests without any social or moral consciousness. I had the privilege of being one of the first members of this group, which I joined in 1926 at the invitation of Max Horkheimer and Friedrich Pollock.

The years of my academic training were devoted to the study of sociology and literature. Later, in my first independent work, I attempted to apply what I had learned from Marx, Freud, and the great philosophical tradition of Europe to a new appraisal of European literature since the Renaissance. Like many other intellectuals in my circles of that time, I was convinced of the decadence of Western society. All of us felt Hitler's threatening advance and by the same token considered the rest of the

First presented in Summer 1981 at the Free University in Berlin and the Max Planck Institute in Starnberg.

1. See Leo Lowenthal, *Schriften, Das burgerliche Bewußtsein in der literatur* (Frankfurt, 1981), 2:301 ff.; in English, see *Communication in Society* (New Brunswick, N.J., 1986), 2:221 ff.

so-called civilized world to be damaged. We strove, each according to his own knowledge and inclination, to interpret historical and contemporary problems in such a way as to reveal their socially regressive or progressive character. We rejected the concept of a "value-free science" as an unpardonable renunciation of the moral responsibility of those who, amid the general misery of average people, had the good fortune to lead the life of an intellectual. If some of the formulations in what follows appear partisan or even angry, I offer no apologies. On the contrary, I would be pleased at such accusations. There was reason enough for anger— in the scientific enterprise as well as in public life.

Since my school days I have been attracted to literature, and it is certainly no coincidence that I spent several years as a German teacher at a *Gymnasium* in Frankfurt before joining the Institute. I suspect that from the onset I tended toward literary criticism, for as a high school student and young teacher I had experienced the utterly banal approach to the teaching of literature practiced by most instructors and supported by the officially approved textbooks. More than anything, however, I was irritated by the utterly conventional choice of literary texts. Since I lived through the years after World War I as a politically rebellious if not out-and-out revolutionary young man, it seemed to me quite natural to apply the practical experience gained in school and in politics to my theoretical endeavors within the academy.

I soon discovered that I was quite isolated in my attempts to pursue the sociology of literature. In any case, one searched almost in vain for allies if one wanted to approach a literary text from the perspective of a critical theory of society. To be sure, there were Franz Mehring's articles which I read with interest and profit; but despite the admirable decency and the uncompromising political radicalism of the author, his writings hardly went beyond the limits of a socialist journalist who wrote in essentially the same style about literature as about politics and the economy. Georg Lukács hadn't yet published his impressive series of essays on Marxist aesthetics and interpretation of literature. Of course, I was deeply touched and influenced by his fine little book, *The Theory of the Novel* (1920), which

---

Leo Lowenthal is professor emeritus of sociology at the University of California, Berkeley. He is also professor emeritus at the University of Frankfurt in West Germany. His collected works have been published in five volumes in German (1980–87) and in a parallel English edition. Lowenthal's autobiographical writings, edited by Martin Jay, will appear in the fall of 1987 under the title *An Unmastered Past*. Lowenthal's present studies deal with German postmodernism. **Ted R. Weeks** is a graduate student at the University of California, Berkeley, specializing in imperial Russian history.

I practically learned by heart. Besides Levin Schücking's small volume on the sociology of literary taste, the only other major influence I can recall was George Brandes' monumental work on the literary currents of the nineteenth century,

Nonetheless, I had the courage, not to say hubris, to plan an ambitious, socially critical series on French, English, Spanish, and German literature, the beginning of which was to be formed by the above-mentioned studies. My attention was especially focused on the writers and literary schools which the German literary establishment either punished by total silence (for example, "Young Germany" and Friedrich Spielhagen) or raised up into the clouds of idealistic babble (Goethe and the Romantics) or relegated to quasi-folkloric anthropology (C. F. Meyer and Gottfried Keller).

In these studies, I limited myself to the narrative forms of literature; for reasons which I hold to be sociologically and artistically valid, I believe that novels and stories represent the most significant aspect of German literature in the nineteenth century. While I in no way feel ashamed of these documents of my youth, I am conscious of their weaknesses. If I were to write them over again, I would certainly be less sure of some of the direct connections I drew between literature and writers on the one hand, and the social infrastructure on the other. In later publications I attempted to analyze with greater circumspection the mediation between substructure and superstructure, between social currents and ideologies; but my views on the social world and the necessity to combine social theory and literary analysis have not changed in any essential way. In the last decades the sociology of literature has become progressively more fashionable. The writings of my contemporaries have often amazed me because some—frequently in unnecessarily complicated and esoteric language—are so concerned with "mediation" that the connections between social being and social consciousness became almost obscured.

1

The first issue of the *Zeitschrift für Sozialforschung*—the only one we managed to publish in Germany before the Hitler-night descended—gives an indication of what Critical Theory means: namely, a perspective, based on a shared critical fundamental attitude, which applies to all cultural phenomena without ever claiming to be a system. It includes critical analysis of philosophy, economics, psychology, music, and literature.

Critical Theory—a term, by the way, which we only began to use in the late thirties—should not, then, be understood as anything more than this collective "common denominator." As the only survivor of the founding years in the twenties, I feel almost ill at ease. . . . Why should I survive and not the others, who in 1926 invited me to join an intellectual alliance they had created in an institutionalized form two years earlier?

We did not speak of "Critical Theory" at that time, and the thought of a "school" was certainly far from us. We were and remained "Nay-sayers" in the tradition of Hegel's particular form of negation; each one of us tried to express what was wrong in his particular field and, therefore, in our society. We were consciously on the periphery of established power. Even now, as you will see, this position on the periphery, this marginality, remains for me in my work and perhaps even in my own perception of life the most important category. I have been guided in the last fifty years by my unbroken commitment to the European literary heritage and simultaneously to the critique of commodity and word production for a manipulated and manipulable mass market. I shall try to sketch my critical approach.

2

To start with the most important thing right away: art and consumer goods are to be strictly held apart, and I cannot accept any of the current attempts by radical circles both here and in the United States to do away with this distinction. To be sure, the consumption of high art can also turn into mass culture and play its part in manipulating society. I only need to remind you of the role of Wagner during the Hitler years, about which Theodor Adorno has written extensively. More peculiar examples are found in the history of theater direction, for example, when bourgeois common sense trivializes the socially inherent tragedy of marriage and love. Here I am thinking, for example, of an English production of *Othello* in the eighteenth century when the Moor does not kill Desdemona in the final scene but rather realizes his own mistake and asks her for forgiveness so that they can be eternally happy on earth; or when at the turn of the century in a staging of Ibsen's *Doll's House* in Munich, at the end of the play, Nora does not close the door from the outside but from within and returns to her boring husband—for, after all, the place of the woman is in the home. These are certainly examples which reflect the social climate. On the other hand, certain materials, originally produced as articles of consumption can sometimes—if seldom—pass into the realm of folk art or rather of folkloric mythology. But those are borderline cases. I also must not neglect to point out certain differences between the American and the European scene. In the United States the sociology of literature is more or less limited to content analysis and the study of the effects of mass culture with particular emphasis on commercial and political propaganda. The model used in these studies is behavioristic, that is, unhistorical. Sociology of literature in the sense of an analysis of art remains suspect. I sense today in Europe an inclination to perceive a work of art merely as a manifestation of ideology, which strips it of its specific integrity, that is, its historically conditioned but also rationally

creative and cognitive role. To put it in a more provocative form: Marxist *Marxist*
literary criticism is not only totally adequate but indispensable in the
analysis of mass culture. However, it must be applied with utter caution
to art itself and must, as a critique of social illusions, limit itself to the
residues which are unequivocally ideological in nature.

In even stronger terms: art teaches and mass culture is learned; that
is to say, a sociological analysis of art must be cautious, supplementary,
and selective while a sociological analysis of mass culture must be all-
inclusive, for its products are nothing less than the phenomena and
symptoms of the process of the individual's self-resignation in a wholly
administered society.

3

I would like now to speak of the sociology of literature as art. Adorno *Adorno*
once said: "Works of art . . . have their greatness only insofar as they let
speak what ideology conceals. They transcend, whether they want to or
not, false consciousness." Literature is not ideology: we are not engaged
in research on ideology; rather, we have to focus our attention on the
special truth, the specifically cognitive aspect, which the literary work
imparts. This focus is not equivalent to any version of "new criticism";
on the contrary, it is a concern with the social history of art and its
reception, as suggested in Marx's comments on Greek tragedy and the
novels of Balzac. At this point I would like to identify the great themes
of literature as I perceive them from a sociologically critical perspective.
First of all, the most general. Literature is the only dependable source
for human consciousness and self-consciousness, for the individual's relationship to the world as experience. The process of socialization, that
is, the social ambience of the private, the intimate, and the individual,
is raised to consciousness by the artist for his time as well as for our time,
and thereby functions as a constant corrective to our false consciousness.
Awareness of this aspect of art has only come to be an important issue
on the intellectual agenda during the last fifty years, as the Western
world entered into a severe crisis with the rise of totalitarianism. The
sociology of art is indeed one of the owls of Minerva. Sociology of literature
rightly understood should interpret what seems most removed from
society as the most valid key to the understanding of society and especially
of its defects. Psychoanalysis, by the way, in revealing the social dimension
of the most intimate aspects of body and psyche, is a good model for
what I am attempting to express. Of particular importance to me is the
role of a critical sociology of literature in the analysis of the social ambience
of the intimate and the private, the revealing of the sociological determination of such phenomena as love, friendship, the relationship to
nature, self-image, and the like. This does not mean reductionism. Lit-

erature is no mere quarry. I reject all attempts to regard literature as a tool to learn data and facts about institutions such as the economy, the state, and the legal system. Social scientists and social historians should be forbidden from regarding literature as a source for raw materials. Literature teaches us to understand the success or failure of the socialization of individuals in concrete historical moments and situations. The novels of Stendhal, for instance, and in particular *Lucien Leuwen,* would be a perfect source for studying the transitions of forms of experience from a feudal to an aristocratic to a bourgeois type of individual.

If you should find what I have said thus far too formalistic, the critical perspective will immediately raise its head again. When I speak of the history of the individual's socialization I also speak of the history of his sufferings, as well as of his passions. The literature with which I am familiar, that is, western European literature since 1600, is the history of human passion in our ever-present crisis, the long-endured story of tension, promises, betrayal, and death. The literature of bourgeois society makes the permanent crisis of the individual manifest. It is a criterion of literature as art whether and to what extent it manifests the crisis as permanent. And thus we enter the precarious realm of the fringe or marginality.

The most extreme form of the marginal existence, that is, the conscious or unconscious critique of society, is expressed in the empathic utterances of those characters who know humanity's death sentence to be already sealed before we enter the so-called fullness of social life. Stendhal has one of the figures, with whom he identifies, say somewhere in *The Red and the Black,* "I can see nothing other than a death sentence which characterizes a real human being. . . . Everything else can be bought." And a half century later, Walter Pater assures us in his *Renaissance: Studies in Art and Poetry,*

> Well! we are all *condamnés,* as Victor Hugo says: we are all under sentence of death but with a sort of indefinite reprieve—*les hommes sont tous condamnés à mort avec des sursis indéfinis:* we have an interval, and then our place knows us no more. Some spend this interval in listlessness, some in high passions, the wisest, at least among "the children of this world," in art and song.[2]

This means, in the language of a neo-romantic, that art alone communicates what is truly good in human life and experience, a promise of happiness which remains unfulfilled.

Here I come to the most significant aspect of marginality, namely, the sociology of the artist himself. He has a skewed view of the world.

2. Walter Pater, *The Renaissance: Studies in Art and Poetry* (London, 1912), pp. 251–52.

By looking at the world obliquely, he sees it correctly, for it is, indeed, distorted. The artist is no Cartesian but a dialectician focusing on the idiosyncratic, on that which does not fit into the system. In short, he is concerned with the human costs and thus becomes an ally of Critical Theory, that is, of the critical perspective which is itself a part of critical praxis.

The marginal in the work of art is represented by groups, situations, and protagonists. First, from the perspective of Critical Theory, the literary artist turns into our ally where he is the spokesman for the *collective of outcasts:* of the poor, the beggars, the criminals, the insane; in short, of all those who bear the burden of society. Here, however, one finds immediately manifested the true dialectic of art which in the sense of the Adorno remark cited above makes its interpretation as mere ideology meaningless. In the writer's representation which comes nearer to reality than unmediated reality itself, the collectivity of those excluded from profits and privileges is shown to be the true first nature of man. In the collectivity of misery, the possibility of true humanity is revealed not as distortion but as an immanent indictment. It is dialectical irony that those who least correspond to a trivial bourgeois ideological concept of the individual bear the mark of a liberated, autonomous humaneness.

Here I may perhaps refer to my analysis of the works of Cervantes as an example of social groups on the periphery:

> There are two, not mutually exclusive, ways of looking at the marginal figures of Cervantes; they are the refuse of a society that has cast them aside, and they are, by virtue of their own right, moralists.
>
> All these marginal creatures, the beggars, the crooks, the gypsies, the insane, constitute "overheads" of society, to which they are either unwilling to belong or from which they are forcibly excluded. But while they are accused, indicted, and confined, they themselves in turn are accusers. Their very existence denounces a world they never made and which wants no part of them. The artist, in giving these people a voice, may seek to inspire uneasiness on the part of those who have profited by the prevailing order. The author's voice is the voice of the losers. The other aspect in which the marginal figures may be viewed leads us back to the concept of the Utopian. The marginal figures not only serve the negative function of indicting the social order; they also positively demonstrate the true idea of man. They all serve to show the possibilities of Utopia, where everyone has the freedom to be his own deviant case—with the result that the very phenomenon of deviation disappears. The outcast society of robbers and thieves who are plying their trade on the fringes of Seville, and the society of gypsies encamped on the outskirts of Madrid, are grotesque Utopian prototypes: everybody works according to his own talents, and everything is shared by everybody.

The meaning of Cervantes' critical idealism is even clearer in *The Little Gypsy*. The tribal chief says: "We observe inviolably the law of friendship; no one solicits the object of another man's affection; we live free from the bitter curse of jealousy." Thus at the threshold of the new society Cervantes describes the law by which it operates and confronts it with its professed measure: the autonomous and morally responsible individual. And this responsible and independent man is to be found only at the margin of society, which at once produces and expels him.[3]

The most extreme case in which a critical perspective attempts to highlight the cognitive character of peripheral groups portrayed by literature is that of woman. Ever since the Renaissance, the literary artist has made female protagonists the true revolutionary critics of a defective society. Ibsen once said, "Modern society is not a human society; it is merely a society of males." However, this disenfranchisement of woman has not only negative but also positive consequences.

Ibsen's men never practice what they preach, and the only principle by which they live—the materialism of personal gain—they never admit. The women, too, are materialistic, but their materialism is clearly of a different nature, and it is, above all, openly articulated. It is a conscious dramatic irony that morality is preached by the egotists while egotism is preached by the moralists.

Second, the *situation-marginality* and group-marginality are very closely related. Significant examples are found in Shakespeare's plays, especially in *The Tempest,* in *King Lear,* and in *Timon of Athens,* where the characters are driven out into the wilderness of unsocialized nature. Here nature is not perceived as raw material to be abused and exploited by a class society's lust for power—an exploitation which parallels that of the marginal groups of society about which I just spoke. When in these plays nature emphatically appears as the untamed elements, it heralds at the same time a reconciliation of nature and man. Outraged nature forms an alliance with outraged man in order to indict an evil society. In *The Tempest* this is made very clear, as unmastered nature leads the human being's second nature, his reified and socialized mask, back to his true nature. The marginal situation of absolute poverty (not to be confused with Robinson Crusoe's situation), which initially besets Prospero, Lear, and Timon, eventually turns into a blessing and thus represents the anticipation of utopia. Implicitly or explicitly (and this I can only boldly assert without proof), utopia—the reconciliation of the first nature of man and nature—remains the fundamental theme of authentic literature.

Third, where the *protagonist* himself appears as a peripheral figure, the synthesis between marginal groups and marginal situations has been

3. Lowenthal, *Literature and the Image of Man* (Boston, 1957), pp. 42–45.

reached or at least anticipated from Rabelais' *Pantagruel* to, if you will, Günter Grass' *Tin Drum,* and on up to the very present time. In these works the identity of the average person in class society and the protagonist are totally incompatible. Don Quixote is the symbol of a critique of bourgeois society, its manipulated conformism from its late feudal forms around 1600 up to the present day. He is the ahistorical symbol of a genuine historical materialism. In every situation he is insane, that is, he is sane; in every encounter he is irrational, that is, he is rational. He is the only one who is really happy, nearly fulfilled—precisely because he sees society from an oblique critical perspective and "straightens it out" by his fantastic deeds. By converting his critical idealism into practice, he represents the fulfillment of the potential of every individual. While he is destroyed and finally dies, he still stands for the premonition of what life could be. His fantasies anticipate what remains invisible in this damaged world. To quote Hegel:

> We find in . . . Don Quixote a noble nature in whose adventures chivalry goes mad, the substance of such adventures being placed as the centre of a stable and well-defined state of things whose external character is copied with exactness from nature. . . . In all the madness of his mind and his enterprise he is a completely consistent soul, or rather his madness lies in this, that he is and remains securely rooted in himself and his enterprise.[4]

In short, in him, through him, the identity of theory and practice is realized.

Before I turn briefly to the topic of mass culture, I would like, as a transition, to refer once more to Stendhal who to my mind is the master of analysis of the experience of socialization, and who, if in a now dated way, anticipates a social climate in which genuine experience becomes completely overpowered by conformism. And this is indeed the essential characteristic of mass culture. When, in *Lucien Leuwen,* Lucien can endure neither the decadent restoration society nor the *juste-milieu* of the new bourgeois world, he toys—as does the hero of *Wilhelm Meister's Travels*—with the idea of emigrating to America. The quotation speaks for itself:

> All Lucien's sensations had been so dreary since he came to Nancy, that, for want of anything better to do, he let this republican epistle absorb his attention. "The best thing would be for them all to sail for America. . . . And would I sail with them? . . . I am not quite such an imbecile! . . . I should be bored in America among

4. G. W. F. Hegel, *The Philosophy of Fine Art,* trans. F. P. B. Osmaston, 2 vols. (New York, 1975), 2:374–75.

men who are, it is true, perfectly just and reasonable, but coarse, and who think of nothing but *dollars*."[5]

Boredom is indeed the key word; it is the form of experience in which nineteenth-century artists express the perspective of Critical Theory in relation to the emerging manifestations of modern life.

4

My own analyses of mass culture employ the term "boredom" because it offers access to the most significant factor: that is, the crippling of imagination which obstructs artistic experience and gives free rein to the forces of manipulation. The extent to which the "administration," that is, the suppression, of the imagination is part of the business of mass culture might be made clear in a few examples. In the United States, as well as in Germany, book clubs are a big business. One enterprise by the name of Time Books promises a "Time Reading Program." For a modest sum, the creators of the program promise the monthly delivery of three or four books and encourage participation in a "planned approach" to reading which guarantees that "though your time may be limited you will be reading widely and profitably . . . many books which are truly timeless in style and significance." The reliability of selection is beyond doubt: "This plan draws its strength from the fact that the editors spent thousands of hours finding the answers to questions that you, too, must have asked yourself many times. . . . It is part of their job to single out the few books that tower over all others." Significance, quality, and relevance of the publications are assured: "In each case, the editors will write special introductions to underline what is unique in the book, what impact it has had or will have, what place it has earned in literature and contemporary thought." In addition, a kind of religious sanction is bestowed upon the wrappings: "The books will be bound in durable, flexible covers similar to those used for binding fine Bibles and Missals."

Another example: the Literary Guild, one of the most successful American book clubs, recently offered an inexpensive special edition of *Anna Karenina, Madame Bovary,* and Dumas' *Camille.* The advertisement for it reads as follows:

These three classical novels which are now published together in an attractively bound series tell the story of a trio of tragic and unforgettable ladies who risked their life for love and thereby lost everything. Tolstoy's Anna Karenina, a woman who gives up her aristocratic society for the cause of an insuperable passion, Dumas's

5. Stendhal, *Lucien Leuwen*, trans. Louise Varèse, 2 vols. (New York, 1950), 1:71.

Camille lady who makes the highest sacrifice for the man she loves, and Flaubert's Madame Bovary, a tender dreamer whose romantic longing leads to an act of violence.

These are illustrations of the degradation of art to commodities of mass culture. After all, the triumphs and tragedies in love experienced by Faust's Gretchen or Anna Karenina are not eternally valid statements about the nature of woman but are to be seen as specific perceptions about women in certain circumstances. It would not be such an outrageous act of manipulated mass culture if, instead of tossing such books cheaply onto the mass market, the experts were to proclaim that these ladies are all neurotics and would certainly be better off today after psychoanalytic treatment! In short, the organization and "administration" of the imagination is taken over by the agencies of social control. The products of this market are legitimate subject matter for the behavioral sciences; in this context reductionism is indeed an adequate model.

Mass culture reinforces and signals the instructions in the late capitalist world that promote a false collective. In this sense, I have always regarded my studies as political. Two examples in particular come to mind which appear to me symptomatic of the shattered bourgeois self-consciousness and the insuperable impotence which characterized the mood of wide strata of the middle classes. One example is related to genre, the other to literary reception. Both phenomena are closely related.

One of my studies had as its subject the reception of Dostoevsky in Germany from the turn of the century as documented in a voluminous corpus of books as well as in articles, journals, and newspapers. It soon became clear to me that the massive reception of Dostoevsky's works was not necessarily a function of their aesthetic quality but rather of deeper sociopsychological needs. With the probable exception of Goethe, Dostoevsky was the literary figure most written about at that time. The analysis of the material showed that the reception of Dostoevsky's works revealed the significant idiosyncracies of German society in a time of total crisis: infatuation with the so-called irrationalism of the artist; the alleged mystery in the life of the individual; the wallowing in the "dark regions of the soul"; the glorification of criminal behavior—in short, indispensable elements later incorporated in the psychological transfiguration of violence by National Socialism.

That studies on reception can have sociopolitical significance was confirmed to me years later when I took a closer look at the reviews of the writer whom I had believed to be—years before the event—a Nazi sympathizer: that is, Knut Hamsun. A history of the reception of Hamsun's works can reflect the development of political consciousness from liberalism to the slogans of the authoritarian state. Bourgeois literary criticism was not nearly as surprising as the Social Democratic responses. If one reads the observations on Hamsun which appeared in the leading theoretical journal of German Social Democracy, *Die Neue Zeit,* one finds in the nineties a clear political stance: Hamsun's novels are to be rejected; they do not portray living human beings but rather vague attitudes which have nothing to do with tendencies directed toward positive change.

When, however, one takes a look at the volumes of *Die Neue Zeit* from the early years of World War I and the immediate postwar years, one finds glowing descriptions of the same writer who twenty years before had been so unambiguously rejected. What had previously been judged as "empty atmosphere" and "mere nervous stimulus" was now perceived as "gripping depictions of life and soul in which the most vivid reality with all its lights and shadows is transposed into the allegory of innermost life." The author who impressed the earlier critics as an "amorous exclamation point in a melancholy easy-chair" had now grown "to that solitary greatness" which one may not compare with others without doing him an injustice. What had previously been seen as "ephemeral as the atmosphere" in his novels suddenly became "a parable of the eternal."

After World War I, the liberal spokesmen of the bourgeoisie joined in this hymn of praise with those of the proletariat that Hamsun so despised. Conventional bourgeois criticism and that of *Die Neue Zeit* belong to the same constellation: that of political resignation and a readiness for ideological seduction among broad social strata in Central Europe.

My studies on genre examined the biographical fashion. I attempted to analyze, in two different societies, popular biographies as an illuminating criterion for significant transformations in political and social structure. The first study was still carried out in Germany, before 1933. Today one can scarcely imagine the flood of popular biographies which inundated Europe and Germany. Already by 1918, the popular biography was the classic example of escapist literature for the German bourgeosie. Biography is both the continuation and the inversion of the novel. In the bourgeois novel, documentation functions as raw material. Quite the contrary is true in the popular biography. Here the various kinds of documentation, that gigantic pageant of fixed data, events, names, letters, and so forth come to take the place of social relationships which have become the individual's fetters; the individual is, so to speak, nothing more than a typographic element, a column heading which winds its way through the book's plot, a mere excuse to attractively arrange a certain body of material. The heroes of popular biographies have no individual destinies; they are nothing but functions of the historic. While rarely the manifest credo of this literature, latent relativism is always present. Conscious cynicism of the masters is completely absent, but what remains is the need to cloak the helplessness of the losers. The aestheticism of the nineties, the *fin de siècle,* could be called the very epitome of activity when compared to the fatigue and weakness emanating from these writers of popular biographies. In these testimonies to the immortality of mortality, in this maze of superlatives and uniquenesses through which reason can never hope to guide us, the writers are every bit as lost as their readers.

Popular biographies in the United States operated in a different social context. What I attempted to show in my work on the triumph of mass idols in several American high-circulation magazines was the structural change in the treatment of popular biographies in the period of transition from liberal capitalism to that of manipulated collectivism. I called it the transition from the idols of production to the idols of consumption. Whereas around the turn of the century, the so-called heroes were the representatives of production, at the end of the thirties and the beginning of the forties, increasingly these "heroes" were replaced by athletes and entertainers, especially those of the cinema, and what appeared to be "newsworthy" about them were their private affairs rather than their productive functions. The identification offered to the reader was no longer that of the rise to enterpreneurial success but rather to the imitation of consumption. Ultimately, the German and the American phenomena share certain identical characteristics, though in a different political context. As I put it then:

> But the distance between what an average individual may do and the forces and powers that determine his life and death has become so unbridgeable that identification with normalcy, even with Philistine boredom becomes a readily grasped empire of refuge and escape. It is some comfort for the little man who has become expelled from the Horatio Alger dream, who despairs of penetrating the thicket of grand strategy in politics and business, to see his heroes as a lot of guys who like or dislike highballs, cigarettes, tomato juice, golf and social gatherings—just like himself. He knows how to converse in the sphere of consumption and here he can make no mistakes. By narrowing his focus of attention, he can experience the gratification of being confirmed in his own pleasures and discomforts by participating in the pleasures and discomforts of the great. The large confusing issues in the political and economic realm and the antagonisms and controversies in the social realm—all these are submerged in the experience of being at one with the lofty and great in the sphere of consumption.[6]

5

With the power of a seemingly prophetic insight Shakespeare suggests the threat to the autonomy of the individual through social manipulation

---

6. Lowenthal, "Biographies in Popular Magazines," in *Radio Research 1942–43*, ed. Paul F. Lazarsfeld and Frank N. Stanton (New York, 1944), pp. 547–48.

in the second scene of the third act of *Hamlet,* although he certainly could not have guessed that finally, nearly four hundred years later, the Guildensterns would defeat the Hamlets:

HAMLET: Will you play upon this pipe?
GUILDENSTERN: My lord, I cannot.
HAMLET: I pray you.
GUILDENSTERN: Believe me, I cannot.
HAMLET: I do beseech you.
GUILDENSTERN: I know no touch of it, my lord.
HAMLET: 'Tis as easy as lying; govern these ventages with your finger and thumb, give it breath with your mouth, and it will discourse most eloquent music. Look you, these are the stops.
GUILDENSTERN: But these cannot I command to any utterance of harmony; I have not the skill.
HAMLET: Why, look you now, how unworthy a thing you make of me. You would play upon me; you would seem to know my stops; you would pluck out the heart of my mystery; you would sound me from my lowest note to the top of my compass; and there is much music, excellent voice, in this little organ, yet cannot you make it speak. 'Sblood! do you think I am easier to be played on than a pipe? Call me what instrument you will, though you can fret me, you cannot play upon me.[7]

Guildenstern represents, if you will, mass culture which mediates social domination, which tries to force the individual to obedience and plays with him as on a passive, but well-prepared instrument.

    What finally happened is clearly expressed in the words of the American poet, Randall Jarrell, who has the following to say in his book, *Poetry and the Age:*

The poet lives in a world whose newspapers and magazines and books and motion pictures and radio stations and television stations have destroyed, in a great many people, even the capacity for understanding real poetry, real art of any kind . . . the average article in our magazines gives any subject whatsoever the same coat of easy, automatic, "human" interest.[8]

Jarrell contrasts Goethe's statement, "The author whom a lexicon can keep up with is worth nothing" with Somerset Maugham's: "The finest compliment he ever received was a letter in which one of his readers said: 'I read your novel without having to look up a single word in the

7. William Shakespeare, *Hamlet, Prince of Denmark,* act 3, sc. 2, ll. 350–72.
8. Randall Jarrell, *Poetry and the Age* (New York, 1957), p. 18.

dictionary.' " And Jarrell closes with the observation that "popular writing has left nothing to the imagination for so long now that imagination too has begun to atrophy." In short, the wasting away, the end of imagination, is the end of freedom.

I cannot say anything definitive about the possibility of genuine artistic experience in the present day. The acquaintance with great art is certainly growing, but an acquaintance without genuine experience, which is rooted in critical openness, only serves to support the system. Acquaintance and experience are mutually exclusive. I am more than concerned about the possibility of the aesthetic experience as experience of freedom in today's world. I can say no more. What I have tried to convey here was perhaps not so much a summary of my work in the sociology of literature as a chapter of a perhaps too presumptuous intellectual autobiography, an autobiography, however, which without false modesty does not lose sight of the marginality of the field. As an intellectual, one certainly can and possibly ought to live on the margins. And for me, sociology of literature has served me there quite adroitly!

Response to Leo Lowenthal

Lewis A. Coser

Much of what I know about the sociology of literature I have learned from my old friend Leo Lowenthal. But I feel obliged, nevertheless, to dissent from one of the central contentions of his present essay ("Sociology of Literature in Retrospect," pp. 11–25). Lowenthal, or so it would seem to me, unduly glorifies by a kind of neoromanticism, the literary vocation. To him, "Literature is the only dependable source for human consciousness and self-consciousness" (p. 15). The writer, to him, is the only truthteller in a world otherwise marked by falsehood and distortion. Art is, or should be, our only dependable guide to feeling and conduct. The literary work embodies a special truth not otherwise available in our fallen world. But is this really the case?

It may be true, as Lowenthal says, that "literature is not ideology" (p. 15), but does it follow from this that it exists in a rarified sphere uncontaminated by the ideological or cultural currents of the age? In one of his earliest writings, Lowenthal himself showed in instructive detail the ideological protofascist distortions in the literary work of Knut Hamsun. Unless he would deny any artistic stature whatsoever to the works of this novelist, Lowenthal gets himself involved in logical confusion. There are, after all, a number of great writers whose works are marked by a variety of judgments that are repugnant to modern liberal sensitivities. T. S. Eliot's "polite" anti-Semitism or Ezra Pound's cruder variety can hardly be overlooked. When they engage in Jew-baiting, they surely do not speak "the truth." Yet who would dare to argue that their writings do not belong to the highest achievements of modern literature? It would seem to me rather silly to argue that they are not major literary figures because they espouse unpalatable and "untrue" sets of ideas.

Writers, I have argued elsewhere, are a bit like those canaries that miners used to take down their shafts hoping that they would give them early warnings of toxic gases that human smell could not discern. Writers, some have argued, have special antennae that enable them to sense things "as they really are," undistorted by the veiled falsehoods and deceits that are manifest in the rest of the cultural environment. But is this really the case?

Even if one may grant that literary artists often have the ability, to use Henry James' expression, to "catch the color of life itself," it also remains the case that the vision of the writer is likely to perceive this color through the lenses of his or her own peculiar sensitivities and angles of vision. Writers do not conceive the whole truth and nothing but the truth. They can convey only a partial truth as refracted through the filters of their own minds and their own sensibilities. How else could one explain the enormously variegated ways in which particular writers have dealt with the same historical events or cultural circumstances? The French Revolution, as seen through the eyes of Thomas Carlyle, is surely different from the same revolution as depicted in, say, Georg Büchner's *Danton's Death*. The Russian Revolution seen through the eyes of Boris Pasternak has little in common with its depiction in the writings of Isaac Babel.

If most historians have given up Leopold von Ranke's grandiose ambition to depict what has happened in the past "as it really has been," why then can we hope that the literary treatment of events or conditions necessarily reveals the unvarnished truth? Literature is not born after immaculate conception; it partakes of the travail, the conflicts, the distortions, yes, even the lies that are in the very saturated atmosphere the imaginative writer, like everyone else, must breathe. It is true that great writers have the uncommon ability to identify with wide ranges of experience and to throw light on the manners and morals of an age that are unperceived or misunderstood by their contemporaries. But this is a far cry from believing with Leo Lowenthal that "literature is the *only* dependable source for human consciousness and self-consciousness" (my emphasis). I am not inclined to deny the achievements of the literary imagination, but I feel strongly that it need not take precedence over the sociological or the historical imagination.

Oscar Wilde once observed in a deliberately paradoxical manner that much that we "know" about Victorian England or nineteenth-century

---

Lewis A. Coser is Distinguished Professor of Sociology Emeritus at the State University of New York at Stony Brook and adjunct professor of sociology at Boston College. His many works include *Men of Ideas* (1970), *Sociology Through Literature* (1972), *Refugee Scholars in America: Their Impact and Their Experiences* (1984), and *A Handful of Thistles: Collected Papers in Moral Conviction* (1988).

Russia is likely to be a collective representation that owes more to Charles Dickens and Fyodor Dostoyevski than to historians. Perhaps, but I would surely not depend on this "knowledge" before having checked it against the great nineteenth-century historians or the sociological insights of, say, Karl Marx.

In a sense, Leo Lowenthal's argument seems to me to deny the significance of the sociology of literature altogether. If literary works are true by definition, what is the use of tracing the social and political influences that have colored the vision of the writer? It is only if we see writing as the complex result flowing from a variety of sources, from the author's private psyche to the ideological currents of the age, that the sociological analysis of works of art becomes a meaningful enterprise. Lowenthal insists that sociological analysis must be applied "with utter caution" and can, in any case, deal only with those "residues which are unequivocally ideological in nature" (p. 15). I see a much less modest role for the sociological study of literary works. Such study, I would contend, may succeed in penetrating to the core of a work of art.

By pushing aside as at best peripheral those studies that attempt to analyze the complex relations between a writer and audience, whether real or imaginary, by relegating almost to the domain of the irrelevant attempts to link literary works to the ideological temper of a society, or a section thereof, by seemingly pushing aside the very notion of a shared cultural universe, Lowenthal now seems to devaluate much that he taught us earlier. Why should one indeed analyze the social and political ideas of, say, Shakespeare and relate them to the cultural ideals and ideas of the Elizabethan age if such endeavor does not contribute in any significant extent to our appreciation of King Lear or Othello?

If the sociologist of literature, like any sociologist of worth, is to contribute to the interpretation of the past and the present of human beings in society, he or she cannot ignore the knowledge that literary works provide. Yet the understanding of literary messages is forcefully enhanced if we are able to decode those messages by continuing reference to the historical situation, the audience, the circle of admirers or detractors in which the author moves. The world of literature provides an enormous variety of textured commentaries on humankind's exhilarating as well as tormented course through the ages. Life is hardly worth living without profiting from the fruits of the labors and commentaries of great writers. But let us not divinize even the greatest of them and pretend that they have privileged access to the truth as a whole.

Text, Author-Function, and Appropriation in Modern Narrative: Toward a Sociology of Representation

Robert Weimann

To talk about the sociology of literary representation is, first and foremost, to propose to historicize representational activity at that crucial point where its social and linguistic dimensions intersect.[1] The troublesome incongruity between these two dimensions need not be minimized, but it can be grappled with as soon as the presuppositions of either the hegemony of the subject or that of language itself are questioned. In this view, the position of Georg Lukács (not to mention that of Erich Auerbach or even that of the more traditional sociologist of literary referentiality) tends to ignore the state of extreme vulnerability and recurrent jeopardy in which representation has always found itself, just as Michel Foucault's diametrically opposed view of the ultimate hegemony of discourse obliterates or displaces a lot of unbroken contemporary representational practice. Even more important, both these quite different approaches may be said to appear monistic in that the gaps and links between what is representing and what is represented are viewed *either* in terms of closure and continuity *or* in terms of rupture and discontinuity. But as I shall proceed to glance at some representational strategies in

---

1. For some theoretical presuppositions, see my critique of post-structuralist concepts of "representation" in "Text and History: Epilogue, 1984," *Structure and Society in Literary History: Studies in the History and Theory of Historical Criticism* (Baltimore, 1984), pp. 267–323. At the same time, the present essay draws substantially on some of the historical materials and texts I first used in a contribution entitled "History, Appropriation, and the Uses of Representation in Modern Narrative," in *The Aims of Representation: Subject/Text/History,* ed. Murray Krieger (New York, 1987), pp. 175–215.

the late modern period, the question needs to be faced whether it is not precisely in these gaps and links, and in the way in which, simultaneously, the gaps are closed and the links are broken up, that historical activity can be seen to assert itself.

If the contradiction of system and event, of predetermination and performance can be seen to affect representational activity, and if this contradiction can at all be formulated in terms of a sociological *Erkenntnisinteresse,* the issue of historicity must be discussed on more than one level: not only on the level of what is represented (which would reduce this project to some genealogy of the signified) but also on the level of who and what is representing. The point is to view these levels (the rupture between them as well as their interdependence) together and to attempt to interconnect the semiotic problematic of signification and the extratextual dimension of representativeness, as involving changeful relations of writing, reading, social reproduction, and political power. In this view, the use of signs, although never quite reducible to a referential function, must be reconsidered and this question needs to be asked: under which conditions and in which respects would it be possible to talk of sociology in that area of instability itself which marks the relations between signifier and signified, between the author's language and the reader's meaning?

1. Uses of Appropriation

This summary, of course, is highly provisional and greatly oversimplifies a theoretical question, but even so it may perhaps suffice to introduce a concept of appropriation (or expropriation) as denoting some social and temporal kind of activity which precedes the problematic of both the subject and the sign. As against both the classical-romantic view of the text as the purely referential activity of some reflecting subject and the (seemingly opposite) view of the text as some autonomous locus of self-determining differentials or epistemes, the concept of appropriation may, I submit, help us to focus on the changeful constellations of the contradiction itself between whatever extralinguistic activity and whatever intralinguistic difference engage in the process of representation. Although,

---

Robert Weimann is professor of English and American literature at the Zentralinstitut für Literaturgeschichte, Akademie der Künste, Berlin DDR. His books in English include *Shakespeare and the Popular Tradition in the Theater* and *Structure and Society in Literary History.* His most recent book-length study in German is *Shakespeare und die Macht der Mimesis: Repräsentation und Autorität im Elisabethanischen Theater.*

ultimately, the contradiction between discourse and production, linguistics and sociology may turn out to be quite irreducible, the links even more than the gaps between them have not been sufficiently explored.

Thus, although the study of discourses as juridical "*objects* of appropriation"[2] is of the greatest importance, it must be complemented by their study as *Subjekte* of appropriation, that is, as historical agencies of knowledge, pleasure, energy, and power. In other words, the question of appropriation must be studied not only in relation to the exchange value of an author's works, that is, their property status, but also, and at the same time, in terms of the use value of *his or her work*, that is, in reference to the changing functions and effects of his or her literary production as an appropriating agency. In regard to the functions of representation, then, appropriation would have to be defined at the intersection of both text-appropriating and world-appropriating activities, in the sense that the concept will, over and beyond its economic and juridical dimensions, encompass noneconomical and nonjuridical activities. These activities will be conceived in terms of *Aneignung*, of making things (relations, books, texts, writings) one's own. Hence it seems possible to say that both the world in the book and the book in the world are *appropriated* through acts of intellectual acquisition and imaginative assimilation on the levels of writing as well as reading. In this connection, the German term *Aneignung* has the advantage of not necessarily involving an ideologically preconceived idea of (private) ownership or (physical) property; instead, it allows for acquisitive behavior as well as for nonacquisitive acts of intellectual energy and assimilation. Since, therefore, the term is not limited by juridical ideas of private property, the sense of "making things one's own" can and, in fact, must be used *literally*, not as a metaphor of some juridical action or condition associated with a certain type of (bourgeois) society.

"Appropriation" so defined would provide us with a concept denoting an activity which, even while it can precede ideology and signification, is not closed to the forces of social struggle and political power or to the acts of the historical consciousness of the signifying subject. Linking the world of prehistory with that of historical activities, Marx was the first to define "appropriation" in relation to *Arbeit* (work, labor): defining *Aneignung* as a function of work, Marx related the varying modes of appropriation not only to the changing conditions of production and ownership but also to changing patterns of relationship between the individual and his or her community.[3] On a theoretical foundation such as this, appropriation may involve events and structures of homogeneity

2. Michel Foucault, "What Is an Author?," in *Textual Strategies: Perspectives in Post-Structuralist Criticism*, ed. Josué V. Harari (London, 1980), p. 148; my italics.

3. See Karl Marx, *Grundrisse: Foundations of the Critique of Political Economy*, trans. Martin Nicolaus (New York, 1973), p. 485.

as well as heterogeneity in the sense that the relationship between the appropriator and his or her property is not a fixed or invariable one but, historically, may allow for varying degrees of identification as well as distance, alienation, and reification. The process of making certain things one's own becomes inseparable from making other things (and persons) alien, so that the act of appropriation must be seen always to involve not only self-projection and assimilation but also alienation through expropriation.

2. Author-function and Appropriation: The Epic and Beyond

To emphasize the potential contradiction between the process and the product of appropriation seems especially important as soon as we return to the task of historicizing the variegated uses of representation. In our context, the changeful nature of the space for (non)identity between what is representing and what is represented emerges perhaps most clearly when we compare representation in modern fiction with, say, that in the heroic and courtly epic up to and including Chrétien de Troyes, Hartmann von Aue, Wolfram von Eschenbach, Gottfried von Strassburg, and, even, late borderline cases like Sir Thomas Malory. In precapitalist societies the distance between the poet's act of appropriating a given text or theme and his or her own intellectual product and property is much smaller: the extent to which his or her *matière* is given, the extent to which "sources," genre, plot patterns, topoi, and so on are preordained is much greater. What is more, the poet's production never attains to a state of personal property or ownership. The amount of assimilating activity, the capacities for self-projection or alienation between the act and the product of representation remain limited. As long as the appropriator related to the means and modes of his or her production for the most part communally, as some unquestionably given, shared property, there is very little that *he or she can make his or her own*. Hence, the epic poet tended to take previously inscribed authority for granted: he or she affirmed the validity of the work of predecessors more readily; he or she accepted as part of his or her own work the labor (as it were) already invested in the invention of a great story with widely known events and characters. But in doing just that, the poet subscribed to a literary mode of production that was in many ways correlated to a socially dominant mode of appropriation in which, as Marx notes, "the chief objective condition of labour does not itself appear as a *product* of labour, but is already there as *nature*."[4] The discontinuity between the act and object of appropriation and its effects and functions is not all that considerable; the act of intellectual assimilation constitutes itself on the basis of the

4. Ibid.

givenness of what is to be assimilated. The author's function is to assert known and publicly acknowledged ideals; it is not to appropriate any area of thought or experience that has not previously been appropriated in feudal society itself.[5]

Thus, the changing context of appropriation can be seen to affect or even help constitute changeful modes and functions of representation: in the absence of deeper divisions between the appropriator and his or her properties the functions of representation remained limited. In premodern narrative there was little need for that romantic and realistic mode of representation, where a deliberate act of self-projection came to interact with the intellectual assimilation of the world and where the universality of the latter helped to intensify the particular expression of individuality in the former. In other words, the self-projecting uses of representation remained limited as long as appropriation was characterized not by dynamic contradictions between individual activities and given objects and relationships but by "the *reproduction* of *presupposed* relations." As long as the appropriator related to his or her objects as, in the words of Marx, some "inorganic part of his own subjectivity,"[6] the uses of representation were restricted.

But at the beginning of the modern period, the process of discursive *Aneignung* in representational form assumes a highly dynamic and unpredictable quality; being less predetermined by the given state of communal property—the givenness of cultural materials, literary conventions, and traditions—the act of representation emerges under conditions where writers are faced with the growing need to appropriate for themselves the means and forms of literary production; they have to make them their own precisely because they confront the conditions and means of literary production and reception as something alien, as produced by others, as something which they cannot unquestionably consider as part of the existence of their own social and self-fashioned intellectual selves. Hence, the *representative* quality of their writing, the very function of representativity itself becomes burdensome. As the writer's and reader's distance from the means and modes of production (including the production of literary texts) grows, there develops new scope for a writer's own individual point of view, for his or her own choice of productive strategies vis-à-vis the increasing availability of those means, modes, and materials which, self-consciously, the writer can self-fashioningly make his or her own.

5. I have developed the problematic of appropriation in late medieval and Renaissance prose narrative in the first two chapters to *Realismus in der Renaissance: Aneignung der Welt in der erzählenden Prosa,* ed. Robert Weimann (Berlin and Weimar, 1977), pp. 47–182. For an English summary and expansion of this approach, see my article " 'Appropriation' and Modern History in Renaissance Prose Narrative," *New Literary History* 14 (Spring 1983): 459–96.

6. Marx, *Grundrisse,* p. 487.

Thus, ever since the Renaissance, the dimension of representativity in discursive utterances can no longer be taken for granted. The representative function of discursive action enters a state of vulnerability and unpredictability which, paradoxically, makes representation—in politics just as in literature—problematic as well as necessary. As Stephen Greenblatt noted, "most great representational art in our culture seems to be generated" out of "a healing of [some] loss or undoing."[7] What representational art presupposes and what it thrives on is more than anything else the loss, the undoing of the plenitude of that property in which the self and the social are mutually engaged and in which their engagement is unquestioningly given and taken for granted.

3. Flaubert and the Crisis in Discursive Appropriation

Since the modern dialectic of representation and appropriation cannot adequately be discussed on a purely theoretical plane, let me at this point introduce two or three narrative texts in which the modern aims and functions of representational discourse have entered—out of their fullness—that state of crisis which makes them particularly illuminating. Although unfinished at the time of the author's death, Gustave Flaubert's *Bouvard et Pécuchet* deserves our special attention because in it a new and highly critical function of representation appears to be closely associated with a radically negative version of the theme of appropriation itself. In fact, it may be said without exaggeration that this narrative comes close to being a *Zurücknahme,* a revulsion from those classical fictions like *Robinson Crusoe* and *Faust,* where the link between appropriation and representativity was particularly strong, where the hero (Robinson Crusoe or Faust) through and in the image of the act of appropriating the world achieves a high status of representativity, where he becomes in fact the representative of a class or even humanity precisely because of the way he copes with and conquers the forces of nature.

As against such representativeness on the levels of both social function and iconic signification, the new departures in Flaubert's narrative can best be characterized by saying that the traditional links between the representational quality of the signified and the social representativity of the signifying activity become tenuous to the degree that the writer's own mode of literary production tends to be isolated or turn away from the material productions and the social mode of economic appropriation in bourgeois society. On the surface, Flaubert's narrative appears to recapitulate the whole sweep and variety of the parable of appropriation but to an altogether different effect. Bouvard and Pécuchet, two Parisian

7. Stephen J. Greenblatt, preface to *Allegory and Representation,* Selected Papers from the English Institute, new series, no. 5, ed. Greenblatt (Baltimore, 1981), p. x.

copy-clerks, resolve to retire to a village in Normandy in order to dedicate the rest of their lives to successive explorations into those areas of nature, experience, and knowledge from which their previous bourgeois existence had effectively debarred them. But for them the challenge of appropriation results in a course of action marked by radical failure, with the effect not of representativity but social isolation. As the two bachelors diligently attempt to make their little world their own, as they set out to appropriate the arts of gardening, agriculture, winery, chemistry, medicine, geology, archaeology, literature, and even criticism, they neither extend the frontiers of knowledge and experience nor, even, confirm and reauthorize any previously appropriated body of knowledge and control over nature. Despite all their dedicated efforts Bouvard and Pécuchet permanently and increasingly "enlarge the distance between what they are studying at any given moment and their abililty to cope with the problems of daily life."[8] As they read and read a vast literature of appropriation, as they proceed from authority to authority, the narrative widens the gulf between the signs of their reading and the symbols of their experience, between the acquired language of their theoretical knowledge and its actual meaning in iconic terms of subsequent actions and images.

There emerges an ever-widening dichotomy between what the words and figures of their reading are representing and what, in the course of following these learned significations, is actually achieved and represented in the narrative of their reception and application. What finally signifies is the narrative of how, in the act of its reception, the inscribed intellectual authority enters a state of crisis. What results is some loss in the applicability of authority, some decline in its validity, the defeat of its representativity. As the two bachelors begin to dabble in the arts of writing and reading, they come up against the "assurance," the "obstinacy," even the "dishonesty" in the critical columns of their day; they are bewildered by the "idiocies of those who pass for learned, and the stupidity of others hailed as witty!" Facing a deep crisis in authority, they themselves discuss the predicament of literary criticism in terms of the loss of its own representativity:

> Perhaps one should rely on the public?
> But works which met with applause sometimes displeased them, and in those that were hissed they found something they liked.
> So the opinion of men of taste is misleading and mass judgement is inconceivable.[9]

Torn between the crumbling authority of intellectual experts and the inconceivable legitimacy of "mass judgement" Bouvard and Pécuchet

---

8. Gustave Flaubert, *Bouvard and Pécuchet,* trans. A. J. Krailsheimer (1881; New York, 1976), p. 10.
9. Ibid., p. 140.

themselves rehearse a crisis in authorizing some representative response and judgement. Their own failure and defeat is so startling because they start out much like the traditional type of appropriating hero in fiction, but rather than assimilating the world that surrounds them so as to represent it—in Hegel's terms—"as some outer reality"[10] of their own striving selves, they utterly fail in their attempt at both world-appropriating and text-appropriating action. Finally, at the end, when they have completely isolated themselves from their community (and this was Flaubert's own, unfinished design) the two inseparable friends end up as copyists at a double-sided desk. *Aneignung* has become an impossible task: to appropriate, to make one's own the world of nature and society, yields nothing but defeat and, finally, despair. Having despaired of appropriating, using, and enjoying the knowledge and the ways of their world they content themselves with copying, that is, rewriting, not the signified of their own experience, but the mere signifiers from the books which they so miserably failed to receive and translate into some meaning of their own.

4. Representations of Self and Society in Henry James

The early decline, in France, of discursive representativeness provides a particularly revealing perspective on the more optimistic and, or so it seemed, democratic links between the American writer and his society. At a time when Charles Baudelaire, Paul Verlaine, Stéphane Mallarmé, and Arthur Rimbaud already exemplified some deep gulf between the verbal representations and the social representativity of the poet, the American writer was prepared, tragically like Herman Melville or comically like Mark Twain, to shoulder the burden of representation on the levels of both textual signification and social function. In the transcendentalist tradition, the poet's version of his own representativeness receives its most sustained affirmation in the writings of Ralph Waldo Emerson, who in one of his most influential essays declares the poet to be "representative man." Coming at the end of a European (largely German) romantic tradition of homogeneity and closure in the relation of text, history, and subject, Emerson says: "the poet is representative. He stands among partial men for the complete man, and apprises us not of his wealth, but of the common wealth."[11] Characteristically, for Emerson, the poet's is "the largest power to receive and to impart," he "re-attaches things to nature and the Whole," ("P," pp. 321, 328) and thus can "raise to a divine

10. G. W. F. Hegel, *Ästhetik*, ed. Friedrich Bassenge (Berlin, 1955), S. 75; my translation.
11. Ralph Waldo Emerson, "The Poet," *The Complete Essays and Other Writings by Ralph Waldo Emerson*, ed. Brooks Atkinson (New York, 1940), p. 320; further references to this work, abbreviated "P," will be included in the text.

use the railroad, the insurance office, the joint-stock company; our law, our primary assemblies, our commerce, the galvanic battery, the electric jar, the prism, and the chemist's retort; in which we seek now only an economical use."[12] This reads like a positive representation of that world of economics, politics, nature, and science which Flaubert had already surrendered as a space for appropriation in his more skeptical narrative. But in Emerson the poetic appropriation of the world is one in which the appropriator is still believed to be close to some universal and, hence, representative human property, which, in Emerson's definition, is "the common wealth." And since this "common wealth" unites the representations of the poet with the appropriations of "hunters, farmers, grooms and butchers" ("P," p. 326) (not to mention the men of politics and business), the social impulse of the representer and the historical interests of the represented appear to be continuous rather than discontinuous, unified rather than heterogeneous. In other words, the authority of what is representing informs, and is informed by, the authority and legitimacy of what is represented: the verbal appropriations of the poet and the material appropriations of "farmers, grooms and butchers," chemists, joint-stock companies, and politicians are made to appear so close and mutually so self-supporting that they ultimately sustain a large space of homogeneity between them.

If this American picture of hope and illusion appears to project the very opposite of Flaubert's burden of representation it may appear ironic that one of the greatest of Emersonian disciples, Henry James, in setting out to revise the social connections of his own narrative, gradually but irresistibly arrives at a position which after all is not so far removed from Flaubert's. Since I have space only to choose one of the great Jamesian themes, the most relevant in our context appears to be the one in which the writing represents the crisis of its own representativeness. As in the work of Thomas Mann, the erosion of representativeness itself is *represented* in its most immediate individual and psychological form: in the fiction and the figure of the artist himself, in his loss of social integration and bourgeois respectability, and in the diminishing range of his own participation in the moral and political consensus. The crisis of representativeness is turned into a theme, into a novelistic representation itself, and its most consistently mimetic form is, of course, the biographical *Darstellung* of characters, such as Tonio Kröger, Gustav von Aschenbach, and Adrian Leverkühn in Mann, or Neil Paraday ("The Death of the Lion"), Paul Overt ("The Lesson of the Master"), Ray Limbert ("The Next Time"), and of course Nick Dormer (*The Tragic Muse*) in James.

In these fictional representations, the artist, far from being representative man, either renounces the claims of middle-class life or is already an outsider, standing (in the sense of Mann) in a queer aloof relationship

12. Emerson, "Art," *Complete Essays*, p. 314.

to the rest of humanity, out of harmony with at least some of the most
broadly received middle-class values and attitudes. Although on the surface,
in the reduced scope and mimetic form of novelistic subject matter, the
gulf between what represents and what is represented appears at least
in part to be bridged once more, yet the underlying tensions in the
identifications of self and society, the contradiction between self-projection and appropriation have vastly increased. This becomes obvious as
soon as the Emersonian conception of the poet as the "sayer" and "namer"
of the "common wealth," as "the only teller" of the news of the world is
critically, not to say sarcastically, redefined in relation to such public
forms of activity as, for instance, a career in journalism and politics
involve.

As in James' *Tragic Muse*, the new perspective on the diminishing
social representativeness of art is exemplified in the antagonism between
the status of the artist and the role of the politician. This conflict leads
to a defiant emphasis on the independence, the self-respect, and the
uniqueness, if not the autonomy, of the function of art in society. The
Emersonian concept of art as the most intensely representative vessel of
life gives way to a sense of its autonomous or redeeming function which,
precisely, resides in its freedom from representativeness. As Stephen
Donadio has suggested in *Nietzsche, Henry James, and the Artistic Will*, this
fiction shares "the impulse to achieve a self-definition independent of
one's national or class origins, the impulse to be free of the limitations
imposed by a particular time."[13]

Such independence characterizes Nick Dormer, the central figure
in *The Tragic Muse*, a promising politician, who begins to conceive of his
future career as liberal member of Parliament as "talking a lot of rot"
which "has nothing to do with the truth or the search for it; nothing to
do with intelligence, or candour, or honour."[14] Authority, in other words
(and Flaubert would have agreed), is not to be found in the public sphere
of power and politics; henceforth, whatever common ground there was
between the representation of politics and the politics of representation
becomes tenuous and dissolves. So Nick Dormer the artist parts with his
politically influential fiancée; he rejects "the old false measure of success"
and chooses to become a painter so as to be able to enjoy "the beauty of
having been disinterested and independent; of having taken the world
in the free, brave, personal way" (*TM*, p. 125).

The longing for a disinterested kind of independence, the preference
for "the free, brave, personal way" must be read as symptomatic not only

13. Stephen Donadio, *Nietzsche, Henry James, and the Artistic Will* (New York, 1978), p.
90. See, in this connection, the cogent reinterpretation of Jamesian formalism by John
Carlos Rowe, *The Theoretical Dimensions of Henry James* (Madison, Wis., 1984), pp. 225–37.
14. Henry James, *The Tragic Muse* (1890; New York, 1978), pp. 74–75; further references
to this work, abbreviated *TM*, will be included in the text.

of the changing position of the artist in bourgeois society but of the new foundations on which James sets out to redefine the function and the art of representation. In that he comes close to the Nietzschean position (as formulated by Mann) " 'that life can be justified only as an aesthetic phenomenon.' "[15] If, up to a point in time, marked perhaps by the Joycean figure of Stephen Dedalus, the erosion of representativeness is rendered in traditionally representational forms of novelistic mimesis, the reason is not of course simply that of their undoubted resiliency. There is, at the very moment of his social alienation, the artist's attempt (as Michael Fried has shown in the work of Gustave Courbet)[16] more resolutely than ever before to efface the distance between creator and art object and, in the teeth of its deepening contradiction, once more to fuse representation with what it represents. In this sense, these late endeavors in the traditional forms of realism do attempt that "healing of some loss or undoing" on which some of the greatest representational activities seemed to have thrived.

However, if it is the gap, the lack of identity between what appropriates and what is appropriated which, in the first place, made representation necessary, this gap, once it is turned into an abyss, begins to affect and put strains on representational form itself. The most immediate modernist link between the deepening crisis in representativeness and the nascent erosion in representational form can be traced on the level of the writer's communication with his public. When, in *The Bostonians,* James satirically recoiled from the vulgar forms of commercialized publishing and when this major novel, just like *The Tragic Muse,* was ill received and spitefully or, at best, indifferently reviewed, the author turned to the theater and, after that, began to experiment in and modify the traditional narrative conventions of representational form. The results are too well known for me to specify them here, but what needs to be emphasized is that there is a connection between the represented artist's option for "the free, brave, personal way" and James' own redefinition of the representational strategy of the novel as a "direct, personal impression of life." The "direct" and "personal" quality of novelistic writing (just like the impressionism in contemporary painting) now serves as a distinguishing mark of the braveness with which the artist breaks away from that ideological authority which, in the form of a social and aesthetic consensus, had hitherto informed the standards of his representation. The "brave, personal way" helps secure a new freedom from representativeness; the very directness of the novel's impression guarantees the related freedom by which the signifying activity of the representer constitutes itself in relative independence of the given signified in the represented.

15. Quoted in Donadio, *Nietzsche,* p. 61.
16. See Michael Fried, "Representing Representation: On the Central Group in Courbet's *Studio,*" in *Allegory and Representation,* pp. 94–127.

Thus, the loss in the artist's representativeness is both redeemed and compensated for in terms of narrative technique: the emerging forms of narrative immediacy, the repudiation of omniscience, the stylized modes of point of view can all, in one important respect, be understood as a formally acknowledged relief from the traditional burden of authorial representativeness. It is the "direct, personal impression," the seemingly authentic flow of individual consciousness, the slice of life itself, which helps the author to leap over the crippling effects in the more homogeneous forms of representational closure, the ideological burden of determinacy in the public uses of language, what James in *The Tragic Muse*, coming now very close to Flaubert's *sottisier*, calls the "ignorance," the "density," "the love of hollow, idiotic words, of shutting the eyes tight and making a noise" (*TM*, p. 75).[17]

5. Modernism and the New Economy of the Signifier

While the later fiction of James reveals the precariousness of the links between the traditional forms of representation and the eroding relations of representativeness, the elements of crisis reach their full force only in the flowering of modernist strategies of narrative. Although it is of course quite impossible here to project the full modernist problematic of narrative representation, let me at least suggest some of the gaps and moments of transition between the Jamesian and the post-Jamesian situation and explore the impact of diminishing appropriation on the rupture between what represents and what is represented (and representable). First, let me glance at Van Wyck Brooks' *Three Essays on America* (written in 1913–14) in which, shortly before the outbreak of World War I the language of the dominant culture is revealingly taken to task. What Brooks, in the following passage, articulates is the complaint that the public language of politics is both unrepresentable and unrepresentative and that "ideals of this kind, in this way presented . . . cannot enrich life, because they are wanting in all the elements of personal contact." Brooks notes the depth of the gulf, in language, between what represents personal consciousness and what is represented in public ideology:

> The recognized divisions of opinion, the recognized issues, the recognized causes in American society are extinct. And although Patriotism, Democracy, the Future, Liberty are still the undefined, unexamined, unapplied catchwords over which the generality of

17. A good deal of the ambivalence of James' position relates to "his posture in the marketplace, his divided ambition for both artistic integrity and popular acceptance" (Michael Anesko, *"Friction with the Market": Henry James and the Profession of Authorship* [New York, 1986], p. 87). See, in this connection, Marcia Ann Jacobson, *Henry James and the Mass Market* (University, Ala., 1983).

our public men dilate, enlarge themselves and float (exact and careful thought being still confined to the level of engineering, finance, advertising and trade)—while this remains true, every one feels that the issues represented by them are no longer genuine or adequate.[18]

The failure, then, in these signifying concepts of politics and morality was that "the issues represented by them" had ceased to communicate any intellectual authority: the traditional signified had exhausted its capacity for legitimation, and the representational function of these signs was gravely impaired. What emerges from the writings of Brooks and those radical intellectuals who disowned the progressivism of the politicians is that the crisis in the representational function of language was primarily related to the erosion of a certain type of social, cultural, and philosophical authority. Whatever stability had remained in the relation between what was representing and what was represented, in the light of this failed authority a good many public significations now appeared as "undefined, unexamined, unapplied." While in Brooks' view this crisis was diagnosed as mainly a rupture "between university ethics and business ethics,"[19] the latter still seemed to retain an element of representability: language on the "level of engineering, finance, advertising and trade" continued to appear intact and was not viewed as subjugated to that crisis in appropriation which the public language of culture and politics had succumbed to.

In early twentieth-century fictional discourse, the inroads into the traditional social function of representation can most conspicuously be traced where during or shortly after World War I the erosion of authority led to a new political economy of signification, as best known to us in Ernest Hemingway's writing. As an illustration let me look at a well-known passage in *A Farewell to Arms* which is revealing and perhaps unique because, paradoxically, what it represents is a crisis of representativeness in the novelist's language itself. The first person singular is of course Frederic Henry's:

> I was always embarrassed by the words sacred, glorious, and sacrifice and the expression in vain. We had heard them, sometimes standing in the rain almost out of earshot, so that only the shouted words came through, and had read them, on proclamations that were slapped up by billposters over other proclamations, now for a long time, and I had seen nothing sacred, and the things that were glorious had no glory and the sacrifices were like the stockyards at Chicago if nothing was done with the meat except to bury it. There were many words that you could not stand to hear and

18. Van Wyck Brooks, *Three Essays on America* (New York, 1934), pp. 28, 101–2.
19. Ibid., p. 17.

finally only the names of places had dignity. Certain numbers were the same way and certain dates and these with the names of the places were all you could say and have them mean anything. Abstract words such as glory, honor, courage, or hallow were obscene beside the concrete names of villages, the numbers of roads, the names of rivers, the numbers of regiments and the dates.[20]

Hemingway's character is embarrassed by the collapse of any representational function on the part of some of his signifiers. But the embarrassment serves more than characterization; it transcends its fictional emitter, the first person singular instance, the "I" as an iconic sign and narrative point of view, so as to embrace the discursive practice of this passage as some strategic economy of writing itself. The crisis in representation remains attached to the characterizing icon of the first person singular and yet goes beyond it; in other words, this crisis is both represented and representing at the same time. Since the problem is articulated so self-consciously, on the level of both iconic sign and narrative activity, representational product and representational process, this text can be read on at least two levels.

First, although my interests now do not point this way, it can be read in terms of the iconic constraints of the fictional product of representation which, most immediately, are revealed in the language of the Hemingway hero, his muteness, and his modernist inability to assert himself anywhere except in the barroom, the bedroom, the arena, and on safari.[21] Second, the crisis in representation can be studied on the level of discourse in terms of the constraints and possibilities that this new rhetoric implicates as some ideological and aesthetic economy of articulation. On this level, our text reveals some extraordinarily articulate reluctance to authorize, let alone to appropriate, the dominant language of politics. There is some stark discontinuity between the given spectrum of public significations and the actually usable, much more limited range of the novelist's signifier. When the use of this signifier appears conditioned by its increasingly tenuous relation to any "abstract words"—to any generalized mode of public signification—the consequences are of course more complex than a naively referential understanding of fictional discourse can ascertain.

This complexity must be emphasized even when, as in other fictions of this period, the mimetically structured narrative of individual experience, especially in the love story, persists virtually unchallenged. As opposed to the as yet unbroken representational forms of this fictional figuration, the representational action on the level of discursive practice is so much

20. Ernest Hemingway, *A Farewell to Arms* (1929; New York, 1957), p. 185.
21. See Stanley Cooperman, *World War I and the American Novel* (Baltimore, 1967), p. 185.

more deeply affected. But there remains an uneasy connection between *histoire* and *discours* when this text goes out of its way to transcribe the dilemma of representational discourse in terms of a soldier's image of a legitimation crisis as a spatial metaphor of the distance to, and the loss of authority in, the official language of war politics. What we have is a spatial icon of physical aloofness distantiating the language of propaganda through the rain and the sheer distance from those who stood there and were told to listen. In this image, just as in that of "proclamations . . . slapped up . . . over other proclamations," the imperfectly achieved or redundantly handled process of communication serves as some register of the inefficacy of the authority transported therein. When Frederic Henry heard these words, "sometimes standing in the rain almost out of earshot, so that only the shouted words came through," the transcendental signified is, as it were, acoustically undermined and any claim of representativity is refuted, precisely because, in Brooks' phrase, "ideals of this kind, in this way presented . . . are wanting in all the elements of personal contact."

In Hemingway's text, "intellectual contact" and of course appropriation remained viable, if not "on the level of . . . finance, advertising and trade," at least perhaps on that of "engineering," geography, and statistics. In *A Farewell to Arms*, "only the names of places" had "dignity," and the irony in the use of a concept like "dignity" must not detract from the fact that place names did retain some representational function and authority, so that "dignity" here, presumably, was associated with a simple, unbroken sense of continuity between signifier and signified. Hence, it was "the concrete names of villages, the numbers of roads, the names of rivers, the numbers of regiments and the dates" which allowed for what Brooks called "careful thought and intellectual contact," and which did not sound "obscene" as against the real obscenity in taking for granted continuity in the representational function of transcendental signifieds with so heavy an ideological liability.

In *A Farewell to Arms* place names were of course foreign, and these foreign signifiers may have been particularly suited to carry the burden of what in our text is called "dignity." At any rate, Hemingway must have gladly used these names (much like the foreign sounds and signs of Paris, Spain, and Africa) to assist in the fictional manufacture of a world that still appeared representable precisely because its rendering was exceedingly selective, projected "piece by piece, out of the most meticulously chosen and crafted materials."[22] It was as if the choice of this material, based on meticulous scrutiny, was designed to intercept the unrepresentable and to withhold anything that did not meet the greatest rigor of authenticity. The authentic world was of course the world of things simple and basic;

22. John W. Aldrige, *"The Sun Also Rises*—Sixty Years Later," *Sewanee Review* 94 (Spring 1986): 340.

it was a world precluding those meanings and experiences which could not positively be measured by such deceptively simple significations as "nice," "clean," and "honest."

For Hemingway, the most crucial problem, then, was one of representability, and his unfailing response to it was a concern with the economy of the signifier. But the simplicity of his language was deceptive when it was not at all designed to convey a comparable simplicity of meaning. This contradiction in the signification process resulted from the twofold demand that writer and readers placed on the signifier: it was to fill in the space which remained representable and, at the same time, to demarcate those regions of fictionalized experience which resisted meaningful articulation. More than anything, this language was a highly fastidious medium, sounding the absence of things and the muteness of emotions in the unrepresentable space between and behind the common, the trivial utterance.

What made the artful inscription of triviality so untrivial and, if I may say so, so meaningful was that behind this fastiduous language there was no blankness, no vacuity but, on the contrary, "the strongly sensed presence of things omitted."[23] The omission itself might constitute some inverted kind of pathos, the effect of understatement, the staccato of refusing to connect. Even more important, this "strongly sensed presence of things omitted" could now serve as a foil to what, preciously, was still representable. Hence the largeness, in Hemingway, of even the most trivial signifier: the nod, the drink, the casual greeting, the fresh shirt, the rain on the tent. The representational efficacy of signs such as these resembled that of the names of places and rivers and the number of regiments in that their authority was not undermined by the legitimation crisis of some ideological signified. So every sign that did manage to be released into signification, against the compulsion of silence and the pressure of the unspeakable, appeared so much larger for having escaped omission or obliteration.

To be sure, the price for all this economizing was high enough: it involved among other things a curb on the project of novelistic representation, the willingness to abstain from previously maintained appropriations of things and relations. But, again, the diminished range of intellectual appropriations and comprehensions was, somehow, compensated for. It was compensated for not just by some extraordinary precision and economy in the use of verbal signs but by some new and problematic dimension in the relations between the fastidious order of the signifier and the submerged presence of disorder on the level of the half-suppressed or silenced signified. In Hemingway, the signifier is held in a state of uncanny balance between its capacity for releasing and its ability to obliterate meaning. To define the quality of this balance involves some awareness

23. Ibid., p. 342.

of what, in my introduction, I have called the historical activity residing in the very links and gaps of representation and in the way that the gaps are closed and the links are broken up. Although such definition can only be verified to the extent that it proceeds from some given text, perhaps it is possible here in conclusion to hazard a generalization and to say that the functioning of this balance can be gauged in relation to both the triumph and the fear associated with the precarious (dis)placement of meaning. The triumph is achieved to the degree that the gap between the speakable sign and the unspeakable meaning is at least temporarily closed and some existential challenge, as in the representation of war, is met through the power and resiliency of language. But, meanwhile, the fear remains, and its register is the sheer amount of silence and invisibility, affecting the whole range of information, insight, and emotion which, in the rupture between the simple signifier and the difficult signified, is darkly withheld. Behind this silence or darkness there is, on the part of the writing or the reading, some anxiety about not being able to relate to the larger issues of suffering and injustice, to the anonymous forces of war, the military, the ideology.

In *A Farewell to Arms,* there are two obvious possibilities of response, but either of these seems incapable of overcoming the futility, the pain, and the muteness inscribed in both the iconicity and the strategy of this writing: To surrender to these uncontrollable forces is not brave; to take up arms against their superior strength is hopeless. Even so, in the face of this alternative, whatever Hemingway's representational strategies can effect finds some correlative on the iconic level of representing his characters' action: Frederic Henry escapes to Switzerland and leaves the war behind. This is his way of responding to (though not controlling) the impossible alternative, and Catherine's death underlines the contingency of this triumph over fear. But what the characters can do and what they cannot do provides a mimetic parable for breaking the links and closing the gaps in this representational discourse. What this modernist discourse finally does is to seek refuge from the verbal obscenities of a murderous language and *Weltanschauung.* And yet, in doing just that, this discourse needs to fortify itself against the temptation of muteness and the threat to be overpowered by silence. Hence, the political economy of this writing calls for another, alternative, and minimalist strategy of representation to be upheld as almost a commission to survive and so, incidentally, to resist.

Reading Revolutionary Paris

Priscilla Parkhurst Ferguson

Reading the modern city compels a sociology of literature. Comprehension requires the reader to decipher the palimpsest of urban space and to integrate the many layers of physical, social, historical, and symbolic associations that determine identity within the city. At issue is not the physical city alone, the topography and toponymy of place, but also the verbal constructs that interpret and define place. The complex textuality resulting from the interaction of these two kinds of urban texts is further complicated in the modern city by the rapidity of growth, the competing frames of reference, and the sheer density of material that characterize the modern urban experience. No single text can do justice to this complex urban textuality; the sociology of literature serves here by looking for interpretations in patterns of meaning across texts. The many ventures that go under the label of the sociology of literature undoubtedly make this intellectual enterprise look very much like the "large loose baggy monsters" that Henry James saw in the novel. Yet, just as the novel is grounded in certain literary practices, a sociological approach to literature is founded on certain practices of texts. The intertextuality engendered by the friction of these texts, the peculiar functions that accrue to those texts designated as literary, the relations among different kinds of texts—these are the recurrent and fundamental concerns of the sociology of literature.

Modern Paris offers a paradigmatic example of urban intertextuality. For Walter Benjamin this Paris became "the capital of the nineteenth

The National Endowment for the Humanities awarded a fellowship that supported much needed and greatly appreciated time to work on revolutionary Paris. A preliminary version of this essay appears in *L'Esprit créatur* (Summer 1989).

century" because this city, better than any other place, illustrated the patterns and complexities of modernity. And Paris defined the age because it symbolized the experience of change. Cities have long been equated with invention, innovation, and the attendant turmoil. Even so, nineteenth-century Paris stands out for the intensity of this experience. The relentless centralization of government, the concentration of cultural institutions, industrialization, and even more in evidence, a rampant commercialism all shaped this experience. But what set Paris apart from other cities and made it the archetype of radical change was the Revolution. The events and the consequences of 1789 haunted the next century. Whether one condemned the specter or celebrated the vision, revolution was both the subject and the paradigm of Paris, and the combination reconstructed the French capital as every observer's laboratory for social change. Just as important for the potential readers of this changing urban text, the crisis of the city was importantly a crisis in meaning. The Revolution separated the primary urban texts that had worked together to identify the city before 1789. Representing the Revolution required representing change, rupture, and disorder, not simply because political events demanded it but because the Revolution had disjoined the physical city from the verbal constructs once associated with it.

1

On 21 January 1793, Louis XVI was driven from the Prison du Temple to what had been inaugurated as the Place Louis-XV and what was then the Place de la Révolution. The journey lasted almost two hours. The closed carriage and its full military escort passed through streets lined with citizens armed with spikes and guns. Drums attached to the horses covered any expression of sympathy for the condemned king. At the scaffold the king declared his innocence and absolved his executioners, more drums muffling his attempts to say more. The deed accomplished, the severed head was paraded before the impatient bystanders whose shouts of "Vive la liberté" and "Vive la république" ended this performance of what Michel Foucault so aptly called the "spectacle of the scaffold."[1]

1. See Abbé Edgeworth de Firmont (the king's confessor), *Dernières heures de Louis XVI, roi de France,* in *Histoire de la captivité de Louis XVI et de la famille royale, tant a la Tour du Temple qu'a la Conciergie* (Paris, 1817), p. 222, and Jean-Louis Soulavie, *Mémoires historiques et politiques du règne de Louis XVI,* 6 vols. (Paris, 1801), 6:517–18. The depiction of Louis XVI's execution by royalists lays great stress on his martyrdom, taken in christological

Priscilla Parkhurst Ferguson is professor of French at the University of Illinois at Chicago; she is the author of *Literary France: The Making of a Culture* (1987).

The conspicuous political dimensions of the execution have over-shadowed its specifically urban consequences. For, in beheading the king, the Revolution not only abolished a central symbol of country, it obliterated a vital emblem of the city. At least since the sixteenth century, monarch and inhabitants alike had boasted of Paris as the "capital of the kingdom." Whose capital could it be henceforth? Decapitation deprived the city of a *chef*, of its symbolic head. Paris became an organism without a head, truncated, incomplete, in sum, a monstrosity. So strong was the association of the city and the monarchy, so visible the imprint of royalty on the city itself, that the execution made much of Paris a symbolic non-sense. The fleur-de-lys (and sometimes a crown) that figured on the seal of the city clearly had to go. What would replace them? Whose city was it? It had been the monarch's city. Who now would, or indeed could, symbolize the comprehension of it? In a very real sense, the city had to be rewritten before it could once again be read.

Most obviously, one regime took over from another and went about the business of creating institutions in its own image. Accordingly, revolutionaries destroyed a number of the more egregious emblems of the past. (The term "vandalism" was coined at the time.) But renewal entails more than demolition. Given the imprint of the monarchy on Paris, symbolic regeneration posed problems of major proportions. The execution of Louis XVI was itself a larger symbol of urban crisis. It bespoke an immediate need for symbolic re-representation. It required a drastic rewriting, or resymbolization, of the urban text.

Although the connections between Paris and the king antedate the Renaissance, it is then, with the consolidation of the monarchy, that the relation acquired new force. A turning point came when the monarchy decisively cast its lot with the capital. In 1528 François I notified municipal officials of his decision to "make henceforth the greatest part of our home and stay in our good city of Paris and environs more than anywhere else in the kingdom."[2]

The wars of religion directed royal attention away from the city, but by the beginning of the seventeenth century, with Henri IV firmly in control of kingdom and capital, Paris figured high on the royal agenda. In the first decade of the century the king and his minister Sully commenced what was in effect the first Parisian urban renewal. Streets were built as was the strikingly innovative Pont Neuf; entire sections were developed, notably the Place Royale (des Vosges) and the Place Dauphine. The

---

terms. At the final parting, the king's confessor fell to his knees and cried out, " '*Allez, fils de St-Louis, montez au ciel*' " (quoted in Firmont, *Dernières heures de Louis XVI*, p. 226, and Soulavie, *Mémoires historiques*, 6:517). See also Michel Foucault, *Surveiller et punir; naissance de la prison* (Paris, 1975); trans. Alan Sheridan, under the title *Discipline and Punish: The Birth of the Prison* (New York, 1979), part 1, chap. 2.

2. Quoted in Jean-Pierre Babelon, *Nouvelle histoire de Paris: Paris au XVIe siècle* (Paris, 1986), p. 45.

honorific system of urban toponymy, instituted at this time, reserved the street names for the royal family (Dauphine, for the future Louis XIII, Royale, Sainte-Anne, for the patron of Anne of Austria) and close associates (Richelieu, Colbert)—so many acts to proclaim the presence and the puissance of the monarch.[3] Royal appropriation of urban space brought Paris into the modern age. Buildings, monuments, statues, streets, and their names heralded the king, impressing his authority in a commanding exercise of symbolic eminent domain.

The extent of the monarchy's demarcation of urban space can scarcely be overestimated. This "sacred geography" dedicated to the monarchy proclaimed the indissolubility of the royal and the sacred.[4] Louis XVI, like his predecessors, ruled by divine right and could even count a royal saint among his ancestors (Louis IX, Saint Louis). Some of the churches in Paris had been built as a result of direct intervention by the king or the royal family (Val-de-Grâce by Anne of Austria, the Invalides by Louis XIV, Sainte-Geneviève—the Pantheon—by Louis XV), but in effect every church impressed the king's stamp upon the city. Despite the removal of king and court to Versailles beginning in the 1670s, Paris continued to glorify the monarchy throughout the eighteenth century, from the inauguration of the Place Louis-le-Grand (Vendôme) in 1699 to that of the Place Louis-XV (Concorde) in 1763.

With 1789 the "sacred geography" had to be desecrated. The intensity of the monarchical urban text placed the leaders of the Revolution in a quandary: how to transform the capital of the kingdom into the center of the Revolution. Only through this dilemma can we comprehend the passion and the energy that revolutionaries brought to their plans for redefining urban space. The insignia of the king had to be eradicated, the emblems of reason and revolution displayed. The Places Louis-le-Grand and Louis-XV were renamed (des Piques, de la Révolution) along with a good many other streets. Royalty and saints yielded to authentic republicans. Montmartre became Montmarat, Hôtel-Dieu turned into Mirabeau-le-Patriote, Sainte-Anne gave way to Helvétius. Republican virtues replaced royalty, as Princesse metamorphosed into Justice, Richelieu into La Loi. It took only a few years for royalty to function as the negative of nomenclature. (Republican habitués of the Café Procope supposedly proposed names of royalist writers for all of the sewers!) The street names that had served as instruments of indirect social control under the ancien régime were recast as flagrantly political weapons. Of course, renaming alone could not exterminate the monarch. The demolition of the royal

3. See my "Reading City Streets," *French Review* 61 (Feb. 1988): 386–97. Here as elsewhere topographical and toponymical detail is taken from the incomparable work by Jacques Hillairet, *Dictionnaire historique des rues de Paris,* 2 vols. (Paris, 1963).
4. The notion of "sacred geography" is developed in Robert Redfield, "The Cultural Role of Cities," *Human Nature and the Study of Society,* the papers of Robert Redfield, ed. Margaret Park Redfield, 2 vols. (Chicago, 1962), 1:326–50.

statues in the Places Louis-le-Grand and Louis-XV in 1792 prefigured and in a sense enabled the execution of Louis XVI a few months later. From elimination of the symbol of monarchy the Revolution progressed logically to the execution of its embodiment in the king.

Because it cannot in itself supply redefinition, mere destruction never suffices. Further, the piecemeal alterations of nomenclature violated every notion of system. Each renaming was partial and, hence, unreasonable. The strategy could never satisfy a regime that sought, as the abbé Grégoire put it in his report to the National Assembly, to "republicanize everything." The only way to realize a wholly rational city would be to start over again, and in fact there was at least one proposal to raze Paris, another to build from scratch a city worthy of the Revolution. Less drastic were the proposals to rename *every* street in Paris according to one system or another.[5]

The many Revolutionary schemes for rationalizing Paris failed. Dreams of a rational, ideologically coherent city dissipated in politics. From the symbolic practices of the Revolution subsequent regimes took the lesson of overt politicization. Competing ideological currents complicated every topographical decision. Squares, streets, monuments, and even buildings in toponymical flux bore witness to a city in search of a symbolic raison d'être. Witness the odyssey of the Panthéon: built as a church (Sainte-Geneviève) at the end of the ancien régime, it became a pantheon under the First Republic, was restored as a church by the Empire (1804–14), the Restoration (1815–30), and the Second Empire (1852–70), after having been a pantheon under the July Monarchy (1830–48). In 1885, for the interment of Victor Hugo, the Third Republic changed it once again, and definitively, into a pantheon. The alterations of the statuary, the removal or relocation of individuals buried there, make the Panthéon a paradigmatic illustration of the volatile politics of urban space.

2

The primary text *of* the city of Paris prompted all kinds of writing *about* the city. The two kinds of urban texts—the physical city in itself and writing about that city—had been linked at least since Guillot's *Dit des rues de Paris* at the beginning of the fourteenth century. The moves of the monarchy to "write" the city in its own image fortified the connection between urban space and its textual rendition. Witness the guidebooks that undertook to explicate the "new" urban text. These guides, which first appeared in the sixteenth century, assumed that unmediated contact with the city was inadequate at best, and likely dangerous. The writer acted as the essential mediator between text and reader, between city

5. See Ferguson, "Reading City Streets," and Bronislaw Baczko, " 'Une ville nommée Liberté'—l'utopie et la ville," *Lumières de l'utopie* (Paris, 1978), pp. 283–399.

and inhabitant, between subject and the king. Royalty adhered in the interminable genealogies and lists of municipal officials and in the prominence accorded residences of the great—greatness in this sense deriving from proximity to the crown. In 1532, in what seems to be the first guidebook of Paris, *La Fleur des Antiquitéz de Paris,* Gilles Corrozet proposed first a history of the city, and then

> all the most praiseworthy things accomplished by princes and kings in Paris and all the edifices built by them from the time that it was first inhabited up to the time of the very Christian king of France, Francis the first of this name.[6]

The success of this first effort led Corrozet as early as 1550 to bring out the far more substantial *Les Antiquitéz, histoires, croniques et singularitez de la grande & excellente cité de Paris,* "where you will find . . . how much our Kings have enriched and decorated this capital city with privileges, with buildings and with their own persons, even after their death."[7]

Later guidebooks celebrated the monarchy in a more sophisticated manner even as they kept the celebratory mode. Thus, it was entirely logical for Germain Brice, author of a guidebook that went through nine editions between 1684 and 1752, to begin his tour of Paris with the official residence of the king in Paris, the Louvre, "the most remarkable place, which makes it the principal ornament of the city by its vast extent and the quantity of buildings of which it is composed."[8]

Throughout the eighteenth century there were numerous other guidebooks as well as histories of Paris, and a good many literary works took Paris as their subject—from Lesage's *Le Diable boiteux* (1707) and Montesquieu's *Les Lettres persanes* (1721) to many of the works of Rétif de la Bretonne, notably *Les Nuits de Paris* (1788–94). However, none of these works influenced nineteenth-century urban journalism nearly so

6. Gilles Corrozet, *La Fleur des Antiquitéz de Paris* (1532; Paris, 1945), p. 28. Corrozet ends with a marvelous genealogy that traces François I back to the royal line of Hector, thereby "substantiating" the origin of Paris in the line of Troy. See also Babelon, "Le Discours sur la ville," *Paris au XVIᵉ siècle,* pp. 15–43, which discusses early maps as well. On Corrozet and a number of later guides through the eighteenth century, see Maurice Dumolin, "Notes sur les vieux guides de Paris," *Mémoires de la société de l'histoire de Paris et de l'Ile de France* 47 (1924): 209–85.

7. Corrozet, introduction, in *Les Antiquitéz, histoires, croniques et singularitez de la grande & excellente cité de Paris, ville capitalle & chef du Royaume de France: Avec les fondations & bastimens des lieux: Les Sepulchres & epitaphes des princes, princesses & autres personnes illustres* [the postmortem influence comes from the epitaphs], authored in part by Corrozet, greatly augmented by Nicolas Bonfons (1550; Paris, 1577). The introduction first appeared in the 1561 edition.

8. Germain Brice, *Description de la ville de Paris et de tout ce qu'elle contient de plus remarquable* (1684; Geneva and Paris, 1971), p. 20. The foreword by Michel Fleury gives a publishing history: fourteen editions, counting reprints and counterfeit editions.

much as Louis Sébastien Mercier's panoramic *Le Tableau de Paris*.[9] Mercier struck out in new directions by his decision to render the city in terms of its inhabitants rather than its masters. He would not talk, he informed his readers at the outset, about the already fixed, about the monuments and buildings that mark urban space. He would himself fix the transient, the ever-mobile public and private behavior. The reader should not expect history or description of topography. Mercier would give neither "inventory nor catalogue" (*TP*, 1:v), and he even directed the historically minded reader to a dictionary of the city in four volumes (*TP*, 1:iv). Instead, what interested Mercier was comportment and its "fugitive nuances" (*TP*, 1:iv). In a credo that pointed to nineteenth-century realism, Mercier claimed to describe what he saw, without the intellectualizing that marred the work of so many of his contemporaries. His was a picture, a tableau, not a meditation: He "drew according to what he saw," he "painted" his tableau. "In this work I have held only the brush of the *painter* & . . . have given almost nothing over to the meditation of the *philosophe*" (*TP*, 1:ix). He wanted only to paint, not to judge or satirize (*TP*, 1:xiii, ix).

Le Tableau de Paris altered the rules of the genre. Mercier did not see himself as a satirist like Lesage or Montesquieu. Rather he approached Paris like an ethnographer, working from within a perspective akin to what social scientists call "participant observation." This was the model on which future generations of urban journalists would base their work on modern Paris. These later observers were fully aware that Mercier's emphasis on fixing changing customs introduced a new level of complexity into the definition of the city, a complexity that seemed peculiarly to suit their own, rapidly changing, uncertain times. The struggles over the designation of city space gave a distinctly urban resonance to the larger political conflicts played out in postrevolutionary France. The successful contestation of authority opened the city to definitions from every quarter. The execution of one king, the defeat and subsequent flight of his successors in 1814, 1815, 1830, 1848, and 1870 bespoke the fragility of political authority. With no center, the urban symbol system was in disarray. Into this symbolic void, writers stepped with varying degrees of assurance, to assert the authority of the written word to interpret the modern city and the society that it both represented and expressed.

The profusion of writing about Paris betrayed a pervasive bewilderment over the state of urban society. If, as Hugo insisted in the 1820s, a postrevolutionary society compelled a postrevolutionary aesthetic, an urbanizing Paris dictated an urban aesthetic. Exactly how that aesthetic

9. See Louis Sebastien Mercier, *Le Tableau de Paris*, 12 vols. (Amsterdam, 1781–88); hereafter abbreviated *TP*. *Tableau de Paris* appeared in one volume in 1781. Its popularity was such that a revised edition in four volumes appeared in 1782, volumes five through eight in 1783, volumes nine through twelve in 1788.

might be revolutionary was a subject of great debate as writers sorted out genres and styles, publics, publishers, and politics. Histories, guidebooks, essays, novels, and poetry about Paris glutted the market, which then asked for more. In 1856, by way of justifying yet another anthology of Paris explorations, Théophile Gautier summed up the situation:

> This magic title of Paris ensures success for a play, a journal, a book. Paris has an inexhaustible curiosity about itself that nothing has been able to satisfy, neither weighty tomes, nor light publications, nor history nor study nor memoirs nor tableaux nor the novel.[10]

Guidebooks proper, with maps and discussions of streets and sights, generally confined themselves to tracking topography and institutions. More indicative of the commotion of the period are the "literary guidebooks" that claimed to portray the Paris emerging after the July Revolution of 1830. The literary guidebook made a signal contribution to the French literary scene during the middle third of the century, from the fifteen-volume *Paris, ou le livre des cent-et-un* (1831–34) to the work that both capped and exhausted the genre, *Paris Guide,* published for the Exposition Universelle of 1867. For Parisians equally interested in and anxious about the world changing before their very eyes, these works furnished both information and assurance.

The multivolume collections of vignettes on people, places, events, and institutions capitalized on the expanding reading public that made the serial novel so successful a formula. Publishers raced to get out the next compilation, and writers from all sectors of the literary field joined in, from Chateaubriand and Charles Nodier among the older generation, to Alphonse de Lamartine, Honoré de Balzac, Gérard de Nerval, Alexandre Dumas, Hugo, and a host of others. Even foreigners, Goethe and James Fenimore Cooper most prominent among them, were pressed into service. Each volume of *Les Français peints par eux-mêmes* carried a front page dedicated to all the contributors from "The Grateful Editor." By the 1840s these literary guidebooks carried lavish illustrations by Paul Gavarni, Henry Monnier, and Honoré Daumier, to mention the best known. The articles ran the gamut from the short sketches known as *physiologies* (Balzac's "Histoire et physiologie des Boulevards de Paris" from *Le Diable à Paris*), semicaricatures (Balzac on "L'Épicier"), to discussions of characteristic or picturesque institutions (the morgue, the insane asylum at Charenton,

---

10. Alexandre Dumas et al., *Paris et les Parisiens au XIXe siècle: moeurs, arts et monuments* (Paris, 1856), p. i. The same subtitle is used in two other works that overlapped considerably: *Le Tiroir du diable* (Paris, 1845), and *Le Diable à Paris* (Paris, 1853). See also *Paris, ou le livre des cent-et-un,* 15 vols. (Paris, 1831–34); hereafter abbreviated *P.* The most extensive collection remains *Les Français peints par eux-mêmes: encyclopédie morale du dix-neuvième siècle,* 9 vols. (Paris, 1842); hereafter abbreviated *F.* See also Paul Lacombe, *Bibliographie parisienne – Tableaux de moeurs (1600–1880)* (Paris, 1887), p. 112.

public libraries), and descriptions of current events (the cholera epidemic, the funeral of the scientist Georges Cuvier). Such collections were, in short, a rag bag, which had something for just about everyone.

Fifty years after the publication of *Le Tableau de Paris* the publisher, Ladvocat, placed *Paris, ou le livre des cent-et-un* (1832) under Mercier's aegis: "we have to do for the Paris of today what Mercier did for the Paris of his time" (*P,* 1:vi). But Mercier's brush would no longer do. A new kind of politics had intervened in that half century. Nor was it simply a question of finding a contemporary Mercier. No single author could encompass the postrevolutionary city: "What writer could suffice for this multiple, tricolor Paris?" (*P,* 1:vi). The national flag joined the white of the monarchy with the red and the blue of the city of Paris. Who could render what the *Journal des Débats* had called the " 'drama of one hundred different acts' " (*P,* 1:ix) of tricolor Paris? This particular genre responded by countering diversity of subject with diversity of execution, which is why the literary guidebook can stand as the paradigmatic genre of urban exploration.

Jules Janin's opening article for the collection reiterated the association between new times and new modes of depicting them. Since everyone had taken to observing contemporary society, nineteenth-century Paris wanted not one but many observers to reveal it all. The contrast with Mercier is striking. Sure of his ability to comprehend everything he saw in the 1780s, the author of *Le Tableau de Paris* clearly gloried in the exuberant diversity he found all around him. His nineteenth-century epigones could not sustain that sense of certainty. They were overwhelmed by multiplicity, by sheer numbers, by strange sectors of society and their even stranger inhabitants. Insofar as the fragmentation of the city precluded encompassing the whole, these works could only enumerate their findings. No single point of view could prevail. Who could guide readers through the long gallery of modern customs, "that two revolutions have made for us" (*P,* 1:1)? The classical unities, and even more modern ones, no longer applied. The complexities of social and political revolution called for the collaborative interpretation: "Since one man can no longer write our drama, we call on over a hundred to do the job. What difference does it make if there are a hundred of us or two? . . . If unity loses, interest wins" (*P,* 1:14–15).

To judge by the number of works that appeared in this format, including reprints of previously published articles, multiple authorship made good commercial sense. (Subscription was the favored sales technique: only subscribers to *Les Français peints par eux-mêmes* received the ninth volume.) It also made good sociological and aesthetic sense. Ten years after *Paris des cent-et-un* Janin restated his convictions in the introduction to the most ambitious of these works, *Les Français peints par eux-mêmes* (five of the nine volumes focused on Paris), which appeared between 1840 and 1842 and was billed as an *encyclopédie morale du dix-neuvième siècle.* The rapidity of change and the fragmentation of Parisian society, Janin observed, forced a new approach to the city. In 100 years, "people will recount . . . that this city, so proud of its unity, was divided into five or six sections, which were like so many separate worlds, more separate than if each one of them were surrounded by the Great Wall of China" (*F*, 1:v–vi). A single writer might just possibly grasp the unitary nature of the king's domain; many chroniclers were needed to comprehend the warring, volatile republics of a postrevolutionary age: "This great kingdom has been cut up into so many little republics." Open any chapter of *Les Caractères,* Janin urged, and you will be convinced that representation of modern society must be divided among many authors: contemporary society boasts (or despairs of) innumerable phenomena La Bruyère never even imagined (*F*, 1:ix).

The very vogue of the literary guidebooks testifies to the failure of the definitions they proposed, the failure, in sum, of what may be termed an "aesthetic of iteration." In these texts the divers parts of the city fail to cohere. The chorus of voices provides no synthesis, no sense of place, no center. The aesthetic of iteration founders on the descriptive because it lacks the author/ity to convert *descriptive* lists into *narrative* order.[11] Coherence resides in the table of contents, where the order is *logical* in the primary, etymological senses of theory (*logia*) and discourse (*logos*). There is no guide, no authority to interpret the city. These tables of contents take the reader on the textual equivalent of the *flâneur*'s promenades.

Through the tables of contents the order of these works becomes *socio-logical,* the order/disorder of society complacently, uncritically reproduced in an urban text designed to reassure. No interpretation was imposed on the city. The multiple authorship vaunted by Janin and so strongly supported by publishers and readers reproduced the diversity and the disorientation of urban life. The city was laid out before the reader like the merchandise displayed in the arcades that Benjamin took as another emblem of Parisian modernity. The reader-shopper sampled, or moved on. The display of the guidebook was designed to diffuse attention onto as many points as possible, to entice the potential consumer or spectator. Thus does the *flâneur,* as Benjamin observed, give himself over to the phantasmagoria of the market.[12]

11. Philippe Hamon identifies this transformation from *description* (lists) to *tableau* (presupposes an order) as a primary problem in the construction of especially realistic narrative. See Hamon, *Introduction à l'analyse du descriptif* (Paris, 1981), p. 183.

12. See Walter Benjamin, "Paris, capitale du XIXe siècle," *Gesammelte Schriften,* ed. Rolf Tiedemann and Hermann Schweppenhäuser, 6 vols. to date (Frankfurt am Main, 1972–), 5:60. This version of the essay was originally written in French in 1939. The German version, written in 1935, does not include the passage cited above. See Benjamin, "Paris, die Hauptstadt des XIX. Jahrhunderts," *Gesammelte Schriften,* 5:45–59; trans. Edmund Jephcott, under the title "Paris, Capital of the Nineteenth Century," *Reflections: Essays,*

The weaknesses of the aesthetic of iteration, the inadequacies of these works as real guides to Paris, and the deficiencies of their interpretations of the rapidly changing urban space are all symbolized in a single recurring figure—the devil. For although the true model of the new urban journalism was Mercier's *Tableau de Paris*, the nominal model was Lesage's *Le Diable boiteux* (1707 and 1726). In this satirical novel Asmodée [Asmodeus], a junior devil of lust and lechery, removes the rooftops of houses in Madrid (read Paris) to display his control over human lives. Immensely popular from its publication, *Le Diable boiteux* offered a convenient tag and conceit for the literary guidebooks. *Paris, ou le livre des cent-et-un* (1831) was originally entitled *Le Diable Boiteux à Paris, ou Paris et les Moeurs comme elles sont.* "You will have something better than *Le Diable boiteux*, believe me," promised the publisher, citing a prepublication journal article (*P,* 1:v, vii, xi). Taking his cue from the original title, Janin entitled his introductory article "Asmodée." The image was subsequently picked up in a series of guidebooks generated by *Le Diable à Paris* of 1845–46 (with reprints or reeditions in 1845, 1852, 1853, and 1868–69).

The eighteenth- and the nineteenth-century devils do not necessarily have much in common. True, Monnier's engraving for the title page shows a peg-leg devil atop the world waving his crutch (fig. 1).[13] On the other hand, the rather elegant devil standing over the map of Paris that Gavarni placed on the title page of *Le Diable à Paris* (1845 and 1853 editions) (fig. 2) looks quite unlike the crippled dwarf sporting a plumed red turban and a great white satin cloak who makes his appearance in the first chapter of *Le Diable boiteux* (though they both have cloven hooves to signal their origins). In any case, beyond the title page or at most the first article, the devil disappears. His guidance is literally superficial as he skims over the surface of the city.

His ostensible disappearance notwithstanding, by his very limitations the lame devil, now multiplied by 100 or more collaborators, performs

---

Aphorisms, Autobiographical Writings (New York, 1986), pp. 146–62. For the connection between *physiologie* and *flânerie*, see Richard Sieburth, "Une idéologie du lisible: le phénomène des physiologies," *Romantisme* 47 (1985): 39–60. These literary guidebooks reproduce the structure of the dominant discourse identified by Richard Terdiman, most particularly the newspaper. See Richard Terdiman, *Discourse/Counter-Discourse: The Theory and Practice of Symbolic Resistance in Nineteenth-Century France* (Ithaca, N.Y., 1985), chap. 2.

13. The devil is surrounded by four figures, two bewigged men (one in the act of writing), a hooded figure with a very pointed goatee, and a half-nude old man, arm outstretched. Back left figures the Panthéon or the Invalides. To the right a scroll lists the names of the predecessors of the one hundred and one: Addison, Sterne, Fielding, Goldsmith, St Foix (author of a popular multivolume series, *Essais historiques sur Paris*, 1754–55), Dulaure (author of eight volumes on the history of Paris, who also figures among the contributors to the collection), and Mercier. It is significant that the French models, with the exception of Mercier, are specialists on Paris, the English models of a particular approach to literature.

PARIS,

ou

LE LIVRE

DES CENT-ET-UN.

TOME PREMIER.

Addison.
Sterne.
Fielding.
Goldsmith.
St Foix.
Dulaure.
Mercier.

HENRY MONNIER

THOMPSON.

A PARIS,

CHEZ LADVOCAT, LIBRAIRE

DE S. A. R. LE DUC D'ORLÉANS.

M DCCC XXXI.

FIG. 1

LE
DIABLE A PARIS

— PARIS ET LES PARISIENS —

TEXTE

PAR GEORGE SAND — P.-J. STAHL (HETZEL) — LÉON GOZLAN
P. PASCAL — FRÉDÉRIC SOULIÉ — CHARLES NODIER — EUGÈNE BRIFFAULT — S. LAVALETTE — DE BALZAC
ALPHONSE KARR — MÉRY — GÉRARD DE NERVAL
ARSÈNE HOUSSAYE — THÉOPHILE GAUTIER — ALFRED DE MUSSET, ETC.

ILLUSTRATIONS

PAR GAVARNI, BERTALL, ANDRIEUX, H. MONNIER, LANCELOT, FABRITZIUS, ETC.

PARIS

MARESCQ ET COMPAGNIE
ÉDITEURS
5, RUE DU PONT-DE-LODI, 5

GUSTAVE HAVARD
LIBRAIRE
15, RUE GUÉNÉGAUD, 15

1855

Fig. 2

an important aesthetic function in the literary guidebooks. Although Lesage's Asmodée may look at his city from above, his view is no less partial than those of the nineteenth-century collaborators. He flits from house to house, just as the guidebooks pass from topic to topic. In both instances the reader must infer Paris from the many and incommensurate parts. Janin and his publisher chose better than they knew. For the devil embodies the need for another vision. Traditionally, the devil sees all, yet his vision is without wisdom. He knows the world only to manipulate it for his own perverse ends. The combination of strength and weakness is figured in the integration of fine clothes and peg leg. In the guidebooks, the two together, splendor and handicap, also point to the inability of an aesthetic of iteration to imagine the city. The guidebooks, like the devil, spread before the reader a glittering array of parts that, finally, do not cohere. For neither the one nor the other does sight lead to insight.

3

Rewriting the city demands a special kind of imagination, one that sees beyond the parts to the whole, one that welcomes system. The great novels of the nineteenth century do just this, and their richness depends in good part on their assumption—quite the contrary of Janin's—that the city existed intact and that, however much attention must be paid to the parts, Paris was more than their sum. The novel replaced the aesthetic of iteration of the literary guidebooks with an "aesthetic of integration." The politics of integration and the definition of city space once imposed by the monarch no longer obtained. In the absence of an urban aesthetic the writer arrogated the authority of definition. The kings of the nineteenth century had lost creative power. Balzac explicitly connected the metamorphosis of the city, in particular its losses, to the absence of royal authority. He saw no king who fulfilled the *idea* of kingship, which he defined in terms of a *gaze* capable of giving life or taking it away or as a *word* endowed with the gift of creation. Balzac, of course, was promoting himself as replacement, the one who could re-create old Paris.[14]

14.

Pour les flâneurs attentifs . . . pour ceux qui savent étudier Paris, mais surtout pour celui qui l'habite en curieux intelligent, il s'y fait une étrange métamorphose sociale depuis quelque trentaine d'années. . . . nous avons vu beaucoup plus de rois qu'autrefois. . . . Plus on a fabriqué de rois, moins il y en a eu. Le roi, ce n'est pas un Louis-Philippe, . . . : le roi, c'était Louis XIV ou Philippe II. Il n'y a plus au monde que le Czar qui réalise l'idée de roi, dont un regard donne ou la vie ou la mort, dont la parole ait le don de la création.

(Honoré de Balzac, "Ce qui disparaît de Paris," *Oeuvres Diverses,* vols. 38–40 of *Oeuvres complètes* [Paris, 1940], 40:607. This essay was originally published in *Le Diable à Paris* [1844]).

The conjunction of literature and the city was already a commonplace by the nineteenth century as urban discourse of every sort threatened to overwhelm the city. In 100 years, Janin assured his contemporaries in his introduction to *Les Français peints par eux-mêmes*:

> People will say that everyone in this capital spent all their time talking, writing, listening, reading: morning speeches written up in your newspapers; spoken speeches in the middle of the day from the courts; printed speeches in the evening. The preoccupation of the entire city was to figure out if it would talk a bit better the next day than the day before. [*F,* 1:v]

Into an urban space flooded with discourse the novel brought a reimagined city. In place of fragments of a city the novel presented a city made whole. It simultaneously expanded the narrative to contain the city and constricted the city to fit its narrative. The simplification involved in these rhetorical strategies of containment is a necessary property of symbolic management. For without such stylization the city muddles the reader trying to read the urban text much as it disorients the inhabitant endeavoring to negotiate the city.[15]

The metaphorization of Paris begins much earlier, but it is in the nineteenth century that metaphors and images acquired a particular, and modern, intensity. The characteristic and appropriate trope for the postrevolutionary city is metonymy. Recourse to metonymic figures, in particular synecdoche, construes the familiar sights of Paris that, topographically and symbolically, tie its many parts: the Seine, the sewers, the catacombs, the cemetery, and latterly, the métro. All of these figures reduce the city to a part, yet this part also contains the city. The reciprocity of synecdoche is vital to the way these metonymic figures define the city in its entirety.[16]

What parts could stand for the whole? Now that the king no longer held sway, what elements could represent Paris? One of the most frequent strategies of writers and tourists alike was to view the city from afar, most strikingly from a height. Early maps tend to place the observer somewhere on the horizon, at a point of view that no one at that time could possibly have. We have all climbed the towers of Notre-Dame or the Tour Eiffel or, hélas, the Tour Montparnasse. An adventurous soul in the nineteenth century might even take a balloon ride.

Or read novels. The view from afar was a staple of city novels in the nineteenth century, a subgenre of a more general romantic taste for

15. See Richard Wohl and Anselm L. Strauss, "Symbolic Representation and the Urban Milieu," *American Journal of Sociology* 63 (Mar. 1958): 523–32.

16. Pierre Citron locates the transformation from theme to myth in just this tendency to conceive of Paris as a whole. See Pierre Citron, *La Poésie de Paris dans la littérature française de Rousseau à Baudelaire,* 2 vols. (Paris, 1961), 2:249–63. See also "Index-Catalogue des images relevées depuis des origines à 1862," 2:407–44.

panoramas. The most famous of these is Hugo's "A Bird's Eye View of Paris" in *Notre-Dame de Paris* (1831), countered in *Les Misérables* (1862) with "An Owl's View of Paris." The mirror image of the aerial panorama is the labyrinth in Hugo's celebrated discourse on the sewers in *Les Misérables*, the one and the other *not* the "real" city but a projection of that city.[17]

The most striking views among Balzac's panoramas, the most pregnant with meaning, are those from Père-Lachaise: Eugène de Rastignac's defiant challenge in *Le Père Goriot*, Jules Desmarets' vision in *Ferragus* of the "microscopic Paris" of the cemetery as a synecdoche for "the true Paris."[18] The cemetery is at once a *site de passage* and a *rite du récit*, a place of passage and a narrative rite, a modern variant of the mediaeval dance of death designed to impress the living with the vanity of life. In M. M. Bakhtin's terms the *topos* of the cemetery constitutes a chronotope, a trope that makes time "artistically visible" and invests space with "the movements of time, plot and history."[19] This chronotope reinvests the landscape with authorial definition, just as the bird's-eye view of the writer substitutes for the superior vantage point that was once the king's.

Here the "melodramatic imagination" is very much an "urban imagination," the ability simultaneously to conceive the part and the whole, and this "synecdochal imagination" is vital to the urban novel because it allows the city to be apprehended.[20] Synecdoche thus bespeaks an "aesthetic of integration." Physiologies and literary guidebooks disperse energy by dividing Paris into parts. The urban textual equivalent of "divide and

17. See Citron, *La Poésie de Paris*, 1:387–409. Judith Wechsler notes that "the mid-nineteenth century is the period of the bird's-eye view" (Judith Wechsler, *A Human Comedy: Physiognomy and Caricature in 19th Century Paris* [Chicago, 1982], p. 20). She points out that three popular literary guidebooks also featured bird's-eye views for their frontispieces: *Le Diable à Paris* (1845–46), Edmond Texier's *Tableau de Paris* (1852–53), and *Paris dans sa splendeur* (1861).

Other examples include four works by Émile Zola: *La Débâcle* (the final view of Paris in flames); *L'Assommoir* (ascent of the wedding party to the top of the column of the Place Vendôme); *Une Page d'amour* (Jeanne's night at the open window, waiting for her mother; Hélène and M. Rambaud at the Passy cemetery); and *Les Trois Villes—Paris* (the final view). Nor is the device limited to French literature. See Charles Dickens, "Town and Todgers's" *Martin Chuzzlewit* (1844), and the historical vision that concludes *A Tale of Two Cities* (1859).

18. Père-Lachaise opened in 1804 and by the 1820s was a favorite promenade. Benjamin points to "Das panoramatische Prinzip bei Balzac" (Benjamin, "Aufzeichnungen und Materialien," *Gesammelte Schriften*, 5:663). See Jeannine Guichardet, *Balzac: "Archéologue" de Paris* (Paris, 1986), pp. 321–27. Other panoramas include *Les Proscrits* (1831); *La Femme de trente ans* (1831), the beginning of Part IV; and *L'Envers de l'histoire contemporaine* (1842–44), where the topographical panorama gives rise to a historical one.

19. Bakhtin was of course interested in the stylistic analysis of literary works, and he defines the chronotope accordingly as "the intrinsic connectedness of temporal and spatial relationships that are artistically expressed in literature" (M.M. Bakhtin, "Forms of Time and of the Chronotope in the Novel," *The Dialogic Imagination: Four Essays*, ed. Michael Holquist, trans. Caryl Emerson and Holquist [Austin, Tex., 1981], p. 84).

20. See Peter Brooks, *The Melodramatic Imagination: Balzac, Henry James, Melodrama, and the Mode of Excess* (New Haven, Conn., 1976).

conquer" is the "segregate and forget" tactic implied by the aesthetic of iteration of the *physiologies*. Those caricatured are safely Other, they live safely Elsewhere. The urban imagination, on the other hand, insists on the connections between those parts, even, or especially the most extreme. Père-Lachaise is part of the city, so are the sewers; the infamous rue Soly, where Ferragus lives, is contiguous with the rue Ménars, where Madame Jules lives; the Montagne-Sainte-Geneviève of the Pension Vauquer is inscribed within the Faubourg Saint Germain of Mme de Beauséant's hotel and vice versa. Balzac does not allow the reader either to forget or dismiss these connections. Each is a necessary function of the other. Each depends on the other. The myth of Paris, which crystallizes in the revolutionary energies released by the July Revolution, becomes a function of the insistence on these almost organic connections. The personification of Paris attests to this organic conception of the city. Integration overcomes iteration to create the unity that cannot be reproduced because it does not exist. This creation is the vocation of the writer, and the city thus created has been called a "utopic."[21] It is precisely this utopic that allows us to identify with the city, to know it, or to feel that we do. The utopic offers a text and a tactic for dealing with the city.[22]

This utopic, properly speaking, is revolutionary. The assimilation of the Revolution into literary France is the task, and the glory, of the writer, and the condition of literature. The writer's creation of symbolic unity replaces the monarchy and does so in full acceptance of the consequences of that which destroyed the monarch. The novel makes its distinctive contribution by restoring the human scale of the city through exemplary (not "typical") figures that give the city expression and definition. Rastignac, Quasimodo, Gavroche, Frédéric, Gervaise, Nana, and others are actors in revolutionary Paris as well as protagonists in novels.

4

The fusion of the writer and Paris, Paris and modernity, modernity and revolution, is nowhere more arresting than in the work and the persona of Victor Hugo. Nowhere does Hugo insist more on the connections than in his outsize introduction to *Paris Guide* of 1867.[23] Given his tenacious and highly publicized opposition to the Second Empire, Hugo was a somewhat audacious choice for a work timed to appear for

21. The concept is Louis Marin's; see his *Utopiques: Jeux d'espace* (Paris, 1973); trans. Robert A. Vollrath, under the title *Utopics: Spatial Play* (Atlantic Highlands, N.J., 1984).

22. See Michel de Certeau, *L'Invention du quotidien* (Paris, 1974); trans. Steven Rendall, under the title *The Practice of Everyday Life* (Berkeley and Los Angeles, 1984), esp. chap. 3.

23. See *Paris Guide par les principaux écrivains et artistes de la France,* introduction by Victor Hugo, 2 vols. (Paris, 1947); hereafter abbreviated *PG*.

the Exposition Universelle sponsored by the government. But any work whose title page boasted authorship *"par les principaux écrivains et artistes de la France"* had to include Hugo, so great was his reputation in France and abroad and so strong were his associations with Paris from *Notre-Dame de Paris* to *Les Misérables* and through thirty years of Parisian literary life. Hugo's identification with the Paris text is so entire that he virtually makes himself part of the text or, to be precise, a "paratext."[24] Alluding to his exile just off the Brittany coast, he notes that "appropriately, we are on the threshold, almost outside. Absent from the city, absent from the book" (*PG,* p. XXXIV). This distance is not fortuitous. It is necessary because it gives Hugo the perspective from which to embrace all of Paris, past, present, and future.

By its format *Paris Guide* belongs squarely within the tradition of the literary guidebook. The editors conceived the two large, closely printed volumes as an "encyclopedic enterprise" and had the "absolute conviction of publishing *the most complete* work on Paris ever undertaken" (*PG,* p. vi). Hugo himself asserted that the work was "an edifice built by a dazzling legion of minds," and if one added "all the other luminous names" which are missing for one reason or another, "it would be Paris itself" (*PG,* p. XXXIV). *Paris Guide* was a salmagundi, with historical pieces (Louis Blanc on Old Paris) and articles on institutions (Sainte-Beuve on the French Academy, Michelet on the Collège de France, Gautier on the Louvre Museum, Viollet-le-Duc on Paris churches, Taine on art), mixed in with practical information (guides to streets and buses). Yet Hugo's grandiloquent introduction of over forty pages subverts the very notion of a guidebook in any ordinary sense of the term. Nothing could be further from the aesthetic of iteration than Hugo's vast panorama of Paris from ancient to modern times and into the future. For the physical and historical Paris receives far less attention than the meaning of the city within the progressive development of Western civilization.

Hugo works with an assumption that by the mid-nineteenth century is certainly a cliché: Paris as head, as brain.[25] But Hugo elaborates this familiar association into a vision of Paris and eternity. The history of Paris becomes the drama of revolution. Paris is more than the head of a people (*PG,* p. XX), it is the brain of the universe, the "nerve center" of the earth (*PG,* p. XXVII), and, hence, vital to its life. "The universe without a head would be like a decapitation. One cannot even imagine an acephalous civilization" (*PG,* p. XXV). Thus Hugo returns to the very source of unmeaning. Decapitation exemplifies the original loss of meaning

24. On the "paratext," see Gérard Genette, *Seuils* (Paris, 1987), a partial translation of which appears as "Structure and Functions of the Title in Literature," trans. Bernard Crampé, *Critical Inquiry* 14 (Summer 1988): 692–720.

25. Citron (*La Poésie de Paris,* 2:413, 441) lists several references for brain [*cerveau*] beginning with Rétif de la Bretonne; head [*tête*] (of France, of the universe) represents a far older association, the first example dating from the twelfth century.

for monarchical Paris in the execution of Louis XVI. Hugo's protest here gives new meaning to a lifelong opposition to capital punishment. The refusal of decapitation accomplishes the impossible. It puts Paris back together again, makes the city whole, and restores its meaning. That meaning has changed. The language through which Hugo accomplishes this miracle has become the language of revolution. The writer, not the monarch, creates meaning.

Clearly, Hugo takes *Paris Guide* in the highest sense: the book is a guide to Paris, Paris is the guide to humanity. The history of Paris is a "microcosm of general history," "the pivot city on which, on a given day, history turned" (*PG,* pp. VI, XVIII).[26]

Paris owes this paradigmatic modernity to the Revolution: "1789. For almost a century, this number has been the preoccupation of the human species. It contains the entire phenomenon of modernity" (*PG,* p. XVIII). Rome is more majestic, Venice more beautiful, London richer. But Paris has the Revolution: "Palermo has Etna, Paris has thought. Constantinople is closer to the sun, Paris is closer to civilization. Athens built the Parthenon, but Paris tore down the Bastille" (*PG,* p. XVIII).

The Revolution supplied Hugo with the synecdoche that he needed to encompass modern Paris. For the Revolution explains as it justifies the postrevolutionary city, including even the decadent Paris of the Empire—"The minute is sick, not the century" (*PG,* p. XXXII). Using a strategy on which he will rely in *Quatrevingt-Treize* (1874), Hugo has recourse to metaphors of nature to explicate the excesses of which, in another mode, he disapproved. The Revolution is a "sublime vaccine" that destroys the "virus" of servitude and superstition. "What is the French Revolution!" Hugo exclaims and answers immediately, "A vast cleansing. There had been a plague, the past. This fiery furnace burned this miasma" (*PG,* p. XXXIII).

The seal of the city reproduced on the frontispiece literalizes Hugo's conception of postrevolutionary Paris in a century of progress (fig. 3). In contrast to the official seal, which displays a three-masted ship viewed from the side, the seal of *Paris Guide* exhibits a galley with a single square sail and with its bank of oars raised, going before the wind. For Hugo, surely the ship is propelled by the winds and the manpower of the Revolution. The great billowing sail heading directly toward the reader pictures Hugo's impassioned affirmation that "Paris is the center of effort [*le point vélique*] on the sail that represents civilization" (*PG,* p. XIX). Like

---

26. Hugo's exaltation of Paris continued a tradition of boasting that dated from the twelfth century. Corrozet's dedication to *Les Antiquitéz* of 1550 (edition of 1577), for example, affirmed not only that Paris had no peer but that the very name of the city ennobled its nobles. On the Latin as well as French sources of what was in effect a literary genre of city praise, see Babelon, *Paris au XVIe siècle,* pp. 18–31. The notion of Paris as world is usually traced to the Emperor Charles V in 1540, who proclaimed that Paris " 'non urbs, sed orbis' " (ibid., p. 28).

PARIS GUIDE

PAR

LES PRINCIPAUX ÉCRIVAINS

ET ARTISTES

DE LA FRANCE

PREMIÈRE PARTIE

LA SCIENCE — L'ART

DEUXIÈME ÉDITION

PARIS
LIBRAIRIE INTERNATIONALE
15, BOULEVARD MONTMARTRE

A. LACROIX, VERBOECKHOVEN ET Cᵉ, ÉDITEURS
A Bruxelles, à Leipzig et à Livourne
1867

FIG. 3

the winds that converge on a single point of the sail, the currents of modern civilization intersect in Paris.[27] This progressive vision of *Paris Guide* thus counters the pessimism of *Notre-Dame de Paris,* with its bitter lamentation on the lost unity of mediaeval civilization. As the mediaeval world cohered around the Church, so modern society finds its raison d'être in the Revolution, "this strong nineteenth century, son of the Revolution and father of liberty" (*PG,* p. XXXIV). As Notre-Dame de Paris signified mediaeval Paris, so the Panthéon, "full of great men and useful heroes," manifests its modern, revolutionary equivalent. Saint Peter's may be the larger dome, but the Panthéon is the more elevated thought (*PG,* p. XXVIII).

Even as Hugo was writing his revolutionary utopic, Baron Haussmann was drastically rewriting the topographical text of Paris, creating a very different city from the one that Hugo knew or imagined. Haussmann produced a Paris to be seen and admired, a bourgeois Paris of parks and broad avenues to compete with the royal Paris of the ancien régime. By way of contrast, Hugo's concern was with the seer not with the seen. His domain was not the material city but the spiritual one. Hugo no longer climbed the towers of Notre-Dame to view the city; he ascended to the dome of the Panthéon, the tomb that, in a startling oxymoron, Hugo sees radiating above the city like a star ("The Panthéon . . . has above the city the radiance of a tomb star [*tombeau étoile*]" [*PG,* p. XXVIII]).

In due time, Hugo himself would lie in the Panthéon, among the great men and useful heroes of France. For the moment, in 1867, for *Paris Guide,* he wrote from afar, the distance of his exile allowing him to imagine Paris without the encumbrance of the visible realities of the bourgeois city. Hugo staked these claims on the very last page of his introduction with the name of his home on the Isle of Guernsey. Hauteville House does not simply tell the reader where Hugo lives; it is a sign that tells the reader where he stands in relationship to Paris—Hauteville House, high above the city, high within the city. Even in exile Hugo claimed Paris as his own.

27. The seal of Paris was officially registered in the Armorial Général de France in 1699. The ship (which also figures in the arms of a number of French port cities) originated in the seal of the Prévôté des Marchands dating from 1412 when the addition of the fleur-de-lys on the top third of the seal graphically demonstrated the imposition of royal power on the city represented by the merchants. The seal decreed by Baron Haussmann in 1853 had a ship that resembled the more elaborate three-masted galleons characteristic of the ancien régime seals. Haussmann's seal also marks the first appearance of the motto *Fluctuat nec mergitur* [It floats and does not sink]. See Anatole de Coëtlogon and Lazare Maurice Tisserand, *Les Armoiries de la Ville de Paris, sceaux, emblèmes, couleurs, devises, livrées et cérémonies publiques,* 2 vols. (Paris, 1874–75), vol. 1. The current seal shows the galley, white against a red background, surmounted by gold fleur-de-lys on blue, the whole enclosed on the bottom by an olive branch with the motto in red and surmounted by a crown-chateau.

It is supremely fitting that Hugo should have been so intimately associated with the Republic and that he, in effect, became its hero. It is also right and proper that the Third Republic should have inscribed this metonym for Paris on the cityscape itself. In 1881, to celebrate the beginning of his eightieth year, the street where he lived became the Avenue Victor Hugo. And it was Hugo's burial in 1885 that finally designated the Panthéon as a republican sanctuary. Thus did the city itself confirm what Hugo believed as firmly as Thomas Carlyle, namely that the writer is the hero of postrevolutionary society, for it is through the writer that Revolutionary Paris becomes literary France. For the third term in the equation of Paris and the Revolution, the term that closes and completes the circle, is art, and most particularly literature. Reason and art make common cause because "great poetry is the solar spectrum of human reason" (*PG*, p. XXIX). The poet claims legitimacy as the descendant of the "trinity of reason," Rabelais, Molière, and Voltaire (*PG*, p. XXVII). Paris is the guide to humanity, and the poet is the guide to Paris.

Once again, the seal of Paris offers an appropriate emblem. In a gesture of political unity the official seal of Paris chosen by Haussmann retained the fleur-de-lys background over the ship, and it retained as well the château-crown at the very top. *Paris Guide*, placed by Hugo under the sign of the Revolution, logically eliminated the fleur-de-lys. But it kept the crown. Surely Hugo, like Balzac, like the other writer-guides, intended that crown for himself, for the writer who had already been "crowned" by the Revolution. Because literature "completes and crowns Paris" (*PG*, p. XXVIII), Hugo in effect claims the crown that the city bears on its coat of arms. The bond with Paris comprehends, or transcends, all regimes.

Revolutionary texts come in many guises, and their multiplicity and diversity go far to explain the difficulty involved in relating profound social, economic, and political change to literary change. Every one of these texts must create its own point of view, and the study of texts almost always reflects in some way on perspective. The tableau of the guidebook and the overview of the novel construct a place to stand within narrative, a place from which to see. In establishing connections between different kinds and levels of texts, the sociology of literature makes its peculiar contribution to the study of texts with a heightened concern with the whole problem of perspective. The shifting bases of the many urban texts disclose the larger difficulty in seeing Paris. Reading the city requires seeing the city, which in turn commands a place of observation.

To understand how the Revolution disrupted the Paris text is to see why Janin made such a virtue of multiple points of view in the literary guidebook or, alternatively, why Hugo would insist so emphatically and so compulsively on Revolutionary unities for his Paris. In both instances, the literary device acknowledges the disorder produced by the Revolution. The first attempts to accommodate that disorder, the second seeks to vanquish the problem by redefining the city in terms of that Revolution. The broader nineteenth-century preoccupation with Paris carried on the battle between accommodation and redefinition.

In a sense, every Parisian, and for that matter every city dweller, in the nineteenth century as today, is caught between Janin's spirit of accommodation and Hugo's spirit of assertion. The complexity of the modern city, of course, requires both. In exploring the connections between social transformation and literary change, the sociology of literature supplies a gauge of the struggles between strategies. And with that gauge it suggests the crucial role that literary discourse plays in interpreting, and thereby constructing, social discourse.

The Reality of Representation:
Between Marx and Balzac

Sandy Petrey

In his celebrated 1888 letter to Margaret Harkness, Engels claimed to have learned more about French society and its history from Balzac "than from all the professed historians, economists and statisticians of the period together."[1] According to Paul Lafargue, Marx's admiration for the *Comédie humaine* was so intense that he intended to write a critical study of Balzac as soon as his studies of economics were complete.[2] Considered in relation to the sociology of literature, such assessments establish extraordinary importance for the intertextual relationship between Balzac's fiction and the founding documents of Marxist thought. Whether we understand the sociology of literature as literary representation of social reality or as social influences on literary creation, Balzac, Marx, and Engels constitute a privileged group. The *Comédie humaine* stands at the origin of the Marxist vision of society, and that vision has in its turn dominated many of the most influential critical studies of literature in its social matrix. The question of what Marx and Engels learned from Balzac is momentous.

The purpose of this essay is to address the learning process as illustrated in one text by Balzac, *Colonel Chabert*, and one by Marx, *The Eighteenth Brumaire of Louis Bonaparte*. My argument is that those two texts share a vision that, while profoundly historical, repudiates theses commonly ascribed to the Marxist and Balzacian understandings of historical existence. In brief, those theses can be summarized as economism,

---

1. Karl Marx and Friedrich Engels, *Marx and Engels on Literature and Art* (Moscow, 1984), p. 91; further references to this work, abbreviated *ME*, will be included in the text.
2. See Paul Lafargue, "Reminiscences of Marx," in *ME*, p. 439.

the assumption that the task of sociology is to cut through the ideological configurations associated with a particular social formation to reveal the economic activity that, by making the social formation what it is, constitutes the ultimate determination of collective existence. *Colonel Chabert* and *The Eighteenth Brumaire* undermine the armature of economism, the hierarchical superiority of material reality over ideological concepts. Because both texts represent ideology as a material reality in its own right, they make every hierarchy based on the opposition between matter and ideology untenable.

The starting point for my reading of the exchanges between Marx and Balzac is the repetition in *The Eighteenth Brumaire* of a striking image employed in *Colonel Chabert* to represent the force of ideology as experienced by a man forcibly set outside the conventions it endorses. Balzac first: "The social and judicial world weighed on his breast like a nightmare."[3] Marx's appropriation occurs in a much-quoted meditation on the past as impediment to the future.

> Men make their own history, but they do not make it just as they please; they do not make it under circumstances chosen by themselves, but under circumstances directly encountered, given and transmitted from the past. *The tradition of all the dead generations weighs like a nightmare on the brain of the living.*[4]

What is the (material) weight of an (immaterial) nightmare, and why do Balzac and Marx agree that invoking it is a valid means to express humanity's relation to its history?[5]

For Balzac, the nightmare is a total destruction of identity. Colonel Chabert is a Napoleonic officer who was grievously wounded and declared

---

3. Honoré de Balzac, *Le Colonel Chabert*, vol. 3 of *La Comédie humaine* (Paris, 1976), p. 343; further references to this work, abbreviated *CC*, will be included in the text. All translations from Balzac are my own.

4. Marx, *The Eighteenth Brumaire of Louis Bonaparte* (New York, 1963), p. 15; my emphasis. Further references to this work, abbreviated *EB*, will be included in the text.

5. In French and German: "Le monde social et judiciare lui pesait sur la poitrine comme un cauchemar"; "Die Tradition aller toten Geschlechter lastet wie ein Alp auf dem Gehirne der Lebenden." This strikes me as so obvious a borrowing that I have to wonder why it does not seem to be generally known. One contributing factor may be that the standard French translation of *The Eighteenth Brumaire* gives a fanciful version of the sentence in Marx: "La tradition de toutes les générations mortes pèse d'un poids très lourd sur le cerveau des vivants" (Marx, *Le 18 brumaire de Louis Bonaparte* [Paris, 1969], p. 15). Does this *poids très lourd* come from a misreading of *ein Alp* as *eine Alp*?

Sandy Petrey is professor of French and comparative literature at the State University of New York at Stony Brook. The author of *History in the Text: Quatrevingt-Treize and the French Revolution,* he is completing a book entitled *Realism and Revolution.*

dead at the battle of Eylau in 1807. After six months of amnesia, he recovers his memory but is incarcerated as a maniac when he tries to reclaim his name and position. Ten years of painful effort culminate in his return to Paris, but Paris is now the seat of the Bourbon Restoration rather than the Napoleonic Empire. In the new capital of a new regime, Chabert learns that his wife has married Count Ferraud, with whom she has had two children. The woman who has become madame la comtesse Ferraud, a countess of the Restoration, absolutely refuses to recognize her first husband, a count of the Empire, and even refuses to give up any part of the fortune she received on being formally declared a widow. Although Chabert secures the services of an honest lawyer willing to defend his right to his name, the thought of a scandalous court case is repugnant to him. He consequently goes back into the humiliation of impoverished anonymity, leaves his wife with her second family, and ends his days in the poorhouse at Bicêtre, where he spends twenty years in semilunacy while his wife shares with another the fortune that rightfully belongs to Chabert.

It is while Chabert is learning from his lawyer all the maneuvers that will be necessary before he can become himself again that the weight of the social and judicial world presses on his breast like a nightmare. He cannot (re)make his own history because the circumstances he encounters have brought a dead generation back to life, have produced a Restoration of the past that resolutely denies this Napoleonic officer a present and a future. Like Marx before the ersatz Napoleon, Chabert experiences the ersatz Old Regime as the radical disruption of every obvious ground for believing that the movement of history is forward. *The Eighteenth Brumaire* copies an image from *Colonel Chabert* in part because the two texts share a single sense of history off track but in control.

In *Revolution and Repetition,* Jeffrey Mehlman argues that Marx experienced the farce of Napoleon III as an uncanny denial of the power of representation to express truth. "To read *The Eighteenth Brumaire of Louis Bonaparte* as the systematic dispersion of the philosopheme of representation"[6] is for Mehlman a straightforward matter of taking seriously Marx's commentary on the break between the Napoleonic state and the dominant class in French society, the bourgeoisie. State power, which in Marxist theory represents a dominant class, in fact has no connection with what it ought to signify; the state becomes independent, a fissure opens between sign and referent.

To this explicitly depicted disruption of political representation corresponds an implicitly celebrated disruption of verbal representation, the

6. Jeffrey Mehlman, *Revolution and Repetition: Marx/Hugo/Balzac* (Berkeley and Los Angeles, 1977), p. 21; further references to this work, abbreviated *RR,* will be included in the text.

Rabelaisian gusto of those words in metonymic eruption that Marx repeatedly chose to "represent" the supporters of Napoleon III. One instance can suffice: "swindlers, mountebanks, *lazzaroni,* pickpockets, tricksters, gamblers, *maquereaus,* brothel keepers, porters, *literati,* organ-grinders" (*EB,* p. 75), and so on. A macaroni language describes not a social formation but its chaotic dissolution.

The philosopheme of representation is faith in a connection between the representing medium and the thing represented. In analyzing state power, *The Eighteenth Brumaire* furnishes an exhaustive commentary on how that connection can be severed. In developing its style, the same text takes elaborate pains to suggest that words are generated by other words rather than by the things they name. As Mehlman says, "Thus, for Marx as analyst—as for us as readers of Marx—reading entails endeavoring to affirm a tertiary instance breaking with the registers of specularity and representation. It is the degree zero of polysemy, the fundamentally *heterogenizing* movement of dissemination" (*RR,* p. 22). Although the philosopheme of representation requires the homogeneity of two terms, Marx's *Eighteenth Brumaire* continuously splinters the representational pair, aggressively refusing to admit any link between entities that ought to be inseparable.

I will later raise the question of what Mehlman neglects in his assessment of *The Eighteenth Brumaire.* For the moment, let me say only that what he asserts is convincing and compelling. Whether we consider its content or its style, *The Eighteenth Brumaire* is a rambunctious insurrection against the belief that political and verbal representations are reliably grounded in unproblematic reality.

Colonel Chabert enacts the same dissociation of representation and reality, sign and referent, through continuous depiction of a living individual unsuccessfully seeking the name of a man declared dead. The sign *Chabert* enters the narrative when its claimant introduces himself to the clerks of the lawyer Derville. The clerks' reaction immediately alienates the proper name from its proprietor and associates it with meaningless signifiers on parade that invite comparison to Marx's list of the supporters of Napoleon III.

> "Chabert."
> "The colonel who died at Eylau? . . .
> "The very one, sir," the man replied with an antique simplicity. And he withdrew.
> [The following interjections, quite untranslatable, greet Chabert's announcement.]
> "Chouit!"
> "Dégommé!"
> "Puff!"
> "Oh!"
> "Ah!"

"Bâoun!"
"Ah! le vieux drôle!"
"Trinn, la, la, trinn, trinn!"
"Enfoncé!" [*CC*, pp. 317–18]

The "antique simplicity" of Chabert's demeanor is vacuous beside the
postmodern gyrations set off by his name, which designates the quick
and the dead with equal unrealiability. The nightmare weighing on Chabert's breast is also a farce rollicking around his identity.

Identity and name properly adhere to a subject. When Chabert loses
his name and identity, subjectivity becomes untenable. Balzac's text emphasizes the importance of its vision of the subject desubjectifying in
several ways, the most striking of which is its use of a preeminently
subjective term, *ego,* more than fifty years before the word's earliest
French occurrence recorded in the *Grand Robert* and the *Trésor de la
langue française.* "The *ego,* in his thought, was now only a secondary effect
. . . for this man rebuffed ten years running by his wife, by the courts,
by the entirety of social creation" (*CC*, p. 329). The irony is insistent.
What may be the first French occurrence of the term *ego* expresses the
loss of a subjectivity before the concerted assaults of a social formation.
With the whole of society on one side and the ego on the other, the latter
must withdraw.

On returning to Paris, Chabert learns not only that his house has
been razed but also that the new regime, in its zeal to remove from the
French language all marks of the French Revolution, has changed the
name of the street where his house used to be. Here is Chabert telling
Derville of his nonreturn to wife and home: "With what joy, what haste
I went to the rue du Mont-Blanc, where my wife should have been living
in a house belonging to me. Bah! The rue du Mont-Blanc had become
the rue de la Chaussée d'Antin. My house was no longer to be seen there,
it had been sold, pulled down" (*CC*, p. 332). As Chabert himself is a
referent without a sign, so all the words that bring him joy are signs
without referents. The rue du Mont-Blanc is not the rue du Mont-Blanc,
his wife is no longer his wife, and his house is nonexistent. Chabert
returns to France to find that what he knows as the French language
has lost its connection to the world.

At the battle of Eylau, Chabert was buried alive. The material fact
that he was indeed alive has become meaningless beside the ideological
fact that his death was duly certified and recorded. "I was buried under
dead men, but now I'm buried under the living, under acts [*sous des actes*],
under facts, under society in its entirety" (*CC*, p. 328). The *acts, facts,
society* series tersely summarizes the ontological vision of Balzac's text.
An *acte* is at the same time an action and an official record that the action
took place. To underscore that only the second element of that definition
counts, the word *acte* prepares the word *fact* used in the sense established

by Vautrin in *Lost Illusions*. "So the fact is no longer anything in itself, it is wholly in the idea others form of it."[7] Vautrin's "others" are what Chabert experiences as "the entirety of social creation" and "society in its entirety." For both characters, the objective fact of a referent existing as itself is inconsequential; only social creation produces social existence. A living man has died if his death certificate is in order, for the fact in itself is nothing. With his name cut away from his self, Chabert has no alternative to letting his self go as well: "My name is offensive to me. I'd like not to be myself" (*CC*, p. 327).

The being that cannot be named is ultimately replaced by a being that proceeds from its name in the old folks' home at Bicêtre. When the attorney Derville, who twenty years earlier had tried vainly to bring Chabert's identity and existence back together, sees his former client at Bicêtre and calls him by his former name, he gets this response: " 'Not Chabert! Not Chabert! I'm named Hyacinthe,' the old man replied. 'I'm no longer a man, I'm number 164, room 7,' he added, looking at Derville with anxious timidity, with the fear of an old man and a child" (*CC*, p. 372). Balzac's ultimate dispersal of the philosopheme of representation is a single referent named both "Chabert" and "Not Chabert," both a man and no longer a man.

Compare the final description of Balzac's protagonist to the same character's introduction. "In sum the absence of any movement in the body, of any warmth in the eyes, was matched by a certain demented expression of sadness, by the debilitating symptoms characteristic of idiocy, to make this figure something baleful that no human speech could express" (*CC*, pp. 321–22). That sentence is the final result of an extensive series of rewritings throughout which two elements are constantly prominent, the absence of signs of human life such as movement and warmth and the impossibility of naming this dead being in any form of human speech. In the received ideology of representation, a name exists because a being requires it. In Balzac's version of representation, a being ceases to exist because there is no name for it. After a decade of helplessly seeking a word to say that he is, Chabert is a semiotic and referential absence when he goes into Derville's office. The failure of Derville's efforts on his client's behalf means that the only way to fill the absence is to accept the presence of the "Not Chabert" named number 164, room 7.

Chabert is therefore the most impertinent of challenges to the philosopheme of representation, a referent separated from its sign and so inexorably diminished that the name does not appear an appendage of the thing but rather the thing an excrescence of the name. If we look at *Colonel Chabert* from the perspective of the fundamental philosophical principles set forth in *The German Ideology*, Balzac's text even seems to

---

7. Balzac, *Illusions perdues*, vol. 5 of *La Comédie humaine* (Paris, 1977), p. 700.

set back on its head the vision of reality Marx and Engels claimed to have set on its feet.

> In direct contrast to German philosophy which descends from heaven to earth, here it is a matter of ascending from earth to heaven. That is to say, not of setting out from what men say, imagine, conceive, nor from men as narrated, thought of, imagined, conceived, in order to arrive at men in the flesh; but of setting out from real, active men, and on the basis of their real life-process demonstrating the development of the ideological reflexes and echoes of this life-process. [*ME*, p. 43]

If we set out from Chabert as a man "in the flesh," as a "real, active man" who is the locus of a "real life-process," we arrive at a stupefying incomprehensibility, a life-process atrophying without cause, flesh without the heat and movement it requires absolutely. But if we set out from Chabert as said, imagined, conceived, narrated, thought of, his story proceeds with the rigor of Aristotelian logic. Instead of echoing his life-process, ideology saps it; instead of the name proceeding from the thing, the thing degenerates from the name. Because Chabert is said, conceived, and narrated as dead, his real life-process ceases to be a matter of practical consequence.

But this negation occurs only if we separate his real life-process from his life as said, imagined, conceived, narrated, and thought of, and it is just this separation that *Colonel Chabert* assertively denies. Balzac's painful descriptions of Chabert's physical deterioration do not reverse a hierarchy so much as undo the opposition on which it is based. The social world that weighs on Chabert's breast is real in exactly the same sense as the body of which the breast is part. What is unreal according to the concept of reality established by *The German Ideology* is the individual, suprasocial subjectivity—the ego—that bourgeois philosophy defines as an inalienable attribute of every living person. The dissolution of Chabert's selfhood repudiates vulgar idealism as well as vulgar materialism by representing Chabert as a socialized subject experiencing reality as a nightmare because human life in a social formation cannot be reduced either to its material or to its subjective components.

In his own illustration of the nightmare's weight in *The Eighteenth Brumaire*, Marx undermines the same opposition by reiterating Balzac's insistence on the material impact of ideological concepts. What happened to France between 1848 and 1851 is no more comprehensible as the effect of a material infrastructure than what happened to Colonel Chabert between 1807 and 1817. In both cases, a discursive practice first declares its independence from a physical life-process and then integrates what it says into the process of real life. "Thus, so long as the *name* of freedom was respected and only its actual realization prevented, of course in a legal way, the constitutional existence of liberty remained intact, inviolate, however mortal the blows dealt to its existence *in actual life*" (*EB,* p. 31). It is Marx who underlines *name* and *actual life,* and his dual emphasis demands contemplation. One purpose of the emphasis is certainly to reproduce the contrast in *The German Ideology* between material reality and what is said and imagined. Yet Marx's own materialist analysis suggests that names cannot be completely ignored by eloquently formulating the lie it is also exposing: "the constitutional guarantee of liberty remained intact, inviolate." In its immediate context, this assertion is an ironic mockery of language cut off from reality. In the larger context of *The Eighteenth Brumaire* as a whole, however, such assertions are an essential constituent of the reality lived by France and its citizens. As befits a man whose power was purely the effect of his name, Napoleon III consolidated his position by making other names change the world despite their ridiculous inability to describe it.

At least since Plato, the contrast between shadow and substance has been a dominant Western metaphor for the distinction between reality and illusion at the core of standard materialist analysis. Yet Marx saw the rise of Napoleon III as a reality proceeding from illusion, as humanity and its history transformed by a shadow with no substance behind it. "Men and events appear as inverted Schlemihls, as shadows that have lost their bodies. The revolution itself paralyzes its own bearers and endows only its adversaries with passionate forcefulness" (*EB,* p. 44). With its bearers paralyzed, the revolution has no material reality. Yet the specter of revolution becomes matter by virtue of the passionate forcefulness it instills in the praxis of those it terrifies. Marx's identification of men and events as shadows without bodies in no way revokes the Marxist imperative to explain the world men and events produce. All that changes is the form explanation must take.

The explanatory method required by the Second Empire accords equal attention to what events are and what they are named.

> . . . wild, inane agitation in the name of tranquillity, most solemn preaching of tranquillity in the name of revolution; passions without truth, truths without passion; heroes without heroic deeds, history without events; development, whose sole driving force seems to be the calendar, wearying with constant repetition of the same tensions and relaxations. [*EB,* p. 43]

Agitation named tranquillity, tranquillity named revolution, chronology named history, repetition named development: the driving force of human existence has become the calendar, and even the calendar is "wearied" of humanity's failure to proceed toward its revolutionary goals.

What prevents revolutionary progress? An ideological configuration for French society that is as unfounded and as unconquerable in *The*

Eighteenth Brumaire as in *Colonel Chabert.* I suggested above that the re-lationship of material reality to ideological representation in Balzac's tale is a direct challenge to simplistic interpretation of the metaphorics of real life and its imaginary narration prominent in *The German Ideology.* I now want to take the argument a step further and consider Balzac's depiction of Colonel Chabert as the model for Marx's depiction of class struggle in *The Eighteenth Brumaire.* Each text invokes a material presence that ought to manifest itself intelligibly in a social setting. But each text also delineates an ideological resistance to this manifestation that leaves material presence indistinguishable from immaterial absence. The fictional Chabert is but cannot be named; the historical class struggle is but cannot affect political events. The theme common to fiction and history is that society can at least temporarily ignore as well as manifest the opposition between base and superstructure on which standardized materialist analysis depends.

To make this argument about *The Eighteenth Brumaire* requires applying to Marx the lesson he and Engels often taught about Balzac: an author's explanation of a work is to be accepted only if the work itself justifies the author's opinion. Balzac defined the *Comédie humaine* as a determined defense of throne and altar. Marx defined *The Eighteenth Brumaire* as a thoroughgoing description of the class struggle in action, most notably in the 1869 preface to the text written seventeen years earlier. There Marx contrasted his methods to those of the other principal chroniclers of the *coup d'état* by insisting that Hugo and Proudhon inadvertently glorified Napoleon III whereas Marx himself concentrated on the material forces that alone make history. "I, on the contrary, demonstrate how the *class struggle* in France created circumstances and relationships that made it possible for a grotesque mediocrity to play a hero's part" (*EB,* p. 8). As with Balzac's *Avant-propos,* so with Marx's preface: introductory theses are valid if and only if they explain what they present, and in neither instance does the proffered explanation bear comparative scrutiny beside what it introduces.

In modern European society, the class struggle pits bourgeoisie against proletariat. In *The Eighteenth Brumaire,* proletariat and bourgeoisie suc-cessively withdraw from the struggle and go home to rest. The proletariat's withdrawal began with their massacre in June of 1848 and was complete with the supremely noneconomic fact of workers' disenfranchisement in May of 1850.

> But the election law of May 31, 1850, excluded [the Paris proletariat] from any participation in political power. It cut it off from the very arena of the struggle. It threw the workers back into the position of pariahs which they had occupied before the February Revolution. By letting themselves be led by the democrats in face of such an event and forgetting the revolutionary interests of their

class for momentary ease and comfort, they renounced the honour
of being a conquering power, surrendered to their fate, proved
that the defeat of June 1848 had put them out of the fight for
years and that the historical process would for the present again
have to go on *over* their heads. [*EB*, p. 77]

Even if we assume that Marx did not fully mean it when he identified
"the very arena of the struggle" as the derivative and epiphenomenal
act of casting ballots in a bourgeois election, the conclusion of this passage
remains unambiguous. The proletariat may be the subject-object of history,
but the history analyzed in *The Eighteenth Brumaire* takes place with neither
workers nor the "revolutionary interests of their class" affecting it.

The proletariat's antithesis, the bourgeoisie, is equally docile. *The
Eighteenth Brumaire* contains masterful examples of classic Marxist interpretation of production and trade as the motive forces of political events.
But that analysis always concludes by showing how production and trade
push producers and traders out of politics to create not a political expression of bourgeois interests but a yawning void that a farcical adventurer
steps in to fill. Although the bourgeoisie's material demands effortlessly
make sense of all French history from the Renaissance to the Second
Republic, the advent of Napoleon III sweeps bourgeois sense into the
ashcan of history.

> But under the absolute monarchy, during the first Revolution,
> under Napoleon, bureaucracy was only the means of preparing
> the class rule of the bourgeoisie. Under the Restoration, under
> Louis Philippe, under the parliamentary republic, it was the in-
> strument of the ruling class, however much it strove for power on
> its own.
> Only under the second Bonaparte does the state seem to have
> made itself completely independent. [*EB*, p. 122]

The class rule of the bourgeoisie becomes the nonclass rule independent
of the bourgeoisie. Rather than the "instrument of the ruling class," the
state comes to act by and for itself.

Compare this celebrated passage from Marx's preface to *A Contribution
to the Critique of Political Economy:* "The mode of production of material
life conditions the social, political and intellectual life process in general.
It is not the consciousness of men that determines their being but, on
the contrary, their social being that determines their consciousness" (*ME*,
p. 41). The theses of that passage, crucial though they are to Marxist
analysis of historical events, are irrelevant to Marx's vision of the Second
Empire, a regime established because the contradiction between social
being and consciousness was resolved in favor of the latter. In 1851,
French capitalists avidly renounced the form of political life dictated by

the capitalist mode of production. "Thus the industrial bourgeoisie applauds with servile bravos the *coup d'état* of December 2, the annihilation of parliament, *the downfall of its own rule,* the dictatorship of Bonaparte" (*EB,* p. 115; my emphasis).

The state is far from the only element of the superstructure to violate proper representational rules connecting it to its material base. All elements of intellectual life become so heterogeneous that France presents the archetypically postmodern spectacle of representation and the thing represented in stridently irreconcilable conflicts. "The spokesmen and scribes of the bourgeoisie, its platform and its press, in short, the ideologists of the bourgeoisie and the bourgeoisie itself, the representatives and the represented, faced one another in estrangement and no longer understood one another" (*EB,* p. 103).

This estrangement of representatives from their referents has special poignancy in *The Eighteenth Brumaire,* which also contains a memorable warning against assuming that petit bourgeois ideologists must themselves lead petit bourgeois lives. To the contrary.

> What makes them representatives of the petty bourgeoisie is the fact that in their minds they do not get beyond the limits which the latter do not get beyond in life, that they are consequently driven, theoretically, to the same problems and solutions to which material interest and social position drive the latter practically. This is, in general, the relationship between the *political* and *literary representatives* of a class and the class they represent. [*EB,* p. 51]

That admonition against vulgar materialism specifies that determination in the last instance by the economic base is indeed a phenomenon of representation rather than direct causality. Ideas are representative because they express (rather than develop from) the operations of material interests. Yet the estrangement of the bourgeoisie's representatives from the bourgeoisie they represent remains disorienting. Even if the sign does not proceed mechanically from the referent, the inability of the two to understand one another makes it hard to see how "limits in minds" and "limits in life" are somehow the same thing. In *The Eighteenth Brumaire,* a single class reality is spoken and lived in unrelievedly disparate ways.

Like Balzac's Chabert, therefore, Marx's class struggle is in *The Eighteenth Brumaire* an indubitable fact that miserably fails to represent itself in the political and ideological forms that shape French society. And the scandal is even more invidious, for class itself is in Marx's text eerily reminiscent of the man who is in Balzac's text both Chabert and "Not Chabert." After separating Napoleon III from bourgeoisie and proletariat, Marx seeks to attach him to another group created by the material conditions of production, the nineteenth-century French peasantry. The pronouncement that state power is after all the representation of material reality is at first unequivocal. "Bonaparte represents a class, and the most numerous class of French society at that, the *small-holding [Parzellen] peasants*" (*EB*, p. 123). Bourgeoisie, proletariat, and the struggle between them have ceased to influence the course of French political history, but the bedrock of the Marxist view of political history, its ultimate determination by class configurations, remains intact.

Yet "class" immediately becomes the same kind of hopelessly shifting signifier as the state, for Marx follows up on his resolution of the problem of the state by making the concept through which he resolved it no less a puzzle than the difficulty the concept was to lay to rest. Instead of a group fused by shared economic interests and the shared ideology appropriate to such interests, French peasants are a serial mass almost wholly ignorant of their common social being.

> In this way, the great mass of the French nation is formed by simple addition of homologous magnitudes, much as potatoes in a sack form a sack of potatoes. In so far as millions of families live under economic conditions of existence that separate their mode of life, their interests and their culture from those of the other classes, and put them in hostile opposition to the latter, they form a class. In so far as there is merely a local interconnection among these small-holding peasants, and the identity of their interests begets no community, no national bond and no political organization among them, they do not form a class. [*EB*, p. 124]

"Am I dead or am I alive?" a bewildered Chabert asks his lawyer (*CC*, p. 333). "Are we a class or are we a sack of potatoes?" the French peasants might well ask Marx. In neither case is the answer definitive.

Because French peasants are both a class and not a class, they "cannot represent themselves, they must be represented" (*EB*, p. 124). Marx's compelling analysis of how the ideology of the Second Empire accomplishes this representation has been much and justly admired. But this analysis often and explicitly announces that the Second Empire represents not the smallholding of 1851 but that of many decades earlier, the smallholding of the period when peasants were newly released from feudal obligations and not yet subjugated to capitalist debt. In other terms, what Napoleon III represents is not the peasantry as it exists in material practice and social process but as it nostalgically imagines itself in (false) consciousness. The ideology of Napoleon III expresses not the concrete reality of economic being but the absurd fantasies of another ideology.

"One sees: *all* 'idées napoléoniennes' *are ideas of the undeveloped small holding in the freshness of its youth;* for the small holding that has outlived its day they are an absurdity. They are only the hallucinations of its death struggle, words that are transformed into phrases, spirits transformed into ghosts" (*EB*, p. 130). That passage from the conclusion of *The Eighteenth*

Brumaire both echoes the invocation of all the dead generations in the introduction and suggests an answer to the question of how much a nightmare weighs. When hallucinations are successfully represented, they become a dictatorship. Words successfully transformed into phrases can produce the world they articulate. Although created in direct and egregious contradiction to all discernible contours of material reality, the Second Empire became an overpowering material reality.

Terry Eagleton's study of Walter Benjamin includes an important discussion of *The Eighteenth Brumaire* that takes as its focus the reading advanced by Mehlman in *Revolution and Repetition*. Whereas Mehlman sees the state's liberation from its economic base as eliciting "a Marx more profoundly anarchical than Anarchism ever dreamed" (*RR*, p. 41), Eagleton contends that the Bonapartist regime fits neatly into Marxist categories as properly understood.

> For Bonapartism is not of course anarchism, and, *pace* Mehlman, there is nothing "uncanny" about it. The state for Marxism is not the direct representation of a class interest (which Bonaparte can then be thought to rupture), but, as Nicos Poulantzas argued, "the strategic site of organization of the dominant class in its relationship to the dominated classes."[8]

Eagleton opposes the state as a class' "direct representation" to the state as the site of a class' "strategic organization." *The Eighteenth Brumaire* contemptuously dismisses the former but respectfully maintains the latter.

Reading Marx together with Balzac, however, makes it clear that the problematic of *The Eighteenth Brumaire* is not *how* a class manifests itself politically but *what* it is that is manifested. From the perspective of a certain materialism, a class is the same kind of unmistakable entity as Dr. Johnson's stone. But in *The Eighteenth Brumaire,* the class being of bourgeoisie and proletariat are more like Colonel Chabert's living body, unquestionably real (Dr. Johnson's foot would not pass through it) but just as unquestionably prevented from making its reality signify. The class being of the peasantry is on the other hand a fully signifying entity that is not real in the material sense. Here the analogy is not Colonel Chabert's living body but his certified death, for the peasantry too comes to be by coming to be represented. If Mehlman confuses the order of *The Eighteenth Brumaire* with anarchy, Eagleton confuses the source of the order Marx describes with the unitary vision of class Marx repudiates. Peasantry, proletariat, and bourgeoisie are all named a class, but no single definition can explain why the name is appropriate in all three cases.

Eagleton highlights the ambiguities of class being in *The Eighteenth Brumaire* when he asserts that the crux of Marx's analysis "can be found

---

8. Terry Eagleton, *Walter Benjamin, or, Towards a Revolutionary Criticism* (London, 1981), p. 162; further references to this work, abbreviated *WB,* will be included in the text.

in the famous enigma that Marx proposes in the text's final pages: when is a class not a class?" (*WB*, p. 167). Essential though that question is, the order of its terms implies the same ontological solidity for the concept of class as Eagleton's earlier discussion of representation versus strategy. Moreover, it is not Marx's final pages on the peasantry that ask when a class is not a class but his earlier pages on a proletariat and a bourgeoisie that do not act as a class should. The final discussion of the peasantry asks a wholly different question: when is a nonclass a class?

Despite his desire to distance his understanding of *The Eighteenth Brumaire* from Mehlman's, Eagleton's phrasing of the question he sees as the crux of Marx's text in fact reiterates the crux of Mehlman's reading, the catastrophic breakdown of the representational bond between a referent and an expression. What distinguishes Marx's Second Empire from the anarchy of unbridled semiosis is not that bourgeoisie and proletariat retain their class being even though that being has become representationally invisible. It is rather that the class being of the peasantry becomes a historical fact by virtue of its successful representation. Mehlman asks, "what is the status of a State that no longer represents anything?" (*RR*, p. 16). Marx responds by demonstrating that anything a state represents is material reality even if the conditions of production militate against its material consolidation. Eagleton's question and Mehlman's analysis suggest that Marx inquires principally into a class becoming a sack of potatoes. But *The Eighteenth Brumaire* takes as its conclusion and theme a sack of potatoes becoming a class.

It is this transformation of something that is not social being into something that is that exemplifies the reality of representation in Marx and Balzac. Both authors pitilessly shed all concepts of realism as accurate depiction of material existence in its materiality, yet both authors brilliantly illustrate realist recognition of the substance *imbued* by social articulation of a material presence. In both, what Engels called the triumph of realism is not penetrating through ideology but affirming that conflicts between ideological and material constructs can go either way.

In discussing Heidegger's concept of the work of art, Fredric Jameson contrasts "the meaningless materiality of the body and nature" to "the meaning-endowment of history and of the social."[9] *Colonel Chabert* and *The Eighteenth Brumaire* foreground an identical contrast. Chabert's body and the class being of the bourgeoisie and the proletariat are meaningless materiality; Chabert's death and the class being of the peasantry exemplify the meaning-endowment of history. Balzac and Marx are in perfect agreement that accurate depiction of social existence requires according equal importance to how the material can become meaningless and how meaning can be material.

9. Fredric Jameson, "Post-Modernism, or The Cultural Logic of Late Capitalism," *New Left Review* 146 (July–Aug. 1984): 59.

Eagleton affirms the value of that agreement when he considers the actual message conveyed by Marx's representation of the peasantry's representation.

> By virtue of Bonaparte the peasantry becomes a class proper, discovers a signifier that redefines its status. Marx's political insight, in other words, is the ruin, not of representation, but of a naive semiotic conception of it. It is not that political signifiers have become free-standing, as the formalism of a Mehlman (or his post-Marxist English equivalents) would suggest; such a claim merely falls prey to the ideology of Bonapartism itself. Bonaparte is indeed a signifier of class interests, but a complex, contradictory one that politically *constitutes* the very interests it signifies. Such complex articulation can be grasped neither by a purely empiricist model of the sign, in which the signified grabs for a signifying form extrinsic to it, nor by the kind of formalism that slides signified under signifier, where the resultant friction wears the former to nothing. [*WB*, p. 168]

With one reservation, I take that passage to be a stunning summary of the vision of reality and representation shared by Marx and Balzac, both of whom deny with equal force the pieties of simplistic materialism and the fireworks of unlimited semantic slippage. The reservation concerns Eagleton's statement that through successful representation "the peasantry becomes a class proper." Although that statement is valid, its validity depends on the fact that a "class proper" is no longer the product of material reality alone. The dialectical semiotics responsible for the peasantry's transformation repudiate received versions of economistic analysis while preserving intact the primacy economism assigns to class being.

The "complex, contradictory" view of representation in *The Eighteenth Brumaire* is that the class interests represented by Napoleon III have the full status of material reality even though no material reality stands prior to the representation that "*constitutes* the very interests it signifies." What Eagleton later names the "wholly new political semiotics" (*WB*, p. 170 n. 105) of *The Eighteenth Brumaire* is a materialist vision of meaning that relentlessly concentrates on what representation does while remaining acutely aware that direct expression of objective existence is one of the things it cannot do.

That is precisely the vision of meaning enacted in *Colonel Chabert*, like *The Eighteenth Brumaire* in combining full modernist delight in the phantasmagoria of signs' unreliability with full realist respect for the referential integrity of signs validated by the collectivity in which they circulate. At the end of *Molloy*, Samuel Beckett gives a celebrated synopsis of writing's complete freedom from descriptive obligations. "I went back into the house and wrote, It is midnight. The rain is beating on the windows. It was not midnight. It was not raining."[10] Throughout *Colonel Chabert,* Balzac teaches the same lesson by describing a living man who is not a man alive, a Chabert who is "Not Chabert." During the conversations between Chabert and Derville, client, attorney, and narrative voice take turns playing with as many ways to say what is not as they can come up with. Chabert introduces himself to Derville as the man "who died at Eylau" and specifies that "my death is a historical fact" (*CC,* pp. 322, 323). Derville responds in kind by saying to Colonel Chabert, "I am the lawyer of Countess Ferraud, the widow of Colonel Chabert" (*CC,* p. 324). As if the game were too enticing to be left to characters, the text joins in: " 'Sir,' said the dead man" (*CC,* p. 323).

The difference between Balzac and Beckett is the same as that between Eagleton's Marx and Mehlman's. In each pair, the latter stops at the sign's freewheeling independence of preexistent reality while the former goes on to recognize semiotic production of the reality lived by those for whom the sign means. When Mark Twain announced that reports of his death were greatly exaggerated, his ability to make the announcement sufficed to make it true as well as comic. When Chabert made the same announcement, his physical presence—as if to exemplify Jameson's "meaningless materiality of the body"—was irrelevant to the social consensus that a report in proper form cannot be an exaggeration because it has become a historical fact.

That is why Balzac's text is completely serious when it refers to Chabert's death in language that, as the text also shows, cannot possibly be serious. "M. Ferraud, at the time of Count Chabert's death, was a young man of twenty-six" (*CC,* p. 347). That particular reference to the nonexistent referent of Chabert's demise comes during a long digression on the man who married Chabert's wife, a digression Balzac made progressively longer in his multiple revisions of *Colonel Chabert.* The digression's theme is that Ferraud, a count of the old aristocracy, is under the Restoration following the line of an ascendant career with as much momentum and as little reason as are apparent in Chabert's descent. Since he plays no part whatever in the action as recounted, Count Ferraud is the converse of Count Chabert. Within the narrative universe, one of Countess Ferraud's two husbands is a person without an identity, the other an identity without a person. In each the dialectic of presence and absence ridicules every concept of existence in itself and affirms the supreme reality of existence as socially represented.

The analogy to Count Ferraud in *The Eighteenth Brumaire* is Napoleon III, the man who also founds a career on a name that history has converted into a force by blithely ignoring that the past is past.

---

10. Samuel Beckett, *Molloy* (London, 1959), p. 176.

Historical tradition gave rise to the belief of the French peasants in the miracle that a man named Napoleon would bring all their glory back to them. And an individual turned up who gives himself out as the man because he bears the name of Napoleon, in consequence of the *Code Napoleon,* which lays down that *la recherche de la paternité est interdite.* [*EB,* p. 124]

Like legitimate class interests and the struggle between them in Marx, Count Chabert is in Balzac a compelling material fact that society is ignoring. Like Napoleon III, Count Ferraud is a narrative nonentity who acquires supreme narrative importance by virtue of society's purely ideological attitude toward his name.

Marx's reference above to the Napoleonic Code alludes to the widespread rumor that Napoleon III was not in fact the son of Napoleon's brother but was the offspring of his mother's adultery. The jibe is petty, but its dissociation of the name of Napoleon from *any* connection with the reality of Napoleon emphasizes that the social function of a name in no way depends on material reality. Like the referent, paternity is not a physical fact but a social performance.

To call the referent a performance is to invoke J. L. Austin's theory of speech acts and suggest a conceptual frame pertinent to the realism of both Balzac and Marx. The peasantry's class being and Chabert's death are ideal instances of the reality produced by what Austin named performative speech, which could not be better defined than by recalling the lesson Eagleton drew from Marx, that under certain conditions expression "*constitutes* the very [thing] it signifies." For Austin, the condition required is codified in Rule A.1, the socially recognized existence of a conventional procedure having conventional effect. Felicitous reference to reality can be adequately understood only if we recognize reality as the consequence rather than the origin of reference to it, and reference is productive only when made so by the collective organization of the society in which it occurs.

From a speech-act perspective, Mehlman is fully justified to insist with such verve that the text of *The Eighteenth Brumaire* utterly dissipates the philosopheme of representation. But from the same perspective, Eagleton is correct to refuse out of hand Mehlman's suggestion that the end of referential representation is the beginning of anarchy. Instead of playfully gamboling about, signs are in Marx and Balzac the hardworking agents of a society that uses them to articulate its being for its constituents. That being is material in every sense of the word except that codified in the philosopheme of representation, which assumes that matter is only what exists independently of the forms through which it is expressed.

In his influential study, "Ideology and Ideological State Apparatuses," Louis Althusser raises several points with direct relevance to the intersection of Marx, Balzac, and Austin. After making and defending his famous statement that the great speech act of ideology is to interpellate individuals as subjects, Althusser reverses the terms to say that the category of the subject also constitutes ideology. Subjectivity therefore constitutes the ideology that constitutes subjectivity.

> I say: the category of the subject is constitutive of all ideology, but at the same time and immediately I add that *the category of the subject is only constitutive of all ideology insofar as all ideology has the function (which defines it) of "constituting" concrete individuals as subjects.* In the interaction of this double constitution exists the functioning of all ideology.[11]

In that passage, what Althusser calls the "concrete individual" seems to possess the nonideological existence of a classic materialist referent, seems to be an objective entity independent of the ideological speech act constituting a subjective entity. Interpreted from this point of view, Colonel Chabert would be a concrete individual who, even though not interpellated as Colonel Chabert, is nonetheless a full human being; Marx's peasants would be a class that, even before they are represented by Napoleon, nonetheless have full class being.

But Althusser goes on to show why neither Marx nor Balzac considers their characters' preideological being worthy of narrative impact. What ideology constitutes as a subject is nothing at all before its ideological interpellation.

> Thus ideology hails or interpellates individuals as subjects. As ideology is eternal, I must now suppress the temporal form in which I have presented the functioning of ideology, and say: ideology has always-already interpellated individuals as subjects, which amounts to making it clear that individuals are always-already interpellated by ideology as subjects, which necessarily leads us to one last proposition: *individuals are always-already subjects.* Hence individuals are "abstract" with respect to the subjects which they always-already are.[12]

What was "concrete" has become "abstract." The referent prior to ideology is now the imaginary derivative of ideological production. Since the individual is always already a subject, the word *individual* denotes nothing if we define it in opposition to the word *subject.* What seemed concrete is the purest abstraction, for we imagine the individual solely through our sense of the subject who is always already there.

    11. Louis Althusser, "Ideology and Ideological State Apparatuses (Notes towards an Investigation)," *Lenin and Philosophy, and Other Essays,* trans. Ben Brewster (New York, 1971), p. 171.
    12. Ibid., pp. 175–76.

Althusser's play with *concrete* and *abstract* is comparable to the vagaries of the *class proper* in Eagleton. First represented as the concrete effect of concrete economic practice, the class interests of the peasantry are then abstracted from Napoleonic performance of the act representing them. In both cases, what is at issue is not a temporal sequence but a semantic contrast. As Austin taught with exemplary rigor, representation in society can never be understood through the classic dichotomy of concrete existence and abstract naming. Abstractions are the concrete itself—a nonclass is a class—when historical conditions make their representation as such felicitous.

Marx elaborates his appropriation of Balzac's weighty nightmare by specifying when and how the dead generations come to life.

> The tradition of all the dead generations weighs like a nightmare on the brain of the living. And just when they seem engaged in revolutionizing themselves and things, in creating something that has never yet existed, precisely in such periods of revolutionary crisis they anxiously conjure up the spirits of the past to their service and borrow from them names, battle cries and costumes in order to present the new scene of world history in this time-honoured disguise and this borrowed language. [*EB*, p. 15]

Marx's French illustrations are the bourgeois revolution that began in 1789, with its heavy use of Rome; the proletarian revolt of 1848, with its use of 1789; and the Napoleonic revolution of 1851, with its repetition of the First Empire. The factor constant across three radically disparate conjunctures of the forces and relations of production is the performative nature of social representation on which Austin's terminology continuously insists.

The Eighteenth Brumaire anticipates that terminology as well as the vision of social reality it articulates. From its opening characterization of history as tragedy and farce, Marx's representation of Napoleon III relies heavily on the language of drama and theatrics underlying the Austinian concept of *performance*. Like Austin, Marx uses theatrical language to make the double point that while nothing objective authorizes a successful performance, something objective can follow it. It was in fact because Napoleon III understood this performative character of representation that he became Napoleon III: "the adventurer, who took the comedy as plain comedy, was bound to win" (*EB*, p. 76). In making his comic performance into world history, Napoleon III did exactly the same thing as the bourgeois revolutionaries of 1789 and after, who had no more right to play the part of Romans than the nephew to play the part of the uncle. Marx's acute sensitivity to the power of "borrowed language" to transform an inherited world introduces his analysis of a bogus political representation constituting the social being it represents.

Whereas Marx assigns equal importance to the positive and negative components of representation as performance, Eagleton foregrounds the negative. His reading of *The Eighteenth Brumaire* conceals the bourgeoisie's massive transformation of reality under the drabness apparent once reality was transformed.

> So it is not just that bourgeois revolution swathes itself in theatrical costume: it *is* theatrical in essence, a matter of panache and breathless rhetoric, a baroque frenzy whose poetic effusions are in inverse proportion to its meagre substance. It is not just that it manipulates past fictions: it *is* a kind of fiction, an ill-made drama that expends itself in Act Three and totters exhausted to its tawdry conclusion. If bourgeois revolutions trick themselves out in flashy tropes it is because there is a kind of fictiveness in their very structure, a hidden flaw that disarticulates form and content. [*WB*, p. 167]

The objection to this refusal of performance is not just that it neglects the immense power of bourgeois role-playing described with such moving power in the *Communist Manifesto*. Eagleton's binary rhetoric contrasting bourgeois fictiveness to proletarian substance undermines one of the crucial points Marx draws from his meditation on role-playing, that workers' liberation will *also* depend on literary representation of a nonexistent referent: "The social revolution of the nineteenth century cannot draw its poetry from the past, but only from the future" (*EB*, p. 18). Not the present, the future: as bourgeois revolutionaries ignore what is for what was, socialist revolutionaries must ignore what is for what will be. Immense as the distance between the two revolutions is, they are identical in performing a reality that is also a fiction. Like the class interests of the peasantry, the class liberation of the proletariat in *The Eighteenth Brumaire* is to be *constituted* by the act that represents it.

Jameson discusses the *Communist Manifesto*'s paean to bourgeois development in these terms.

> Marx powerfully urges us to do the impossible, namely to think this development positively *and* negatively all at once; to achieve, in other words, a type of thinking that would be capable of grasping the demonstrably baleful features of capitalism along with its extraordinary and liberating dynamism simultaneously, within a single thought, and without attenuating any of the force of either judgement.[13]

As the *Communist Manifesto* urges us to think bourgeois revolution positively and negatively all at once, *The Eighteenth Brumaire* urges us no less powerfully to make the same dialectical evaluation of bourgeois fictiveness.

13. Jameson, "Post-Modernism, or The Cultural Logic of Late Capitalism," p. 86.

Marx's description of the Second Empire argues in its entirety that representation must be taken with the utmost seriousness because what it performs is inseparable from what the world will be. Poetry from the future and dramatis personae from the past are equally false to the present and equally crucial to historical change. Fictions are not that which Marxism must refuse but that which it must incorporate. As a type of fiction, ideology presents the same duality. Marx's task is not only to show what ideology falsifies but also to appreciate what it performs.

This is the lesson of *Colonel Chabert* brilliantly applied in *The Eighteenth Brumaire*. Those whom Engels considered Balzac's inadequate surrogates, "all the professed historians, economists and statisticians of the period together," could easily have taught him and Marx all they needed to know about society's material base. What Balzac taught was that the material base was not all they needed to know. Marxist analysis and the *Comédie humaine* establish a special meaning for the sociology of literature, a sense in which neither social nor literary realism can be understood apart from the other because each reveals the conditions on which the other depends. Society in Balzacian fiction and fiction in Marxist society are simultaneously imaginary and real. To paraphrase Jameson, their truth and their lies must be grasped in a single thought without attenuating the force of either attribute.

Two Approaches in the Sociology of Literature

Terry Eagleton

There are two main ways in which an interest in the sociology of literature can be justified. The first form of justification is (in the epistemological sense of the term) realist: literature *is* in fact deeply conditioned by its social context, and any critical account of it which omits this fact is therefore automatically deficient. The second way is pragmatist: literature is in fact shaped by all kinds of factors and readable in all sorts of contexts, but highlighting its social determinants is useful and desirable from a particular political standpoint.

Both of these cases would seem to have something going for them. Hardly anybody would want to deny that literature is in an important sense a social product; but this claim is so general that a specifically "sociological" treatment of literary works does not necessarily follow from it. Metaphors and line endings, after all, are also in some sense social products, so that to attend to these elements of a literary text is not necessarily to deny the work's sociality. "Social product" would seem too comfortably broad a category, just as "economic product" would seem too cripplingly narrow. A problem with the realist case about the sociology of literature, then, is that it is not very clear what exactly is being claimed. The pragmatist case would seem a persuasive rationale for, say, a feminist reading of Alexander Pope's *Essay on Criticism,* since few people would want to claim that the poem was in some central way *about* patriarchal relations in the sense that *The Rape of the Lock* is. A Marxist critic who attended to questions of social class in *Treasure Island,* perhaps placing Long John Silver in the context of the British shop stewards' movement and celebrating his antagonism to the gentry, would not necessarily be committed to holding that these issues were "in fact" crucial to the text; he or she would insist instead that they should be brought to light because they were crucial to history and society in general.

The problem with this summary, however, is that it merely pushes the realist/pragmatist issue one stage back to the interpretation of history and society themselves. Is the pragmatist critic arguing that such questions are *really* central to history, in which case he or she is a pragmatist about literature but a realist about society? Or do such issues emerge, as a certain kind of pragmatist would want to hold, only within a particular way of constructing history from the viewpoint of certain political needs and desires in the present? A "sociological" critic, in other words, can be pragmatist about both history and literature together, realist about history but pragmatist about literature, or realist about them both. One can hold that structures such as class and patriarchy genuinely are vitally determining forces in historical development but see no reason why every literary work should be centrally concerned with them, and so justify one's attention to such themes in a particular work from a pragmatist perspective. What one cannot be, surely, is a pragmatist about history and a realist about literature.

Pragmatist positions of one kind or another are at the moment rather popular with some feminist critics, who suspect, often rightly, that epistemological realism involves a form of male objectivism. But it would surely be very strange for a feminist to hold that her account of men's oppression of women was not in some sense actually true. Perhaps "in some sense" makes the vital difference: realists and pragmatists may wrangle over what this means, but any political critic has surely to hold to *some* notion of truth, otherwise his or her case merely undercuts itself. There is something odd in hearing certain feminist critics denounce truth in one breath and patriarchy in the next. In pulling the carpet out from under one's political enemy, one has to be careful that one has not pulled it out from beneath oneself. Perhaps what is being denounced is something called "transcendental" truth; but not all realists are transcendental realists, and indeed it is very difficult these days to find anybody at all who will defend such claims. They are increasingly a straw target to be piously set up and ritually bowled over. The same applies to many deconstructive critiques of truth, which usually turn out to be no more than the flip side of obviously untenable metaphysical claims. The problem for prag-

Terry Eagleton's recent works include collected essays—*Against the Grain* and *William Shakespeare*—as well as a novel, *Saints and Scholars*. His work in progress is on the ideology of the aesthetic.

matists here is that their accounts of their interests, needs, and desires would seem inescapably to entail certain implicit views as to what is actually the case. To talk in a broadly pragmatist way about "strategic calculations" and "tactical interventions" unavoidably entails some claim to knowledge of how the world is; otherwise such talk is merely empty. If it is not in some sense true that South Africa is a racist society, then the desires and interests of the African National Congress are entirely pointless. There is no point in Marxists desiring a classless society if we have one already and have simply not noticed. If men do not in fact oppress women, there is no point in being a feminist. To abandon epistemology for politics is not undesirable but impossible: all statements of political interest are always implicitly theories of reality.[1] Realists and pragmatists may disagree over how we *know* that men oppress women, but it is self-contradictory to hold, as some radicals would appear to, that truth is, *tout court,* an objectionable notion. The present fashion for placing the word coyly in scare quotes merely suggests that however much we rail against positivism we are still secretly in thrall to it. Similarly, those who hold that it cannot be a *fact* that South African blacks are exploited, since "exploitation" is after all a value term dependent for its force on one's political interests and desires, are covertly or explicitly in thrall to a subjectivist ideology of value.

This is not to argue that cognition is the "ground" of interest and desire; it is simply to deny that it is their obedient servant. To desire uselessly, rather than feasibly, is to risk falling ill. If I could be shown tomorrow that there never were any such things as social classes, then I would try to stop desiring a classless society for fear of becoming psychotic or hopelessly boring. The position of a pragmatist who takes "interest," "power," or "desire" as his or her epistemological baseline (which is really no more than a modish contemporary version of the old-fashioned moral "decisionism" of R. M. Hare or the existentialist "commitment" of Sartre) is still open to argument: are such interests and desires actually *worth* holding in the sense that they might, for example, have beneficial effects?

1. A fact notably overlooked by Jean-François Lyotard in his and Jean-Loup Thébaud's *Just Gaming* (trans. Wlad Godzich, Theory and History of Literature, vol. 20 [Minneapolis, 1985]). Lyotard holds to a rigorous duality between descriptive and prescriptive statements. The most amusing feature of his argument is that, having apparently not read David Hume, he spontaneously reinvents his notorious dichotomy of "fact" and "value," without, it would seem, the slightest awareness of the hammering to which this case has been submitted, and not only by Marxists. Hume's coupling of positivism and idealism, the most banal gesture of bourgeois ideology, has quite specific historical conditions and is uncritically reproduced in rather different political conditions by the "anti-bourgeois" Lyotard. It is as though an English philosopher blissfully unaware of Descartes was to announce triumphantly, at the conclusion of some contorted argument, "I think, therefore I am!" Significantly, the well-known deconstructionist Samuel Weber, in his afterword to Lyotard's volume, leaves this rigid dichotomy of prescriptive and descriptive quite undeconstructed; for to deconstruct it would be to strike at one of the theoretical dogmas of post-structuralism.

This questioning will inevitably involve debate about how things are out there in the world. At some point or another in the process of reality testing, the ego might have to acknowledge that its desires are unrealizable and adjust them accordingly. What Lenin called "infantile communism" finds this process particularly hard to engage in. To talk about how things are out there in the world is not necessarily to imply that things are ever only one way or that such knowledge is transcendentally uncontaminated by interest and desire. There is no knockdown transcendental appeal against those who believe South Africa to be history's most shining instance of racial harmony; one just has to argue with them about this and that, show them a few townships, and so on. The transcendentalist case is a tiresome red herring which is currently driving some people into flagrantly self-contradictory positions when, in fact, they actually have forceful, interesting truth claims to advance.

If Marxists manage to bring down the bourgeois state, socialize the means of production, and institute full socialist democracy, then we really do not mind being told by people like Richard Rorty that all we are doing is carrying on the conversation. If that is what one prefers to call what we are doing, for some philosophical reason of one's own, then this is perfectly alright with us as long as we are still allowed to do it. If, on the other hand, Rorty and people like him began to produce some cogent theories of what is actually the case in order to stop us (and it would no doubt require a real political assault on middle-class America for them to be driven to this dreary extreme), then we might become rather worried. There is no point in organizing one's forces against the bourgeois state if it doesn't exist.

If there are problems with pragmatism, however, there would also seem to be real difficulties with realism. In its classical forms, Marxism is a strong epistemological realism which claims, for example, that all history actually *is* the history of class struggle. Even allowing for the properly sloganeering nature of this proposition, and the *genre* of the text in which it occurs (the *Communist Manifesto*), it is surely not true. There is no important sense in which, say, the oppression of women or homosexuals can be said to be just a product of class struggle, deeply imbricated with capitalism though such conditions may be. There is also no important sense in which the fact that road signs are painted green in the United States and white in the United Kingdom may be seen as a product of class struggle. There is not even any sense in which all of the activities of the state, media, or educational system are directly relevant to the reproduction of class rule. If this is the case, then perhaps it would be wiser for Marxists to choose the pragmatist path and argue that, though they are not of course claiming that all social products (literature, for example) are directly relevant to class struggle, they are deliberately focusing on those which are, or on those aspects of social phenomena which are, in order to further their own particular political desires.

My own view is that each of these cases, realist and pragmatist, has something to be said for it, but that neither is wholly adequate in itself. In his essay "Base and Superstructure in Marxist Cultural Theory," Raymond Williams confesses himself as having "great difficulty in seeing processes of art and thought as superstructural in the sense of the formula as it is commonly used."[2] One response to this doubt is to point out that whether art is superstructural or not is not necessarily a question to be decided once and for all. It depends, rather, on what one, as a critic, happens to be doing at the time. Thus, if one is checking the date of the work's publication or counting the recurrence of flower imagery in it, there is probably no very relevant sense in which one might be said to be treating it superstructurally. If on the other hand one is inquiring into the way the ideology of the work may support certain dominant social relations, then one is indeed submitting it to a superstructural reading. "Superstructural," that is to say, designates less a fixed ontological realm of phenomena than a particular standpoint or form of discursive activity. When the bourgeois state takes action to mobilize its emergency services in the event of flood or famine, it is not, generally speaking, behaving as part of the superstructure; when it mobilizes its troops to break a strike, then it is. When American schoolchildren salute the flag, the educational system is a superstructure; when they are taught how to fasten their shoelaces it is not. Superstructural is as superstructural does: some features of a social institution may be superstructural and some not, and these same features may change their status from one situation to another.

I am suggesting, in other words, that the base/superstructure model is most illuminating if the superstructure is regarded as a set of variable functions rather than as a given realm. One of the gains of such a functional emphasis is, ironically, to avoid the functional*ism* which some Marxist theory has embarrassingly, unwittingly taken over from bourgeois sociology, whereby the character of an institution is thought to be exhaustively definable in terms of its functional relations to other institutions. To claim that, say, literature is superstructural *tout court* is thus to fall prey to bourgeois ideology, suppressing the contradictory features of such a phenomenon by characterizing it wholly in terms of a certain unvariably supportive role in the process of exploitation.

I want to shift the argument, then, from the functional character of the superstructure to the functional character of the *term* "superstructure"—to effect a slide from the substantive to the adjectival. This position involves a fairly strong revisionist reading of Marx himself, who in at least some of his major formulations of the model would seem to hold to a sort of genetic-functional interpretation of the superstructure. A

2. Raymond Williams, "Base and Superstructure in Marxist Cultural Theory," *Problems in Materialism and Culture: Selected Essays* (London, 1980), p. 36.

Marxist should always be wary of swerving from tradition in this way, since "tradition" means those beliefs which many hundreds and thousands of men and women in active struggle over the generations have found it possible and necessary to hold, rather than some bright idea dreamt up overnight by an intellectual. But an ontologizing of the superstructure seems to me in the end an impediment to effective political practice, and in any case Marx himself was the first Marxist revisionist. Roughly speaking, a phenomenon is superstructural when and only when it plays some active, reasonably direct role in the power struggles of class society; and to this extent what is and what isn't superstructural at any given point is a matter of political contention, not a question of looking up the books. The superstructure is defined precisely by *its action on the base:* it is, as Marx himself once commented, a *relational* term, or, as we might say, a contextual one. To examine a phenomenon like literature superstructurally is to contextualize it in a particular way—to highlight those aspects of it which act as hegemonic supports. (One might add: as antihegemonic subversions, too. But one would be opening up a different, difficult matter in the theory of ideology.) There thus need be no implication here that the work does not reveal other aspects distinct from or irreconcilable with these specific features; but there is also an implicit claim that *any* social object, such as rhubarb pie or the size of one's feet, could in some appropriate context begin to behave superstructurally.

An example of functionalist theory in Marxist views of the superstructure would be a certain classical Marxist view of the state. According to this view, the political state is the instrument of the ruling class; it is directly defined in terms of its efficacy in executing dominant social interests. This view merely suppresses the fact that the state is, among other things, a terrain of political *struggle*—that, as with the relations between parliamentary democracy and monopoly capitalism, it is a contradictory, internally conflictual process within which certain working-class advances are usually possible. (Lenin, after all, once led the Bolsheviks into the Duma.) The state is not only an agency of class rule but a means by which the *unity* of any social formation is produced and reproduced, and these roles may prove mutually contradictory. In seeking to further dominant interests in the long term, the state may find itself forced to negotiate with oppositional interests in the short term, trim its sails, and make concessions. But there is a distinction between this dialectical view and a kind of leftist reformism which would see the state simply, so to speak, as up for grabs, a field of political contention *unweighted* in a particular direction. The state does indeed strive to reproduce the unity of the social formation, to act as the cement of civil society, but it seeks to maintain this unity on the basis and beneath the aegis of a certain political power. Both excessively realist and excessively pragmatist views of the state are likely to lead to mistaken, ineffectual political strategies.

My argument, then, has tried to balance between realist and pragmatist accounts. Insofar as "superstructural" is a functional term, we cannot simply read off, in the manner of a strong epistemological realism, what is superstructural and what is not. Something can be *made* superstructural, focused and defined as such by the contention of political forces; and to this extent my case gives some comfort to the pragmatists. But since I also want to maintain that the functional use of the term "superstructure" answers to some definite social reality, to that degree I want to preserve a certain realism. In an "extreme" version of the functional case, it would be possible in principle for governments, law courts, churches, schools, television stations, and literary texts almost *never* to behave superstructurally. Perhaps they do so only sporadically and untypically, in crisis situations. One reason why I am a Marxist is that this case strikes me as grossly implausible. An enormous range of the routine activities of such institutions would seem to me unintelligible if one did not posit this activity as in some sense supportive of political hegemony. But to claim this is quite distinct from claiming that these social institutions came into existence expressly for such a purpose—a genetic-functional case—or that their whole mode of operation can be exhausted by such an account.

The reason why many social institutions, "literature" among them, behave for much of the time in superstructural fashion can be found in the nature of the base. Put briefly, superstructural activity is essential because the base is itself divided. If social relations were conducted without oppression and exploitation there would be no need for a superstructure. The superstructure is an "imaginary" response to a real contradiction in the mode of production. This is why some Marxists speak of a communist society as one in which the superstructure will have disappeared. They do not, presumably, mean by this that there will be no schools, artifacts, television stations, or administrative bodies (though they might mean there will be no churches and strip joints); they mean that these apparatuses will have ceased to behave in the manner characteristic of them in class society. Schools will doubtless still exist in communism, though in a greatly transformed way, but they will not be superstructural. The British monarchy, however, will not exist because there is no way in which such a phenomenon can *not* be superstructural. Milton will still exist, but critical accounts of him which show what a rogue he was to support the beheading of Charles will not, or at least will wither away. As long as social relations continue to depend on exploitation, superstructural functions are necessary to regulate and mystify the social conflict to which this will inevitably give rise. It is in this sense, not in some genetic-functional way, that the secret of the superstructure is to be found in the base—in a certain set of social and economic relations. It is not so much that the superstructure has its *roots* in the base as that it has its *reasons* there.

Since oppression and exploitation are routine facts of late capitalist society, it follows that much of the "culture" of that society will in fact, though not for all of the time, be explicable by that form of contextualization for which the word "superstructure" is traditional Marxist shorthand.

In this sense, then, my case is a realist one; but it is not the strong, inflexible realism of a certain Marxist tradition, and it makes room for the pragmatic position of deciding, for reasons of one's own particular political interests and desires, to focus on those aspects of social phenomena which are in any given situation supportive of hegemony. Insofar as I want to say that there are central aspects of literature which actually are, regardless of my own political predilections, closely bound up with social exploitation, I give offence to a certain kind of pragmatist; insofar as I also want to argue that there are social phenomena which at particular times are in no very relevant sense so bound up, I give offence to a certain kind of Marxist realist. Whether this position is called dialectical, cunningly judicious, sitting on the fence, or having your cake and eating it no doubt depends on one's political predilections.

Molière and the Sociology of Exchange

Jean-Marie Apostolidès

Translated by Alice Musick McLean

The advent of a market economy led European society to invent new spaces to facilitate the circulation of consumer goods and of values. The market, understood less as a concrete than as an abstract place—a "public sphere"[1]—constitutes the space of merchandise and of monetary exchange. When the theater broke away from religious tradition, gained autonomy as an art, and fell under the governance of aesthetic laws, it became the space for the circulation of new values. In seventeenth-century France comedy made its claim as a neutral, autonomous space for the confrontation of old ideologies, stemming from Christianity, and new ones, rooted in the absolute monarchy. The theater offered a space for simulation where new behaviors were subjected to imaginary testing, by trial and error. The author of comedies tried out different solutions in front of the spectators and explored different paths before settling on an implicit choice.

This space of simulation was imposed by the fact that while social roles and status still constituted an "essence" (the place of each man on earth as willed by God), they nevertheless underwent a profound transformation when certain individuals conceived the possibility of changing roles. Even though the model of the three orders (clergy, nobility, third estate) still functioned as a general reference, the tripartite division failed to conceal the social changes since the mid-sixteenth century and especially

---

1. Jürgen Habermas, *L'Espace public: archéologie de la publicité comme dimension constitutive de la société bourgeoise*, trans. Marc B. de Launay (Paris, 1978).

since the early seventeenth century. Under Louis XIV, the feudal nobility, which lived off its property, was displaced by an urban nobility, for whom ground rents no longer provided the principal source of revenue. The aristocrat of old gave way to the courtier; the values of urban society, propagated by the salons and the entourage of the king, took precedence over military values. At the height of the revival of the aristocracy, another group of men, not originally of the *noblesse d'épée*, enriched itself and acquired power—judges or merchants made up the bureaucracy of the royal administration, developed commerce, controlled the finances of the kingdom. In other words, they laid the foundations of modernity, a task which the Revolution finished up.[2] In addition considerable numbers of artisans, servants, and laborers, many barely out of the peasantry, settled in cities and likewise confronted a double system of values. Everywhere, society moved from a social system in which the mode of differentiation was stratified and organized hierarchically to another in which the mode of differentiation was becoming functional.[3]

At every level, the values of Christianity, still the ideological soil for the French, were undermined by new activities and attitudes—the loaning of money, market practice, religious skepticism, philosophical rationalism—that transgressed them. The conflicts that came from this double ideological standard were taken on by preachers in the religious domain, and by the *moralistes* and the dramatic authors in the field of literature. It is in this general intellectual climate that we must place Molière if we wish to understand the extent to which he wrote primarily for his own time before he made his claim to put on stage the universal man. More precisely, we need to understand how the values of universal man— *l'honnête homme*—offer an acceptable alternative to the conflict between the feudal and the modern mode of existence.

Molière's theater presents a gallery of dangerous personalities whose maladjustment threatens the security of a new institution, the nuclear family.[4] These individuals are often delinquent fathers, rebellious sons, or bachelors whose ambition has turned them into criminals. These char-

2. See Alexis de Tocqueville, *The Old Régime and the French Revolution*, trans. Stuart Gilbert (Garden City, N.Y., 1955).
3. See Niklas Luhmann, *Love as Passion: The Codification of Intimacy*, trans. Jerry Gaines and Doris L. Jones (Cambridge, Mass., 1986).
4. The expression is Ralph Albanese's, used in his *Le Dynamisme de la peur chez Molière: une analyse socio-culturelle de Dom Juan, Tartuffe et L'Ecole des femmes* (University, Miss., 1976).

Jean-Marie Apostolidès is professor of French literature at Stanford University. His publications include *Le roi-machine*, *Les métamorphoses de Tintin*, and *Le prince sacrifié*. **Alice Musick McLean,** a Ph.D. student at the University of Chicago, is specializing in medieval narrative and the literature of the fantastic.

acters are dangerous because they are appealing, and they are captivating because they play on social contradictions, moving back and forth from one system of values to another. Instead of finding the "golden mean," they behave unacceptably, either by exchanging too much and in an unorthodox manner, or by refusing to exchange altogether. By excess or by default, they imperil the fragile balance in the model of the *honnête homme.*

Two of Molière's plays, *The Miser* and *Don Juan,* will put us in a better position to understand the mechanisms of simulation. In both cases, the main character is unable to unite the different values that divide his world, and consequently he favors some values to the detriment of the others. The social group reacts to these transgressions, but, in doing so, they come to regard the dangerous individual as sacred. The latter is not understood in his identity with the others but rather in his difference. The stage makes it possible to ostracize this individual by giving him the mask of a monster (Harpagon) or even that of a devil (Don Juan). The staging then moves away from psychological realism to mythology. In the guise of a devil Don Juan, like Faust, appears to us as one of the founding figures of modernity.[5]

The method chosen here draws on concepts borrowed from sociology and anthropology. This double conceptual approach is necessary for a society divided between values inherited from medieval Christianity and precapitalist practices. Seventeenth-century France did not think of itself as a class society but as a society of orders. Since sociology is a system of knowledge whose concepts are taken from an imaginary construct, it is thus more suited to analyzing bourgeois society than societies in transition.[6] In trying to measure the past with the aid of tools forged in and for contemporary societies, the sociologist runs the risk of only measuring an artifact, produced by his theories in the field of history. Hence the need for the anthropological concepts, including the notion of exchange, among others, whether material (the exchange of goods), symbolic (the exchange of signs), or sexual (the exchange of women).

This approach will bring to light the contradictions underlying the society of the ancien régime. Whereas an ordinary sociohistorical approach views the reign of Louis XIV as unified under a dogmatic classicism, the socioanthropological approach stresses the tensions and oppositions running through this society. Classicism appears then as a façade covering up the change that it cannot imagine. This "spectacle"[7] makes it possible to unite contradictory social practices, both those produced by consumption

5. See André Dabezies, *Visages de Faust au XXe siècle: Littérature, idéologie et mythe* (Paris, 1967).

6. See Cornelius Castoriadis, *The Imaginary Institution of Society,* trans. Kathleen Blamey (Cambridge, Mass., 1987).

7. See Guy Debord, *Society of the Spectacle,* rev. English ed. (Detroit, 1977).

and which originate in the medieval economy (based on the gift/counter-gift and service) and those belonging to the early accumulation of capital which sketch future bourgeois economic practices.

With regard to the literary field, this method has the great advantage of "historicizing" the very notion of literature and its various genres. The literary sphere did not become autonomous until the eighteenth century when the novel became the dominant genre. Novels then gave independent expression to the new interiority specific to the bourgeois sensitivity.[8] The three domains—psychological interiority, market exchange, and literature as a field of free expression—were linked. In the seventeenth century, however, fiction was still in its formative stages; it was not yet totally free. The theater thus formed an intermediary universe between religious representation and literary expression. On the one hand, the theater extricated itself from faith, while remaining obsessed with evil; on the other, it constituted a locus of research, less at the level of content than at that of form. It strove to become a literary genre. Nevertheless, the small share of interiority it presupposed on the part of the spectators, as well as the absence of fiction admitted in its narratives, prevented the theater from going over entirely to the side of literature. This double status gave the theater a unique place in social history because it allowed the mourning of old values and the trying out of new values which in traditional terms were judged criminal. The theater thus turned into a testing ground for modernity.[9] Understood in this fashion, the theatrical stage constitutes a first form, simple and archaic, of the field of simulation necessary to modern societies. Simulation came into play as soon as social roles were freed from their religious ties and as soon as society came to think of itself as a functional whole, changes brought about by classical political philosophy.[10] The same holds true for the twentieth century, apart from the enormous difference that today simulation no longer relies on the theater but on technology.[11]

The Exchange of Money: Harpagon

Harpagon is a seventeenth-century miser, that is to say, a usurer. He makes money work for what it will yield, and, on this account, he is one of the most important precapitalist figures in French theater. However, Molière portrays him from a moral standpoint and is interested less in

8. Reinhart Koselleck, *Critique and Crisis: Enlightenment and the Pathogenesis of Modern Society* (Cambridge, Mass., 1988).

9. Jean Duvignaud was the first to attribute this function to the theater in *Les Ombres collectives* (Paris, 1973).

10. See Nannerl O. Keohane, *Philosophy and the State in France: The Renaissance to the Enlightenment* (Princeton, N.J., 1980).

11. See Philippe Quéau, *Eloge de la simulation* (Paris, 1986).

the social mechanisms that favor the usurer than in the disastrous effects of this practice on Harpagon's family. Harpagon is a widower of about sixty, the father of two children he hopes to marry off, and he has a fairly large number of servants, at the head of whom is a steward named Valère. Unlike most of the leading bourgeois characters Molière puts on stage who use their fortune to monopolize an imaginary capital of honor, Harpagon assumes his bourgeois ignominy and wants instead to augment his usurious and commercial capital. He is detached from traditional values. He is not impressed by nobility, he spurns family conventions, and he entertains solely financially advantageous relations with others. He is a father in name only and considers himself rather an individual with no attachments, someone to whom everyone is a potential rival or enemy. With his own son, he finds himself involved first of all in a relationship of amorous rivalry, later in the relationship of usurer to borrower. The monetary tie takes the place that should belong to the affective tie, and Harpagon even tries to get rid of his children with the least possible expense: "without dowry!"[12] For their part, the children dream only of running away from home. At least Cléante does; he wants to start a family with Marianne far from his childhood milieu: "I'm determined to run away with my beloved and take whatever fortune Heaven may vouchsafe us" (M, p. 115).

If we accept Henri Bergson's definition of comedy—"*Something me-chanical encrusted on the living*"[13]—Harpagon presents himself as an adding machine. As soon as he enters into contact with someone, he does not perceive who that person is, but rather what he owns. With a surprising degree of precision, he can say how much what someone has can yield under any given circumstances. The energy that drives Harpagon is not expressed in affective or amorous behaviors but is converted directly into money. Since he feels neither love nor hate, he does not understand these feelings in others, whom he treats as abstract forces to be turned into profit.

This inversion of values that dehumanizes human beings likewise humanizes things, at least the most essential thing: money. Harpagon treats it as if it possessed a soul, since, according to him, money is the energy that sustains the world. When his cash box is taken from him, he is deprived of his vital energy; this is why he yells that a murder has taken place. In his delirium, he calls his money his "beloved," his "con-solation," his "joy" (M, p. 159). When later there is a quid pro quo between him and Valère (Valère is speaking of women, and Harpagon, of money), the misunderstanding can be prolonged only because gold

12. Molière, *The Miser and Other Plays*, trans. John Wood (1953; New York, 1985), p. 123; further references to this play, abbreviated M, will be included in the text.
13. Henri Bergson, *Laughter: An Essay on the Meaning of the Comic*, trans. Cloudesley Brereton and Fred Rothwell (London, 1911), p. 37.

has been humanized: Harpagon cannot imagine that anyone could be attached to anything else. In Valère, who flatters him constantly, he recognizes his own character traits, the same obsession with possession. Indeed, Harpagon dreams of a world without loss, without waste, a world where it would be possible to accumulate ad infinitum, without expending any energy. In this sense, he already embodies a certain "capitalist" spirit for which everything represents progress, and linear time points to an ever-larger conquest, to an ever-more-dominant rationality. And since Harpagon identifies his existence with gold, he thinks he will live indefinitely since he spends only the bare minimum necessary to restore his ability to calculate.

This obsessive fear of spending is characteristic of the behavior of a miser. There is no scrap, no rag that cannot serve as currency, as one can note in the list of assorted objects that Harpagon slips into the terms of his loan agreement unbeknownst to his borrowers and which he requires them to sell as a substitute for a part of the principal. These cast-offs of aristocratic and bourgeois wealth have lost their use value for Harpagon, who reassigns them a reduced exchange value and puts them back into circulation in usurious exchange. But the refusal of any expenditure, any loss, amounts to repression and comes out as absolute loss, that is, death. In no other play by Molière does death have a stronger presence than in *The Miser*. It is the reverse of the wish for total accumulation, the other symptom of Harpagon's folly. The myth of Midas enables us to understand: like the legendary king, the usurer transforms everything he touches into gold but in doing so he loses his life.[14] His children flee from him, his servants lie to him and steal from him, his horses, reduced to skeletons, are of no use to him. Every relationship that is not monetary is struck with sterility. Verbal or affective exchanges are reduced to an illusion due to the dominance of the exchange of money. The only sincere wishes are death wishes: Cléante promises his father will die within eight months, Frosine advises Marianne not to sign the marriage contract except on the condition that Harpagon will die soon, and she herself wishes that he rot in hell (*M*, p. 138). In his answers to these wishes, Harpagon expresses delight at the thought that he will see his children buried. In this comedy where human beings are reified by the relationship to money, death is only the final consequence of their transformation into abstract things, quantifiable and negotiable.

The only characters who retain a bit of humanity, even though they themselves are treated as merchandise, are Master Jacques, among the servants, and Elise, among the children. If the coachman-cook shows some tenderness for his master, the miser's daughter is undoubtedly more complex than she appears. Her age is not given, but she is so sensible that she must be about thirty. She has in fact taken on the

14. Judd Hubert has already made the comparison between Harpagon and Midas; see his *Molière and the Comedy of Intellect* (Berkeley and Los Angeles, 1962), p. 213.

mother's role. Although she no doubt loves Valère sincerely, she cannot bring herself to act, that is, to flee the house. She encourages her fiancé to keep his mask. Despite the promise of marriage that he has gotten her to sign, she holds to the status quo: "I must confess I am concerned about the outcome," she confides (*M*, p. 111). She treats her father considerately, never criticizes him openly, unlike her brother, and cannot even bear for anyone to criticize him in her presence. When Valère tries to do so, albeit with restraint, he has to apologize for having offended her. As we learn at the beginning of the play, Elise is of a melancholy temperament. Her fears concern not only her father but her fiancé as well. When Valère talks about going to find his parents, a move which would provide an avenue of escape from a difficult situation, Elise holds him back: "Oh no, Valère. Do not go away, I beseech you! Stay and give your whole attention to gaining my father's confidence" (*M*, p. 112). She encourages him in his role as a hypocritical financier who not only indulges the boss' whims but above all follows his example.

By imitating Harpagon's behavior, Valère acquires the same power in Harpagon's family as Tartuffe does in Orgon's, and sometimes he even uses practically the same phrases as Tartuffe. As for Elise, she acts like an Elmire who has succumbed to the hypocrite's charm. If she owes her life to her father, does she not owe it just as much to the lover who saved her from drowning? And does her affection not have as its origin the debt that she cannot repay in any other way? Elise justifies her indecision by conjuring up to Valère the inevitable disappointment that marriage brings; she fears, she says, "the cruel indifference with which men so often requite an innocent love too ardently offered them" (*M*, p. 111). And, in the face of her lover's protests, she voices an opinion that puts all men in the same category: "you all talk like that. Men are all alike in their promises" (*M*, p. 111). In short, she wants to be the eternal fiancée, because marriage would bring about an affective loss. She makes a fetish of absolute love, perhaps because it is of Oedipal origin, but mostly because she does not want to tap the sentimental capital it represents. Like her father, but in the domain of libidinal economy, Elise fears loss, the deterioration of feeling and death. By refusing to consummate the marriage, she keeps absolute love (and her virginity) like a treasure.

This interpretation of Harpagon's daughter helps us understand the father. Just before the play begins, two parallel and independent events have taken place in the household: first, the promise of marriage between Elise and Valère, and second, the settlement of a long-standing obligation: a debtor came to repay Harpagon the considerable sum of 10,000 pounds. With no time to invest this gold, the miser buried it at the far end of the garden. During the course of the play, he keeps going to check on it and ends up having it stolen. Even though Harpagon generally puts his money to work, here he contemplates it. He takes it out of circulation and momentarily suspends its double value of usage and exchange. The gold becomes his fetish, his God, a hieratic object he literally adores. He treats it the way his daughter treats love, as an absolute. Ordinarily, when money works, it gets used up in the process of circulation; the owner must separate himself from it and make it take risks so that it will yield. Here, Harpagon cannot bring himself to do so, and prefers the phantasm of economic omnipotence (the fact that money theoretically permits a multitude of purchases among which one must choose) to the loss due to a particular investment.[15]

We find the same structure in the libidinal economy. The period of engagement is the short time when the woman is taken out of circulation yet remains "un-consumed," suspended between use and exchange. During the ancien régime, it was an extremely codified ceremony because bringing together two families, unknown to each other, entailed considerable risk.[16] It was thus a period where the decrees of society corresponded closely to the individual's personal *habitus,* a period during which the actors involved enjoyed a high degree of prestige, precisely because of this close correspondence. Finally, the engagement is also, in the West, the time of passionate love, that is, of the phantasm of eternal pleasure, of an absolute feeling, absolute because it has not yet been confronted with history and with ordinary life. We can now appreciate the full force of the quid pro quo that structures act 5: the fiancée and the cash box are equivalent objects for two men, one of whom "has ingratiated himself in the favor" of the other that is, Valère and Harpagon. The fetishism of the monetary sign and absolute love are a single deviation, in the double domain of monetary economy and libidinal economy. This deviation corresponds to a fixation on the sign of exchange (gold/love), to a refusal of loss, a mocking return to the sacred, which the characters are unable to mourn.

The Universal Exchange: Don Juan

All exchangers are epitomized in Don Juan, who surpasses the type and attains the dimensions of a myth.[17] On two occasions during the

15. For a sociological analysis that compares Harpagon's practice with the ideal of Colbertian mercantilism, see Ralph Albanese, "Argent et réification dans *L'Avare,*" *L'Esprit Créateur* 21 (1981): 35–50.

16. "We can posit as a general law that the more dangerous the situation is, the more the practice tends to be codified. The degree of codification varies with the degree of risk. This can clearly be seen in the case of marriage: ... the more the marriage unifies distant, therefore prestigious, groups, the greater the symbolic profit, but so also the risk. It is in this case that there will be a very high degree of formalization of practices; this is where there will be the most refined polite expressions, the most elaborate rites" (Pierre Bourdieu, *Choses dites* [Paris, 1987], p. 96).

17. See Georges Gendarme de Bévotte, *La Légende de Dom Juan: son évolution dans la littérature des origines au romantisme* (Paris, 1906), and Leo Weinstein, *The Metamorphoses of Don Juan* (Stanford, Calif., 1959).

course of Molière's play, allusion is made to the clothes Don Juan is wearing, first by Sganarelle, then, after the drowning, by Peter: "A regular gentleman, 'e be—gold lace on his clothes from head to foot."[18] With the gold, Don Juan sports ribbons the color of fire ("There bain't no part of 'em, even their shoes, that don't be a-loaded down with 'em" [*M*, p. 210]). What we know about Sganarelle's costume, from the postmortem inventory of Molière's personal effects, proves that he wears clothes matching those of his master.[19] Don Juan appears under the double sign of gold and of fire, and it is through these two emblems that we will interpret him.

From Tirso de Molina to Molière, the theological importance of the drama of the *burlador* diminishes, but the protagonists of Molière's version appeal to Christian values to judge Don Juan. All of them refer to the ethics of the Gospel to condemn the seducer, to condemn the man that broke the oaths traditionally binding men together. Upon seeing the multiple transgressions perpetrated by Don Juan, the clan delegates Don Louis as its chief, who judges the guilty party and sanctions the rupture the seducer himself had sought: "You claim descent from your ancestors in vain. They disown you" (*DJ*, p. 237). Don Juan causes yet another rupture by destroying the bipolarity that is the foundation of traditional society, that of the sacred and of the profane. In abducting Elvira, he violates the convent and commits sacrilege by putting the inside world in contact with the outside. Then, having married the nun, he breaks the bonds of marriage once again to devote himself to new conquests. This act, his claim to rival God Himself, is the heinous crime, the sin for which there is no forgiveness. He feels strong enough to taunt his Creator by stealing a virgin consecrated to Him.

According to a religious interpretation of the world, Don Juan assumes a diabolical role. He tempts each of the characters in turn, traps them with fallacious words. Those who enter into contact with him find themselves being offered, in exchange for their salvation, valorized things they cannot acquire without transgressing Christian morals. To each person, Don Juan proposes new values which not only cannot be offered by the religious universe, but whose acquisition could very well weaken long-standing solidarities. The first victim of the seduction is of course Sganarelle, who gave himself to the devil not only in the hope of a reward (his wages) but also because the light emanating from the evil angel has dazzled him and because he has made Don Juan his captivating model. Don Juan plays the seducer with women too, by making them glimpse

18. Molière, *Don Juan or the Statue at the Feast,* in *The Miser and Other Plays,* p. 210; further references to this play, abbreviated *DJ*, will be included in the text.
19. Among the lot of Molière's clothing, "a cloth camisole with gold facings," "two sleeves of taffeta the color of fire and of green moire," and "a short-sleeved shirt of red taffeta" identified as costumes for characters in *Don Juan* (Madeleine Jurgens and E. Maxfield-Miller, *Cent ans de recherches sur Molière* [Paris, 1983], p. 569).

a richer life, affectively or materially. The only character of the play who does not succumb to the devil is Francisco, the destitute pauper who has put his absolute trust in Heaven. Don Juan asks him to swear, that is, to commit a mortal sin, in divine as well as human law. He proposes to the pauper to exchange his soul for a gold louis and repeats the temptation three times while making the coin shine in his hand. And Francisco, poverty notwithstanding, and with an unparalleled dignity, refuses what he considers to be a fool's bargain: "No sir, I'd rather starve" (*DJ*, p. 225).

Nevertheless, it is by another aspect of his personality that Don Juan appears as the incarnation of the devil. At a time when everyone possesses sufficient grace (the Jesuits maintain it against the Jansenists), he is the exception. He accepts damnation voluntarily. He is the damned par excellence, he to whom Lucifer has granted his "grace," an infernal grace that is the negative of God's. From the beginning of the play to the end, from Sganarelle to the Specter of the last act, from the sublunar world to the celestial universe, everyone and everything comes to warn Don Juan of the risks his soul runs. He pays no attention and denies everything until the last moment. Not only does he refuse the gift of prophecy that emerges from his entourage (Sganarelle, Elvira, and Don Louis prophesy in turn), but also he ridicules the miracles God has allowed to happen, the transgressions of the order of things that He has accepted to convert the infidel. Whether before the miracle of the statue, three times repeated, or faced with the apparition of the Specter, Don Juan dismisses Heaven's grace. He returns God's own gifts to Him in order to owe Him nothing: "those who reject Heaven's mercy bring down its wrath" (*DJ*, p. 247) is the final judgment uttered by the statue of the Commander while he transmits the divine Fire. During five acts, the flight of the hero is crossed by many hands held out to him, that of Sganarelle who tries to convert him, of Elvira and Don Louis who attempt to put him back on the straight and narrow, of Peter who pulls him out of the water, and even the hand held out by Monsieur Dimanche to obtain his money. Don Juan refuses these various extended hands[20] and only takes hold of those who can lead him into hell—Charlotte's hand, promised to Peter ("only give me your hand . . ." [*DJ*, p. 215]) and the statue's:

THE STATUE: Give me your hand.
DON JUAN: There. [*DJ*, p. 247]

Don Juan's wandering turns into one big mistake. Not one of his criminal plans succeeds, because each time someone stands in the way

20. On the social symbolism of the hand, see Eugène Marsan, *Savoir-vivre en France* (Paris, 1926), pp. 26–31.

to point him in a different direction, even the pauper whom he questions about the way to town and who indicates the way to go to heaven, that is, the practice of charity. Each defeat, each aborted project is a new extension of credit offered to Don Juan by Heaven. This is particularly clear in act 4 when the deceiver finds himself saddled with a fast despite himself. He fails to see, in the impossibility of eating, a sign urging him to mortify the flesh; he helps himself to terrestrial nourishment before divine nourishment, about which Don Louis, Elvira, and the statue come to talk with him. He especially does not understand that the supper he is in a hurry to eat will be the last, that it will resemble a demoniacal counter-Last Supper where everything will be "consumed."

Molière's play should first be read from a Christian perspective because the religious pole unifies all the divided social structures, that of the family, of politics, or of exchange. Each of the protagonists comes to condemn Don Juan, but Heaven alone is powerful enought to execute the sentence. Whereas in other comedies by Molière the threatened characters do not have much difficulty in driving away the *pharmakos* (scapegoat), in *Don Juan* they are all scattered, split up, and do not communicate among themselves except through the intermediary of the hero.[21] Don Juan restores the unity of the world, but against him, and only in the theological meaning of the play. He is marked with the *minus* sign and permits the coherence of the divine word by the promise of Fire. It is the progressively stronger assurance of his eternal damnation that solidifies the values of the group; God needs the devil to manifest His existence to the world.

The first universe is religious, structured around two poles, the sacred and the profane; it is placed under the sign of Fire. The second universe, superimposed on the first, is secular, egalitarian, and no longer hierarchical. Don Juan does not wear the sign *minus* there, but rather the *plus* sign. Gold has succeeded Fire. All of the characters of the drama are conscious of the coexistence of the two universes and of the tug-of-war between them, engendered by their opposite values. The temptation to which Don Juan submits them consists precisely in his proposing to be their intermediary, allowing them to pass from one universe to the other, from the religious world to that of the market. And if, with the exception of the pauper, each gives in to a greater or lesser degree, it is because each one's confidence in Christian values has already been shaken. Elvira has doubted the divine promise and doubts it still at the time of her first meeting with Don Juan; when she leaves the husband who has abandoned her, she does not know which, if any, of her brothers or if God will be able to avenge her honor. Monsieur Dimanche, Charlotte, and Mathurine

21. As Jules Brody has shown in "*Don Juan* and *Le Misanthrope,* or the Esthetics of Individualism in Molière," *PMLA* 84 (May 1969): 559–76.

apparently also doubt divine wisdom since they wish to leave the place where God put them to save them. The Christian universe is being shaken by secular values.

Don Juan's strength and power over the world are apparent in his ability to displace. He pulls all of the other characters along in his wake displacing them in not only geographical but also social space: Charlotte dreams of becoming mistress of the chateau, Monsieur Dimanche is treated like a prince, Peter is promoted to the rank of chateau supplier, and Sganarelle achieves equality with his master by sharing his table. Customs and language undergo the same magnetization: Elvira goes from the vocabulary of mystical love to that of carnal love, but in the end she returns to the convent vocabulary; Sganarelle, who wants to rival his master, talks like a book before he, along with his reasoning, collapses; Charlotte switches from using a country jargon to that of urbane civility. By unconscious mimicry, she speaks differently with Peter and Don Juan and resumes speaking in dialect with the latter only when she doubts his word, in order to keep a distance between them. And the statue of the Commander breaks its stony silence to transmit the divine word.

Don Juan's power to change his fellow human beings recalls the power of gold when it comes into contact with objects: he transforms people into merchandise, he attributes a quantifiable value to them, and he makes them circulate. This process of market transformation manifests itself in his relationships as seducer with women. What he says about them boils down to this: all women are equal and cannot be distinguished except by the time required to conquer them. As with merchandise, it is the quantity of time spent to *produce* them that determines their value. What differentiates Elvira from Charlotte is the seduction time, since it takes Don Juan several weeks to seduce the former but only a quarter of an hour to persuade the latter to marry him. The difference between people is no longer qualitative but quantitative and thus measurable. All women are inherently desirable, for they are, in Don Juan's eyes, merely transitory incarnations of the abstract Woman he seeks to reproduce, an imaginary being invented by his calculating desire. Beyond concrete, carnal individuals, with their qualities and their faults, above all with their vile or noble essences, their common or aristocratic blood, Don Juan searches for the common denominator. This is the reason all women seem lovable to him and that he dreams of passing from one to another as if he were making perpetual rounds.

Don Juan does not transfer his desire onto gold as Harpagon does; rather, he is the incarnation of that desire, which looks like precious metal to him. It never wears out, it is never used up, and the seducer thinks he has enough love for all the women in the world. In fact, he is able to go so quickly from one to another because he does not wear them out, nor does he wear himself out. He transforms them into merchandise, but this metamorphosis is carried out for the benefit of others. As far as he is concerned, he is careful not to consume them entirely; he sizes them up, evaluates them, compares them, seduces them, and abandons them. Above all, he interferes in the lives of couples, that of God and Elvira, of Peter and his Charlotte, of the young engaged couple we glimpse, just as the serpent came between Adam and Eve. He gleans his pleasure in passing, before sending the transformed lovers back to each other. He extracts, as it were, an erotic surplus value by prohibiting the free exchange of desire, by opposing any amorous behavior in which he does not take part. For him, there is no pleasure except in a love triangle in which he mimics the desire of the other. His pleasure seems to derive from anticipation, at the mere sight of requited love.[22] Hence he does not exhaust the use value of the women he transforms into marketable objects; he only uses what is necessary to determine their exchange value, that is to say, to fix their price. Then, once the women are uprooted from their universe, Don Juan puts them into circulation and takes no more interest in them. He has succeeded in freeing them from their essence and in endowing them with a new value, an erotic value, which will subsequently permit a free seduction of new partners.

As a figure of gold, Don Juan plays in the economic universe the same role the devil plays in the theological universe. He is a transforming force, wearing the *minus* sign in one world, the *plus* sign in the other. He is a counter-God who frees beings from the weight of tradition, he is the very principle of movement. He becomes something of an alchemist and achieves the synthesis at which Harpagon fails. His contact with women gives them another value, no longer linked to who they are but to what they own, no longer qualitative but quantitative; he gives them a price and thus enables their general exchange, under a "perverse" system in which the market economy imposes its model on the libidinal economy. The play is structured around this double universe. In both worlds, it is a matter of conversion. The group tries to convert Don Juan to Christian values, while the seducer converts women to erotic and market values. But, since no one speaks the same language, they cannot understand each other. Only Sganarelle, the pivotal character of the play, is able to use the double language, which is why he can switch so easily from religious values to those of his master. He is the universal translator, the one who attempts a halfhearted osmosis between the two worlds with incompatible values.

At the end of the comedy, Heaven learns accounting, and Don Juan agrees to speak the language of religion. Gold and Fire, emblems of the

22. See on this subject the description he gives (*DJ*, p. 205) to Sganarelle of the engaged couple he has been pursuing for several days. A psychological analysis of the character would bring to the fore the homosexual component of this triangular desire, Don Juan's coming back to the trio situation in the very fact of telling Sganarelle his phantasms and of making him intervene in all the relationships the master entertains with women.

two contradictory universes, grow closer in the fifth act; theology finds a common ground with economics. But the latter is not well thought out in the seventeenth century. Although the market structure is in place, the economic vocabulary is not yet well established. Myth bolsters scientific analysis. By participating in the elimination of Don Juan, the group of protagonists (and the spectators) tries to reject the new generalized principle of circulation and exchange. Thus, it economizes its collective guilt by finding a scapegoat for the transgressions which have thrown traditional society out of joint. Nevertheless, the punishment of "a nobleman who has given himself over to wickedness" (*DJ*, p. 201) in the theological universe which administers the sacred brings forth the modern figure of Don Juan. As in primitive societies, but on another level, communication between two universes occurs through the sacrifice of the negative. For Don Juan to attain the level of myth, he must be eliminated. His annihilation will make possible the movement from the Christian feudal world to the market world, which is still ours today. Modernity begins with the solemn sacrifice of this Antichrist, who thereby attains exemplary status and enters the pantheon of contemporary gods. By offering his hand to the statue of the Commander, Don Juan sanctions the fusion of the contradictory values he incarnates.

Conclusion

Molière's theater stands out as a testing ground and a judgment place where new social behaviors are tried out and sanctioned by laughter. Although rarely given directly, the implicit model against which deviant characters are measured is the *honnête homme*. Whereas during the preceding generations this model was normative, transmitted through multiple treatises on manners, during the reign of Louis XIV it becomes implicit. It is hidden, but it can be tacitly inferred from all unacceptable behavior, which is stigmatized by ridicule. This situation leaves the norm in a gray area, which allows for flexible social strategies at a time marked by a double system of values.

The staging of social deviations or failures of the collectivity takes the form of a denunciation. With the tacit complicity of a reference group (court society, the *honnêtes gens*), the author focuses attention on those individuals unable to correctly master the double system of values, all of those unsuccessful in achieving the "golden mean," classical France's ideal. The staging is tantamount to an "imaging," that is, to an abstraction. The real Harpagons or Don Juans of the seventeenth century doubtlessly did not completely understand the conduct Molière attributed to them. They did not think out their behavior, a practice akin to cynicism, but instead came up on a day-to-day basis with solutions to new problems. Because of his intellectual stance, Molière endows them with a logic that is actually derived from the imaging. Putting characters on stage amounts to choosing such exemplary traits as Harpagon's miserliness or Don Juan's sexual obsession and transforming these characteristics, divorced from their context, into characters. In creating "types," Molière constructs a sharp, recognizable image, which he exposes to the condemnation of his contemporaries, who, in turn, will be able to recognize among their peers a Harpagon or a Don Juan. Imaging is thus a social power, an appropriation by which the author undertakes to raise himself above his condition. We know that Molière, by becoming one of the principal artisans of the "pleasures of the king," was able to escape his original background and to acquire a familiarity with the court that he could never have acquired had he carried on his father's upholstery business.

To be complete, any sociology of theater should therefore include some reflections on staging, and on the denunciation, because every imaging seems like a verdict. It is in effect an act which enables us to move from concrete cases (the Harpagons or Don Juans Molière may have known) to the abstract ones (the miser or the seducer). It lets us go beyond the particular to the general, but only by transforming the real. To produce on stage is therefore to act on the social fabric by manipulating symbolic signs. Classical theater as a genre is no more neutral or objective than the bourgeois novel or contemporary cinema. It is an intellectual instrument whose content cannot be separated from its form.

Seen from this angle, literary activity complements law. It is a technique akin to a science of manners that allows us to generalize about different activities by reducing them to their common denominator. It accounts for behavior that falls outside of the law or that the judiciary system cannot entirely resolve. Although this behavior may flout the moral code, it is not clearly illegal. Whereas the law sanctions past conduct, acts which actually did take place, the theater sanctions possible conduct. (We note in passing that the majority of classical playwrights studied law.) It is in this sense that the theater deals with the imaginary, has a great capacity for invention, and breaks away from realism. Nevertheless, in the history of the West, the autonomy of theatrical representation is connected with the autonomy of law. They are two parallel systems whose function is to equate action and behavior, and to sanction them.

One last point remains—the relationship between the activity of the dramatic author (the imaging) and that of the critic. In fact a theoretical approach is also an imaging, a representation, though with other instruments, except that it does not find its original material in concrete behavior, as the playwright does, but rather in texts, that is, in a material that has already been treated. This article has taken two plays, written a few years apart by the same author, and has identified their unity in the notion of exchange. In doing so, we have pushed Molière's text one more step in the process of abstraction. More than three hundred years separate us from the creation of these works, and we have analyzed them "from a distance" by valorizing the particular themes that interest our history (simulation). The same reduction Molière imposed on the concrete behaviors of his contemporaries is the very one we now apply to him, but on a higher degree of abstraction. And in both cases, this return to treating behavior in discourse implies, on the part of the author, a gain of power in the cultural field specific to him: court society for Molière, the academic institution for this author. Critical activity is no more innocent than dramatic activity; it is literary judgment and as such implies competition for legitimacy. If criticism does not succeed in questioning its own foundations, it runs the risk, as Pierre Bourdieu has observed, of taking these artifacts for the reality of what it describes.[23]

The sociological approach advocated here differs from others in that it regards literature neither as a reflection nor as the expression of the ideology of a group. It makes literature an imaginary construct which, although its roots are buried in history, nevertheless escapes historical determinism by becoming simulation. In this manner, literature opens out to the future, becomes a producer of meaning and a place of experimentation with new sensibilities. It allows the testing of new behaviors without legal sanction because it is a complement of law just this side of legality. Its domain is parallel to that of scientific research; it is social and imaginary experimentation.

Our method also infers an understanding of literary form and content in dynamic interaction and not as fixed essences. It postulates that there exists no absolute point of view from which the truth of the text can be understood. It requires then not only a historical understanding of the conditions of production of the work but also an analysis of the critic's point of view and of his or her tools of critical knowledge. In this sense, this sociological method posits a criticism of criticism, it urges a theory of theory.

---

23. Bourdieu, *Choses dites*, p. 137.

"News, and new Things": Contemporaneity and the Early English Novel

J. Paul Hunter

Long before Samuel Richardson showed readers and writers of fiction how to savor a single human instant a thousand ways, the world of print had begun its long liaison with the up-to-date, the latest news, the present moment, trying to provide a sense that the printing press offered a technology for nearly instant replay of human experience. Such a sense was crucial to many varieties of art and cultural experience in England in the late seventeenth and early eighteenth centuries because the culture itself had developed a fixation on contemporaneity, part of its larger interest in discovery, enlightenment, and novelty. When the journalist, publisher, and would-be narrative-writer John Dunton insisted (repeatedly) that "News, and new Things do the whole World bewitch,"[1] he was characteristically blurring a distinction, this time between intellectual curiosity and the desire to be au courant, the fundamental motivations, respectively, for readers of science and journalism. But the blur represents a shrewd perception of connection between acute awareness of the latest events and the desire for innovation and originality. Both features of contemporary consciousness were crucial to the emergence of the peculiar, present-centered form of narrative that we have come to call (appropriately enough) the novel, and in fact the fusion of the two helps create the cultural mind that makes the novel possible.

1. Dunton repeatedly used the line in his various works, often as an epigraph, but it was actually written by Robert Wilde. In one sense, Dunton's whole career is a gloss upon the line: "We are all tainted with the *Athenian* Itch, / News, and new Things do the whole World bewitch" (*Poems on Several Occasions* [London, 1683], p. 83).

The preoccupation with novelty, often motivated by a simple desire to be thought trendy and in-the-know, developed in one of its aspects into pure ephemeral silliness. Publishing ventures, including most of Dunton's, often tried to read fickle public taste in the simplest and most obvious ways. A proliferation of anonymous ballads, broadsides, narratives of public or private intrigue, prophecies, criminal confessions, and other ephemera took events and rumors of the street and returned them to the street in printed form. But in other aspects, the attraction to novelty represents the legitimate line—from Francis Bacon through Isaac Newton, a line that later moved through Charles Darwin and Albert Einstein to Werner Heisenberg and Barbara McClintock—which refused to allow the Stagirite his traditional authority and which opened genuinely new directions of thought and human behavior. And the desire for "news," although it frequently ends also in byways, utter trivia, and solipsism, represents as well the higher and broader reaches of communicative possibility, the side of the Enlightenment that leads away from elitism and toward political as well as literary radicalism.[2]

The sense that the moment (any isolated moment potentially, but some species of moment in particular) was in itself a kind of art object— to be adored, meditated upon, fondled, and contemplated again and again—had far-reaching, long-term implications for literature. Three major intellectual thrusts—philosophical explorations of time; psychological interests in memory, continuity of consciousness, and the nature of personal identity; and the new theological concerns with conversion, the individual epiphany, and the enlightened inner instant—all relate to (and in some sense grow out of) the developing concern with contemporaneity, the desire to recognize the momentous in the momentary and to feel the power of all time in its most fleeting moment. By the

---

2. For an extended argument that the novel derives directly from journalism, see Lennard J. Davis, *Factual Fictions: The Origins of the English Novel* (New York, 1983). The issue of origins seems to me much more complex than Davis suggests; a number of cultural forces converge to make the novel possible, and a great variety of literary and paraliterary forms provide crucial paradigms for the novel. For a good critique of Davis, see Michael McKeon, "The Origins of the English Novel," *Modern Philology* 82 (Aug. 1984): 76–86. In his recent book, *The Origins of the English Novel, 1600–1740* (Baltimore, 1987), McKeon himself offers a sensible balance on the issue and provides a rich sense of contextual complexity. In my forthcoming study, *Before Novels*, I discuss journalistic materials as one of several kinds of reading materials that helped prepare audiences for strategies used in novels. It takes much more than journalism, however, to make novels the characteristic expression of modern English culture.

J. Paul Hunter, professor of English at the University of Chicago, is the author of *The Reluctant Pilgrim, Occasional Form,* and of a forthcoming book on literacy, readership, and the contexts of early English fiction, *Before Novels.*

time the novel began to emerge even in its most elemental and tentative stages, English culture had given its tacit approval to a widespread devotion to radical contemporaneity, an urgent sense of now.

The novel represents a formal attempt to come to terms with innovation and originality and to accept the limitations of tradition; it reflects the larger cultural embracing of the present moment as a legitimate subject not only for passing conversation but for serious discourse. For at least a half century before the novel emerged, the world of print had experimented in assuming, absorbing, and exploiting that new cultural consciousness based on human curiosity—on the one hand "preparing" readers for novels and on the other offering later writers of novels some sense of potential subject matter and potential form, a sense of how the present could be won over to serious literature. The process was a curious and unstructured one; in its early manifestations it hardly seemed destined to lead to a significant new literary form. Even in retrospect, the print novelties of the turn of the century hardly seem part of a teleology of form or thought, but the broad ferment that authenticated the new, together with the apparent permanence that print seemed to bestow on accounts of the temporary and passing, ultimately led to a mind and art that transcended occasions and individuals even though it engaged them first of all—energetically, enthusiastically, evangelically. The first fruits of the modern moment-centered consciousness were not very promising, but the emergence of that consciousness enabled, when other cultural contexts were right, an altogether new aesthetic and a wholly different relation between life and literature.

1

It is hard to say exactly when the present time became such an urgent issue in the English cultural consciousness. In one sense, of course, contemporaneity is and has always been of the essence in every culture, the immediacy of human needs and fears putting into shade all more abstract concerns. But long before the advent of print, or even of any means of written communication, art had taken as one of its essential functions the need to steer the human mind away from immediate gratification toward some longer and larger view—toward distancing, abstraction, perspective, a historical view that saw the present as a result, and largely as a reiteration, of a past that stretched amiably across a canvas as large as the mind of humankind itself. Literature (like painting, music, and told tales) had certainly celebrated or encompassed events, occurrences, and occasions, many of them recent or even urgently contemporary. But in traditional literature—oral creations that aspire to be etiological and formally satisfying—the demands of the moment are subordinated to a concern with the larger story of the culture that includes but quickly transcends individuals and individual times, putting them into a perspective of history and slow time.[3] Print technology, whatever its inherent attraction to the quick and the new, for the most part inherited and extended the assumption that human beings needed to be pried away from the immediate and the momentary to consider greater matters. It saw its function primarily as the need to educate people rather than just inform them, to delight with lasting joys rather than repeat the passing effects of conversation or oral discourse, to extend and expand human considerations rather than narrow, intensify, and gratify the immediate. And so printed books early on primarily consisted of works that offered, or aspired to, perspective: classics from the past; attempts to describe the universals of human experience; works of theology, philosophy, or history; narratives of long ago and far away.

The seeds of dissension are, of course, early visible in the world of print, especially at moments when "art" is not such a secure notion or when traditional forms and audiences are under close scrutiny. Certainly in Elizabethan times one can spot tares prospering outside the traditional enclosed garden. The urban paraliterature in the time of Thomas Nashe, Thomas Dekker, Stephen Gosson, and Ben Jonson instantly suggests that print had uses that could extend well beyond the traditional and invade unaccustomed social groups. It is in this sense (rather than in the existence of particular novel-resembling books) that the novel—with its distinctively modern and antiaristocratic tendency to encompass the daily, the trivial, the common, and the immediate—has roots that reach well back into older times and domestic traditions.[4] But the relationship to that curious paraliterary past is a complicated one because definitions of "literature" hardened during the seventeenth century, and the gap between "art" and popular culture increased enormously before the novel was (finally) able to narrow it again much later.

The formal programs for serious literature in the Restoration and early eighteenth century betray a divided heart about present events. Certainly the poets wanted to feel themselves an integral part of their own culture and its public faces, and they sought, as in few ages before or since, to affect the direction of politics and social history in their own

3. Superb work on the oral tradition and on the difference between oral and written modes has appeared in recent years, although literary history has yet to absorb its conclusions. For a good characterization of the tendencies of oral literature, see John Miles Foley, *Oral-Formulaic Theory and Research: An Introduction and Annotated Bibliography* (New York and London, 1985). For ongoing discussion of the literary implications of oral literature for literary theory and history, see the journal that Foley founded in 1986, *Oral Tradition*.

4. The old view that the novel began in Elizabethan times, or perhaps even in classical Greece, has largely disappeared in the wake of increasingly precise definitions of how the novel differs from other types of fiction, but in the past few years, narratology (despite numerous virtues and accomplishments) has tended to lose track again of distinctions, historical and otherwise, among different kinds of narrative.

time. They often seem obsessed with even the most minor happenings around them. Their accounts of public affairs, their concern with the current health of the state, and their anxieties about social change are seldom far from the surface in what they write, even when they address the eternal issues of a *Religio Laici*, a *Solomon*, or an *Essay on Man*. And when they set themselves, as they often do, the task of evaluating critically the directions of modern life—in poems like *Absalom and Achitophel* or *The Dispensary* or *The Rape of the Lock*—they regularly treat contemporary matters in great, often painful, detail, regarding themselves as legitimate heirs of the Roman tradition of public commentary and responsibility. Still, there is among the public poets and aspiring men of letters always a decorum. It is not so much that they hold back in detail or restrain themselves in tone as that they try to restrict their subjects—the persons, events, *and* ideas they treat—to ones generally thought available and appropriate to public consideration. Among themselves they play and take holidays in verse or prose, and the range of banter and facetiousness in personal letters and light verse is sometimes astonishing. But until their exasperation is heightened and their anger turned to righteous indignation, they avoid the contexts of common debate and street life unless they are trying to locate it in a larger context (as in *A Description of the Morning*, or *Trivia, or, The Art of Walking the Streets of London*) or undermining its values in some sort of mock-heroic contrast (as in *MacFlecknoe*). When they turn desperately to full programs of satire that engage the present as the nearly full burden of their content, they have been driven to it largely by the energies of what has begun to happen in the popular mind. Certainly it is accurate to think of Augustan literature as aggressively public and heatedly anti-innovative, so that prose attacks on novelty like *A Tale of a Tub* or poetic ones like *The Dunciad* contain as much energy and vitality as the newly funded creativities they oppose. Writers like Jonathan Swift and Alexander Pope come to their position and achieve much of the force that drives their writing from a basic change in the culture. The best taste and the best brains in literature in the early years of the eighteenth century fought the change nearly every step of the way. While getting enormous mileage out of its weaknesses and silliness, they never came to terms with its virtues or its implications for future writing except as blind, often inarticulate and indiscriminate, hatred. The justification for public poetry and occasional literature that Augustans took from their Roman models, while always the putative sponsor of high art about contemporaneity, does not account fully for the best of Augustan addresses to the present time. Much as Pope or Swift would have dreaded to think it, popular culture not only provided grist for the Augustan mill but also the energy for doing the grinding.[5]

---

5. Recent social history has had so far too little effect on eighteenth-century studies, and the impact of popular culture—on the novel, let alone canonical forms—has been

What was most significant about early innovation had less to do with specific literary accomplishments than with the very idea that experimentation could be defended vigorously and sometimes plausibly and that modern occasional writing seemed to fit the mood, tone, and needs of the culture even when it was not very good. The defenses of the moderns against the ancients—whether by John Dryden or John Dunton, Robert Boyle or Richard Bentley—ring with a surprising energy, even when they argue or illustrate foolishly, and in retrospect it seems quite astonishing that traditionalists like William Temple and Swift took the new movement seriously enough to answer in such detail. In an important sense, the recognition that such works as *A Tale of a Tub* and *The Dunciad* bestowed on literary modernism legitimized the issue, and the "popular culture" aspects of novelty and journalism, ironically, come to exist in a canonical literature because the most traditional rivals, for reasons never yet fully explained, put them there.

Not all the energies of "literary" innovation resided in journalistic efforts to celebrate the present moment, but many of them did, and it is important to recognize the cultural depth and breadth beneath and around the surface signs. Perhaps the cultural anxiety about present time intensified gradually throughout the seventeenth century, or perhaps by fits and starts, but by the 1690s, the world of print had clearly joined the world of conversation, gossip, and rumor in a singular devotion to issues of the moment. The directions of publishing in the 1690s represent a milestone in the developing concern with contemporaneity. The pragmatic social and ethical concerns of the reign of William and Mary, manifested in such phenomena as the Societies for the Reformation of Manners, are one sign of the cultural mania for news.[6] But there are many other signs as well: the publications of the 1690s and the early years of the new century generally suggest both how fully the concerns

---

largely unexamined. For a promising direction, see Pat Rogers, *Literature and Popular Culture in Eighteenth-Century England* (Brighton, Sussex, and Totowa, N.J., 1985). Ronald Paulson's provocative *Popular and Polite Art in the Age of Hogarth and Fielding* (Notre Dame, Ind., 1979) stands almost alone among earlier studies, although C. J. Rawson's *Gulliver and the Gentle Reader: Studies in Swift and Our Time* (London and Boston, 1973) is brilliantly suggestive about the popular origins of Swift's creative energy.

6. The moral fervor of reform during the reign of William and Mary was heavily dependent on public accounts, awareness, and outrage. Whether vice flourished more successfully or even more openly then is questionable, but the proliferation of accounts convinced the public that "the times" were especially desperate, and newspapers and pamphlets became the most significant weapon in the reformation-of-manners craze.

The question of when and why the preoccupation with contemporaneity became so obsessive in England is too complex for an essay in literary history to address, but the proliferation of printed materials at the time of the Civil Wars suggests that some combination of ideology and concern for personal safety must have been involved. Certainly the growing presence of pamphlets about contemporary events in the 1640s and 1650s helped to create the taste that printers tried in wider ways to satisfy near the end of the century.

of the moment had absorbed the world of print and how the world of print interacted with conversation and the oral culture, especially in London where pamphlets, periodicals, and informal talk fed each other in an ever-intensifying attention to the latest news or pseudonews.

2

Histories of English journalism seriously begin with the 1690s, for the sharp increase in the number of periodicals published in London in this decade and the proliferation of news pamphlets and news sheets that eventuate in the founding of a London daily in 1702 suggest that the cultural moment for journalism had just then come.[7] The term "journalism" apparently did not enter the English language until 1833,[8] but according to the *Oxford English Dictionary*, the term "journalist" came into use as early as 1693 to describe those who wrote for the public press of the daily doings of life. In their etymology, "journalist" and "journalism" appropriately suggest the whole range of preoccupation with contemporaneity, with the daily and the ordinary, that characterized the 1690s and the following decades. The French word *jour* is, of course, the root from which "journalist" and "journalism" spring, and "journal" and "journey" have their derivation there as well. In its original meaning, a "journey" was a day's travel (although it quickly became extended to cover travels that could be measured by a specific number of days required), and "journal," both in its sense as a public account of daily events and as a private account of the personal details of daily life, in its origins emphasizes the centrality for the recording and receiving consciousness of immediate moments in time.[9] Significantly, the term "journal" and its several derivatives separated themselves from the sense of order and predictable repetition that a word like "diurnal" has continued to carry in English, so that the term "journalism" in the sense that it is popularly used today carries (much like the term novel) historically accurate connotations that suggest what was happening in the culture at a very deep level.[10] By the 1690s, the English consciousness had become so obsessed

7. "Periodical" publication, defined broadly enough, dates from antiquity, and something vaguely resembling newspapers may be traced back at least as far as 1620 in England. For detailed information on the early history of newspapers, see Joseph Frank, *The Beginnings of the English Newspaper, 1620–1660* (Cambridge, Mass., 1961); R. M. Wiles, *Freshest Advices: Early Provincial Newspapers in England* (Columbus, Ohio, 1965); G. A. Cranfield, *The Development of the Provincial Newspaper 1700–1760* (Oxford, 1962); and J. A. Downie, *Robert Harley and the Press: Propaganda and Public Opinion in the Age of Swift and Defoe* (Cambridge, 1979).

8. C. T. Onions et al., *The Oxford Dictionary of English Etymology* (Oxford, 1966), p. 498.

9. I discuss the matter in more detail in *Before Novels*.

10. For a provocative account of a complex set of historical interrelationships, see the entry under "Diana" in Eric Partridge, *Origins: A Short Etymological Dictionary of Modern English* (New York, 1983).

with the potential significance of any single isolated instant that an immediate written record needed to be created. The preoccupations with news and novelty in fact coalesce in the popular consciousness much as Dunton suggests.

Journalism was beginning to "rise" elsewhere in Europe too, but it became culturally significant rather more slowly and tentatively in other countries. Nowhere else does there seem to be, so early, the obsession with contemporaneity that characterizes English culture at the beginning of the eighteenth century. The English were notorious among Europeans both for their attraction to novelty and their devotion to news. An eighteenth-century French traveler to England concludes that "the melancholy temper of the English has rendered them, in all ages, exceeding fond of every thing which appears to be out of the common order."[11] The English fondness for wide-ranging gossip, masquerading as news of foreign affairs, was regarded as beyond debate, although Englishmen regularly took umbrage at that "common Imputation cast upon *Englishmen* by Forreigners."[12] "The writings most in fashion at the present period," writes a Swiss visitor to England in 1727, "are pamphlets for and against the government, on politics and different subjects of interest relating to England and her allies. Almost every day some of these works appear and are eagerly sought after, for politics in this country seem to interest everyone."[13] The Frenchman Pierre Jean Grosley, visiting London in 1765, found the English still "infatuated with politics" and "passionate for news," with newspapers "thrown about upon the tables in coffeehouses." He seems puzzled that "these news-papers are regularly filed, kept from year to year, and are referred to in public and in private, like the records of law in Westminster-hall."[14] Almost a century before, a proud but troubled native, Richard Baxter, already lamented that "all men are affected most with things that seem new and strange to them." He linked the taste for novelty with the lust for news, insisting that the famous national characteristic was in fact a manifestation of universal desires: "If nature were not much for Novelty, the publishing of *Newsbooks* would not have been so gainful a Trade so long."[15] Another sort

11. Pierre Jean Grosley, *A Tour to London; or, New Observations on England, and its Inhabitants*, trans. Thomas Nugent, 2 vols. (London, 1772), 1:239.

12. Nathaniel Crouch, *England's Monarchs* (London, 1685), fol. A2.

13. César de Saussure, *A Foreign View of England in the Reigns of George I & George II: The Letters of Monsieur César de Saussure to His Family*, ed. and trans. Madame van Muyden (London, 1902), pp. 178–79; further references to this work, abbreviated *FV*, will be included in the text.

14. Grosley, *A Tour to London*, 2:75.

15. Richard Baxter, *A Christian Directory; or, A Summ of Practical Theologie, and Cases of Conscience* (London, 1673), p. 36. Baxter, anticipating Dunton's etiology and analysis, goes on to quote the biblical passage about the Athenians who "spent their time in nothing else, but to tell or hear some new thing" (Acts 17).

of traveler, Lemuel Gulliver, makes a similar observation about the strange land of Laputa, ultimately concluding the same thing about his fellow Englishmen: "But, what I chiefly admired, and thought altogether un-accountable," he says of the otherworldly mathematicians, "was the strong Disposition I observed in them towards News and Politicks; perpetually enquiring into publick Affairs, giving their Judgments in Matters of State; and passionately disputing every Inch of a Party Opinion."[16]

The creation of such a public consciousness in England was probably not engineered so much as just permitted, although the new brand of party politician and information manipulator like Robert Walpole obviously perceived advantages to be gained from heightened public consciousness of public events and attitudes loosened from their traditional moorings. The cultural institution that finally had the most to do with encouraging the new consciousness has usually been studied in literary history only in a somewhat precious way. That institution is the coffeehouse, often treasured for its benign and lovable (if somewhat obtuse) denizens who value good conversation, or praised for its attempts to raise the cultural level of cits and tradesmen, or gently teased for the foibles of sotted squires or sparks gone to embers. A more important cultural contribution resides, I believe, in the structural tendency of the institution to bridge a variety of social levels of discourse (with at least as much influence from below as above) and to blur the distinction between oral and written discourse.[17]

The conversation of the coffeehouse, while sometimes perhaps as "improving" and high-minded as its literary admirers would have us believe and sometimes as irrelevant and banal as satires on it suggest,[18] most often seems to have been determined not by abstract or "universal" human concerns but by the events of the day—or rather by what public gossipmongers defined as "events" of the day. Timeliness was the crucial element in the conversation; talking to the moment was as crucial to the

16. Jonathan Swift, *Gulliver's Travels, The Prose Works of Jonathan Swift,* ed. Herbert Davis, 14 vols. (Oxford, 1939–68), 11:148.

17. For all the anxiety to define and separate genres and kinds in the eighteenth century, there is a remarkable tendency, in practice, to blur and merge, a tendency that has been insufficiently discussed, especially in relation to oral traditions.

18. In a letter of 29 October 1726, Saussure reported that "Some coffee-houses are a resort for learned scholars and for wits; others are the resort of dandies or of politicians, or again of professional newsmongers; and many others are temples of Venus" (*FV,* p. 164). He seems to be reflecting prevalent clichés and oversimplifications, which are still honored. Although the leading coffeehouses no doubt did attract distinctive audiences, contemporary treatments of the phenomenon suggest that all or most were characterized nearly equally by newsmongering and a love of gossip about current topics. The classic treatment of the coffeehouse phenomenon is still Robert J. Allen's *The Clubs of Augustan London* (Cambridge, Mass., 1933), although it badly needs updating. For details of individual houses, see Bryant Lillywhite, *London Coffee Houses: A Reference Book of Coffee Houses of the Seventeenth, Eighteenth, and Nineteenth Centuries* (London, 1963).

coffeehouse consciousness (and ultimately to daily life in London) as writing to the moment ever became to the novel. Reports, rumors, and stories from the street vied with printed "news" and speculations from the regular periodicals and the daily variety of occasional publications as the subject of conversation. It may have been amusing to hear the mixture of information, misinformation, speculation, and opinion that resulted, and apparently the joy of participating was widely prized. Not many major decisions about government or trade (or anything else) resulted from these conversations (although journalists and spies for various groups regularly listened in, used them as sounding boards, and probably planted additional "information"), but the illusion of being "involved" in matters of moment and of "knowing" the state of London and the world seems to have appealed mightily to late seventeenth- and early eighteenth-century Londoners of many classes and stripes. "What attracts enormously in these coffee-houses," writes the visitor César de Saussure in 1726, "are the gazettes and other public papers. All Englishmen are great newsmongers. Workmen habitually begin the day by going to coffee-rooms in order to read the latest news. I have often seen shoeblacks and other persons of that class club together to purchase a farthing paper. Nothing is more entertaining than hearing men of this class discussing politics and topics of interest concerning royalty. You often see an Englishman taking a treaty of peace more to heart than he does his own affairs" (*FV*, p. 162). Even allowing for the bemused chauvinism of a visitor bent on entertaining the folks at home, the picture confirms in its basic outline the view from English observers. The virtuosi and coffeehouse politicians widely portrayed in plays and other records of the time were essentially the "Athenians" with an itch for news and novelty that Dunton described, and their significance lies not in what they actually knew, said, or accomplished but in the expectations they set for eighteenth-century conduct and consciousness. As early as 1667, a London broadside, *News from the Coffe-house*, satirized the already-accepted expectations:

> You that delight in Wit and Mirth
> And long to hear such News
> As comes from all Parts of the *Earth* . . .
> Go hear it at a *Coffe house*
> *It cannot but be true.*

> . . . .

> There's nothing done in all the World,
> From *Monarch* to the *Mouse*
> But every Day or Night 'tis hurld
> Into the *Coffe-house.*

> . . . .

> So great a *Vniversitie,*
> I think there ne're was any;
> In which you may a Schoolar be
> For spending of a Penny.[19]

Seven decades later, the expectations and jokes were still the same. A 1733 satire invites its readers to

> See yon spruce busy *Man,* he asks you hasty,
> What News from *Coffee-Club,* or who just past ye?[20]

No doubt real news did sometimes get passed on in such company, for real doers as well as imaginary ones did in fact frequent coffeehouses—often with their judgment fully intact—but a "Coffee-house Tale" was considered synonymous with unreliability, the love of stories for their own sake, and ultimately with triviality.[21]

In the mixture of journalism and conversation, print record and loose talk, fiction and fact, informed opinion and baseless speculation, the oral and written cultures dramatically meet and interact in the coffeehouse milieu, reflecting changes in the larger world and demonstrating not only how quickly booksellers had learned to exploit the daily possibilities of print but also how "talk" and current opinion joined and enlarged the cycle of "now" consciousness. And, like the influence of books and booksellers, the effect spread outward from London with a sense of what was appropriate, timely, and "in." The result was felt not so much in the provincial proliferation of coffeehouses themselves but in the acceptance of London values and conversation as normative. For many in villages and in the countryside, the sense of the city and its alluring fashions of busyness and knowledge of the world set expectations that profoundly affected the sense of what was worth talking about, thinking about, and reading about. And if such a cycle of communication and such a mixture of human modes characterized daily London life and set a pattern elsewhere for those who aspired to live a fashionable modern life, they also led to an important conditioning of the reading public and those who wrote for it. As the reading public for journalism, didactic works, biography and travel, history, and literature in the late seventeenth century became (without much alteration) the reading public for the novel a generation later, the sense of urgency about present time and current concerns was deeply built into the public consciousness. The private reading of novels

19. *News from the Coffe-house* (London, 1667). I quote from the first, sixth, and tenth stanzas.

20. *News. A Burlesque Poem* (London, 1733), p. 6. "And here I'll stop," the poem ends, "lest I'm with *News* confounded" (p. 12).

21. See, for example, the way Sir Roger L'Estrange uses the term in *Citt and Bumpkin* (1680; Los Angeles, 1965), p. 32.

in a sense displaced the taste for public discussion.[22] The early novelists shared the public taste for contemporaneity and novelty and quickly discovered how to blend it into a substantial and complex web of narrative and discursive prose, creating in effect a kind of portable coffeehouse of elongated conversation in print.[23] For Henry Fielding the world is a stagecoach in which a narrator can nudge and twit hearers, and for Laurence Sterne it is a library where readers are present with the author as he writes, but the effect is finally just as evident in the expository "dear Reader" world of Daniel Defoe or the epistolary totality of shared circumstance in Richardson or Fanny Burney.

3

Works that detail a single event or a series of related ones had been fairly common early in the seventeenth century. In titles such as *A Wonderfull and most Lamentable Declaration of the great hurt done, and mighty losse sustained by Fire . . . ; . . . Winde, Thunder, Lightning, Haile, and Raine* and *The Wonders of this windie winter* (both 1613) one can readily see the interests of those who wrote about the contemporary scene, an interest that lay primarily in natural disasters or other dramatic events and their role in human destiny. The emphasis was continuously on patterns, their supernatural origins, and the human implications. Every event, no matter how small or apparently isolated, was put into larger perspective as a detail in some larger plan. The woodcut that serves as a frontispiece to *Wonders of this windie winter* suggests that recurrent theme. There two heavenly figures are shown blowing toward earth, while in the ensuing wind trees and houses fall, and people and ships tumble helplessly about in the sea. No event is altogether independent; nothing just happens.

A similar thematic emphasis continues in much of the material published about contemporary events throughout the late seventeenth century and into the eighteenth, especially when some dramatic natural occurrence

22. The importance of women in the reading public for novels has much to do with this displacement. Women were largely excluded from, or at least underrepresented in, coffeehouses, and thus were denied access to the most direct means of hearing and sharing news, but if I am right that the novel became a kind of substitute for news and gossip, the importance of novels to female readers and soon to female writers suggests the way women came quickly to relate to the deep cultural phenomenon. I have discussed the evidence for female literacy and readership of novels in my essay " 'The Young, the Ignorant, and the Idle,' " in *Anticipations of the Enlightenment in England, France, and Germany,* ed. Paul J. Korshin and Alan C. Kors (Philadelphia, 1987), pp. 259–81.

23. On gossip and the novel, see Homer Obed Brown, "The Errant Letter and the Whispering Gallery," *Genre* 10 (Winter 1977): 573–99, and Patricia Meyer Spacks, *Gossip* (New York, 1985). The illusion of companionship that both Fielding and Sterne try to further relates to the tendency of the novel to associate itself with gossip and with oral discourse more generally.

focuses attention on human limits in the face of earthquake, wind, or fire. The prodigious storm of November 1703, for example, inspired a number of detailed accounts of destruction and the frustration of human efforts. There was virtual unanimity in regarding the event as a divine visitation upon England, although the precise grounds for divine anger were located variously, depending upon the assumptions, affiliations, and biases of the individual writer. Defoe's artful account, *The Storm, Or, A Collection Of the most Remarkable Casualties And Disasters Which happen'd in the Late Dreadful Tempest, Both by Sea and Land* (1704), one of the best of his early blends of narrative interest and thematic coherence, is one of the most detailed and comprehensive treatments (285 pages long), and it is probably the best. But there were many other notable accounts as well, including *The Terrible Stormy Wind and Tempest . . . Consider'd, Improv'd, and Collected, to be had In Everlasting Remembrance* (1705), *A Wonderful History of All the Storms, Hurricanes, Earthquakes, &c. That have happen'd in England for above 500 years past* (1704), and *An Exact Relation Of the Late Dreadful Tempest: or, a Faithful Account Of the Most Remarkable Disasters which hapned on that occasion . . . Faithfully collected by an Ingenious Hand, to preserve the Memory of so Terrible a Judgment* (1704). "So remarkable and signal a Judgment of God on this Nation," the latter pamphlet argues, "no History either forreign or domestick, can parallel," claiming that the storm was more destructive than the great fire. "To transmit therefore a distinct and true Account of that unheard of and fatal Accident, and to observe an exact Decorum in each particular as much as possible, we hope, will not be unacceptable to the Reader; since a matter of this important Consequence must and will stand as a Monument of the Anger of Heaven, justly pour'd down upon this Kingdom to all posterity."[24] Accounts like these repeatedly emphasize, usually through key words in their titles as well as by repetition in the body of the text, their factuality and particularity ("Exact Relation," "Faithful Account"). Details are in fact very important to their effect, but the emphasis still falls, as it did a century earlier, on meanings that can be assigned to the storm. Those meanings remain old-fashioned in their reliance on traditional religious and moral assumptions about how human events are, and should be, controlled, and in their insistence that such events can be "read" as God's judgment on human behavior and events. "Readings" often differed, of course, the storm being regarded alternatively as God's displeasure with Queen Anne or with those who frustrated her plans, but however doctors disagreed in the applications of their theology, they agreed that such events had dramatic, often deep, meanings. One popular interpretation of the storm, especially among Dissenters, was as a judgment on playgoers

24. *An Exact Relation Of the Late Dreadful Tempest; or, a Faithful Account Of the Most Remarkable Disasters which hapned on that occasion . . . Faithfully collected by an Ingenious Hand, to preserve the Memory of so Terrible a Judgment* (London, 1704), pp. 24, 3.

(the Collier controversy was still running full speed). When *The Tempest* was produced just after the storm, in what was widely regarded as an irreverent and sacrilegious act, many predicted disasters even more dire.[25]

And so it went. Every natural event offered lively possibilities, and every context had multiple referents. Sometimes the emphasis in such accounts stayed on the details of the event and left readers on their own to draw conclusions. *A True and Perfect Narrative of the Great and Dreadful Damages Susteyned in Several Parts of England by the Late Extraordinary Snovvs* (1674), for example, describes on its title page snow "covering the Tops of . . . Houses" and people burning "all their Goods to keep them warm" but avoids blaming the event on any particular evil practice. More judgmental, but equally detailed, is an account of rains and floods in 1683, *A Strange and Wonderful Account of the Great Mischiefs, Sustained by the late Dreadful Thunder, Lightening, And Terrible Land-Floods Caused by the Immoderate Rain in England, Scotland, & Holland, Giving an Exact Relation of the Men, Cattle, Houses, &c that have been Thunderstruck,* although blame is cast rather broadly and generally.

It is tempting for modern readers to look in such accounts for increasing evidence of insincerity and erosion of belief in divine control and divine intervention, a temptation that literary historians fall for much more frequently than do intellectual or cultural historians. The climate of religious belief is in fact much different in 1703 from that in 1613, but if the nation in general is more secular in 1703 (as it surely is), those who continue to be believers are not less sincere and not noticeably less certain themselves. Accelerated secularism and diminished religious faith are facts of life in the early eighteenth century, but the change is one of degree, and the degree is less radical than some literary historians think. The restoration of the monarchy, the plague of 1665, the Great Fire of 1666, the Glorious Revolution of 1688, the storm of 1703, the peace of

---

25. "Are we not . . . loudly called upon to lay aside this prophane Diversion, by the late dreadful Storm?" asked the anonymous author of *A Representation of the Impiety & Immorality of the English Stage,* 3d ed. (1704; Los Angeles, 1947), p. 4. One pamphlet suggests that the defiant production of *The Tempest* could close theaters by producing a popular outcry against such blasphemy or at least might mean tight regulation. Other events inspired similar interpretations. John Barnard, for example, interpreted a contemporary earthquake in New England as displeasure with sabbath-breaking. A sermon preached in Colchester on the "providential" victories of the Duke of Marlborough created such a fuss that its author claimed he was invited to the local coffeehouse to hear himself parodied and scoffed at, an indication of how wide a net was cast by providentiality and how controversial even patriotic interpretations could become. See Josiah Woodward (?), *Some Thoughts Concerning the Stage in a Letter to a Lady* (1704; Los Angeles, 1947), p. 12; John Barnard, "Earthquakes under the Divine Government," *Two Discourses Address'd to Young Persons* (Boston, 1727), pp. 71–99; and the preface to William Smithies, Jr., *The Coffee-House Preachers* (London, 1706), esp. fols. [A4,]–B1. The latter title was once regarded as Defoe's, and it may well be invented—its rhetoric is somewhat suspicious, but even if the episode is invented out of whole cloth, the pamphlet accurately suggests the terms and tones of contemporary debate.

Utrecht, and every major military and political event throughout the seventeenth century and well into the eighteenth were accompanied by pamphlets and in many cases long books that argued traditional providential interpretations of the events. The difference between early seventeenth- and early eighteenth-century accounts involves the fact that earlier writers can readily assume that their audience will already believe that *some* sort of religious and moral interpretation is true and relevant, whereas later accounts have to be prepared to argue in a context of less certainty about ultimate causes. The change in rhetoric is indeed an index of contexts beginning to change, but most interpreters continue to be supported by the same philosophical and theological assumptions, while being aware that their task of persuasion became every day more difficult because of cultural slippage. Later accounts tend to be more detailed and conscious of piling up the evidence for a particular interpretation. Accounts alternate radically between the precise details of a particular episode and generalizations about the meaning of such events for an interpretation of the direction and fabric of English culture; they illustrate both the importance accorded to authentic human experiences and the deep desire to interpret by accumulation. Many pamphlets, booklets, and single sheets told a particular story and provided explicit or implicit interpretations, usually along moral or religious lines. And ultimately huge collections and anthologies of such stories and anecdotes, usually organized by subject (stories of storms, for example, or famous murders) and by theme (that murder will out, for example, and murderers be punished) became popular and readily available.

But journalism did change dramatically during the seventeenth century, reflecting broadened curiosity more than abandoned commitments. If readers continued to be fascinated with accounts of storms and ship-wrecks, they also developed an interest in lesser, more private and personal events. Everyday and domestic events began to appear more and more frequently in print, both in periodicals and in separate titles. Even at the beginning of the seventeenth century, pamphlets sometimes described murders, acts of treason, and other acts of individual behavior that seemed to threaten the public peace or the social fabric. For example, *A true relation of a most desperate murder committed vpon the body of Sir John Tindall, knight, one of the maisters of the Chancery,* appeared in 1617; in 1605, *A True relation of Gods vvonderfull mercies, in preseruing one aliue, which hanged fiue dayes, who was falsely accused.* By the 1670s, individual accounts of murders appeared routinely almost every week, no doubt reflecting increased crime (especially in London) but also demonstrating the heightened interest of the general public in a more individualized definition of current events. In late 1677, for example, an extensive collection of stories, *A true relation of all the bloody murders that have been committed in and about the citie and suburbs of London, since the 4th of this instant Jnne 1677,* was published. The range had extended by then to accounts of robberies, fires, household quarrels, discoveries of witchcraft, and all sorts of out-of-the-ordinary events occurring to ordinary people in ordinary circumstances. In 1676, a short (eight-page) pamphlet provided *A Brief Narrative of A Strange and Wonderful Old Woman that hath A Pair of Horns Growing upon her Head,* and another "brief and true Relation" purported to describe *The Miraculous Recovery of A Dumb Man at Lambeth.* In 1678 readers were offered such items as *A Strange, but true Relation Of the Discovery of a most horrid and bloudy Murder Committed on the Body of a Traveller About Thirty Years Ago in the West of England* and *Strange and wonderful News from . . . Ireland, or, A Full and True Relation of what Happened to one Dr. Moore.* In the highly charged political year 1679, the following, among many others, appeared: *A True Account of The Horrid Murther Committed upon His Grace, The Late Archbishop of Saint Andrews; A true Account of divers most strange and prodigious Apparitions; A True Narrative of the Horrid Hellish Popish Plot* (a lengthy, illustrated ballad with elaborate references to other published accounts); *A True Narrative and Discovery of several very Remarkable Passages Relating to the Horrid Popish Plot; A True Narrative of that Grand Jesvite Father Andrews; A True Relation of a Devilish Attempt to Fire the Town of Barnet; A True Narrative Of the Late Design of the Papists to Charge Their Horrid Plot Upon the Protestants; A Full Narrative, or, a Discovery of the Priests and Jesuites.*

Many "events," such as those referred to in these titles, were tied to political concerns, rumored occurrences, and suspicions of deep plots. The "Popish Plot" was responsible for literally hundreds of titles that promised the "exact relation" of this or the "true narrative" of that. The term "narrative," in fact, although occasionally used on title pages earlier, became a title catchword in the late 1670s to signal accounts of events that seemed related to Catholic Europe's intrusive interest in English affairs. Although the terms "narrative," "relation," "account," and "news" strictly speaking only indicate that contemporary events are to be the center of attention, such code terms were used to imply a connection with intrigue of some larger, ongoing sort, an implication of human conspiracy nearly as useful as providential explanations to make sense of random, apparently isolated events.

4

Timeliness was essential for most of the separate journalistic publications; ordinarily accounts were rushed into print within days, or even hours, of a dramatic event. Publishers usually preferred personal confessions of horrible conduct, when available, to simple accounts of the events, apparently because such statements seemed to finesse the issue of authenticity while often providing vivid, immediate, and convincing detail. *A Narrative of the Extraordinary Penitence of Rob. Maynard, Who was Condemnd For the Murder of John Stockton, Late Victualler in Grub-street* (1696), for example, includes both an account of "Several Conferences Held with him in Newgate" and "a Copy of the *Papers* which he left to be Published after his Death." *A Full and True Relation of the Examination and Confession of W. Barwick and E. Mangall, of two Horrid Murders* (1690) typically glories in the discovery of the real facts, after an initial uncertainty or cover-up, as does a single sheet, *Concealed Murther Reveil'd,* of 1699.[26] The sense of filling in the details, helping to write the full history of the times and ultimately of reality itself, is prominent in most of these titles, however hurried on by sensationalism or commercial greed. Behind the formerly-concealed-but-now-revealed motif is a powerful sense that great chunks of reality are liable to escape detection or get by without being recorded; the journalistic writers seem to see themselves as sleuths whose duty it is to capture it all for print. Swift thought it was just plain silly to be the universe's amanuensis,[27] but for many of his contemporaries it was not just a living and a comprehensive record of the times that was at stake but also a view of reality. For the Puritans—and their view of history largely becomes the Whig version of reality—nothing could be known without a full and complete account of events: that was where meaning lay.

Other events less momentous than political treason and less horrendous than murder were swept into the public record as well. Physical ailments and cures were often detailed (*A Narrative Of the Late Extraordinary Cure Wrought in an Instant upon Mrs. Eliz. Savage . . . With an Appendix, attempting to prove, That Miracles are not ceas'd* [1694]), local instances of detected witchcraft were described (*A True Narrative of the Sufferings and Relief of a Young Girle, . . . Strangely Molested By Evil Spirits and their Instruments* [1698]), and news was brought in from remoter places (*A True Narrative of the Murders, Cruelties and Oppressions, Perpetrated on the Protestants in Ireland* [1690]). Sometimes collections of miscellaneous events were pulled together to provide the equivalent of annals for a particular year, as, for example, *God's Marvellous Wonders in England: Containing divers strange and wonderful Relations that have happened since the beginning of June, this present Year 1694,* a work that includes accounts of murders discovered, destructive hailstorms, the surprising sprouting of corn in barren fields, a "Shower of Wheat that fell in *Wiltshire,*" and the appearance of a whale near the mouth of the River Humber. Sometimes the record reads like the *Daily Mail* or the *National Enquirer,* but serious cosmic assumptions support its desire to be all-encompassing.

26. *Concealed Murther Reveil'd. Being a Strange Discovery of a most Horrid and Barbarous Murther . . . By Mary Anderson . . . On the Body of Hannah Jones an Infant of 8 Weeks Old . . . As also How it was Conceal'd 3 Years, and not Discovered till Monday last . . .* (London, 1699).

27. The narrator of *A Tale of a Tub* is made to sound utterly foolish when he declares, "This, O Universe, is the Adventurous Attempt of me thy Secretary" (Swift, *A Tale of a Tub, The Prose Works of Jonathan Swift,* 1:77).

Many other short narratives of the 1690–1710 period come from, or purport to come from, documents such as diaries, packets of letters, or notes taken by someone present at the occurrence or at an eyewitness account of it.[28] Other narratives purport to derive from court documents and proceedings.[29] As full, or at least as detailed, as many such accounts were, their truth is sometimes a matter of doubt, regardless of the claims of their titles.[30] The important thing is that they claim factuality, for whether they were literally and completely true, based upon facts but liberally embroidered, or made up out of whole cloth, the narratives achieved much of their appeal through their claim to represent what the present-day world was like, what kinds of amazement and surprise and horror were available to those whose lives were drab, uneventful, and apparently trivial, increasingly buried in the routine impersonality of modern life.

Between 1700 and 1710, a large number of eight-page pamphlets focused on contemporary life with a vengeance. Most of them were half-sheet octavos or half-sheet duodecimos, designed (like chapbooks) to sell cheaply. Some are dated and some are not (the ones that are date mostly from 1705–9), but most recount events of recent date—often startling or at least surprising ones—and all are anecdotal in the new journalistic spirit. Many are told in a spirited, comic, and frolicsome way, while others point toward pathos, poignancy, or even tragedy. What these short episodic pamphlets have in common is that they seem to commit to print the sorts of "surprising" and "wonderful" tales of contemporary life which in another age would have found room, at least passingly, in oral traditions transmitted within families or villages or groups of workers. A few such stories had found their way into print as exempla in moral works or as instances in the anthologies put together to prove or illustrate some theological, philosophical, political, or social point, but very few of them in earlier times would have been preserved at all beyond their immediate

28. An item from 1700 typifies the kind of narrative designed to illustrate providential influence on human destiny by recording a story in detail, in this case in journal form. See Jonathan Dickinson, *God's Protecting Providence, Man's Surest Help and Defence, in Times of the Greatest Difficulty, and Most Eminent Danger. Evidenced In the Remarkable Deliverance of Robert Barrow, with divers other Persons, from the Devouring Waves of the Sea; amongst which they suffered Shipwrack: And also, From the cruel Devouring Jaws of the Inhumane Canibals of Florida* (1699; London, 1700).

29. See, for example, these two brief, single-page items from 1706: *A Full and True Account of the Examination and Condemnation of Handsome Fielding This 6th of December 1706. For Having Two Wives . . . For which he was found Guilty* and *A faithful Account of the Examination of Robert Feilding, Esq.; before the Rt. Hon. the Ld. Chief Justice Holt, and his Commitment to Newgate.*

30. An example is the thirty-eight-page folio transcript of *The Tryal of Spencer Cowper. Esq.; John Marson, Ellis Stevens, and William Rogers, Gent. Upon an Indictment for the Murther of Mrs. Sarah Stout, a Quaker . . . July 18, 1699. Of Which they were acquitted.* Faithful full-transcript accounts of law trials were frequently printed as well.

geographical area or contemporary moment. One can find scattered instances of such short anecdotal pamphlets earlier and elsewhere in Europe, but the sudden appearance of a great number of them in England just after the turn of the century is a new historical phenomenon, marking a perceived desire for access to narrative that is neither primarily moral nor primary political in thrust but that regards the present as crucial to be recorded.

The "plot" of most of these short narratives is given away entirely in the lengthy title, and the writing is usually indifferent, but the tone is sometimes experimental and the subject matter daring. Thus, *An Almanack-Husband: or, a Wife a Month: Being A very Comical and Pleasant Relation of a Merchants Son near the Monument, who Married a Wife every Month, for a Year together* . . . (1708) takes a detached and tolerant view of polygamy and the confusion of progeny that ensues. The "Almanack-Husband" gets all his wives pregnant "and being discovered, gave them all an Invitation to a Tavern, where they were exceeding Merry"; the tone (if not the syntax) is maintained in "A commical *Dialogue* which pass'd between him and his Wives, and after parted very lovingly," an outcome that Captain Macheath must have envied offered in a spirit that, in its broader cultural version, helped to nurture Gay's anti-Augustan side. Only the few cautionary words at the end violate the spirit of the piece: "but I would have the Reader not to mind a Libertine's Advice, for nothing but Destruction attends such lewd Debauchees."[31] An obvious example of thin, after-the-fact, disingenuous moralizing, this kind of brittle postscript is, however, much less common in these narratives (and other works of many kinds) than is usually thought. The moralizing tendency which is native to the period usually results in works that are wholeheartedly didactic; the quick moral gloss that is antithetical to the spirit and tone of the whole is nearly as rare as the total lack of any moral or religious sentiment whatever.

Most of the comic narratives involve male–female relationships and domestic deception. Their plots resemble stage plays, even if the details don't usually derive from this source. The emphasis on literal factuality and currency is heavy, and many contain directions for verification. *The Comical Bargain: or, Trick upon Trick. Being A Pleasant and True Relation of one Thomas Bocks, a Baker's Prentice, near Milk-Street, that . . . courted an Eminent Doctor's Daughter near King-Street in Bloomsbury* (1707), a story of two sharpers who deserve and get each other, contains this "authentication" on the title page: "*If any one Question the Truth of this Relation,* let them En[quire] for the New-married Couple at the Sign of the Dog and Cat in Bread-street, London."

31. *An Almanack-Husband: or, a Wife a Month: Being a very Comical and Pleasant Relation of a Merchants Son near the Monument, who Married a Wife every Month, for a Year together* . . . (London, 1708), title page, p. 8.

More common than comic stories are ones which purport to be serious or tragic and which narrate occurrences that are often violent and brutal. Typical are such titles as *The Cruel Son, or, the Unhappy Mother. Being a Dismal Relation of one Mr. Palmer and Three Ruffins, who Barbarously Murder'd his own Mother and her Maid . . . November the 7th, 1707. by Cutting their Throats from Ear to Ear, in a Cruel and Unnatural manner; and afterwards setting the House on Fire* (1707) and *The Cruel Mother. Being a strange and unheard-of Account of one Mrs. Elizabeth Cole . . . that threw her own Child into the Thames* (1708). Less typical but equally interesting are titles which include several different stories: *Wonder upon Wonders, or, the London Histories* (1710), for example, which includes several separate brief narrations, some of them quite fanciful, and *Eight Dreadful Examples* (also 1710), which includes as one of its examples a story of "How a cruel Tax-gatherer taking away a poor Womans Cows wrongfully, his own Died, and for blaspheming God he was turned into a Dog."[32]

5

"Reader," begins the narration proper of a 1707 eight-pager called *The Horrors of Jealousie, or, The Fatal Mistake,* "I here present you with a very amazing and dreadful Relation." Adjectives such as "amazing," "dreadful," "terrible," and "horrible" are as common in the body of these texts as on their title pages, as is the repeated insistence on the immediacy and literal truth of the accounts. They are "true relations," "exact accounts," and "faithful narratives," and they are located and dated precisely. For most of the episodes described, a basis in fact is quite likely, and the suggestion of larger human patterns—whether they involve the certainty of remorse and punishment or the tendencies of a sizable minority of human beings toward behavior that ends in robbery, rape, murder, and incest—is secondary to the emphasis on accurate recording of historic particulars. But it would be foolish to separate these narratives too rigidly from fictional ones or to discount what they tell us about contemporary taste for narrative because of their insistence on truth. Novels written in the years that follow insist just as strongly on the factual basis of their events, and early novels repeatedly verify their claims by citing or "quoting" documents or referring readers outside their texts to actual (and verifiable) persons, places, and events.

What readers found in such narratives as the eight-pagers is similar to what they sought in the longer narratives of "real" life written by

32. Some of the eight-pagers included straight didactic and hortatory material as well; a few were practical guides to vocations or crafts. Most eight-pagers were similar in intent, narrative structure, and quality of printing to chapbooks, which were generally twenty-four pages in length but smaller in page format.

Defoe and his successors a few years later. If the style and artistic structure of narratives like these do not seem to offer a model for potential novels—any more than the brief moments used here to capture some surprising aspect of life in eight pages resemble the resonant length and complexity of Defoe's narratives—the subject matter and focus of these narratives does suggest what interested readers in the generation before they had novels to read. It is not that the eight-pagers are novels in miniature or even protonovels of some sort. But like other journalistic phenomena of the late seventeenth and early eighteenth centuries, they suggest both what was on the minds of large numbers of people in the culture and how the ground was prepared for print strategies that became characteristic of the novel.

In the increasing variety of events that inspired short journalistic narratives in the final years of the seventeenth century and the early years of the eighteenth, we can readily see audience tastes expanding and growing even more voracious as well as intensifying toward matters of the moment. In sheer quantity the number of "news" accounts increases sharply during the 1680s and then even more dramatically near the turn of the century.[33] Part of the reason may reside in the tendency of journalistic interest to beget journalistic interest: the taste for news clearly had developed during the Civil Wars, when average Englishmen and Englishwomen felt they had much personally at stake in every public event. By the 1690s, with subject matter rapidly expanding, an audience of eavesdroppers was in effect creating itself. When the Licensing Act was finally relaxed for good in 1695, after several temporary lapses earlier, the amount of publication increased generally. But the major reason for expanded journalistic subject matter seems to involve a discernible shift in taste toward a greater interest in private life, the personal, and the subjective. There is increasing emphasis on the personal feelings of those involved in significant occurrences, and quite a number of short narratives (like *A True and Perfective Narrative of the . . . Snovvs*) seem almost to be interested in narrative for its own sake. Few of those narratives lack moral or religious application of some kind; in most of them the application seems natural and genuine enough, but an interest in other effects is obvious as well. Many intend primarily to amaze or amuse, and many others blend delight and instruction attractively. Cumulatively these narratives suggest a nearly infinite variety in human events and feelings. In the way they blend contemporaneity, subjectivity, concentration on detail, emphasis on the unusual which happens even to the most ordinary of mortals, and sponsoring interest in the patterns of human events, we can readily see a number of novelistic features that had not been comfortably present in romance or other earlier narratives.

33. On the issue of whether the increased number is related to licensing, see the extended discussion in Downie, *Robert Harley and the Press.*

Some of the early English novelists, most notably Defoe, cut their teeth in print journalism, learning narrative and expository craft by interpreting what was happening almost at the moment of action. For others, like Richardson, the routines of their daily lives meant that journalistic accounts of the times were more immediate to them than belles lettres, and their notion of the present was firmly shaped by the way their journalistic contemporaries saw and phrased it. Still others, like Fielding and in a sense Sterne, although less personally involved in popular print culture during their formative years, ultimately discovered just how steeped they were in journalistic assumptions and found themselves later in their careers shifting back and forth between fictional narratives of a certain magnitude, scope, and literary pretension and journalistic treatments of the everyday. For Burney, devotion to a personal and private account of everyday events amounts to almost the same thing as journalism, and the sense of immediacy and of minutiae in her fiction depends upon ways of thinking, perceiving, and articulating that she developed for her diaries, a record of daily life that depended on a crucial sense of immediacy and the values of contemporaneity.

For almost all the early novelists, individual segments of what they wrote when they wrote novels might easily be mistaken for the stuff of everyday popular print. Both the matters they wrote about and the way they wrote about them owed much to the journalistic context of the previous half century. Distasteful as it may be to traditional literary history, the relationship between ephemera and serious literature in the mid-eighteenth century was a very close one, not always clear even to the writers who were producing one or the other, and these writers moved back and forth in their commitments and accomplishments in a very confusing way. A literature of the everyday ultimately cannot make very persuasive high-flown claims to be high-born and elitist. Despite Fielding's attempts to establish a literary and classical heritage (as well as many subsequent critical sophistries), the novel has seldom had much luck in dissociating itself from origins in a broad popular consciousness and allegiances that are broad rather than narrow, leveling rather than hierarchical.

More important, however, than any apprenticeship individual writers got or direct influence that they felt was the context of expectation that they inherited, participated in, and ultimately enhanced. A significant aspect of that contextual inheritance involved the belief that contemporary events demanded attention and interpretation, and the cultural consciousness of contemporaneity meant that the narrative intention and definitions that they developed had a fertile ground. Telling the story of what life is like now and helping to explain how it got that way—the literary job that novelists defined for themselves—could hardly have come about without such a friendly everyday context, and an important aspect of what the novel came to do is a palpable result of the journalistic agenda. Other aspects of popular consciousness also conditioned novelists, the readers of all kinds of print material, and the preoccupations of the culture more generally. Journalism is not *the* explanation of where the novel comes from or why it developed when it did. But the consciousness that made the present moment the center of human attention and led to the directions of modern journalism helped prepare the cultural context for novelists' preoccupations, too. Crucial dimensions of the modern novel seem unimaginable without the peculiar combination of "News, and new Things" that obsessed English culture at the turn of the eighteenth century, dominated most of the directions of the print culture, and refused, for just one brief moment before the novel took over as the dominant form of modern discourse, the written and oral worlds, the sign of one world dying and another newly born.

Literary Field and Classes of Texts

Jacques Dubois and Pascal Durand

Translated by Priscilla Parkhurst Ferguson

An *objet d'art* creates a public that has artistic taste and is able to enjoy beauty—and the same can be said of any other product. Production accordingly produces not only an object for the subject, but also a subject for the object.

Hence production produces consumption: 1) by providing the material of consumption; 2) by determining the mode of consumption; 3) by creating in the consumer a need for the objects which it first presents as products. It therefore produces the object of consumption, the mode of consumption and the urge to consume. Similarly, consumption produces the *predisposition* of the producer by positing him as a purposive requirement.

—KARL MARX, "Introduction" to *A Contribution to the Critique of Political Economy* (1857)

An Outclassed Concept

Like the theories and the individuals by which they are produced, concepts are at once obsolete and mortal. Certain concepts, in favor for a time, are replaced by others dictated by what is convenient or in vogue. Others fall out of favor bit by bit, and still others suddenly find themselves read out of court. Such today is the case with the concept of "social class," which seems to be excluded from general discourse. Even in the discourse where it originated—sociology—it makes only discreet appearances, and then it is enveloped with all kinds of qualifications. The ideological stakes

An earlier version of this article appeared as "Champ littéraire et classes de textes," *Littérature* 70 (May 1988): 5–23.

of such repression are clear enough (get rid of the word to deny what it represents), as is the sociopolitical context of those stakes (a society where the liberal illusion of "mobility" papers over the cleavages and antagonisms between classes). The decline of the concept also has a good deal to do with our modern skepticism toward the schematic divisions and prophetic visions inherited from the last century. The final confrontation of classes will not take place, at least not within the framework predicted by Marxism. And if the class struggle continues, it now only appears surreptitiously and indirectly. The relations of production and domination become more and more abstract and oblique. Even the apparently simple fact of belonging to a given segment of society within a generally mobile society like ours has become more than ever a complex and diffuse fact. All in all, it is far too easy to think that classes exist solely as superficial or peripheral effects, as in the attitudes and behavior by which individuals seek to set themselves apart from others.

Must we then give up inquiry into social relations and their power over human action? Every society is endowed with codes that sanction hierarchical structures as well as forms or forces of domination. Every society divides and classifies the diffuse masses of which it is composed. In short, every society practices social classification and institutes (when it does not institutionalize) relations between those classes.

Perhaps this outclassed and outdated concept will recover some of its acuity and its pertinence when it is introduced into the explanation of literary facts. Such an endeavor is simple though heavy with implications we shall endeavor to sketch out through a proposition that is intentionally limited and one-sided. How and to what extent can the operating notion of *class* be applied not to populations of authors or readers but to "populations" of texts? In fact, this is exactly what we do when we talk about the "society novel" or "popular literature" or when we classify cultural products as highbrow, middlebrow, or lowbrow. Yet literary sociology has never generalized or even theorized the concept of "textual classes." The discussion below is intended to lay the foundation for such a theoretical approach.

Jacques Dubois is Professor of French Literature of the Nineteenth and Twentieth Centuries and of the Sociology of Cultural Institutions at the University of Liège. He is the author of *L'Institution de la littérature: Introduction à une sociologie* (1978). **Pascal Durand** teaches in the same department at the University of Liège. **Priscilla Parkhurst Ferguson** is professor of French at the University of Illinois at Chicago. She is the author of *Literary France: The Making of a Culture* (1987).

Texts and Classes

Marxist in inspiration, early work in the sociology of literature gave social class a prominent place. The primary objective was to define, in a given period, the relations between a social group and a group of authors or works, in other words, the ties between a class and a literary genre. This sociology of literature essentially aimed at confirming the hypothesis according to which given textual products express, in content and formal structure, the collective existence and the ideology of the social group from which they issue. Lucien Goldmann's work on seventeenth-century French literature and Erich Köhler's analyses of medieval genres uncovered convincing homologies.[1] More generally, the rigor and the success of this work did much to legitimize a sociological orientation within the study of literature.

At the same time, the work of Goldmann and Köhler showed that homologies between texts and social class could not account for every situation. Furthermore, homologies became especially problematic and difficult to verify for aesthetic products closer to modern times. As society became more mobile and more complex, the literary sphere of this bourgeois regime and its market economy asserted an unprecedented autonomy. The essential claim and result of that autonomy consisted in the mediation of the connections between literature and the larger cultural field. This autonomy obliged the theoreticians of homologies to concede that the systematic division of which they dreamed—the distribution and distinction of aesthetic works according to social class—had little relevance or concrete correlation in the social system of the nineteenth and twentieth centuries. Two divergent side paths then showed the way out of this dead-end street. One path led them to assimilate authors and works to a vast bourgeois (or petit-bourgeois) order that literature ineluctably either reproduced or opposed. The other path brought them to a complex set of mediations between literature and society. In both cases, whether by excess or by default, the reference to specific social conditions tended to evaporate, leaving very little of the original objective.

Texts and Institutions

More recently, the theory of symbolic fields or of the literary institution has posed in other terms and on other bases the question of the social

---

1. See Lucien Goldmann, *The Hidden God: A Study of Tragic Vision in the "Pensées" of Pascal and the Tragedies of Racine*, trans. Philip Thody (London and New York, 1964), and Erich Köhler, *Ideal und Wirklichkeit in der höfischen Epik; Studien zur Form der frühen Artus- und Graal- dictung* (Tübingen, 1956); translated into French by Éliane Kaufholz, under the title *L'Aventure chevaleresque: Idéal et réalité dans le roman courtois, études sur la forme des plus anciens poèmes d'Arthur et du Graal* (Paris, 1974).

determination of aesthetic products.[2] This theory posits that in the modern world artistic creation and its agents operate in a specific space contained within the larger society where they function with relative autonomy. Literature thus becomes the concern of a self-regulating caste living partially within a closed space. The relative independence of this literary caste means that the symbolic profit taken by writers from the expansion of the book market frees them from their erstwhile guardians (principally individual or institutional patrons). The institutional theory can therefore no longer accept a simple homology between classes on the one hand and authors and works on the other. The apparatus that regulates literary activity serves as a screen between the two terms of the relationship. Does this theory set social divisions and distinctions outside the scope of its investigations? Of course not. On the contrary, one of its goals is to integrate those divisions in its explanatory models in a more dialetical mode, by defining the complex and often ambiguous relationships between the literary and the social spheres in modern society.

The period in which literature set itself up in a closed field and gave institutional form to its practices was also the time during which society showed a marked split between its components, a split characterized by violent antagonisms that were radicalized by class ideologies. However, the foundation of the literary field is not the general sphere of social conflict. Rather, the literary field follows the contours of the bourgeois sphere, which it sets up as an indefinite space that is both contained in and contains the bourgeois sphere. Literature thus belongs to the bourgeois order and goes beyond it. A mixed class, the bourgeoisie assimilated new social strata and was propelled by principles of progress and mobility. Since the nineteenth century it has fought to extend its prerogatives and its field of action, which is why it produces more and more strata between which there are very real possibilities of circulation. Education, marriage, careers, and money open many paths, which license changes of position. This mobility, celebrated by the liberal credo and described by contemporary novelists, is no doubt curbed by the forces of inertia that govern the reproduction of elites. Nevertheless, by virtue of their connections with several fractions of their own class, or even with one or more neighboring classes, more and more bourgeois eventually turn into social hybrids.

In its new definition, the literary sphere accelerates this mobility and the production of social hybrids. By vocation this is a domain of weak endogenous reproduction where sons seldom follow in their fathers' footsteps and where every new position originates in either a promotion or demotion. Upstarts and failures, social climbers and marginal figures

2. On symbolic fields, see the work of Pierre Bourdieu, especially "Le Marché des biens symboliques," *L'Année sociologique* 22 (1971): 49–126; on the literary institution, see Jacques Dubois, *L'Institution de la littérature: Introduction à une sociologie* (Paris and Brussels, 1978).

all inhabit the world of letters. Their interaction is facilitated in that the writer's professional status is very uncertain. Many authors take on a second job, which may well be in another socioprofessional category altogether. Thus, more than any other professional corporation, literature is permeable to social struggles and tensions and to ideological compromises, although these operate only indirectly. This is so because literature turns rivalries that are collective in origin into distinctive classifications of people and personages. The faint echoes of class conflict filter through countless networks of interpersonal relationships.

This indirection is an effect of the autonomy of literary activity, and once again that effect is ambiguous. If, on the one hand, the autonomy of the literary field favors hybridization, on the other, it tends to contain or even to neutralize such hybridization. To the extent that it strives to equalize its agents, every institution operates in the same way. But the literary institution goes about this crossbreeding by a sort of power play. Relatively unstructured and devoid of any explicit code (subject to no jurisdiction), the literary institution engenders an intense ideology, which is no doubt tied to its symbolic function but most particularly translates its marginal position within the overall system. Thus the literary institution transcends the specific social logic on which it is grounded and institutes a system of rivalries and classifications that seems like one big metaphor for more general social conflict. It has often been said that writers belong to a dominated segment of the dominant class. Strengthened by the ministry on which they depend and the mission which they internalize, writers recast their anomic status in positive terms. Anomie signals either membership in a community of the elect or a subversive distance from the establishment. In both cases, as Jean-Paul Sartre pointed out in his studies of Baudelaire and especially Flaubert, the writer claims to escape the hold of social determinants and class relationships.[3]

The Production of Differences

These determinisms are so veiled in the modern literary field as to seem devoid of substance. More than simply participating in class antagonisms, the rivalries of literary groups and authors parody those antagonisms. This impression obtains only for the narrow scene of institutional infighting. It disappears as soon as one considers not the fine points of literary activity but that activity as a whole, as part of a vast system joining production and consumption. This broader point of view discloses a

---

3. See Bourdieu's essay on Flaubert in this volume, "Flaubert's Point of View," trans. Priscilla Parkhurst Ferguson, pp. 211–34. See also Jean-Paul Sartre, *Baudelaire*, trans. Martin Turnell (Norfolk, Conn., 1950), and *The Family Idiot: Gustave Flaubert, 1821–1857*, trans. Carol Cosman, 2 vols. (Chicago, 1981–87).

social dimension that appeared lost, from the supposedly passive pole of this system, namely, the reading public [*le lectorat*], receivers in the communication model, consumers for economics.

Beginning in the nineteenth century, and far more than in earlier periods—when the potential reading public was not very diversified—literature stratifies according to highly differentiated publics. Outside the literary field, these publics are distributed along a scale of cultural levels and unwittingly reintroduce social effects into the autonomous literary order. The desocialization of producers, which correlates with the institutionalization of their practice, is balanced by the social diversification of consumers, who inscribe their class on the literary texts that, by implication, they order. This stratification of the field of texts by the reading public results from introducing literary production into a market economy where production has to cover all of the potential public and therefore meet the specific demand of every segment of that public. Each level of the reading public has the appropriate reading material and texts with which it can identify. There is a strong tendency for contemporary literature to classify its production (and to produce classified products) with reference to the real, assumed, or constructed classifications of the different reading publics in question.[4]

But who classifies? In principle, the producers create a hierarchy as a function of consumers.[5] Still, it would be wrong to assume perfect awareness and command of these classificatory maneuvers. The action in question—along with the "politics" implicit therein—is caught in a circular logic: whoever classifies also classifies himself or herself, and vice versa. This "tourniquet" originates in the fundamental fact, already noted by Marx, that the object produces the subject, the subject of consumption and, also, to a certain extent, the subject of production itself. Authors are the children of their texts, publishers of their books; texts and books are always implicated and defined in the vast system of modes and models.

---

4. Bourdieu notes, "The struggle over classification is a basic dimension of the class struggle." Political power works the same way, because to classify is to "impose a vision of divisions" and therefore exhibit one's "power to create groups, to manipulate the objective structure of society" ("Espace social et pouvoir symbolique," *Choses dites* [Paris, 1987], p. 164). Thus there exists a "politics of literature" that acts through and on the scale of cultural degrees and plays on a subtle dialogue between production and consumption. This stratifying politics is already at work in classical literature in the three styles of poetics, but in modern literature it attains a degree of complexity (and perhaps duplicity as well) theretofore unknown.

5. That is, not only writers but all those who regulate literary institutions from within or without: publishers, critics, professors. Publishers determine the series that will present the product; critics select the works that they think are aimed at the public they represent; professors ratify "posterity's triage" and stratify the literary corpus according to the degrees and the network of their teaching and according to their own conception of a given body of texts.

Asking "who classifies?" sets off an interminable process whose origin cannot be determined.

Thus, within the very heart of literary institutions, the procedures of classification along with the grid or grids of textual classes establish a discriminatory and distinctive system that serves as the symbolic guarantor for the social class system and its antagonisms. If this system is immediately recognizable in its crude form (everyone acknowledges the stratification of what we call literature among texts oriented toward distinct reading publics), it is misunderstood in its social extent and meaning (the only accepted criterion for selection is the quality of the work, and the only argument admitted is the intended public). This is why the social effects on textual categories have not really been examined very carefully. The omission is all the more astonishing because modern research, in scrutinizing the more readily accepted concept of genre, has explored an area where such effects are exceptionally dynamic.

Genres

Genres represent the great literary classificatory form that subsumes all other modes of categorization. From the beginning genres have a determinant form insofar as they constitute the sole prescriptive code instituted as such. They are also a determining form to the degree that they designate what is literary and what is not. One should, perhaps, be wary of the notion of literature. Still, poetry or tragedy seem to have a universal acceptance that resolves all doubt. Basic givens of perception and experience, regulatory forms of the literary system, genres nevertheless occupy varying positions with respect to each other. Their value, their effect, what they look like—all can vary from one period to the next. Up to a certain point, genres bear the historical function Roland Barthes assigned to "écritures."[6] For genres like "écritures" testify to a specific commitment on the part of the writer vis-à-vis society and the institution of literature. Choosing poetry in France meant something very different in 1820, in 1870, and 1920. To choose the sonnet over a free form in 1980 is an act that is every bit as "political" as it is aesthetic.

Governing from on high the space of forms, genres place that space under the double principle of liberty (the possibility of choice) and constraint (the necessity of choosing among limited possibilities). However, although genres are essentially prescriptive codes, their prescriptions vary in content and in severity from one time to another, from one aesthetic to another. The single law that is never abrogated is the proscription against mixing genres.

6. See Roland Barthes, *Writing Degree Zero*, trans. Annette Lavers and Colin Smith (New York, 1968). Lavers and Smith translate "écriture" as "writing."

The preeminence and the overdetermination of the major genres are such that they tend to form institutions within the larger institution of literature. The novel, poetry, and the drama make up enclaves within the literary field. Their actors and their products come out of "separate worlds."[7] Each genre institutes and manages its own code (styles, attitudes, behavior, and so on) and at the same time competes with all the other genres. In France over the course of the nineteenth century the novel dispossessed poetry and drama of their exclusive prestige in order to express its conquest of vast territory, not to conquer great prestige. The essay tagged along. Drama and poetry found themselves relegated to minority positions that situated them in so many "separate worlds"— outmoded insofar as they rely on a symbolic capital that may well be depleted, and representing *en abîme* the closure of the system as a whole.

Besides guaranteeing literarity, a genre inscribes texts and authors within a specific population of texts and authors. It thereby contributes to the symbolic and/or institutional socialization of texts and authors that heed its injunctions. To select a genre is to pledge allegiance to a patrimony by grafting one's product onto the intertextual body of products that correspond to that canon. This same choice also accredits the symbolic guarantee that the genre confers on the literary product and its producer. To the degree that the modern literary system, at least the traditional pole of that system, favors generic specialization, it is at a loss with someone like Victor Hugo, an institution and counterinstitution all by himself.

Genres in the Literary Institution

According to their major institutional effect, which joins authority and prestige, stability and segregation, genres give themselves as their own origin: they have the force of law and always appear to antedate any text. Whenever poetics has tried to translate generic order into ontological terms (or principles into what Gérard Genette has called "patchwork"), it only goes further in this same direction, in search of the originating essential category(ies) under the manifest literary product.[8] To a large extent this point of view reverses the actual order of things. For one, it neglects the historically defined status of many generic forms. Moreover, the systemic conception implies that genre depends on a construction after the fact. Thus, and first of all, today's generic system is

7. That we are more likely to speak of the "novelist" or the "poet" than the "writer" attests to the hold of particularistic generic representations, which also result, perhaps even more so, from transferring into the literary order the bourgeois principle of the division of labor.

8. "Bricolages" is Gérard Genette's term for the systematic constructions of poeticians. See Genette, "Introduction à l'architexte," in Genette et al., *Théorie des genres* (Paris, 1986), pp. 89–159.

only too visibly an aggregate of forms tied to very diverse social strata. Further, even where it proves possible to assign an anthropological base to certain genres—narrative, for instance—their definition rests on the crystallization of circumstances around a few texts that serve as reference.

In sum, texts produce genres more than they reproduce them (the object always seeming to contain the category to which it belongs). This point brings us to the notion of textual classes, which Jean-Marie Schaeffer has proposed to counter simplistic classificatory schemes that neglect the dynamic dimension of genres.[9] Breaking with dominant ontological doctrine, Schaeffer confines himself to a strictly phenomenological point of view (moving from text to genre) to demonstrate the work of the *instituting force* under the *instituted product*. The instituted product corresponds to the normative power and the systemic regularity that lead us to contend that genres act as institutions. The instituting force covers the work of founding and transformation exercised by texts on genres, work that proves especially intense for modern literature. Thus, within a shifting field, a genre is not only a class but a class in the process of making and unmaking itself according to a dual logic of identity and difference, or better yet, of identity *in* difference. The preservation of a genre depends on its transformation, its paradoxical mobility in this sense recalling the mobility of bourgeois social structures.

Genres or Classes, Genres and Classes

The order that directs the reader's orientation and the distribution of texts into categories is much more than an innocuous preliminary step: within this field of competing forces constituted by literature, genres and classes are at one and the same time the stakes and the weapons of continual confrontation. With these weapons actors conquer their status, and thanks to them, their rank in the institution. And so we come to the central question: if texts belong in generic classes, do these classes have a social dimension? In other words, are genres classes in themselves or do they simply enter into relationships with classes?

A relationship invariably links genres and classes, though it is neither univocal nor constant. Historically, this relationship seems to be expressed according to two distinct forms of competing alliances. The first tends to superimpose genres and classes on the assumption that social and generic hierarchies coincide. For the classical and romantic periods, poetry was a noble genre legitimated by its noble or upper-class practitioners. By the middle of the nineteenth century, with practitioners (like Paul Verlaine or Stéphane Mallarmé) who were petit-bourgeois civil servants,

9. See Jean-Marie Schaeffer, "Du texte au genre: Notes sur la problématique générique," in *Théorie des genres*, esp. pp. 186 and 202.

poetry had to invent a mythifying discourse to compensate for its social decline. It adopted a luxuriating opacity of language to preserve its endangered legitimacy. The second form of alliance between genres and classes resembles a vertical intersection between the two scales. Genres are stratified into hierarchical classes, and, by implication, classes are subdivided into genres. Next to high-level poetry there is a middle-level or bourgeois poetry and a low-level or popular poetry.

It is tempting to assume that genres and classes coincide in a traditional literary field and that genres are stratified into classes when literature is on the open market. From this point of view the second half of the nineteenth century proves especially interesting. The collision of the two systems ended up producing some flagrant distortions. The Parnassian poetry of Charles-Marie Leconte de Lisle, Théophile Gautier, and their disciples in the 1850s and 1860s, and even the symbolism of Mallarmé and others later in the century, could still claim first place according to the first system. But the novel had already won the game in terms of the second system, which also led it to diversify ("popular novel," "experimental novel," "psychological novel"). Even as the democratization of literature produced the novel for "everybody," it produced a novel for each social class, heavily dependent on the market.[10]

In either the first or the second system, to what extent are the hierarchical arrangements admitted, displayed, accepted, recognized? The point calls for investigation, grounded in contemporary practices and the sliding scales of legitimacy. The last two centuries reveal certain tendencies. As a general rule, genre is not aligned on class. However simple they may seem, the exceptions to the rule—the "popular novel" or the "society novel"—turn out to be ambiguous. Are these novels *by,* *for,* or *about* the lower classes/high society? To the degree that a genre carries a social connotation, it prefers to sidestep the whole question. Until late in the nineteenth century and despite the evident triumph of the genre, "novel" sounded so trivial that the term was left off the cover of most novels. Does this mean that genre systematically erases its social referents? It is more accurate to say that it reveals these referents in the very act of hiding them. Because genre functions as an indicator, it always more or less serves as a metonym for its class and the properties of that class. Whatever their position, users never make a mistake. They recognize themselves in the genres made for them and which, albeit obliquely, are aimed at them.

Take, for examples, four current labels, which can be distributed along a single scale: (1) "gothic novel," (2) "detective novel," (3) "novel,"

---

10. For the second half of the nineteenth century in France, Charles Grivel has described the modern structure of the novel, set out in four levels: realist or naturalist, bourgeois, honnête, and popular. See Grivel, *Production de l'intérêt romanesque: un état du texte (1870–1880), un essai de constitution de sa théorie* (The Hague, 1973).

(4) "fiction." The most neutral of these—"novel"—seems to fit the average (traditional) production for any average (general) public. The other terms go in two directions. Avant-garde literature pares down to essentials or covers its tracks with "fictions" or "narratives" at the same time that production for a mass or semi-mass public embellishes the base term by specifying content, for example, "detective novel" or "gothic novel." Although they move in opposite directions, these two extreme tendencies represent the same process of diversification and specification. The aim is not only to refine the classification (a genre for everyone) but just as much to refine the classification code itself. Neither understatement nor hyperbole deludes readers, who all know which side they are on and happily recognize a familiar code.

From Hierarchy to Layers

Thus, under the (pseudo)system of genres lies a more organic and more determined system of textual classes. Far from being a closed or fixed structure, this system of classes is continually enriched and remodeled by additions. Further, beyond the overall division into spheres of production and consumption on which this system of classes is based, there is a potentially unlimited layering into strata that cut across subclasses. How can such a distributive scale be objectified? How can levels be fixed, if only for a given state of the literary field? Two types of criteria—external and internal—point to a preliminary model. External criteria isolate these strata in terms of the choices and practices of given readers.[11] Such an approach, however, runs the risk of foundering on the difficulty of merging textual classes with the classes of the groups receiving those texts, groups that may or may not be those intended by the textual classes. There is no dearth of examples of such discrepancies. Hermetic poetry is enjoyed by middle-class readers who ratify their social promotion by such prestigious reading, whereas the detective novel appeals to intellectuals who like to slum about in a popular genre and also to play around with a strictly regulated narrative form. Recourse to internal criteria means picking up on the semiological indicators that configure a classification and operate as much in literary terms as in sociocultural ones.[12] In this

11. For a good example of this approach, see Patrick Parmentier, "Bon ou mauvais genre. La classification des lectures et le classement des lecteurs," *Bulletin des Bibliothèques de France* 31 (1986): 202–23.

12. The social destination of aesthetic products can be seen in a series of recurring elements within and especially at the periphery of texts, which essentially function as semiological indicators of classification. On the "threshold" of the book, the producers (and particularly publishers) make use of a set of marks more or less under their control but that sooner or later end up by getting out of their control, even, in certain cases, taking on a meaning other than the original one. In *Seuils* (Paris, 1987), Genette gives a very

case the risk is having to work within parameters as strict as they are plentiful, and sometimes imponderable.

Although this type of study or inventory can certainly yield forms of measurement, the theory of textual classes must take specific note of the fact that these classes are fully recognizable and definable only in conjunction with certain *relationships* and certain *effects*. Evanescent entities that fade away as soon as the classified and classifying subjects (readers, publishers, authors) cease to be aware of them, textual classes belong above all to the order of representation. In part, today, the role of the production system is to outline these subjects (without too much emphasis) and to remodel them according to the possible development of the market.

As for the "relationships," they are absolutely basic. Every class is defined dialectically according to its position with respect to others. Better yet, there is no classification that is not subject to reciprocal definition and readjustment. This is the heart of the theory of distinction, according to which anyone who classifies anything is necessarily classified in the process [*quiconque classe se classe en classant*].[13] Our options and our preferences steer us toward objects or practices that are already socially defined and that send us back to our class origins in such a way as to confirm those choices. The circular movement reinforces the social definitions of the objects chosen.

The relationship between publishers and readers gives a good sense of the importance of this interaction. Publishers confer certain generic marks on their products in order to reach certain groups of readers. The signs of these choices are displayed, but as a function of a public which, at that moment, remains potential, even fictive. Even as they classify products and their hoped-for consumers, publishers also classify themselves. To this we should add that they classify products only according to their notions of their own classification. At this point the actual public enters the scene and reproduces the same procedure in the opposite direction. The choices of these consumers, who of course are also socially defined, reinsert the publisher's position into the heart of sociosymbolic hierarchies, and, in so doing, give a subtle definition of their own position. However it may occur, classification is both reproduction and adjustment. On the one hand, individuals reflect and reproduce their social status by the

detailed inventory of this territory of the authorial and editorial paratext made up of these indicators. (For a partial translation of *Seuils,* see "Structure and Functions of the Title in Literature," trans. Bernard Crampé, *Critical Inquiry* 14 [Summer 1988]: 692–720.) From the point of view of their classificatory effect, the most efficacious indicators are the cover design (figurative or abstract), the title, the generic notation, the names of the publisher and the series, and the acknowledgments. They constitute a summary code of proven efficiency in book sales where the book is an object first of all. It is unfortunate that Genette does not get beyond the perspective of poetics, which leads him to overlook the social investment of these paratextual markings, on the (to us fallacious) pretext that this investment is not easily theorized.

13. See Bourdieu, *Distinction: A Social Critique of the Judgement of Taste,* trans. Richard Nice (Cambridge, Mass., 1984).

interplay of their choices; on the other hand, and in a perpetual movement of refinement, they project into their choices an idea of themselves that touches up their reality. In this way this circular classificatory process escapes a vicious circle.

Autonomy/Heteronomy of Genres or Textual Classes

If literary classifications are able to resist a theoretical mode, it is undoubtedly because they come from a complex interaction between the forces of production and consumption. But this resistance also stems from their ability to produce or reproduce themselves at the crossroads of two great orders of determination, one symbolic, the other social. Here we find not only the most basic economic requirements (making a profit from a particular genre, like "bodice-ripper romances") but also the subtlest symbolic marks (supplying a small group of intellectuals with their signs of distinction).

It would be unwise to limit the establishment of textual classes to the reciprocal action of the literary field and those fractions of the larger society—reading publics—oriented toward the literary field and toward which in turn that field is oriented. It is essential to recognize the capacity of this field to exercise its own logic. The ceaseless remodeling of genres and the variation in their hierarchical distribution result partially from a strictly institutional regulatory apparatus. In other words, internal factors mediate, in various ways and according to specific times and conditions, the influence of external factors. Beginning with romanticism, genres joined in the competition between writers seeking symbolic glory and power. Starting with the Parnassian poets and the realist novelists at mid-century, rival aesthetic programs played one genre against another, even one genre against itself. From the Parnassians to surrealism, from Émile Zola to Alain Robbe-Grillet, the duel between poetry and novel fed a century of controversy. Subgenres and minor forms like the avant-garde theater (symbolist and postexistentialist) or the essay (from Jules Michelet to Barthes) joined in these quarrels from a distance.

Genre and Behavior

For those who believe in them, genres are not simply strategic instruments or means for conveying a message that alone counts. For if the generic system constitutes a socializing medium that guarantees a status for writers and literarity for their products, every genre tends as well to impose thematic or formal structures on texts and also to dictate a code of behavior and a mode of being to authors. Thus the symbolists, Mallarmé in the lead, translated the principles of their generic credo into the ritual of their meetings and into certain strategic behavior. The surrealists' concern with restoring an "aura" to poetry led them to raise this credo into an existential principle that was meant to provoke revolutionary action. This much said, we may legitimately wonder whether such objectifications result from an identification with the genre in question or from an aesthetic program invested in that genre. An "arty" novelist like Barbey d'Aurevilly—or Oscar Wilde, for an English example in drama as well as the novel—undoubtedly owed less to the genre that he practiced than to his aesthetic credo, his reactionary dandyism, and his somewhat scandalous behavior. Still, from romanticism to surrealism, and in spite of programmatic variation of different schools, a strongly codified genre like poetry provokes similar attitudes in all of its adherents and the same quasi-religious consciousness of their status and their "mission."

Transfers and Transactions

The struggle over classifications, which correlates with competition between schools, undoubtedly opposes very localized strata of the textual field. At the same time this struggle engages the system as a whole. In principle, because each category or class is defined relative to the others, every transformation at one point of the literary structure can diffuse from stratum to stratum, eventually altering the whole. This rather excessive theoretical perspective is at least partially confirmed by the series of intermutations that appear in the historical analysis of textual classes. Thus, innovative breaks set off a regulatory process, itself self-regulated, which guarantees the "economic" stability of the system. On the one hand, this regulatory process checks the momentum of chain reactions, and on the other, it initiates the necessary reciprocal reorganization.

Three examples, of increasing complexity, reveal this process in action. The first covers the simple case of two subgenres that begin to interact whenever one of them is caught in a transformative movement against which the other reacts. The second case is already more subtle, since it shows a dialectical adjustment between two separate genres. The third example represents a complex case of symbolic "transaction" insofar as this transaction no longer takes place between two types of literary production but, more broadly, between two types of discursive production.

The last five years of the Second Empire, 1865–70, witnessed the double appearance of the "artistic novel" of Edmond and Jules de Goncourt and the judicial novel of Émile Gaboriau, ancestor of today's detective novel. No one noticed this coincidence, which was overlooked all the more easily in that these two types of novels originated in very different sectors of the literary institution. With *Manette Salomon* (1867) and *Madame Gervaisais* (1869) the Goncourt brothers firmly committed the novel to "modernity," which in literary terms meant a weakened plot, fragmented narrative, indirect point of view, and ineffectual hero-subject. From the serial novel Gaboriau appropriated a type of fiction that adheres to a strict narrative logic and whose authoritative investigator-hero is always on center stage running everything. In sum, what one subgenre gave up, another took up in an insistent, hyperbolic form. Compensation was thus provided by a new "genre," which started from the "bottom" of the generic hierarchy and rose step by step on the scale of values. The judicial novel occupied abandoned territory at the same time that the very excess of its narrative structure alerted "literary consciousness" that the rejections of the avant-garde endangered the system. In any case, the two competing forms realigned the novelistic sector.[14]

A few years later, in the 1880s, an analogous phenomenon of compensatory competition occurred between the novel on the rise and poetry on the decline. Its credo of a purely linguistic and self-reflexive practice prompted symbolist poetry to question the subject of poetic enunciation in negative and radical terms. Pushing to its limits the Parnassian precept of impassivity, Mallarmé and his disciples preached and practiced an "impersonal" poetry, which resulted in "the elocutionary disappearance of the poet."[15] In this way the poetic movement that dominated the end of the century broke with the romantic representation of lyricism as a mirror of the self or a diary of complex and subtle emotions. It is striking that a new school emerged at the same time, led by the novelists Paul Bourget and Maurice Barrès, which proclaimed the absolute primacy of the individual subject, exalted the "cult of the self," and endorsed the psychology of the passions as an explanatory model for social behavior and as the scientific basis of narrative imagination. On the basis of a process already at work for the Goncourt/Gaboriau duo, these "psychological novelists" built their school on the ruins of a domain that had been deserted by the poets. This opportunistic occupation of an abandoned site was also a strategic takeover of a traditional canon whose abandonment had been roundly condemned by a public confused by strange new poetic practices. In this instance, the transposition of one genre to the other was probably mediated by the symbolist novel, which transferred to the novel the Mallarmean precept of the eradication of the self through a constant decentering of a fragmented subject, diffused in the wanderings of a fading consciousness (as in Edouard Dujardin's *Les Lauriers sont coupés* [1888], which anticipated the interior monologue later associated with James Joyce and the novels of Rémy de Gourmont). In this fashion the psychological novelists maneuvered on two fronts. They blocked the avant-garde novel tied to symbolism and proved their conformity with an established literary canon. At the same time they offered the ordinary reader "realistic" novels validated by their supposed scientific base. These essentially strategic stakes testify to the competition and the domination at work in the reciprocal redeployment of textual classes.

14. See Dubois, "Un Cas de transfert symbolique. Roman artiste et roman judiciaire à la fin du second Empire," *Oeuvres et critiques* 12 (1987): 35–47.

15. Stéphane Mallarmé, "Crise de vers," *Oeuvres complètes*, ed. Henri Mondor and G. Jean-Aubry (Paris, 1945), pp. 360–61.

Strictly speaking, the final exemplary case concerns the consequences for the literary field of the expansion, after 1885, of mass-produced news media and the concomitant accelerated growth of a "para-" or "infra-" literary production. Literary milieux at the time hotly debated the rapid development of newspapers, fearful that mass media would destroy the aura of "the written word" by offering the public a lesser version of written culture. This fear was at least partially founded. Around 1890 the press inundated the market with mediocre works, thereby undermining the prestige of the book and producing what contemporaries called the "publishing crash." Marc Angenot has suggested that journalism provoked writers, and notably poets, to reactions of defensiveness and withdrawal, which they expressed in aesthetic programs that broke totally with the aggressive discourse of the mass media.[16] And in fact, symbolist manifestos frequently referred to the menace of journalism. Moreover, Mallarmé's definition of poetic language as anticommunication, as well as the hermeticism included in and legitimated by that definition, depended in large part on this rivalry between literature and the media.

Thus once again there was a reactive and negative redeployment. However, a closer look shows that certain agents of elite literary production adopted a position that was both less radical and more dialectic. Mallarmé presents the most interesting case. His theoretical work, which talks endlessly about the newspaper, sought to go beyond this crisis, and it did so no longer, or not only, by enjoining the poet to set poetic practice apart from media discourse. Mallarmé also invited the poet to reclaim from the newspaper what in fact belongs to poetry, that is, to convert to aesthetic ends that which in the newspaper has a solely pragmatic and informational purpose (for example, the double and extra-large sheet, the interplay of typographical styles, and so on). Mallarmé himself at the end of his life gave a stunning example of this conversion. *Un Coup de dés* (1897) uses typographical variation to great effect. Scattered throughout the "book" and set out on different levels on each page, titles made up of entire sentences stand out in big, thick capital letters against the mosaic of the text. That this poetic transposition of the newspaper model has attracted so little attention has to do with a complex phenomenon of assimilation and differentiation, which cleared the way for numerous avant-garde projects of the twentieth century.[17]

The Symbolic (Re)production of Social Classes

These transactions, with their dialectic of takeover and rejection, disclose the imaginative conflict of form and theme in and behind the

16. See Marc Angenot, "Ceci tuera cela, ou: la chose imprimée contre le livre," *Romantisme* 44 (1984): 83–103.

17. See Pascal Durand, "D'une rupture intégrante: Avant-gardes et transactions symboliques," *Pratiques* 50 (June 1986): 31–45.

conflict of classes and classifications, of which the former seems partly the cause and partly the effect. In this manner we have stressed the capacity of the system to constitute itself, to produce and to reproduce itself. The objection might be raised that, without realizing it, we have only transposed into the order of textual classes the system logic of the order of genres as elaborated by poeticians.[18] Such an objection would disregard what we have stressed all along, namely that these classes, precisely because they mask their impact of division and stratification, never cease to bear a social signification as active as it is hidden. Our current research focuses on the points and modalities of engagement between this social sense of textual classes and, on the one hand, the configuration of collective literary institutions and, on the other, the general economy of the larger society.

Unless it reverts to illusions of homology, this research will not be able to overlook the fact that, however immersed in this social sense, these symbolic divisions undoubtedly have their share of autonomy. Moreover, from within a cultural system as highly structured as literature, these divisions are capable of producing effects of social construction, either fictive or operative. A given group of texts can aim at, or rather generate, a class of readers that straddle two or more social fragments, readers who are socially disparate though united by a secondary collusion that turns out to be their (aesthetic) class-consciousness. The public for detective novels, for example, mixes intellectuals and nonintellectuals, lower middle-class and lower-class readers.

Literature does not only stand humbly before (or in) society as a passive receiver of determining stimuli, which it then translates into symbolic classifications. Literature is also in the position of analyzing, of dissecting and rearticulating the social system according to its own logic. At once the terrain and the instrument of analysis, literature offers sociologists one of the most powerful instruments available for their criticism, on the condition that they keep in mind the specificity of literature and avoid turning it into a mirror and, hence, the accomplice of the social order. Without going as far as Mallarmé's contention that "social relationships and their measurement . . . constitute a fiction, which belongs to literature,"[19] it seems clear that sociology ought to learn from literature, among other things, that the symbolic never stops manipulating the social.

---

18. This is the place to specify that if this article has sometimes given the impression of basing the hierarchy of classes as a function of the distribution of genres, this methodologically convenient procedure in no way precludes further research from taking into account classificatory criteria other than genres. It is clear, to take a couple of examples, that certain authors (for example, James Michener, Joyce Carol Oates) or certain publishers (Harlequin, Reader's Digest Books) virtually function as classes unto themselves. The class effect of Reader's Digest Books is to level out texts previously published elsewhere (in their entirety).

19. Mallarmé, "Sauvegarde," *Oeuvres complètes,* p. 420.

The Book-of-the-Month Club and the General Reader: On the Uses of "Serious" Fiction

Janice Radway

In 1986, the Book-of-the-Month Club celebrated its sixtieth anniversary with special promotions and publicity campaigns. Club officials offered their members a company-sponsored history of the institution, special editions of "BOMC Classics," including J. D. Salinger's *Catcher in the Rye* and Isak Dinesen's *Seven Gothic Tales,* and two commemorative posters proclaiming "The Joys of Reading." In addition, the Club mounted an elaborate exhibition at the New York Public Library celebrating "America's coming of age in literature, culture and the arts."[1] Designed to chronicle significant cultural events both high *and* popular from the years 1926 to 1986, the exhibition nevertheless entwined Club history with the high cultural tradition by prominently featuring books selected by the Club that have since been recognized as major artistic achievements.

I would like to thank Lawrence Crutcher, Nancy Evans, Lorraine Shanley, and Al Silverman for allowing me to conduct this study and for granting access to internal Club documents. I would especially like to thank William Zinsser for his support and encouragement of my research as well as all the editors who took time from their busy schedules to talk with me about their ways of reading. I am also indebted to the John Simon Guggenheim Memorial Foundation for its generous support of this project. Finally, I would like to dedicate this article to the memory of Joseph J. Savago.

1. See, for instance, the September and October 1986 issues of the *Book-of-the-Month Club News,* the catalog distributed to Club members fifteen times a year, which is available at the Club or at the New York Public Library. On the exhibition, which was designed by William Zinsser and Jessica Weber, see the Club pamphlet, "Extraordinary Years, 1926–1986," and a short description of it in "The Talk of the Town: Books," *New Yorker* (28 Apr. 1986): 25–26.

Although these activities were designed in part to garner publicity and thus to help in the Club's membership drive, they were also the creation of editors who are cognizant of the company's past and self-conscious about its cultural role as "an American institution." Its editors often characterize the company as "the book club of record" where "serious book readers" can find "the best new books" in every field imaginable.[2] In fact, the Book-of-the-Month Club is well regarded within the publishing industry as an institution that manages to combine commercial goals with a concern for "quality."[3] The company is attended to, of course, because a Club bid can be an important source of revenue for publishers. But industry executives also respect the skill with which its editors sift through more than five thousand manuscripts annually to choose approximately 250 books that the Club eventually offers to its membership.

In spite of the esteem it now enjoys within the publishing world, the Club's reputation in what might be called "the literary world" remains that of the quintessential "middlebrow" forum.[4] The spatial placement is assigned to the Club's selections by those who define literary culture in America, the critics of the literary press and scholars in the academic world. The Book-of-the-Month Club offers, in such a view, neither the best works of contemporary literature nor the worst examples of mindless

2. The data for this paper include interviews with Book-of-the-Month Club officials and editors as well as a systematic survey of the Club's readers' reports for serious fiction during the years 1984, 1985, and 1986.

3. "Quality" is an adjective used throughout the publishing industry to describe both books and publishing houses themselves. A "quality house" is one that publishes a significant number of literary titles as well as a considerable amount of serious nonfiction. "Quality books" are thus generally distinguished from those intended for the mass market. In conducting interviews with the subsidiary rights directors of major publishing houses, I have discovered that most believe that the Book-of-the-Month Club is interested in distributing "quality books" to its members. On the various sectors in the publishing industry, see Lewis A. Coser, Charles Kadushin, and Walter W. Powell, *Books: The Culture and Commerce of Publishing* (New York, 1982), pp. 36–69.

4. See, for example, Dwight Macdonald, "Masscult and Midcult: II," *Partisan Review* 27 (Fall 1960): 589–631. See also Joan Shelley Rubin's important discussion of the early years of the Club's history in "Self, Culture, and Self-Culture in Modern America: The Early History of the Book-of-the-Month Club," *Journal of American History* 71 (Mar. 1985): 782–806. There Rubin distinguishes herself from the most negative of the Club's critics, acknowledges that the BOMC probably has enlarged the audience for books, and develops a complex argument about the particular historical mediations the "middlebrow" accomplished.

Janice Radway is an associate professor of American civilization at the University of Pennsylvania. She is the author of *Reading the Romance: Women, Patriarchy, and Popular Literature* (1984) and is a former editor of *American Quarterly*. This article is part of a larger study, the working title of which is "The Book-of-the-Month Club and the General Reader: The Transformation of Literary Production in the Twentieth Century."

"trash." Its books, rather, fall into that large amorphous middle ground of the unremarkable but respectable. It is worth keeping in mind, however, that this linear display is arranged mentally as a hierarchy and that mid-range books are seen by such commentators not simply as different from those occupying higher positions but as failed attempts to approximate the achievement of the best books.

This should come as no surprise given recent discussions of the social construction of taste by Pierre Bourdieu, Barbara Herrnstein Smith, and Richard Ohmann among others.[5] As Smith has reminded us, "Like its price in the marketplace, the value of an entity to an individual subject is *also* the product of the dynamics of an economic system, specifically the personal economy constituted by the subject's needs, interests, and resources—biological, psychological, material, and experiential."[6] To dismiss the middle range as products of a fundamental insufficiency, therefore, as the result of a certain incompetence, is to accomplish several other goals simultaneously, all of which have relevance to the self-interest of those making the distinction. It is to state, first, that there is a single hierarchy of value on which all verbal products are ranged and that all such works aspire to the highest position. It is also to affirm the validity and preeminence of that single set of criteria against which all works are measured and thus to insist that there is only one appropriate way to read. Finally, it is to value reflexively and in a hierarchical way those individuals who are able to recognize such value and to appreciate it by reading properly. To label the Club middlebrow, therefore, is to damn it with faint praise and to legitimate the social role of the intellectual who has not only the ability but the authority to make such distinctions and to dictate them to others.[7]

If one accepts the social hierarchy that this taste structure masks, it is easy to accept the validity of the particular criteria which serve as the working test of excellence. In fact, the high value placed on rationality, complexity, irony, reflexivity, linguistic innovation, and the "disinterested" contemplation of the well-wrought artifact makes sense within cultural institutions devoted to the improvement of the individuality, autonomy, and productive competence of the already privileged individuals who come to them for instruction and advice.[8] Appreciation for the technical

---

5. See Pierre Bourdieu, *Distinction: A Social Critique of the Judgment of Taste*, trans. Richard Nice (Cambridge, Mass., 1984); further references to this work, abbreviated *D*, will be included in the text. See also Barbara Herrnstein Smith, "Contingencies of Value," *Critical Inquiry* 10 (Sept. 1983): 1–35, and Richard Ohmann, "The Shaping of a Canon: U.S. Fiction, 1960–1975," *Critical Inquiry* 10 (Sept. 1983): 199–223; further references to Ohmann's article, abbreviated "SC," will be included in the text.

6. Smith, "Contingencies of Value," pp. 11–12.

7. For a somewhat different formulation of this argument, see ibid., pp. 18–19.

8. For a discussion of the connections between the social position and role of literary academics and the values they promote through the process of canonization, see Jane Tompkins, *Sensational Designs: The Cultural Work of American Fiction, 1790–1860* (New York, 1985), esp. pp. 186–201.

fine points of aesthetic achievement is also understandable among people whose daily work centers on the business of discrimination. But it is worth keeping in mind that the critical dismissal of literary works and institutions that do not embody these values *as failures* is an exercise of power which rules out the possibility of recognizing that such works and institutions might be valuable to others because they perform functions more in keeping with their own somewhat different social position, its material constraints, and ideological concerns. The easy critical dismissal of the Club and other "popularizers" is an act of exclusion that banishes those who might mount even the most minimal of challenges to the culture and role of the contemporary intellectual by proclaiming their own right to create, use, and value books for different purposes.

My preoccupation with the Book-of-the-Month Club arises, then, out of a prior interest in the way books are variously written, produced, marketed, read, and evaluated in contemporary American culture. My subjects might best be described as ways of writing rather than Literature, ways of reading rather than texts.[9] I have begun to examine the Club's editorial operation with the intention of eventually comparing the manner, purpose, and substance of the editors' choice of books with the choices of actual Book-of-the-Month Club members. Such a comparison seems potentially interesting for a variety of reasons.

Although the Club has only recently begun the process of compiling large quantities of information about its membership, it seems unlikely that more than a very small portion is composed of literary intellectuals given its reputation among them as the purveyor of the middlebrow and the mediocre.[10] It seems probable, therefore, that for a significant number of Club members, books play a quite different role in their lives and serve other purposes than they do for people who make their living producing, analyzing, and distinguishing among cultural products. Furthermore, because Book-of-the-Month Club editors know from long experience that they can sell a fairly predictable number of books in any

9. See, for instance, my earlier effort to specify how a group of women actually read and evaluate individual books in the much-maligned romance genre, *Reading the Romance: Women, Patriarchy, and Popular Culture* (Chapel Hill, N.C., 1984). I am indebted to Mary Pratt's discussion ("Towards a Critical Cultural Practice," paper presented at the Conference on the Agenda of Literary Studies, Marquette University, 8–9 Oct. 1982) of the concept of "literariness" and the way it disciplines ideologically this particular way of describing my own interests.

10. There are some statistics available that tend to corroborate this inference. A 1958 Club survey of the membership indicated that while eighty-three percent of its members had a college education, only thirteen percent of the members were teachers of one sort or another. This may have changed recently with the Club's use of the *Oxford English Dictionary* as a Club premium, but the continuing difference between the Club's selections and those of the Reader's Subscription Book Club, associated with the *New York Review of Books*, the literary journal read by many American intellectuals, suggests that the Book-of-the-Month Club still does not cater to this group. On the *New York Review*, see "SC," p. 205, and Kadushin, *The American Intellectual Elite* (Boston, 1974).

one of several informally defined "categories," it also seems likely that their membership is not homogeneous. They may in fact be serving different kinds of readers who use books for different purposes and thus judge them according to divergent criteria.

The editors themselves also occupy an interesting social position. It is not well known that the heart of the Book-of-the-Month Club's operation is located in midtown Manhattan. In fact, if they are familiar with the Club at all, most Americans place it somewhere in middle America and attribute its selections to a small group of judges. Although all distribution and membership correspondence originates in Mechanicsburg (near Harrisburg), Pennsylvania, and a group of six judges chooses the monthly main selection, the editorial process is actually initiated, overseen, and carried out by a group of twenty or so individuals who live in and around New York City. Those "editors" are responsible for reading most of the five thousand yearly submissions, for writing the readers' reports that are generated for *every* book the Club receives, and for the selection of alternates offered to the membership as supplements to the actual book-of-the-month. Like most people who work in the publishing industry, they are well educated, overwhelmingly white, and solidly middle class. Most are former English or history majors trained in the close reading of texts. In fact, the two editors in charge of the editorial operation at the time this research was conducted had completed substantial graduate work in literature. Many of their colleagues are published authors themselves. Lunching regularly with friends and professional acquaintances from within the publishing industry, the BOMC editors are well integrated into what Coser, Kadushin, and Powell have called the "culture of publishing."[11]

For the most part, Book-of-the-Month Club editors read typescripts or bound galleys six to nine months before they are published as books. Those editors, therefore, are among the first readers from outside the publishing house to encounter a book, to react to it formally, and to judge both its quality and its commercial possibilities. Indeed they see books many months before even the most prominent reviewers. In most cases, they have only a page or two of introductory material from a subsidiary rights director or the memory of a ten-minute phone call to orient their reading.[12] With little more to go on than a paragraph or two

11. See Coser, Kadushin, and Powell, *Books,* esp. chap. 3, "Networks, Connections, and Circles," pp. 70–93.

12. It is the subsidiary rights director at a publishing house who is responsible for getting a manuscript to the Book-of-the-Month Club, for writing the introductory material, for alerting the individual editors to the impending arrival of the manuscript, and for the negotiation of the contract. According to Coser, Kadushin, and Powell, they are increasingly the key people in trade publishing. For an extremely negative view of the power of the subsidiary rights departments in contemporary publishing, see Thomas Whiteside, *The Blockbuster Complex: Conglomerates, Show Business, and Book Publishing* (Middletown, Conn., 1981).

of description and a few sketchy plans for future publicity, they must "place" the book, evaluate it, and decide whether they can convey their enthusiasm to a potential reader in a description that is routinely two hundred to three hundred, and no more than one thousand, words long.[13] Their reading is governed finally not only by their own preferences and training but by the fact that the Club is a business designed to sell books to others. They are always trying to read as they believe their members do.

A study of the editorial selection process at the Book-of-the-Month Club, therefore, should allow us to witness the complex ideological calculations and negotiations of a particular fraction of the American middle class as it attempts to define itself with respect to the already established taste hierarchy while simultaneously trying to function commercially as the servant of less culturally oriented sections of that class. By tracing the well-documented editorial deliberations of the only group that reads virtually all of the adult trade hardcover books published in contemporary America, we should be able to learn something about the taste and underlying ideological assumptions of those key individuals who are controlling the gate, deciding not only what cultural creations will be formally produced but also which among those will be distributed in "an urgent or attractive way."[14] The BOMC editors are, after all, much like the publishers, editors, and agents of the Professional-Managerial class discussed by Ohmann who are responsible for deciding on the actual content of our literary culture ("SC," pp. 209–10). It is important to note as well that like the publishers and editors they resemble, the BOMC editors are cultural workers. They possess a substantial measure of what Bourdieu has called "cultural capital," and they exercise a certain amount of power in contemporary society by helping to determine what will count as culture for others.[15] Given the relatively minor role of publishing in the larger economy and the pay scale in the industry, it also seems likely that they command somewhat less economic capital. Not unlike the academics who trained them and the literary critics whose job their own resembles, the BOMC editors' social position is a function of their

13. These are the approximate word limits for the descriptive material for alternate and main selections in the *Book-of-the-Month Club News*. The magazine is an interesting cross between a merchandise catalog and a literary review.

14. Ohmann uses this phrase to describe the process by which agents, editors, and reviewers together decide which books will receive special production and critical attention ("SC," p. 202). See also his discussion of publishing officials as gatekeepers ("SC," pp. 202–12).

15. What this means in Bourdieu's universe is that they have acquired extensive familiarity with the legitimate cultural tradition through the process of familial and academic education. There is danger, of course, in an incautious mapping of Bourdieu's findings onto an American context. My goal here is not to superimpose his entire system on American social and cultural reality but to show how suggestive his approach can be in beginning to explore the social determinants of aesthetic judgments which have heretofore been dismissed as insufficiently rigorous, lacking high seriousness, and middlebrow.

economic situation, but it is also a function of their capacity and authority to discriminate and to identify artistic and cultural excellence.

At the same time, because the membership of the Club is broader, more diverse and dispersed than they are, the editors control or rein in their own preferences and attempt to read as they believe their "general" readers do. When asked whether they consider their own taste representative of their readers' taste, nearly all the editors replied that only a small segment of the membership shares their preferences. Their assumption results regularly in a winnowing process based on their perception of the nature of a "popular," though again middle-class, taste. As a consequence they are always attending to what individuals outside the cultural industry actually do with books. They have their own theories about why people buy cookbooks and diet books, for instance, and they regularly turn down books of fiction and history which they themselves appreciated but felt would be uninteresting to their membership. Therefore, their deliberations should also reveal much about variations, rifts, and even contradictions within middle-class taste and the various ideologies of which it is a product. The editors' readers' reports and decisions may permit us finally to begin to trace the interactions among the different fractions of what Bourdieu calls the dominant class: among those who already possess cultural capital, those who lack confidence about their continuing mastery of it and therefore desire a continuing connection to some cultural establishment, and those willing to mediate between the two by assisting the culturally insecure to find new examples of the high tradition. The editors' deliberations should be particularly interesting, finally, because the commercial interests of the Club militate against their sharing in the common assumptions of the cultural elite with whom they identify, the assumption that appreciation and understanding of art and cultural tradition can come *only* with long acquaintance and careful education, and the further assumption that once one has acquired such a capacity, one will not need the advisory service of expert others.

The New York editorial office of the Book-of-the-Month Club employs about 135 people. The warehouse, distribution, and membership operation in Mechanicsburg (or Camp Hill, as it was referred to in the past) provides work for another six hundred. Until recently, connections between the two units were conducted fairly informally. As a consequence, editors rarely gauged their selections formally to sales statistics. The Club functioned editorially without market research largely as a consequence of founder Harry Scherman's original decision to keep the marketing operation of the Club separate from the process of book selection. Although Scherman and his managers knew a great deal about the Club audience because they worked closely with George Gallup as early as the 1930s, they did not permit the editorial judges to see this data because Scherman did not believe it could predict future critical or market success and because he wanted to demonstrate that the process of selection was unbiased. As a legacy of this decision, the Club's past editorial operations have been based on surprisingly little hard data. Most of the information that was amassed was used only to structure new membership drives and to design initial-offer advertising. Although the situation is changing rapidly at the moment, the editorial decisions upon which the present study are based were still grounded predominantly in hunch, intuition, and luck.[16] This is not to say that the editors knew little about their audience, only that the knowledge they had of it was not in quantifiable form but existed as the tacit, relatively unconscious product of long personal experience.

To date, my interviews with editors and my systematic review of the Club's readers' reports for the years 1984, 1985, and 1986 suggest that while commercial concerns frequently dictate Club choices, especially main selections, many alternate selections are made simply because individual editors like particular books and believe that they should be brought to the attention of other readers even if that group potentially numbers no more than two or three thousand. As a consequence, the Club often seems to function as a small bookstore with an idiosyncratic backlist designed to appeal to many different readers rather than as a homogenizing, mass-market distribution operation pitched always and only to the lowest common denominator.[17]One of the justifications editors give for this sort of operation is identical to that cited by Al Silverman, the Club's chairman, in a mission statement written for all company

16. The Book-of-the-Month Club was a family-owned business until 1977 when it was sold to Time, Incorporated by Axel Rosin, the son-in-law of company founder Harry Scherman. Time, Inc. did little with the Club until last year when major changes were instituted. Although the new president, Lawrence Crutcher, has done little to affect the day-to-day editorial operation, he has recently overseen the institution of a sophisticated market research program under a new marketing manager, called for new product initiatives, and instituted major cost-cutting activities. Since all of this is clearly designed to increase the profits of the Club, it is possible that the nature of the editorial operation may be changed at some point. This remains to be seen, however. Because the readers' reports I have read in preparation for this paper were written before the results of the first market surveys began to come in, the aesthetic judgments and decisions discussed here were based largely on assumptions about the Club's membership. I know from informal conversations with the editors that many of their assumptions were borne out by the research, although they were surprised by a few of the demographic findings. Their membership seems to be younger than they had suspected, for instance, and even more conversant with "book culture" than they had supposed.

17. At one point, the Club made an effort to capitalize on this feature of its operation and referred to itself as "America's Bookstore." In elaborating on this view of the Club, former editor-in-chief Nancy Evans (she left the Club in January 1987 to become president and publisher of Doubleday, Inc.'s trade division) has said in an interview with William Zinsser, "Our strength is that there is no book that we stock in our store that we have not read. There is no book in our store that we can't say, 'Read this book. We put it in our store because one of us here, or two of us here, or three of us, think that it's the best book of its kind, or that it's a special book that's worth your time'" (typescript of an interview between Nancy Evans and William Zinsser, 2 Aug. 1985, p. 2; quoted with their permission).

employees. Recounting that he had been asked by someone why a book that had sold poorly had been offered as a selection, he explained, "I told him that we took it because it was a wonderful book, that we knew it probably wouldn't sell much but that it was one of those silent, long-term investments that might pay off in member satisfaction for a segment of our audience." He continued, "Every year we need our Ludlums, our le Carrés, our Kings, and our sure-fire non-fiction books. But we also need the kind of books that are not sure bestsellers, and not faddish, but that delight our audience, and surprise them, a book that members buy not just to read, but also to keep."[18] Silverman's statement implicitly acknowledges the values grounding the taste hierarchy and characteristically identifies the Club as an institution with the search for enduring excellence. With equal frequency, however, one also hears editors justify selections by noting that people have different tastes and that those tastes ought to be satisfied without making judgments about them.

One of the most striking things about the Book-of-the-Month Club, in fact, as a *social* organization, is its effort to create and maintain a nonhierarchical, nonelitist atmosphere even as it identifies itself as a cultural institution with the values associated with high culture. Indeed I think it is this atmosphere, as it is embodied in regular editorial procedures, which is largely responsible for the catholic character of the Club's offerings despite its recurring nods to cultural authority. In fact, it is a remarkably collegial organization where editors and management work hard to value each other's contributions equally. This collegiality is realized most visibly in the company's tendency to promote from within. It is not uncommon for a copywriter at the Book-of-the-Month Club to move up to an editorial chair. Indeed, Joe Savago, who was executive editor at the time this research was conducted, had begun working for the Club only twelve years previously, first as an outside reader and then as a copy editor for the *BOMC News.* In 1986, Savago worked more closely with editor-in-chief Nancy Evans than almost anyone in the Club and was promoted at her departure in January 1987. Jill Sansone, a senior editor at the time these interviews were conducted, was responsible for assigning manuscripts both to outside and in-house readers. She started in the production department working on layout and copy for the *News;* Anne Close, another editor, first worked for the Club as an executive secretary.

The collegial nature of the Club's atmosphere is well known within the publishing industry and prized by those who work there. Indeed I have been struck by the intensity with which its editors discuss their jobs. Every editor I have spoken with sees that job as one of reading. "What could be better," they all ask rhetorically, "than to be paid to read books?" Furthermore, every editor seems to feel supported and trusted both by

18. Al Silverman, "The Book-of-the-Month Club—What We Stand For: A Message from the Chief Executive Officer," p. 6; quoted with the permission of Mr. Silverman.

his or her colleagues and by the Club's top management. All are convinced that if they argue vociferously for a book, they will be listened to and, for the most part, heeded. Nothing I have seen to date contradicts that view or the following picture of the Club drawn by Evans in an interview with executive editor William Zinsser, who was eliciting her opinions for the anniversary history of the Club. Evans observed that "it's quite extraordinary to have this group of people who truly love books." She continued, "There's not a soul here who doesn't. We are all honest-to-God readers. Of couse we have a million other things to do all day, but at bottom this is an intense group of book lovers. Sure we have to make money, and sure we make marketing decisions, but if there's passion for a book, that passion can prevail here, and if we can just get that passion through the pages of the *News* we get it back in kind."[19] Evans' view of the company as a community of book lovers is voiced independently by everyone involved in the actual editorial operation. They also repeat her emphasis on the importance of individual judgment. As Eve Tulipan, another senior editor remarked, the spoken folk wisdom of the Club is "do what you like."

In fact, a hierarchy of taste has not developed within the Club in the sense that some editors' views or tastes are valued more than others. Such a potentially divisive structure has been avoided by a fairly elaborate though informal scheme of horizontal specialization. Each editor reads regularly in one or two fields and is regarded as the resident expert on previous publications, genre conventions and expectations, and standards of assessment within those particular categories. Distinctions are made by individuals *within* equivalent categories rather than among them or their champions. The need for internal social harmony, therefore, seems to foreclose any tendency toward a hierarchical ranking of the categories along a single scale of value.

This process of horizontal categorization dominates the Book-of-the-Month Club's editorial operation. From the moment a book first arrives in the manuscript room, it is treated as a particular example of any one of a number of loosely defined categories.[20] It is tacitly given its first label by Sansone or one of the other senior editors when they decide on the best readers for the book. Sansone makes the assignments on the basis of the publicity material the Club has received from the publisher, on past experience with a known author, on the reputation of the publishing house itself, and on her own broad knowledge of the

---

19. Typescript of interview between Evans and Zinsser, p. 5; quoted with permission.

20. It is apparently the case that the publishing houses do little preliminary screening of the material they send to the Book-of-the-Month Club. When asked, subsidiary rights directors indicate that they send ninety-eight to one hundred percent of the adult trade hardcover books they publish. This is not true, however, of university presses or more specialized publishing houses.

industry. Although she does not indicate in any formal way that a book is "military history," "self-help health," or "popular business management" when an editor receives a manuscript to read, the very fact that it has come to him or her already indicates that it is probably a particular kind of book and thus ought to be read in a certain way. In evaluating the assigned manuscript, every editor seems to judge that book primarily against other similar books published previously in the category. As Zinsser observed, the Club's "basic operating principle is that we should offer the best book in the field." His view was corroborated not only by Savago, who remarked that the editors are "dedicated to presenting a book as exactly what it is," but by virtually all of the Club's editorial procedures: readers' reports nearly always "place" a book in a certain category and frequently refer to the need to fill a particular categorical "slot"; the weekly list of books for Thursday morning editorial conferences notes in a sentence or two just what sort of book the manuscript is; and the copy for a book in the *News* also prominently features a statement about the book's genre.

No one currently at the Club can recall a moment when this categorization process was instituted. Indeed it seems likely that it evolved over time in part out of material necessity. As Savago explained, books are nearly always "blind purchases" in the sense that buyers know next to nothing about the book and therefore cannot predict how it will satisfy them. Since the Book-of-the-Month Club is clearly in the business of selling books to readers who presumably come to it with already defined tastes and "needs," it must find some way to indicate to its members that they are in fact likely to enjoy a certain title—hence the need for a "handle" that will position the book for its members. The Club must manage this categorization process, furthermore, with enough accuracy to ensure that readers will not feel "burned" by the Club and thus refuse to return to it for assistance. The practice of nonhierarchical categorization, then, is also the product of the commercial desire to satisfy as many preexisting tastes as possible.

A relatively small number of operative categories dominates readers' reports, informal discussion, and the *BOMC News*. Among them are popular history, which seems to include the subfields of military history, Civil War history, and World War II history; popular biography; self-help health; popular business management; popular science; fitness; cookbooks and crafts; reference books; classic English mysteries; crime fiction and thrillers; and the final, amorphous category of general fiction, which is informally subdivided into the commercial and the serious. It is especially important to note that this last division, despite the name, is treated editorially as only one more genre or category that must be covered rather than as the apogee toward which all else aspires. The list is a varied one and it points, I think, to different uses of books and different ways of reading. Although I cannot be sure of this until I interview actual Club members, it seems entirely plausible that these categories have evolved because they roughly describe discrete ways of reading and distinct functions for a varied assortment of books. If true, the categories would function as Fredric Jameson claims literary genres do; in *The Political Unconscious* he observes that "genres are essentially literary *institutions,* or social contracts between a writer and a specific public, whose function is to specify the proper use of a particular cultural artifact."[21] Categorical placement within the *BOMC News,* then, may not only serve to identify books for readers but may tell them *how* to read them as well.

Eventually I hope to explore just how the social contract between writers and readers varies across these categories. What, for instance, are the proper uses of the cultural artifacts, biography or popular history, and how are they different from the Club reader's use of serious fiction? Is a Book-of-the-Month Club member's or editor's understanding of the proper use of serious fiction the same as the understanding embodied in academic exercises in literary criticism? If all Club categories prescribe uses that are related to each other in some fundamental way, which is yet different from the use made of literature by intellectuals with the highest cultural authority, will an understanding of those uses tell us something more about the variations in the content of middle-class taste in contemporary America or the functions of literacy outside the academy? For that matter, will it help us to better refine our understanding of middle-class ideology by specifying more clearly how actual subjects define and experience the contemporary world? As a way of initiating such an inquiry, I would like to concentrate for the rest of this paper on the editorial decisions surrounding the selection of what is usually called serious fiction at the Book-of-the-Month Club in order to explain how its editors define the category and what they think its functions ought to be.

The Book-of-the-Month Club has never formalized its definition of serious fiction, its characterization of what it offers within the category, or its criteria for selection. Outside readers do not receive directions about how to make judgments nor are Club editors ever formally instructed by a superior as to what exactly makes a manuscript Club material. While some editors use the term "serious" frequently, others are uncomfortable with it because it connotes something that is "boring." Indeed in reports on serious fiction titles, one regularly encounters a certain hostility toward the academy and the institutionalized teaching of literature which the editors seem to believe transforms fascinating books into dry exercises in analysis. Thus, although they use the term because it is convenient, the editors are careful to insist that serious literature can still be a pleasure

21. Fredric Jameson, *The Political Unconscious: Narrative as a Socially Symbolic Act* (Ithaca, N.Y., 1981), p. 106.

to read. "Serious" should not be synonymous with "dour" in their view or, for that matter, with the gratuitously obscure. The conflict we saw earlier between the public rhetoric of the Club, which emphasizes cultural authority and artistic excellence, and its more catholic editorial operations, which concede the diversity of books for both social and commercial reasons, is played out here as an ambivalence about the nature of serious fiction. On the one hand, the editors seem to share the assumption of the high-culture aesthetic that fiction should be technically complex and self-consciously *about* significant issues. On the other, they demand that such fiction be pleasurable to read, a stipulation that differs little from that made regularly by readers of best-sellers and genre fiction who desire always to be entertained.

In fact, when asked to discuss the category of serious fiction, Book-of-the-Month Club editors begin by opposing it to what it is not. They observe first that what they are trying to eliminate is "trash" or "junk" and proceed to the claim that they are striving to find "intelligent" novels that will "stretch" their readers. Pressed further to elaborate on the distinction, the editors almost always settle on the issue of language and say that trash is sloppily written. Indeed, the single most common complaint in readers' reports which eventually judge a work of fiction to be "trash" involves the charge of linguistic excess. Book-of-the-Month Club editors regularly exclude books whose writing they characterize as self-consciously descriptive, effusive, sentimental, or melodramatic. What they dismiss most frequently, of course, are romance novels and some historical fiction, in large part because their prose is overly "lush," a word used regularly to disparage such writing.

Furthermore, Book-of-the Month Club editors regularly praise the writing in the serious fiction they consider and accept. For them, writing is good if it is characterized by economy, condensation, and precision. In praising Martin Cruz Smith's recent novel, *Stallion Gate*, for instance, Savago characterized Smith's prose as "clean," "supple," and "without cliché." Later he described elements of the book as "tight," "flawless," and "brilliantly, seamlessly melded." It would seem then that the categorical distinction between the worst of the commercial, which is to say "trash" in Club parlance, and the "serious" is grounded first on the binary opposition lush/spare. This would seem, furthermore, a simple instance of the distinction Bourdieu has elaborated on so extensively, the distinction between a popular aesthetic celebrating sensibility and sensation and a bourgeois aesthetic (synonymous in his view with the high-culture aesthetic) recommending reflection and understanding.[22] As Bourdieu notes, "'Pure' taste and the aesthetics which provides its theory are founded on a refusal of 'impure' taste and of *aisthesis* (sensation), the simple, primitive form of pleasure reduced to a pleasure of the senses" (*D*, p.

22. See *D*, esp. pp. 30–50.

486). In making this initial distinction between serious fiction and trash, the BOMC editors again seem to be locating themselves along the same hierarchical continuum employed by literary critics and academics and to be associating themselves, in opposition to the taste of the masses, with the higher, more culturally respectable pole. A function, perhaps, of their training, this move also establishes their cultural authority and asserts their right to select books for others.

Having said that, however, it is important to insist again that neither the distinctions nor the categories are that simple at the Book-of-the-Month Club. The Club prominently features entertainment and genre fiction and sells both by highlighting the visceral pleasures they produce. It is true that this is done for commercial reasons and that in making such selections the editors still take care to choose the "best" books they can find. They admit, even, to a search for "class trash." Yet it is equally important to note that the editors are also genuinely uncomfortable with arraying the categories along a simple hierarchy and prefer to view them as different sorts of books for different purposes. Silverman articulated this other component of the Club view in his mission statement when he cautioned that the "serious book reader is not one who reads *serious* books only—Proust, Rilke, Dostoevsky. A serious book reader is one who buys loads of books a year, most to be educated and entertained, but sometimes to be uplifted."[23] Although the Club *is* more likely to offer a commercial book as the monthly main selection, it also regularly features at least one serious fiction title as a new featured alternate. In any given month, of the roughly twenty to thirty fiction titles listed in the 250-book catalog, about eight to eighteen might be considered serious fiction.

The BOMC editors believe strongly that some books can simultaneously excite the senses and stand up to aesthetic contemplation and evaluation. Savago's review of *Stallion Gate* suggests as much in a conclusion which itself challenges the familiar categorical opposition that is the object of Bourdieu's analysis. I would like to quote Savago at some length, for he demonstrates here the limits of aesthetic distancing in the BOMC version of the high-culture aesthetic:

> Line for line this is the best *writing* I've read in years—Cruz Smith can do anything he wants, from dialogue to nature writing, humor to menace, in a prose that's clean and supple and contains not one single (I was waiting for one) cliché. He writes as an insider, an expert, on whatever subject's at hand—and there are many: the science and the nuts-and-bolts of the bomb and its assembly; the art and psychology of boxing; Indian mores and the New Mexican landscape; jazz music, jazz piano playing and improvisation; the war in the Pacific. The details, everywhere, seem not lifted from some hastily done "research" but to spring from vivid memory,

23. Silverman, "The Book-of-the-Month Club—What We Stand For," p. 4.

intimate experience. The plotting and the sheer craftsmanship of the scenes, of the movement back and forth in time, is tight and flawless. This is the sort of book you'd be a fool to call commercial as opposed to literary, or vice versa. It is simply a wonderful book, period, in which story, character, prose and craft are all brilliant and brilliantly, seamlessly melded. Terrific.

In Savago's mind, carefully crafted prose could be harnessed to larger unities which themselves produce different kinds of pleasure. Serious fiction or the literary, then, was not for him necessarily synonymous with the poetic exploration of the limitations and possibilities of language itself, that which Jameson has labeled the molecular project of modernism and which Savago himself termed "autistic."[24] While Savago appreciated deftly woven sentences and intelligent metaphors, his reports also always focused on a few of the abstract molar unities (constructions produced by the reader to create plot, personality, coherent character, and so on) cited by Jameson which have traditionally been used to recontain the molecular. In fact, his reports were dominated by a concern for "the continuity of personal identity, the organizing unity of the . . . personality," and the role the two play in the creation of a significant narrative.[25]

Savago's opinions are shared widely at the Club. One of the most explicit statements I have yet seen by a Book-of-the-Month Club official about the question of aesthetics was made by Lucy Rosenthal, a former judge and senior editor in an interview with the *Missouri Review* on literary culture in contemporary America. Discussing both her own work as a novelist and the standards she employed at the Club, she discriminated between different kinds of writing in a way that seems to approximate the working definition of "the serious" used by most of the other editors. In response to the interviewer's question about whom she writes for, Rosenthal replied, "I want my writing to be accessible. I want people not to be bored. So I wrote the kind of book that would not bore me." She continued, "I'm not a snob. I don't think I write for an audience directly. I write to tell a story."[26] Storytelling, evidently, at least in Rosenthal's view, is a democratic art that must be defended because some people— "snobs" in her view—do not value it. Comments she has made elsewhere provide some insight as to what she may believe they value in its place. In discussing the writer Norma Klein, in a review of *Give Me One Good Reason,* Rosenthal observed that " 'Klein's novel . . . is more lifelike than literary, a storyteller's book, not a poet's, the work of a writer engaged

24. See Jameson, "Towards a Libidinal Economy of Three Modern Painters," *Social Text* 1 (Winter 1979): 193–94, and *Fables of Aggression: Wyndham Lewis, the Modernist as Fascist* (Berkeley and Los Angeles, 1979), pp. 7–10.

25. Jameson, *Fables of Aggression,* p. 8.

26. Catherine Parke, "An Interview with Lucy Rosenthal," *Missouri Review* 8 (1984): 164–65.

more with life and its possibilities than with language, and its resources for language's own sake.' "[27] While Rosenthal would not dismiss all poetry, it does appear that, like Savago, she is not interested solely in the refined, distanced contemplation of the aesthetic signifier but is searching for a way to attend both to the particularities of individual words *and* to the larger, more utilitarian work they can do in telling a story about coherently formed, interesting individuals.

The typical form of a Club reader's report on fiction suggests that the other editors are similarly engaged. Neither an exercise in textual exegesis nor one in aesthetic connoisseurship, these reports are first and foremost records of the temporal *experience* of encountering characters and only secondarily critical evaluations of a book's mastery of its materials. Although many reports begin with a sentence or two placing the author or the book itself in terms of genre, the first three-quarters of most of them are devoted to detailed descriptions of the characters, their histories, and their activities in the fiction. For most BOMC editors, the crucial molar unity seems to be the coherent, unified personality. They approach the books they read as stories about people. It is only after the editor has attempted to give an account of what it's like to read through a piece of fiction, to spend time with the characters involved, that he or she assesses its consequence or its literary skill. The criteria of significance and craft are always applied, but if a writer does not also produce an encounter with a recognizable and interesting individual of one sort or another, his or her book will likely be rejected by the Club.

When reading with their members in mind, then, the editors of the Book-of-the-Month Club are not seeking the pleasures produced by a historically informed and technically sophisticated appreciation of language-play itself. Although they themselves are capable of such readings and they often display fine passages for their colleagues or note literary lineages and genealogies, their reports are dominated by a preoccupation with what language brings into being. Listen, here, to the distinctions drawn by Savago in his report on the well-reviewed 1983 novel by Stephen Wright, *Meditations in Green: A Novel of Vietnam.*

> Yes, this is easily the best writing I've read in many months, the book is a kind of masterpiece and the author a kind of genius, but no, it's probably not for us. What? Is the BOMC member beneath Good Writing? No, not per se, of course. Good Writing in the service of a fairly conventional, generic effort is certainly *not* wasted on your average literate reader. John le Carré sells almost as well as [X] and mostly, I suspect, to a class of reader which appreciates the difference—and le Carré is a primo BOMC author. But *Meditations in Green* is an essentially formless series of vignettes and

27. Ibid., p. 168.

scenes and surrealities and ironies with a large and shifting cast of occasional characters, not a straightforward story-novel with a plot. It doesn't try to "go anywhere," it just *goes,* brilliantly.[28]

Because Wright's "novel" lacked the conventional generic structure, Savago was not at all sure it could be sold to the Club's members. His reservations were echoed by another reader who judged the book's innovations "failures." "The author's experiments with form and style do not pay off," the reader wrote. Wright "has tried to create a virtuosically controlled chaos, but what results is merely chaos. Plainly, this novel is a mess. The first 100 pages or so are so difficult and obscure that I gave up reading about a dozen times. The lack of plot makes for a terrible predictability and repetition." "With a very strong editor and couple of rewrites," this reader concluded, "we would probably have a good novel here. As it stands, few will get through it."

Within the category of "serious fiction," it seems, the Book-of-the-Month Club is looking for works that are carefully written but which manage to combine an aesthetic, formalist focus with the referential act of designation. They are not interested in those books that foreground their interest in language to such an extent that they are *about* language, its possibilities and constraints. Having said, however, that it is personality, character, and story that such language must bring into being, I also want to add that Club editors are additionally preoccupied with the search for a "new voice" and have frequently selected books that do not foreground character and plot in the traditional nineteenth-century way. Although this may at first sound like the reassertion of the value of style, the BOMC editors do not necessarily equate voice with a personal, idiosyncratic language. For them, the voice must never be disembodied. Their particular demand that the literary voice issue from a recognizable personality and therefore from an identifiable place provides the key, I think, to the meaning of the molar unities in the BOMC aesthetic and ultimately to the function or use of the category of serious fiction, at least as the editors conceive it within the parameters prescribed by the commercial goals of the Club.

Although the term formally refers to a publicity category of the Quality Paperback Book Club, "new voice" is also used as a general critical term by all the editors. When I asked Savago about the term, he explained that when *he* read, he was not so much interested in characters *in* the story as he was in listening to the author speak. His interest in the voice, however, was neither purely aural nor stylistic for he added that what he listened for was "intelligence." As he said, "I hear them as smart or

28. The X is used here to replace the name of a popular thriller writer. Because the Club must continue to work with living writers, I have offered to remove names of people who might be offended by the Club's internal editorial commentary.

not-smart, ardent or not-ardent persons, basically giving me the inside of their heads, via a fiction." He continued, "What I come away with from a book is not a memory of the characters . . . but a sense of who the author is and whether the author is someone I would like to get to know . . . by reading other books of theirs." Of Don DeLillo, whom he admired greatly and championed successfully at the Club, he said, "I want to know what DeLillo has to say every two years about the world we live in now because I believe he is really on top of it." "And I want to know what Kundera has to say about anything," he added.

Indeed of Milan Kundera's *Unbearable Lightness of Being* (1984), Savago wrote in his report that it was "probably the most intelligent novel I've read in years." He added immediately, ". . . which is to say that it's not much of a novel—conventionally speaking—at all." Savago's report went on in the following fashion:

> The traditional imperative of the novel—to move, dammit; to absorb (which is to say, drown) the reader in the *motion* of other people's lives has never left much room for ideas. Most novels have none at all—no fresh or distinctive ones, in any case; others seem founded upon ideas, but ideas so embedded that we must critically extract them via such formulations as "well, what Dickens is *saying* here is that. . . . " Kundera . . . has broken free of this injunction against discursive intelligence, authorial intrusion.

Savago went on to argue in the report that the essential value of Kundera's book rested on his own authorial meditations about issues raised by the actions of characters in the fiction. He claimed further that "the quantity and quality of thought which Kundera has given to these and dozens of other questions would be compromised if he put a slick, compressed version of this thought into some character's mouth, or created a character here and there to 'embody' this or that insight." Indeed it was the very brilliance of Kundera's perceptions that convinced Savago that the Club ought to consider the novel. For him, voice was not an idiosyncratic mode of speech, an idiolect, as it were, but rather a linguistic embodiment of a distinctive, significant point of view on familiar problems and an iden-tifiable world.

Given Savago's reservations about Kundera's book and the additional fact that most Club fiction, even of the "serious" sort, does indeed locate the coherence of personality in its characters, it may be surprising to note that both the Wright and Kundera novels, as well as titles by DeLillo (*White Noise*, 1985), Thomas Pynchon (*Gravity's Rainbow*, 1973), Russell Banks (*Continental Drift*, 1985), and E. L. Doctorow (*World's Fair*, 1985) have all been offered as Club alternates. Although it is impossible to reconstruct the editorial debate that led to selection in each case, Savago's final observations with respect to *The Unbearable Lightness of Being* provide a suggestive clue. He ended his report with the following summary:

And so this novel moves with consummate grace, I think, between the intensely concrete, lyrical evocative novelistic moment in its characters' lives and the discursive analysis of what is at stake, how the characters came to be here, what they are seeking and what they, in fact, find. You can't read it fast, you can't get swept away by it, lost in it, but you can be shocked continually by all that's unexamined in your own life, turn to your own life, and do something about it, with Kundera's intellectual rigor and clarity as a model.

In these remarks, Savago seems to be focusing on the "aptness" of Kundera's ruminations, on their relevance to the lives of contemporary readers. The book will be useful, he implies, to those people searching for suggestions, models, and directions about "how to live." If an unconventional novel can still be read as "equipment for living," in Kenneth Burke's phrase, that quality can overcome the problems posed by a failure to fulfill the more common expectation that fiction must be about recognizable characters with recognizable problems.[29] Thus a book can experiment with novelistic form, and it can even foreground a unique and unusual way of using language. But if that language cannot be construed by a reader as the speech of a recognizable personality with something to say about the world he or she shares with the reader, the book will likely be judged by the BOMC editors as too distant, too boring. Kundera and DeLillo could be "used" because, as Savago remarked in an interview, they "are like the world, your world, as seen by DeLillo and Kundera." Perspective really is the right word here. What such writers create is a peculiarly inflected, uniquely skewed perspective on a *common* world. They do not, as in the case of Savago's autistic writers, "bring a world into being *sui generis*."

In fact, when one looks at the various titles in the category of "serious fiction" that did make their way onto the Book-of-the-Month Club lists for 1985 and 1986 and correlates them with the relevant readers' reports, it becomes clear that most of the books were chosen because their fine prose produced either an affecting and absorbing monologue or a more traditional narrative about recognizable characters. But even the traditional narratives were always treated as recitations that bore the marks of their

29. Kenneth Burke, "Literature as Equipment for Living," *The Philosophy of Literary Form: Studies in Symbolic Action,* 3d ed. (Berkeley and Los Angeles, 1973), pp. 293–304. I would like to thank Peter Rabinowitz for directing my attention to this essay. My findings here are remarkably similar to those of Elizabeth Long who has been working on middle-class women's reading groups. She first reported these findings in her paper, "Literary Judgment and Women's Reading Groups," presented at the 1985 meeting of the American Studies Association, where I first reported these findings about the Book-of-the-Month Club. The congruence of our findings suggests that the patterns of reading we have detected in our separate data are widespread throughout certain segments of the middle-class reading population.

enunciation by an identifiable and critical intelligence speaking always to the reader about the world held in common. Thus the editors demanded always that both monologues and more traditional narratives permit readers to map the insights gained from the experience of reading onto the terrain of their own lives. The BOMC editors seem to believe, finally, that their readers purchase serious fiction because they value verbal facility but also, and perhaps more important, because they are seeking a model for contemporary living and even practical advice about appropriate behavior in a changing world.

It is interesting to note in this context that although BOMC readers' reports about commercial fiction also focus on character, virtually no attention is paid to the larger significance of the characters' fate or to the intelligence of the individual controlling their action. Although it will require more sustained research to be sure, it now appears to me that what matters in commercial fiction is not primarily the congruence between fiction and the "real" but the capacity to catch the reader up in a story that seems to propel itself forward with force. The elementary pleasures of plot are the test of achievement here and, apparently, the more accomplished the concealment of the fact that the story has been conceived and ordered by an author, the more intense the necessary experience of transport provided for the reader.

If the editors are right about "serious fiction," it may well be the case that books in this category function for Club members in a way similar to the many self-help manuals, advice books, and reference volumes that make up the majority of the Club's alternate list. Indeed literacy may still serve primarily as a tool or a technology for such people, which is to say, a device for doing something, for bringing about change, for accomplishing some purpose. If true, it is understandable why fiction would be valuable to the extent that it is readily applicable to one's own life, problems, and concerns. No less relevant to daily life than self-consciously didactic manuals, the artfulness of fiction is subordinated in this evaluative system to its pragmatic possibilities for application.

I think it important to highlight this preoccupation with relevance and the functionality of fiction because it is almost too easy to interpret the editors' preoccupation with character and "the illusion of the coherent self" as evidence of a simple, conservative, middle-class humanism.[30] In such a reading, the BOMC's interest in the individual voice and coherent character might be read as the reactionary refusal of the middle class to encounter the social world it has made, which is to say, a discontinuous universe produced by advanced commodification. The BOMC aesthetic would then be seen as the product of an earlier stage in the development

30. On this point, see Long's argument in "Women, Reading, and Cultural Authority: Some Implications of the Audience Perspective in Cultural Studies," *American Quarterly* 38 (Fall 1986): 610.

of a unified ideology, a stage associated above all with a confident, nine-teenth-century individualism. But recent Club selections such as *White Noise, The Unbearable Lightness of Being, Continental Drift,* and Margaret Atwood's *Handmaid's Tale* give pause about the validity of such an inter-pretation since each in its own way self-consciously explores the nature of the postmodern universe and the fragmentation of the unified subject. Even if these selections are not enough to suggest that the ideology grounding the Club's decisions is multiply constructed of historical survivals, emerging positions, and even contradictory views, then I think the particular way books are *made* to be of use should.[31]

It is clear that in their wish to distinguish their books from those they consider "trash," the BOMC editors are engaging in the familiar move of disparaging the pleasures of the mass, the facile, and the shallow. And yet their demand that fiction be useful is most often articulated through the more specific requirement that if a book does not provide a character or a voice with whom the reader can identify completely, it must at least include one who is admirable enough to function as the moral center of the story. This helps to explain a characteristic feature of readers' reports on rejected novels: their insistent focus on the moral and ethical failings of characters in the fictions. In many cases where books are otherwise acceptable, the editors reject them because the char-acters are morally reprehensible and without redeeming virtue; the preeminent failure of such books is their failure to engage the reader's *sympathy.*

The reading strategies employed by the editors seem to be based in the end on a certain bedrock assumption about the congruence of art and life, the very same assumption Bourdieu identifies as the foundation of the popular aesthetic (see *D,* pp. 4–7 and 32–34). As he says of the aesthetic judgments made by working-class individuals in France, "every-thing takes place as if the 'popular aesthetic' were based on the affirmation of continuity between art and life, which implies the subordination of form to function, or, one might say, on a refusal of the refusal which is the starting point of the high aesthetic, i.e., the clear-cut separation of ordinary dispositions from the specifically aesthetic disposition." Bourdieu notes further that such judgments are produced by an ethos rather than an aesthetic since contemplation is neither distanced nor disinterested but produced by ethical and moral norms that perform a systematic reduction of the things of art to things of life. Whereas Bourdieu's bourgeois aesthetic is predicated on an "elective distance from the necessities of

---

31. My own understanding of the conflicted nature of ideology has been influenced by the work of Raymond Williams and Stuart Hall. See especially Williams, *Marxism and Literature* (Oxford, 1977) and *The Sociology of Culture* (New York, 1982). For a clear formulation of Hall's argument, see "Notes on Deconstructing 'the Popular,' " in *People's History and Socialist Theory,* ed. Raphael Samuel (London, 1981), pp. 227–40.

the natural and social world," the popular aesthetic springs from "a deep-rooted demand for participation" (*D*, p. 32).

Indeed what the Book-of-the-Month Club editors demand most of writers they are to honor as serious is an ability to make them *care*. A stance that might be labeled by others as one of intellectual rigor or critical distance is therefore experienced by them as one characterized only by "coldness." They complain frequently about novels that view their characters too coolly, from too much distance, or without compassion.[32] So while it seems clear that in their distaste for the lushness of trash the editors are asserting the distinctiveness of a high-culture aesthetic based on the rational and the refined, they are also refusing that refusal of the world which has permitted the isolation and enshrinement of the aesthetic as something valuable in and for itself. The artistic is valuable to them only insofar as it does not declare its utter separation from the world. It must first draw the reader *into* its world by appearing to erase the boundaries between the book and external reality. Having thus assured communion and participation, it then must provide the occasion for moral and ethical judgments which can be turned reflexively upon the reader and later used as guidelines for behavior. The value of "serious fiction," in fact, is a function of its capacity to be used as a map which is, despite its status as a representation, a tool for enabling its reader to move about more effectively in the world to which it refers.

My point, finally, is that this emphasis on functionality suggests that what we see at the Book-of-the-Month Club is not simply an earlier stage in the development of a single reified ideology but a complex and conflicted aesthetic system that shares some assumptions about the role of art with what has been called the high-culture aesthetic even while it preserves the demands and accompanying criteria associated with a more popular aesthetic. Whether the core conflict is simply the product of the editor's own ambiguous social position as a well-educated and trained cultural worker charged with serving commercially those with different, less trained taste is difficult to say at this point. In fact, I think that explanation is probably too mechanical. The editors' enthusiasm for the serious fiction they choose *because* it is so deeply involving seems too intense to be entirely calculated. Rather, I suspect that the aesthetic judgments made by the Club editors with respect to serious fiction are representative of an evaluative system that is their own and that works for them precisely because it is constructed of contradictory elements.

It is, first of all, an aesthetic system that in its bow to cultural authority and artistic excellence affirms the validity of the traditional hierarchy of taste. The editors' choices and their justifications for those choices regularly

32. In commenting, for instance, on the heroine of Reynolds Price's *Kate Vaiden* (1986), one editor observed that "she seemed cold and undisciplined in an uninteresting kind of way. Some people might find the book mesmerizing, but I found it only mildly absorbing."

underscore their identification with the keepers of the dominant cultural traditions of the West. This ought not to surprise, of course, since the editors themselves are middle-class individuals possessing much in common with those of the dominant class who define and maintain the value of high culture. In associating themselves with that tradition, therefore, they reflexively assert their right to choose books for others and exercise, even if inadvertently, their power to define what will count as culture for people outside the culture industry as well.

Yet the system's emphasis on the pleasures, even passion, generated by reading and on its capacity to instruct seems carefully calibrated to the interests of people caught up in the daily round of quotidian activities and responsibilities who have little time for leisurely intellectual contemplation or meditation on the fine points of technical achievements in the arts. Neither distanced from the immediate dilemmas of their own lives nor fully confident enough to approach them without respite or advice, the editors of the Book-of-the-Month Club seem to be engaged in a quest for a literature that can operate transitively as a set of strategies to help them and their members cope with the world that surrounds and holds them. They seem to experience that world as a place that still has some unnameable power over them, as a universe they do not fully control. Their persistent preoccupation with the values associated with the popular aesthetic of the dominated classes may be a token, finally, of their own ongoing sense of domination from outside, perhaps in this case by the very institutions and material constraints their own class is responsible for calling into being. Their aesthetic system therefore seems at once to reveal their power and to perpetuate it even as it gives us evidence that they do not understand themselves to be fully in control of that power, their world, or themselves. If this is true, then the particular dilemmas returned to repeatedly in the stories they are led to select may tell us much about the particular problems of middle-class life and thus something about the utopian longings it generates in some of its subjects. Exact specification of those dilemmas will have to await a systematic analysis of the fiction offered to its members by the Book-of-the-Month Club.

Cultural Production as Routine:
Some Thoughts on "America's Bookstore"

Walter W. Powell

Janice Radway adopts a "user's perspective" in her discriminating analysis of the Book-of-the-Month Club ("The Book-of-the-Month Club and the General Reader: On the Uses of 'Serious' Fiction," pp. 154–76). She is interested in the purposes that books serve for their audiences: how editors at the Book-of-the-Month Club read and assess manuscripts and to what extent book buyers find the written word applicable to their own lives, problems, and concerns. This approach enables us to see how tastes or a cultural tradition are put to use: how books are categorized and located, the functions they are intended to serve, and the role that book clubs play in contemporary culture. I have a good deal of sympathy for her line of inquiry; thus I will try to expand only briefly on the questions that she has posed. But I will also suggest a different focus and argue that an audience perspective deflects attention from an alternative way of understanding the activities of the Book-of-the-Month Club.

Radway's major contribution is to illuminate the process by which professional readers both evaluate and classify contemporary fiction. The fact that people distinguish among types of books, locating them categorically, is of course nothing new. But these categories are, as Radway shows, neither natural nor readily identifiable; they are socially constructed. The Book-of-the-Month Club does not operate with a single criterion of taste nor a simple hierarchy of values. The assessments by BOMC editors are self-conscious attempts (indeed, to judge by the quotations from readers' reports, especially those by Joe Savago, these are quite sophisticated efforts) to situate writers and their work within a cultural universe. This cataloging of styles and genres is not readily accessible to everyone, not even to all intelligent readers of serious fiction. " 'Supple' " writing that "'spring[s] from vivid memory, and intimate experience'" (pp. 166, 167–68) is not a category that will be quickly recognized by even an elite audience.

Radway illustrates that this process of "typifying" books in terms of whether they present characters as wholes or as disembodied entities, or with regard to what it is like to read a particular piece of fiction, enables the Book-of-the-Month Club to determine whether a piece of fiction serves as "'equipment for living'" (p. 172). In so doing, Radway not only offers insight into the selection process at the Book-of-the-Month Club, but she also suggests how certain serious writers and their themes are introduced into "middlebrow" culture. One comes away from Radway's discussion impressed with the energy and the discourse that characterizes the BOMC selection process. The book club does seem to be that rare bookstore where the employees have not only read all the books on the shelves but debated and argued about them as well.

This "community of book lovers" (p. 163) does not, however, appear to be immune to the general process of rationalization that has transformed many sectors of the book-publishing industry.[1] Radway notes that, subsequent to her interviews in 1986, a new concern arose at the Book-of-the-Month Club for market research, new product initiatives, and cost-savings (pp. 160–61). Throughout the book trade, the introduction of such policies has typically accompanied the decline of editorial autonomy (that is, an end to the era of decisions based on intuition and luck) and the increasing importance of financial and marketing criteria in the decision-making process. Whether these changes signal a new regime at the Book-of-the-Month Club is not clear from Radway's analysis, but recently the club has asked three of its five judges to resign. The judges pick the main selections, while the in-house editors choose the four hundred or so alternate selections that are offered to members. The stepping-down of three judges may not seem consequential, but two of the judges—Wilfred Sheed and Mordecai Richler—have been with the Club for more than a decade. The Book-of-the-Month Club has had only eighteen judges in its sixty-two-year history, so this restructuring may well reflect an important change in its strategy and operations.

---

1. For a general discussion of this "managerial revolution," see Walter W. Powell, "The Organization of American Book Publishing," *Getting into Print: The Decision-Making Process in Scholarly Publishing* (Chicago, 1985), pp. 1–35.

Walter W. Powell is associate professor of sociology and management at the University of Arizona. He is the author of *Getting into Print: The Decision-Making Process in Scholarly Publishing* (1985) and coauthor, with Lewis A. Coser and Charles Kadushin, of *Books: The Culture and Commerce of Publishing* (1982).

While it may be true that the Book-of-the-Month Club's membership of 1.7 million readers is not aware that its operations are centered in midtown Manhattan, this fact is known all too well by writers and publishers. The Book-of-the-Month Club is highly integrated into the culture of publishing; moreover, it is one of the most influential institutions in the industry. Radway observes that BOMC editors, like the preponderant majority of editors in book publishing, "are well educated, overwhelmingly white, and solidly middle class" (p. 158), with backgrounds in the humanities.[2] These similarities, however, may mask the power of the book club within the industry. It is much more than just "an important source of revenue for publishers" (p. 155). A selection by the Book-of-the-Month Club is a corroborating sign of a book's commercial potential. Recall that BOMC editors are among the first readers from outside the publishing house to evaluate a book. Their decision to take or reject a book influences a publisher's commitment to that book. Thus, book clubs are part of a general screening process that takes place prior to publication. Book clubs, paperback publishers, magazines, bookstore chains, and film studios all decide on a book's commercial prospects. Their choices help determine the size of a book's print run, the publisher's promotional strategy, and the size of the advertising budget. For serious fiction, the Book-of-the-Month Club's decision is a major step in determining whether or not a new work will be promoted to a wide audience. By focusing on how BOMC editors typify various books and sort them into categories meaningful to their members, Radway downplays the important gatekeeper role that the Book-of-the-Month Club plays within the book industry.

This neglect seems to be a general shortcoming in Radway's otherwise fine analysis. By looking at ways of reading, she tends to underemphasize any consideration of the Book-of-the-Month Club as a commercial enterprise, as but one operation within the Time, Inc. media empire. The Book-of-the-Month Club's main task is to turn out a diverse, albeit highly predictable, selection of books for its members on a regular basis. Much of what the book club does is based on successful routines. As Radway notes, the editors at the Book-of-the-Month Club "know from long experience that they can sell a fairly predictable number of books in any one of several informally defined 'categories'" (pp. 157–58). After all, the Book-of-the-Month Club dubs itself "America's Bookstore since 1926." *The book club,* in my view, *is the product.* What is sold to the membership is not, I would argue, a choice of particular new books but rather the Club's taste in books. That taste is relatively unchanging, even though various titles and categories of books may come and go.

This theme is not discordant with Radway's analysis, but it is played softly. Indeed, she tells us that categorical placement in the *BOMC News*

---

2. See Lewis A. Coser, Charles Kadushin, and Powell, "Climbing the Editorial Ladder," *Books: The Culture and Commerce of Publishing* (New York, 1982), pp. 97–117.

not only identifies new books to readers but may tell them how to read the books as well. Moreover, she shows that editors constantly search for "handles" that will position books for their members (p. 164). But by focusing on the uses of fiction and how BOMC editors read manuscripts, she neglects the larger collective product that the Book-of-the-Month Club represents.

The BOMC editors told Radway that they try to read as they believe their members do. They suggested that their preferences differ from those of their membership; thus they must endeavor to assume the role of the "general" reader (p. 160). I fail to find this "story" credible for several reasons. The editors knew, in Radway's words, surprisingly little about who their membership is or what their tastes are. Not only do the editors have scant knowledge of their readers, but they were, at the time of her study, remarkably buffered from audience feedback. They have, she tells us, functioned in the past without knowledge of their choices. The club has pursued, until recently, a strategy in which selections were "unbiased" by sales data (pp. 160–61). The fact that editors know little about their readers or the performance of their selections suggests to me that the individual titles are not what matters; rather it is the overall package and the image of the book club as an authoritative ("the book club of record") guide to contemporary books that is of consequence.

Each year thousands of new books are released—the latest diets, the newest in popular psychology, new fiction from established writers as well as new authors, nonfiction from writers of authority and those with fifteen seconds' claim to fame. Out of this welter of material, the Book-of-the-Month Club presents its membership with a dependable cross section: the appropriate cookbooks, the solid historical biography, the most useful new approach to career management. Even the new discoveries, those titles that may be categorized as novel, experimental, or perhaps a tad racy, are properly labeled in a special category, suggesting the book may not be apt for all members but recommended for the younger and/or hipper set. There is an evenness, a fidelity, to the monthly choices.

The notion of the book club as an identifiable product is critical to its success as an enterprise. It is an effective strategy to reach book buyers who live in areas not well served by bookstores and/or to supply consumers with books that have been preselected for them by "experts." This dependable image of the Book-of-the-Month Club is crucial to the Club's identity. Its constant character also helps us to understand why the Book-of-the-Month Club can be much more selective than editors in publishing houses. The latter cannot afford to eschew "lush" historical fiction, which may make up for its lack of literary grace with great commercial potential. Similarly, BOMC editors forego many new writers, deeming their work too experimental or abstract. Publishers, on the other hand, cannot ignore writers who may represent the next generation or a new wave. But the

Book-of-the-Month Club has a credible image to convey, and thus it can (must?) be both more selective and risk-averse. The book club takes the high ground when it comes to the simple "pleasures of the mass, the facile, and the shallow," but it refrains from embracing a high-culture aesthetic when such works fail "to engage the reader's *sympathy*" (p. 174). America's Bookstore, then, is certainly catholic: it is both somewhat tony and tastefully eclectic, but most of all it is reliable. The fortunes of the Club are bound up in its identity, its ability to produce an accountable, recognizable, and legitimate selection of books fifteen times a year.

Poetry and Politics: Lamartine's Revolutions

Philippe Desan

Translated by Priscilla Parkhurst Ferguson

> I might have lacked genius (I say so though I doubt it) but never propriety. I have been political to the point of self-abnegation.[1]
> —ALPHONSE DE LAMARTINE, *Mémoires politiques*

Is it possible to approach the social discourse of a group, a movement, a class, even a period, starting with a single individual, even one as eminent as Lamartine? This is exactly the methodological question that this essay addresses. We immediately confront the old trap of "reflection," which tells us to read Lamartine to better understand nineteenth-century French society. It would in fact be tempting to generalize the linguistic performance of a single writer and to fuse the literary production of an individual with the discourse of French society. At this point a second question arises: can society be reified from a work of art? Of course not. And yet the text *speaks,* and not only in the name of its author, since it also is written into a larger text that can be defined as a "social text." Every "literary" text is inscribed within a "social" text, or rather every literary text is *also* a social text. And yet there is a marked tendency to separate the literary text from its context, thereby turning it into an object with its own endogenous logic and claiming its autonomy from the "noise" of society. One would like to believe that, since it tends toward the universal, the work of art transcends the daily preoccupations of ordinary people. In which case, the critic need only concentrate on the text by itself, relegating everything that surrounds the text to the category of "noise." The same principle turns text and context into the two irreconcilable poles between which contemporary criticism oscillates.

---

1. Alphonse de Lamartine, *Mémoires politiques, Oeuvres complètes de Lamartine,* 40 vols. (Paris, 1860–63), 37:101; hereafter abbreviated *MP*.

Without positing a unidirectional relationship between these two poles, we shall see that the writer's text and the social text often enter into a dialogue that brings out the points of friction characteristic of a given period. These points of friction shape and structure ideology. Such encounters between the literary text and the social text prompt us to reflect on the ideology of the text in general—the sum of individual (authorial) and social discourses. The role of sociocriticism is to bring out these moments of intersection between the discourses of author and society. This is not the psychological determinism characteristic of criticism of the beginning of the century, which explained the work by the life of the author. Even less is it an attempt to learn about the man through his writings. Still, it is also important not to lose sight of the fact that every text is written by *someone* at a given moment and in a given context. A cliché perhaps, but one to which we do well to attend at a time when text and author seem separated for good.

The discursive intersection that concerns us here examines the romantic discourse on the French Revolution of 1848 and the relationship between poetry and politics as they were brought together in February of that year. The idea of a "romantic" discourse obviously represents an analysis a posteriori. We could be criticized for skipping steps and proceeding by critical suppositions that are in fact the product of a post-Lamartinian literary history. When Lamartine writes, he obviously does not have the ideological benchmarks that we have constructed since, and yet the analysis "in the present" of past discourse is still possible, even desirable. An essential postulate accompanies every analysis of social discourse: a critic must be aware of his or her own position vis-à-vis the work under analysis. One has to know what one wants to prove and why one undertakes such criticism. After all, what good is it to reconstruct the discursive modes of past times if not better to grasp how, via linguistic and ideological ramifications, these words keep sending us back to the present. At this point the notion of a "romantic" discourse acquires meaning since, in the last analysis, sociocriticism ought to lead into a reflection on the present. The concepts discussed and the discursive strategies brought to light ought to build a bridge between the period under examination and the approach of the sociocritic. Our reading of the past intersects in turn with current problems. Perhaps the need to speak comes

Philippe Desan is an assistant professor of French at the University of Chicago. The author of *Naissance de la méthode: Machiavel, La Ramée, Bodin, Montaigne, Descartes* (1987), he is completing a book entitled *Les Commerces de Montaigne: l'émergence du discours économique au XVIe siècle*. **Priscilla Parkhurst Ferguson** is professor of French at the University of Illinois at Chicago; she is the author of *Literary France: The Making of a Culture* (1987).

from a desire to continue that very social text whose extent we hope to grasp and whose ideological contours we hope to trace. Sociocriticism, and particularly the analysis of social discourse, accepts fully and consciously its method as one more mark on the vast palimpsest that forms society.

A corpus has to be established for this kind of analysis. The division between literature and other forms of expression creates great difficulties for anyone interested in social discourse. First, the problematic term "literature" has to be defined. Even though critics often turn to the canon (a definition of literature governed by an institution, principally the academy), we have not retained this highly ideological distinction, but shall look instead at novels along with newspaper articles, public letters, correspondence, political speeches, historical treatises, and of course those poems that directly or indirectly concern political events. This corpus/cumulative text constitutes Lamartine's discourse on revolution.

In this we are following Lamartine's example. For he paid no attention to the critical distinction between the political sphere and his poetic activity. He wrote political pamphlets at the same time as mystical poems. The division between Lamartine the politician and Lamartine the poet, even if accepted by critics today, is totally arbitrary. The author of "Le Lac" and "La Vigne et la maison" was undoubtedly a great poet if one is to judge by the central place that he occupies in the anthologies of French poetry. Library shelves are full of works about Lamartine the poet, but only a few dusty works (and mostly out of date) discuss Lamartine the politician and more specifically his role during the revolutionary days of February 1848.[2] The dichotomy between art and politics is obvious only if we confine our perspective to the way Lamartine is perceived today. The works that examine his public life offer very little on his career as a poet, and vice versa. And yet Lamartine himself, very early on, wanted to bring the two together. The Lamartinian discourse is the sum of his writings, whatever the form or the genre, whether oral or written. Similarly, the term "revolution" must be taken in its broadest meaning, to signify poetic as well as political revolution, all the more so since, for Lamartine, the two merge.

The revolution of 1848 and the great number of discourses that it produced is therefore not a localized problem. It takes its place in the

---

2. However, see the suggestive studies of William Fortescue, *Alphonse de Lamartine: A Political Biography* (London and New York, 1983); Ethel Harris, *Lamartine et le peuple* (Paris, 1932); Henri Guillemin, *Lamartine et la question sociale* (Paris, 1946) and *Lamartine en 1848* (Paris, 1948); Paul Bert, *Lamartine "homme social"; son action dans la région natale* (Paris, 1947); Camille Latreille, *Lamartine: poète politique* (Paris, 1924); Gordon Wright, "A Poet in Politics: Lamartine and the Revolution of 1848," *History Today* 8 (Sept. 1958): 616–27; Leo Gershoy, "Three French Historians and the Revolution of 1848," *Journal of the History of Ideas* 12 (Jan. 1951): 131–46; Jacques Madaule, "La Politique de Lamartine," *Europe: Revue mensuelle* (July–Aug. 1969); and Pierre Clarac, "Aspects de la vie politique de Lamartine," parts I and II, *Revue des deux mondes* (June and July 1981): 580–92, 61–67.

discursive continuity from 1789 and enriches the "general" discourse on revolution (which has become a generic term). The social discourse *around* the events of February 1848 has never ceased to be present. What interests us here is the formation of a new discursive field that used poetry to talk about the revolution (and which perceived the revolution as a poem). What are, for example, the discursive signs used by Lamartine when he decided to speak against the red flag adopted by the insurgents? The reader can decide if we are correct in believing that these references continue to function today. For reasons of space, the discussion is confined to an analysis of three events of the revolution of 1848 (Lamartine's speech before the Chamber of Deputies and his harangues at the Hôtel de Ville in front of the armed crowd on 24 February, and the incident of the red flag the following day) to determine how a single author extends and at the same time limits the discourse on revolution. For Lamartine is only an archetype of a discourse that goes well beyond his text but that, like every archetype, presents itself as a revelatory sign, and hence, as valuable as any other sign, of the redefinition of the idea of revolution during the nineteenth century—a redefinition that hinges on an opposition to 1789 and is based on events of 1830 and 1848.

The Poetic Revolution

Lamartine is not an isolated case. His poetic and political behavior fits within the framework of the romantic movement, which in turn brings to light distinctive aspects of the relationship between poetry and politics at the beginning of the nineteenth century. Romanticism is first of all a reaction against the rational equilibrium defended by the Enlightenment. Their reasoned empiricism led the philosophes to reject every form of spontaneous engagement; the heart had yielded to reason. The "romantic" authors at the beginning of the century rediscovered the senses and the divine. The idea of "genius" symbolizes the "nonrational" side of man, whose innate qualities raise him above the common and bring him close to God. The poet incarnates this superior being placed between God and man. Indeed the romantics all claim to be "geniuses." Even Madame de Staël is described as "a man's genius in a woman's body."[3] Since this genius is universal, it carries beyond the artistic sphere to the social sphere, which is why the romantics tied the poet's genius to the larger benefit to society. François-René de Chateaubriand (1768– 1848), Alfred de Vigny (1797–1863), Victor Hugo (1802–85), and Al-

---

3. Lamartine locates the origin of de Staël's genius in her relationship to the revolution: "Her cradle was that of the Revolution" (Lamartine, *History of the Girondists, or, Personal Memoirs of the Patriots of the French Revolution*, trans. H. T. Ryde, 3 vols. [London, 1856– 64], 1:203; hereafter abbreviated *HG*).

phonse de Lamartine (1790–1869) each in turn claimed active participation in current political life. As "geniuses," they are above all "universal men." The romantic revolution projects the poet above society and transforms him into the "good conscience" of humanity. Writing thus becomes a necessity. "I frankly admit it," Lamartine tells us, "I do not write from piety or vanity or meanness or personality or as a vainglorious poet, politician or writer. I write—do I have to say it—out of necessity!" (*MP*, 37:6).

However difficult it is to generalize intellectual behavior between figures as different as the four romantic poets mentioned above, and despite their political differences, it seems that a definite form of commitment appears in each case. Politics appears to be a necessity for these poets. They have to try their hand at it, even if they give it up eventually. Chateaubriand, the very model of the romantic and often mentioned by Lamartine, was Peer of the Realm, ambassador to Berlin, England, and the Holy See, Minister of State without portfolio, and Minister of Foreign Affairs.[4] A text like *De Buonaparte et des Bourbons* (1814) combines the two. Chateaubriand conceived of politics as essentially literary, and he saw his own role as a writer as a political commitment, acknowledged by everyone, to serve the people. In order to represent the people, which becomes the goal, Chateaubriand stood for election to the Chamber of Deputies (and was indeed elected).

For Chateaubriand as for many romantics the revolution of 1789 supplied the starting point for the discovery of politics. This process was almost always accompanied by writing about this discovery. Chateaubriand undertook *Essai historique, politique, et moral sur les révolutions anciennes et modernes dans leur rapports avec la révolution française* (written in London in 1794), which tries to prove that the revolution of 1789 is only the "evolving" result of previous revolutions. When all is said and done, the poet is a poet even immeshed in politics. *Mémoires d'outre-tombe* (1848–50) was the last poetic preoccupation of a man who appeared to have given up political life. But *Mémoires* is also a text written *against* politics and therefore political. The poetic revolution started by Chateaubriand can be understood only as a simultaneous rapprochement and distancing with respect to politics. More generally, the poetry of the romantics is either communion with or reaction against a given social practice.

---

4. Lamartine will follow in these steps. Both men had the advantage of having traveled and partly established their poetic careers thanks to these trips. Thus Chateaubriand went to America (*Atala, ou les amours de deux sauvages dans le désert*), then to the Near East (*Itinéraire de Paris à Jérusalem*), and Lamartine to Italy (*Graziella*), Lebanon, Galilee, and Palestine (*Souvenirs, impressions, pensées et paysages pendant un voyage en Orient*), then to Asia Minor (*Le Nouveau Voyage en Orient*). It was logical for their political careers as well to tend toward responsibilities that made use of this familiarity with foreign countries. The parallels between the political career and the writing are striking.

Victor Hugo followed more or less the same path. His life can be divided into three periods. The first, from 1822 to 1843, is a time that was especially fertile for the poet, when politics remained in the background. Next comes a political period that is itself divided in two. From 1843 to 1851, though he continued to write, Hugo finished nothing, published no work, but he founded a newspaper, *L'Événement,* to get closer to the people. During the final period, his exile (1851–70), he fully joined politics and literature. This is when Hugo protested most vociferously against the death penalty and called for political commitment on the part of the poet.[5] But even in much earlier writing, Hugo gives more and more space to the role of the poet in society. Thus the preface to *Les Voix intérieures* (1837) leaves no doubt concerning the function of the poet in writing the history that is taking place before his very eyes: "the poet has a serious task to perform. Without going into his civilizing function here, it is for the poet to underscore political events as historical events when they merit such attention."[6]

This notion of the poet as guide appears in "Fonction du poète" (1839), which evokes the genius given by God to the poet whose inspiration will light the way for the world:

> Peoples! listen to the poet!
> Listen to the sacred dreamer!
> In your night, utter without him,
> His face alone is enlightened!
> . . . .
> Because poetry is the star
> That leads kings as well as shepherds to God![7]

In the last period of his life (1870–85) Hugo involved himself less and less in politics (despite his election as senator from Paris in 1876) and spent his time finishing works begun during his exile.

5. See Philippe Desan, "Entre Moloch et Teutatès: Victor Hugo et le discours sur la peine de mort," *Revue de l'Institut de Sociologie* 1–2 (1986–87): 199–211.

6. Quoted by Robert T. Denommé, *Nineteenth-Century French Romantic Poets* (Carbondale and Edwardsville, Ill., 1969), p. 35.

7. Peuples! écoutez le poète!
Écoutez le rêveur sacré!
Dans votre nuit, sans lui complète,
Lui seul a le front éclairé!

. . . .

Car la poésie est l'étoile
Qui mène à Dieu rois et pasteurs!

(Victor Hugo, "Fonction du poète," *Les Rayons et les ombres,* ed. Jean-Pierre Reynaud, *Poésie I,* vol. 4 of *Oeuvres complètes* [Paris, 1985], p. 929).

Lamartine's career offers striking parallels with those of Chateaubriand and Hugo. Poet in his youth, he soon discovered his role as the "representative of the people" and presented himself in turn as the voice of humanity. It is noteworthy that all three of these romantic authors turned toward political journalism at the end of their lives. The common denominator for most of the romantics is the division of their lives into three sharply separated periods defined by the relationship to poetry and politics. In all three cases there is first the poetry of youth, exuberant and passionate, followed by intense political activity and the dismissal of poetry as puerile, and finally a return to "a more religious poetry . . . which aspires solely to God."[8] The wisdom of this last poetry is accompanied by a return to stylistic simplicity and journalistic writing. Better than anyone else, Lamartine sums up the significance of this tripartite division for the romantic poet:

> Once we sang in the language of poets for the happy and the leisured few of the earth; later we spoke the language of orators before statesmen and in the civil storms of the country. Humbler today, and perhaps more useful, we do not blush to learn the language that goes to your intelligence via your heart, and to become simple with those who are simple and little with those who are little.[9]

It will become apparent that these three periods in fact cover a particular conception of man and society in the nineteenth century. First, however, it is important to note that in almost all of the cases, the romantics threw themselves into politics as they threw themselves into poetry, with an inescapable mysticism and a spontaneous fervor where the heart alone speaks.[10] Robert Denommé has argued that "French Romanticism may be defined by the exalted fervor and the messianic zeal that motivates the greater number of messages that it imparts."[11] Their politics, like their poetry, were unpremeditated and sincere (even if a statement contradicted, as it often happened, the positions held the day before). As the agent of Providence on earth, the poetic genius spreads over the masses he endeavors to enlighten with his visions. Illumination and inspiration thus become the privileged instruments of the poet as of the politician, which is why, especially for romanticism, it is impossible to isolate the two "occupations." Vigny was certainly the least "political" of the romantics (though he did join with Hugo to found first *Le Conservateur*

8. Lamartine, *Le Conseiller du peuple*, 3 vols. (Paris, 1849–51), 1:579; hereafter abbreviated *CP*.

9. Lamartine, *Le Civilisateur: histoire de l'humanité par les grands hommes*, 3 vols. (Paris, 1852–56), 1:23.

10. See A. Cherel, "Le Mysticisme politique de Lamartine," *Revue bleue*, no. 5 (May 1939): 188–91.

11. Denommé, *Nineteenth-Century French Romantic Poets*, p. 31.

littéraire and later *La Muse française*). Yet even he harbored the same aspirations as Chateaubriand and Lamartine, and he showed conspicuous interest in Lamennais' democratic version of Christianity and in Saint-Simonianism. Only after failing miserably in the elections of 1849 did Vigny decide to devote himself entirely to poetry. But, once again, the temptation that politics exemplifed for Vigny sheds light on the close bond between poetry and politics for the romantics.

If Chateaubriand represented a model for Lamartine, Lord Byron was the figure who struck the deepest poetic chord. Byron's political engagement in Greece was the ideal for Lamartine and for a number of other romantics. Byron is, for example, the model of "L'Homme" in *Méditations*. Lamartine regretted not having met Byron, whom he admired without reservation. The poet's exile, after his various political misadventures, placed him so to speak above events. But Byron effected the greatest of reconciliations between politics and poetry when he joined the war for independence in Greece. This commitment inspired Lamartine in his second meditation to associate himself with Byron's project:

> Alas! such was your fate, such is my destiny.
> Like you I have emptied the poisoned cup;
> Without seeing, my eyes, like yours, have opened;
> I have searched in vain for the word of the universe.[12]

The "word of the universe" symbolizes the quest for the universal discourse. However, man searches in vain since it is Providence that procures for man both his innate genius and the song with which he will soothe humanity. The poet has only to follow his destiny, and it is expressly as a destiny that poetry and politics are to be conceived. This theoretical position, which could easily be applied to the romantic movement in general, turns up in a striking and little-known text by Lamartine, *Des destinées de la poésie* [*On the Destiny of Poetry*].

Since genius elevates the individual, the poet is above humanity and is able to see better what happens on earth. Poetry will therefore be the mirror of the world in which humanity will be reflected. Lyrical poetry will speak the language of the people. *Des destinées de la poésie,* which is one of the early critical texts by Lamartine and could have served as a romantic manifesto, already announces the overlapping of poetry and politics. Dated 11 February 1834, it was first published in fragmentary form in the *Revue des deux mondes* on 15 March 1834 and soon thereafter

---

12.   Hélas! tel fut ton sort, telle est ma destinée.
       J'ai vidé comme toi la coupe empoisonnée;
       Mes yeux, comme les tiens, sans voir se sont ouverts;
       J'ai cherché vainement le mot de l'univers.

(Lamartine, "Méditation deuxième: L'Homme," *Méditations,* ed. Fernand Letessier [Paris, 1968], p. 8).

in a seventy-five-page brochure published by Charles Gosselin. This text aims at establishing a "unifying" tie between poetry and politics. It is scarcely coincidental that this text was republished at the apogee of Lamartine's political life as the second preface of *Méditations* (1849), right on the heels of the 1848 revolution.

The events of 1848 will put Lamartine's vision of poetry and its mission into practice. The earlier critical text is the linchpin of the poetic revolution proclaimed by Lamartine and most of the other romantic poets. This poetic revolution goes hand in hand with another revolution (1789, then 1848). "Poetry is the idea," Lamartine asserts, "politics is the fact; as the idea is above the fact, so poetry is above politics."[13] But if the idea and the fact (poetry and politics) are hierarchically separate, since the poet stands between God and man, they are nevertheless closely tied. Poetry and politics reconnect in the idea of revolution to create a perfect symbiosis, which obtains for the poetic revolution of romanticism as well as for the revolutions of 1789 and 1848 as viewed by the romantics.

Poetry precedes and is in some fashion superior to politics because it comes from the soul. Inspiration prevails over reflection, and revolutions are poetic to the extent that they begin in an unreasoned inspiration that brings them closer to poetry. In the commentary on his eighth meditation Lamartine establishes an essential difference between "inspirational" poems and "reflective" poems. The first always prevail over the second. Thus, he regarded his eighth meditation, "La Providence à l'homme," inferior to the earlier "Le Désespoir": "This Méditation is not worth the preceding one, and here is why: the first comes from inspiration, the second from reflection."[14]

Lamartine discerns a poetic "revival" in Chateaubriand and de Staël, but he hastens to specify what this renewal owes to a new political context: "It seems that the return of the Bourbon monarchy [in 1814] and of liberty in France gave a new inspiration, another soul to the oppressed or sleeping literature of the period" (*DP*, 1:36). Like an "oppressed" class waking up, literature chooses its representatives; like a social movement, it leads the crowd. Its force comes from its language: "This is why this language, when it is spoken well, strikes man down like lightning, annihilating him with inner conviction and unreflective evidence, or again enchants him like a philtre, rocks him, charms him, like a child in the cradle listening to the sympathetic strains of a mother's voice!" (*DP*, 1:37). Here we find all the favorite images of the romantics, which Lamartine will take up again during the February Revolution, first the idea of the people as a child, next the language-philtre that enables the poet to win over the masses.

13. Lamartine, *Des destinées de la poésie*, second preface to *Méditations poétiques, Oeuvres complètes de Lamartine*, 1:64; hereafter abbreviated *DP*.
14. Lamartine, "Commentaires des premières méditations," *Méditations*, p. 334.

Lamartine attributes an exalted destiny to poetry, which like the masses will no longer be reflective but spontaneous.[15] The juvenile, impulsive nature of poetry makes it run over its imposed cadre. Like every revolution it turns into an excessive, unreflective enthusiasm that dissipates in an instant. But poetry will also become an inherent part of the masses; thus the poet, who will sing *for* the people, can only be elected by the people. Lamartine never forgets this universal aspect of poetry: "Besides this philosophical, rational, political, and social destiny of the poetry of the future, it has a new destiny: it must become part of the people and become popular like religion, reason and philosophy" (*DP*, 1:60). Yet, the romantic revolution is an idea before it is action since, for Lamartine and the romantics, the revolution, like poetry, is idea first, then action.

The Revolution as Idea

Clearly, the poetic revolution of the romantics goes hand in hand with active participation in politics. The poetic revolution derives from a tormented vision of French society at the end of the eighteenth century. All the romantics were deeply marked by the revolution of 1789, which serves as the point of departure for their political reflection. The idea of the people is central to the romantic revolution. The poet must commune with humanity. In *Recueillements poétiques* (1839), "Utopie," dedicated to a young poet, offers Lamartine's vision of the poet's charge:

> He must plunge his senses in the vast sensate world
> Which our mind confuses with the spirit of the times,
> Palpate its every artery and every beat,
> And merge with humanity through every pore.[16]

---

15. Elle ne sera plus lyrique dans le sens où nous prenons ce mot; elle n'a plus assez de jeunesse, de fraîcheur, de spontanéité d'impression, pour chanter comme au premier réveil de la pensée humaine. Elle ne sera plus épique; l'homme a trop vécu, trop réfléchi pour se laisser amuser, intéresser par les longs écrits de l'épopée, et l'expérience a détruit sa foi aux merveilles dont le poëme épique enchantait la crédulité. Elle ne sera plus dramatique, parce que la scène de la vie réelle a, dans nos temps de liberté et d'action politique, un intérêt plus pressant, plus réel et plus intime que la scène du théâtre. . . . La poésie sera de la raison chantée, voilà sa destinée pour longtemps; elle sera philosophique, religieuse, politique, sociale, comme les époques que le genre humain va traverser; elle sera intime surtout, personnelle, méditative et grave; non plus un jeu de l'esprit, un caprice mélodieux de la pensée légère et superficielle, mais l'écho profond, réel, sincère, des plus hautes conceptions de l'intelligence, des plus mystérieuses impressions de l'âme. [*DP*, 1:57–58]

16.   Il faut plonger ses sens dans le grand sens du monde,
            Qu'avec l'esprit des temps notre esprit s'y confonde,
            En palper chaque artère et chaque battement,
            Avec l'humanité s'unir par chaque pore.

(Lamartine, "Utopie," *Recueillements poétiques* [1839; Paris, 1954], p. 89).

Because the feeling of uncertainty and the lack of vision convert the people into an unformed mass that explodes from time to time, it is imperative that revolution be controlled in order to transform it into evolution. Revolution is not a bad idea (to the extent that it is unintentional and spontaneous), but its lack of direction makes it dangerous. Faced with the chaos of the people, wandering about on the bloody paths of his destiny, the poet assumes the function of leading the masses by providing them with divine visions.

Jules Michelet's *Histoire de la Révolution française* (1847–53) and the historian's idea of the people as the motor force of history constitute one of the romantic poets' favorite themes. Since the poet claims to be the voice of the people, he recognizes and accepts his proper place in history. Poetry is not cut off from the vicissitudes of ordinary life, and indeed the poet claims a place in the constitution of this life. The events themselves interest the poet less than their origin as ideas and their transmission to the people. Yet this transmission is itself problematic. For Lamartine there is always a discrepancy between theory and practice, and the failure of revolutions as ideas resides in the fact that events only seldom follow the ideas in which they originate.

Just like Chateaubriand and Michelet, Lamartine constructs a romantic vision of the French Revolution. His *Histoire des Girondins,* published in 1847 just before the February Revolution, clearly reveals his conception of revolution. Lamartine announces the goal of his book at the outset: "As to the title of this book, we have only assumed it, as being unable to find any other which can so well define this recital, which has none of the pretensions of history, and therefore should not affect its gravity. It is an intermediate labour between history and memoirs. Events do not herein occupy so much space as men and ideas" (*HG,* 1:iv). For Lamartine the revolution does not seem to have any material cause; it is solely an idea for which men fight. As with poetry, words do not necessarily correspond to the things they designate. Words are only the signs that evoke those things; they reflect visions that transcend the material needs of the people. As a concept, abstracted from its real conditions, the people is the only thing at stake in revolutions; it has to be won over. For this reason the people are cherished and fed with ideas. On this subject of the "causes" of revolution, Lamartine has been reproached for losing sight of the original objective of 1789 and having fallen into a series of tableaux with no relationship to each other. The reproach is justified. The *Histoire des Girondins* usually jumbles events and episodes unconnected by any general analysis.[17]

Abrupt and ephemeral illuminations of the people, revolutions exist only in the moment when they occur. Lamartine conceives of no possible

17. See Fabienne Reboul, "Histoire ou feuilleton? La Révolution française vue par Lamartine," *Romantisme* 52 (1986): 19–33.

finality for these explosive moments except the revelation of a few individual geniuses who stand apart from the people the better to enlighten them. The true idea of revolution is to bring forth poets from the people.[18] The childlike nature of the people appears several times in Lamartine's poems: "Children six thousand years old startled by a bit of noise" ("Les Révolutions"). Only the genius of a few men can master the uncontrolled excesses of revolutions. Since Lamartine considers that revolutions serve to reveal genius, he is most interested in the orators—the true revolutionary poets. Thus, *Histoire des Girondins* begins with the fall of Mirabeau, "his star [*génie*] had paled its fire before that of the Revolution" (*HG*, 1:2).

The term "genius" is a veritable leitmotif in the *Histoire*, where it is most often associated with the idea of the Revolution itself. The person closest to Lamartine's revolutionary ideal is probably the Girondist deputy Pierre Vergniaud. He possessed "facility, that agreeable concomitant of genius, [which] had rendered alike pliable his talents, his character, and even the position he assumed" (*HG*, 1:240). With his look that bespoke assurance, his "somewhat sad" mouth, and the carefree insouciance of youth, Vergniaud symbolizes the poet of the Girondists. "He was an instrument of enthusiasm, whose value and whose place was in his inspiration. . . . his sentences had all the images and harmony of poesy, and if he had not been the orator of a democracy he would have been its philosopher and its poet" (*HG*, 1:241).

But these poets of the Revolution as idea were as well both guilty and victims. Almost all of them got caught up in the events that destroyed the very idea of revolution: "All was thus blind, except the Revolution itself. The virtue of the Revolution was in the idea which forced these

---

18. Lamartine's poem "Les Révolutions" reveals his conception of the people and of revolutions:

> Mais vous, peuples assis de l'Occident stupide,
> Hommes pétrifiés dans votre orgueil timide,
> Partout où le hasard sème vos tourbillons
> Vous germez comme un gland sur vos sombres collines,
> Vous poussez dans le roc vos stériles racines,
>   Vous végétez sur vos sillons!

. . . .

> Regardez donc, race insensée,
> Les pas des générations!
> Toute la route n'est tracée
> Que des débris des nations:
> Trônes, autels, temples, portiques,
> Peuples, royaumes, républiques,
> Sont la poussière du chemin;
> Et l'histoire, écho de la tombe,
> N'est que le bruit de ce qui tombe
> Sur la route du genre humain.

(Lamartine, "Les Révolutions," *Recueillements poétiques*, pp. 209, 213).

men on to accomplish it, and not in those who actually accomplished it; all its instruments were vitiated, corrupt, or personal; but the idea was pure, incorruptible, divine" (*HG*, 1:41). The first chapter of the *Histoire des Girondins* predicts the importance of Providence for these men of genius, through whose voice it finds expression. The divine voice of Providence means that this word [*parole*] can be transmitted only by poets: "I now undertake to write the history of a small party of men who, cast by Providence into the very centre of the greatest drama of modern times, comprise in themselves the ideas, the passions, the faults, the virtues of their epoch" (*HG*, 1:1).

Only retroactively do revolutions appear necessary. Modern society can only know progressive improvement. On this point Lamartine joined Hugo and several other writers who turned the French Revolution into a romantic myth. As long as a revolution describes the past, it can stand as a theoretical model and literary commonplace. But as a social practice and project for social change, it becomes dangerous. Hugo saw revolutions as "heat explosions."[19] Lamartine viewed them as abstract ideas, never specific actions. Only after the fact, in 1849 and in the light of the events of 1848, can he offer a definition of revolution: "What is a revolution? It is an explosion of opinions or interests which ferment for a certain time in a people, under the name of opposition to the government, and then one day, out of anger, lassitude and impatience, overturns this government and quickly creates another one in its place" (*CP*, 1:559). Here is a simple and closed definition—the revolution as a passing reflex. Lamartine's dream, like that of Hugo, is to reintegrate this barbarianism of revolution within a didactic model that would allow reinterpreting history as a simple search for progress. Henceforth, "the revolution of France will be called the evolution of peoples."[20] Since ideas are often outdistanced by actions, Providence then seeks new geniuses who will commence a counterrevolution necessary to the success of every revolution. Progress, for Lamartine, is possible only beginning from a "counter-revolution." Thus his declaration in 1830 that "a system of counter-revolution alone could have given life to the revolution."[21]

Language and Revolution

In the introduction to *Le Civilisateur*, published from 1852 to 1854, and in spite of the three stages into which he divided his life, Lamartine

19. Victor Hugo, "La Liberté," letter to Clément Duvernois, 19 Mar. 1866, *Actes et paroles II*, ed. Josette Acher, *Politique*, vol. 10 of *Oeuvres complètes*, p. 573.

20. Hugo, "Le Droit et la loi," *Actes et paroles I*, ed. Michèle Fizaine, *Politique*, vol. 10 of *Oeuvre complètes*, p. 66.

21. To the count of Virieu, 1830, *Correspondance de Lamartine*, 6 vols. (Paris, 1873–75), 4:342; hereafter abbreviated *C*.

himself recognized that his poetic, political, and educational careers were all tied by a common denominator: the mastery of "language." Every revolution is in fact accompanied by a revolutionary discourse that makes it possible to circumscribe and fix facts and that often determines action, interprets, explains, rationalizes that action and turns it into "history." This discourse *around* revolution is of course part of a larger structure, namely, the ideology of the moment that produces, defends, or opposes the revolution. This discourse includes and surrounds events, and the narrative often plays a key role in the action. Thus when Lamartine rejected the red flag, he threw words back at the insurgents. When he was forced to commit himself more and more deeply to the revolution, it was once again through words that he was able to push aside the demands made on him and to impose himself as the legitimate leader of the insurrection without having participated in the campaign of banquets organized by republicans in the preceding year.

Lamartinian discourse during the revolutionary days of February 1848 presents a paradigm of a problem that Lamartine poses in all its ambiguity, that of "change in continuity," or evolution in revolution. Lamartine worked on perfecting the form of his speeches at the same time as the content—his politics are poetic and his poetry reflects his politics. Never had anyone stuck to an event in this way. This identification of man and event continued long after February 1848. Outside of systems, political parties, and social classes Lamartine threw himself into the revolution as he threw himself into his poems. He marveled at the enthusiasm of the revolution more than the goal, as Karl Marx's astute observation makes clear: "The working class had only two representatives, Louis Blanc and Albert. Finally, Lamartine as a member of the Provisional Government; that was actually no real interest, no definite class that was the February Revolution itself, the common uprising with its illusions, its poetry, its imagined content and its phrases."[22] Friedrich Engels was even more severe in the *Neue Rheinische Zeitung* of 28 June 1848: "The unanimity of the February revolution, that poetic unanimity full of dazzling delusions and beautiful lies so appropriately symbolized by that windbag and traitor Lamartine, has disappeared."[23] Despite their harshness, these words accurately convey Lamartine's conception of revolution as essentially illusory, spontaneous, verbal, and hence poetic.

Accordingly, most modern critics have taken Lamartine as a poet lost in the corridors of power, the tacit assumption being that poetry and politics can have nothing to do with each other. This prejudice against poetry where affairs of state are concerned was already apparent among Lamartine's contemporaries. Numerous caricatures show Lamartine, lyre

22. Karl Marx, *The Class Struggles in France (1848–1850)* (New York, 1964), p. 39.
23. Friedrich Engels, "The 23rd of June," in Marx and Engels, *Collected Works,* 42 vols. (Moscow and New York, 1975–87), 8:130–31.

in hand, leading the people (fig. 1). The poet himself had to struggle against these caricatures. Lamartine, conscious of the difficulties for a poet to be accepted as a political leader, at the very beginning of his political career asked a friend to place a few chosen words on the subject in his newspaper in order to transfer a bit of poetic glory into the political domain: "Here in essence is what should be said in five or six lines, repeated every week in different terms in a patched up form: We hear that M. de Lamartine is the favorite in several electoral districts. Our hope is to divert this talent from poetry to oratory, etc. etc." (to Aimé Martin, 10 May 1831; *C*, 4:404).

Politics attracted the poet well before 1848. Beginning in 1829 Lamartine perceived that he would never attain the glory that he coveted if he continued to write poetry. Writing to a friend Lamartine remarked: "I see coming to pass what I had always felt, that eloquence was in me more than poetry (which indeed is only one of its forms), and that it would one day come to the surface if it were not too late" (to the count of Virieu, 22 September 1835; *C*, 5:103). He thought poetry "in its form a puerility beneath a thirty-eight year old man" (to the count of Virieu, 16 March 1829; *C*, 4:228). After his election to the French Academy (in 1830), he had nothing more to wish for as a poet. In 1843 his decision was made. He declared grandly, "I no longer wish to write poetry."[24] When his political ambitions began to take form, and even though poetry remained a sure way of earning a living (his poetry was a certain bestseller), Lamartine went so far as to hide his habit of scribbling verse. Clearly he felt that poetry would hamper him in political life.

> I have written five or six novellas . . . ; but do not tell anyone about it, I would be lost with the politicians. Thiers and Guizot, Dufaure, Dupin, Berryer and Barrot have never written anything but bad puns in verse. My poetry is acceptable. Therefore they are great men and I am an idiot, according to administrative logic! What would be the response of Solon, Cicero or Caesar, those divine poets. [to the marquis of Grange, 9 June 1845; *C*, 6:165–66]

This says it all. Lamartine will look to antiquity for his models. He will depend on eloquence and flights of lyricism to establish his political authority. Lamartine discovers that the mastery of language can place him at the center of political life and secure for him the eternal glory of great men. He soon realizes the power of words and decides to play up his oratorical talent and his poetic enthusiasm to win over the masses. He appreciates that in poetry as in politics "words are not what they are; they are what they are made to be" (*CP*, 1:23). As Paul Hazard has

24. To Charles Gosselin, 15 Sept. 1843, *Lettres inédites (1821–1851)* (Porrentruy, 1944), p. 73.

FIG. 1.—Caricature of Lamartine, 1848.

correctly noted, Lamartine soon became aware that politics, above all else, is words placed one after the other, a speech where form prevails over content. With some information on current problems and with a necessary bit of economic jargon, Lamartine was soon capable of talking on any subject: railroads, beet sugar, property income, and so on.[25] History has shown that rhetorician and politician are often one and the same, and never more so than during revolutions. If we consider the revolution of 1789 and the inflation of words that went along with it, we can say that 1848—at least the February days—was above all a "revolution of words." The "fight over words" of 1789 took place again in 1848.[26]

How do words and ideas react to events? The following analysis focuses on three key revolutionary events: first, the proclamation of the provisional government on 24 February; second, Lamartine's proclamation of the Republic at the Hôtel de Ville on the same day; and third, the rejection of the red flag on 25 February. In these three decisive moments Lamartine captured the attention of the crowd. Each time words carried the day. The causes of the revolution are not at issue here but rather the revolutionary "moment" and its accompanying discourse, reduced to three typical, paradigmatic incidents. We follow Lamartine's own account. After venturing to write a history of 1789 (*Histoire des Girondins*), Lamartine took on 1848 in the *Histoire de la Révolution de 1848*. It is noteworthy that Lamartine wrote this latter work in the third person; Lamartine the historian talks about Lamartine the member of the provisional government with a pseudo-"objective" detachment that aims at separating the author from the actor.

The Revolution as Action

What is interesting here is the overlap of events and a particular lyricism. Whatever his detractors may say, Lamartine must be rated one of the most important statesmen of his time. He held—or thought he held—the destiny of France in his hands from February to June 1848. As a member of the provisional government, minister of Foreign Affairs, and unquestionably the best orator (with Ledru-Rollin) of the 1848 revolution, Lamartine played a leading role in the episodes that marked the revolutionary days of February. There are times when one cannot escape the action of revolutions, even when they begin as ideas. This is what happened in 1848, when Lamartine moved from the revolution as idea to the revolution as action.

The 24th of February was undeniably Lamartine's best day. During this eventful afternoon he reached the apogee of his glory. That morning

25. See Paul Hazard, *Lamartine* (Paris, 1925), p. 68.
26. Marc Eli Blanchard, *Saint-Just & Cie: La Révolution et les mots* (Paris, 1980), p. 10.

Paris awoke to find itself in the hands of the insurgents. Even though the king had fled, the royal family had not given up all hope of saving the crown, and there was still the possibility of a regency for Louis-Philippe's grandson. In the beginning of the afternoon, the duchess of Orléans, widow of Louis-Philippe's son, arrived at the Chamber of Deputies with her ten-year-old son. Everything was still possible, and an air of irresolution dominated the session. As soon as Louis-Philippe's abdication was announced, lists with names for a new government began to circulate. Some demanded a provisional government, others a regency. Lamartine had not yet been heard. The conservative right was counting on his eloquence to determine a vote for a regency. He had after all once been in the service of the Bourbons (as an army officer). The republican left knew that it was close to its goal and was not counting much on Lamartine. Ledru-Rollin all by himself could create a majority in the National Assembly. In any case, who still needed a National Assembly? The people were outside, in arms. A veritable oratorical duel pitted Odilon Barrot, from the royalist right, against Ledru-Rollin, on the republican left. Everyone felt that the best speech would win. And yet none of the orators was victorious. At this point Colonel Dunoyer entered, interrupting Barrot and declaring that there was no longer any authority except that of the National Guard represented by him and that of the people represented by the forty thousand men surrounding the Assembly. Crémieux, Ledru-Rollin, and Lamartine rushed toward the podium. Ledru-Rollin took over and called for a provisional government. Finally Lamartine was called on.

At this point no one knew exactly where Lamartine stood politically. For the past ten years he had been "tacking about" (to the count of Circourt, 6 September 1842; *C,* 6:20) without ever throwing out an anchor. He was nowhere and everywhere. As he observed to his friend the count of Virieu as early as 1835, "I am neither more nor less part of the opposition or the government. I very consciously refuse to settle on any definite territory, neither legitimist nor republican nor the middle" (17 January 1835; *C,* 5:77). The royalists made signs, in hopes that he would follow Barrot. Lamartine began to speak without much of an idea where his words would take him. He was in fact living the "poetic" moment of inspiration, as he described it, "with a voice deep as the abyss of destiny he was about to fathom."[27] In his first sentences he sympathized with the fallen crown and evoked the touching scene of the princess protecting her "innocent son." Protests from the crowd. Sensing that his future lay with the people, in short order, at 2:30 P.M., Lamartine was a republican.

---

27. Lamartine, *History of the French Revolution of 1848* (London, 1852), p. 118; hereafter abbreviated *HR.*

Whereupon he launched into a harangue filled with sonorous words—equality, harmony, public peace, the empire of order, the empire of liberty, wisdom, unity, and the like. Yet what is so striking in this speech is not so much the lyrical genius of the orator but rather his steady concern to counterbalance the revolutionary enthusiasm necessary for him to be acclaimed by the insurgents with an attenuation of the action itself. Lamartine worked to diminish and restrain the hold of the people on the future of the nation. The proletariat had to get back down off the stage and accept the leadership of enlightened leaders. Lamartine thus put the brake on revolutionary action by combining key words like liberty, equality, and universal suffrage with a parallel discourse invoking order, public peace, and harmony. The rhetoric on two levels reflects all Lamartine's brio. He perceived that, if it were no longer possible to save the crown and if it were necessary to accept the insurrection, there would still be time to temporize and to limit that insurrection even while claiming to be one of its leaders. In the middle of a revolution Lamartine opted for a reformist discourse. He rejected the proposal to make him head of the provisional government. "A thousand voices cried, 'Take the chair; let Lamartine preside over us.' This he declined. He knew that the chair was too remote from the people, and that they needed at this moment a guiding voice close to their ear, and not a guiding president" (*HR*, p. 125). Lamartine refused the role of politician and chose to remain a poet, closer to the people. He preferred words to acts. It is after all words and ideas that defined his role in the revolution, the role of the poet as politician. He distrusted those who saw in the revolution simply a chance to act.

With this in mind, when the lists were circulating and members of the provisional government had to be chosen, Lamartine systematically eliminated candidates who looked too radical. Thus, as he admits in his *Histoire de la révolution de 1848,* he was directly responsible for evicting Louis Blanc, a definite favorite of the crowd. His strategy was simply to pass over this name that figured on the vast majority of lists: "He [Lamartine] was aware of the popular power of that young writer [Louis Blanc], and appreciated his talents; but he dreaded the spirit of a foregone conclusion in a government of pacification and concord" (*HR*, p. 127). When the members of the provisional government were finally announced, there were no surprises. Lamartine's satisfaction with the way the revolution was going is evident in his later account:

> Dupont de l'Eure represented public virtue; Lamartine, the fraternization of classes in a democracy; Garnier Pagès [the father of Étienne, who played a key role in the July Revolution of 1830 and died in 1841], hereditary esteem and popular gratitude paid to a tomb; Marie, stern authority, combined with moderation; Ledru Rollin, the impetuosity, the enthusiasm, and perhaps the excess of republicanism; Crémieux, the power of debate suited to every

purpose, and liberty of conscience embodied in the government. [*HR*, p. 127]

Nothing very revolutionary in this jumble of hereditary esteem, public virtue, austerity, and useful language. One is struck by the absence of radicals in this revolution begun by the people. Of the eleven members of the provisional government, nine were bourgeois; only one (Albert) was a worker. Even so, the three true representatives of the people (Louis Blanc, Flocon, and Albert) were only secretaries.

Lamartine finally dragged the unruly crowd to the Hôtel de Ville where the provisional government retired to private rooms to decide on a plan of action. During this tumultuous evening, the delegates of the people interrupted the deliberations of the provisional leaders seven times to make sure that they were not going to be deceived and that no one was going to make away with their revolution as happened in 1830. Each time Lamartine was sent to proffer reassurance, "his lofty stature and his sonorous voice peculiarly adapted him to these encounters with the mob" (*HR*, p. 160). His eloquence calmed the crowd as he embroidered endlessly on the favorite themes of every revolution: liberty, equality, fraternity. Every speech resembled an ode: "Oh people. . . . Oh, yes, let us embrace one another, love one another, let us fraternize like a single family from position to position, from class to class, from opulence to indigence" (*MP*, 38:380). A few brave souls called him a "bore," which only prompted him to even more vertiginous words. Caught in a lyric whirlwind, dumbfounded and dazzled by so many beautiful sentences, the delegates of the people eventually left. Finally, around midnight, the central question became more pressing than ever. "Are you going to proclaim the Republic?" he was asked. " 'Well,' said he, 'it is you who have pronounced. You shall be a republic' " (*HR*, p. 177). And so the Republic was proclaimed (figs. 2 and 3).

Lamartine is the living expression of what we could call change in continuity. What he wants is not a revolution but "a complement of revolution" (*HR*, p. 83). Lamartine offered a new vision, a vision of political compromise adapted to the moment. This political pragmatism is common enough for us today but was not usual in Lamartine's time. His setback with the regime of Louis-Philippe forced Lamartine to face reality. It was no longer a time for authoritarian regimes. Lamartine was well aware that power had to make concessions to the rising proletariat; thus his "progressivism," which now seems a matter of course, was greatly misunderstood in his own time. He was even accused of betraying his class. Neither the monarchy nor the bourgeois opposition conceived for a moment that their legitimacy could reside in the masses. From this perspective, nineteenth-century French society is manichean, a period that fully justifies Marx's vision of an antagonism between dominant and dominated classes. In the nineteenth century, power is not shared.

FIG. 2.—Lamartine at the Hôtel de Ville, 25 February 1848.

FIG. 3. — Lamartine at the Hôtel de Ville, 25 February 1848.

Defender of private property like most of the members of the provisional government, Lamartine nevertheless had a different political strategy from that of his colleagues to reinforce power. In 1848 he suggested a means more powerful and more sure than bayonets to safeguard property. He simply proposed to open up property to the greatest possible number of workers. Through order, economy, and work the poet hoped to transform workers into owners and thus to erase the growing popularity of socialist ideas. He dreamed of giving " 'the pledge of property into every hand. It [property] will thus recruit, from the far limits of the population, force, partisans, defenders of the propertied society!' "[28] These prophetic words seem to have been heard.

Lamartine was one of the first to see that control of the people depends, at least in theory, on their participation in the direction of the state. Established authority must endeavor to demonstrate that it can satisfy the expectations and the claims of the masses. From this type of power emerged an opportunistic discourse, unpremeditated and lyrical, which adapted to the requirements of the moment. From this point of view Lamartine was ahead of his time and shows us a new political strategy. Less static and more favorable to openness than all his colleagues among the deputies, he announced, in his political vacillation, what seems today to be the norm. Modern political authority, if it wants to survive, sooner or later has to come to terms with the masses and pay them court. As early as 1843 Lamartine determined that if he wanted to be exalted to the skies and recognized as a genius, he had to rally to the people. Nonetheless, if he wanted to be both guide and poet, he still had to convince the masses to let themselves be guided. Lamartine criticized the July Monarchy on just this account, for not having known how to be the "poetry of the people."

> Every government without poetry is petty. Louis XIV was the poetry of the throne, which is why he is Louis XIV. Napoleon was the poetry of power; 1792 was the poetry of patriotism. The Convention itself was the nefarious poetry of crime. If the July Government had fallen in other hands . . . it could have been the poetry of the people. Is France not the poet of nations?[29]

In spite of his aversion for the crowd, Lamartine grasped the need to compromise and to convert the actions of the masses into words. He claimed his right as the poet of the people and wished to tie his work to the desires of the underprivileged classes. He knew that this people needed guides. When the first barricades were erected in Paris, Lamartine was still hesitating. On that afternoon of 24 February, at the Chamber

28. Quoted in Bert, *Lamartine "homme social,"* p. 176.
29. Quoted in Latreille, *Lamartine: poète politique,* p. 92.

of Deputies and then at the Hôtel de Ville, he sensed that his hour had come. He saw the possibility of becoming a Caesar, at once politician and poet.

It is therefore not at all surprising that Lamartine called for universal suffrage. The idea alarmed the National Assembly, but we should not make the mistake of seeing Lamartine as the representative of the people. He knew perfectly well that universal suffrage would scarcely alter the political map. On the contrary, it would facilitate his own ascent to power. Lamartine hoped to rely on numbers to legitimate his role as guide to the people since, as he speculated, "without a base in universal suffrage, a government is suspended in a void" (*CP,* 2:407). Lamartine applied the same strategy when he asked for the abolition of slavery: "Blacks, some 300,000 [Lamartine refers to Haiti] will accept being subjects but never slaves in a country that has slaves" (to Mr. Champrans, 26 May 1844; *C,* 6:112). It is no longer a question of power dependent on a minority but a universal authority claiming to represent *all* of the people. The universality of poetry turns up in practical politics.

Since it is evident that such an authority must also watch out for revolutionary acts that might affect its legitimacy, we have the explanation for Lamartine's displacement of the concept of "revolution as action" toward the term of "revolution as principle." On this subject of the revolution as idea or principle, Lamartine had already expressed his views to his friend Virieu in 1830: "We agree only on our horror for the Revolution as action, not for the Revolution as principle. The Revolution as principle is one of those great and fertile ideas that renew the form of human society from time to time" (to the count of Virieu, 24 October 1830; *C,* 4:355). Leo Gershoy has demonstrated that Lamartine's adherence to the revolution is purely Hegelian.[30] History is only an *idea*. And as Lamartine had already announced in *Des destinées de la poésie,* the idea precedes and always prevails over action. Lamartine understood that words are the daily bread that those in authority, through the intermediary of the poetic genius, must offer the masses. To attract the people it is necessary to talk to them, charm them. It is then perfectly obvious that Lamartine reduces politics, just like poetry, to a science of speeches full of lofty, sonorous words. Take, for example, his outline for a speech on liberty in 1837: "What will become of true liberty, etc., etc., etc.?" (to Mr. Dubois, 1837; *C,* 5:209)—one word and lots of et ceteras. The idea alone counts, improvisation will take care of the rest.

This "modern" aspect of the Lamartinian discourse is not the only one. If one cannot count on the ideological apparatus at one's disposal, and if demands go too far, the established power (of which Lamartine is now an integral part) can always fall back on reaction and repression. The episode in which Lamartine rejected the red flag as the new emblem

---

30. See Gershoy, "Three French Historians and the Revolution of 1848," p. 139.

of the Republic shows how this discourse could modulate and suddenly turn hard.

When the crowd returned to the Hôtel de Ville on 25 February and demanded a decree that would make the red flag the national flag, Lamartine confronted them alone. His respect for tradition and his distaste for this symbol of the Terror of 1793 led him vehemently to oppose the revolutionaries' demand. Once again, Lamartinian discourse turned the situation around. The principle was the same as the evening before, but the struggle was closer, revelatory of the full force of Lamartine's poetics. As he boasted in the *Histoire de la Révolution de 1848*, "he [Lamartine] commenced by soothing the assemblage by a species of hymn upon the victory, so sudden, so complete, and unhoped for, even by the republicans most ardent for liberty" (*HR*, p. 228). With a few words Lamartine endeavored to subdue the people. But this time victory did not come so easily. A few rebels took aim. Lamartine abruptly changed his tone, speaking of the "flag of terror" and threatening to quit the provisional government. However, the poet realized his mistake. Action would get him nowhere. His genius lay in words. He took hold of himself and launched into the grandiloquent phrases that have become part of French history:

> "I will reject, even to death, this banner of blood,—and you should repudiate it still more than myself; for this red flag you offer us, has only made the circuit of the Champ de Mars, through the people's blood in 1791 and 1793; while the tri-coloured banner has made the circuit of the world, with the name, with the glory and liberty of your country!" [*HR*, p. 230]

Interrupted by enthusiastic cries, Lamartine fell from the chair on which he had stood to deliver his speech. Words conquered once again. "The crowd . . . carried away by the words it had just heard" finally accepted "the flag regained by the persuasions [*paroles*] of Lamartine" (*HR*, p. 230). Once again Lamartine mastered action by ideas, the sign of true genius and true poets.

During the evening of 25 February Paris walls were covered with a poster that contained the following words: "The provisional Government of the Republic declares that the nation adopts the *Three Colors* set out as THEY were during the REPUBLIC. The flag will bear these words: French Republic."[31] This proclamation, no doubt drawn up by Lamartine himself and signed by the members of the provisional government, underscores two words that give a sense of continuity to the revolution. The people of 24 February must comprehend that this revolution did not belong to them but was the remains of a bourgeois revolutionary

31. *Les Murailles révolutionnaires de 1848*, ed. Charles Boutin, 2 vols. (Paris, 1868), 1:41.

process begun over a half century before. Here we find once again Lamartine's favored theme of a "complement of revolution." On 25 February the victorious bourgeoisie reinstated the tricolor flag. Less than twenty-four hours after his accession to power, Lamartine's rejection of the red flag symbolized the people's impotence.

This fight over the red flag must not be taken lightly. Symbols often reflect the events that create them. Underrepresented in the provisional government, the people, who were celebrating their victory only the evening before, were now striving to preserve their gains and to ratify them by the symbolic adoption of a flag with which the working class had been associated since 1793. Thus, it was the future of the revolution, far more than the tricolor flag, that was at stake. The rejection of the red flag portended the reaction that culminated in bloody repression the following June. As Jean Pommier has noted, this defeat of the red flag was in effect a good sign for conservatives who could see it as a positive sign for the preservation of a bourgeois revolution. Once again, the proletariat was overrun by the bourgeoisie, which assigned to the fallen emblem the ideas that it feared.[32] This reaction seemed a necessary one for Lamartine who had once declared that a counterrevolution alone could give new life to the revolution.

Here Lamartine abandoned the liberalism of the 24th and hardened his discourse to defend bourgeois principles, for, as Marx saw so clearly, Lamartine, "the spokesman of the February Revolution, by his position and his views, belonged to the bourgeoisie."[33] Lamartine associated himself with the later repression precisely because he judged reaction indispensable to put an end to what he called the "anarchy of the people." On the very next day the proletariat, complimented so effusively the previous day for its role in the overthrow of the monarchy, had to accede to the values and decisions of the provisional government. Lamartine remained the trump card of this new authority. By his mastery of the tirade and lyric discourse, he enabled the ratification of actions, which, from 25 February on, were already slipping away from the people. Only a poet of genius could win such a combat of words.

The victory did not last long. Misunderstood by the bourgeoisie and overlooked by the people, Lamartine was abandoned by everyone in the June days. His failure in the December presidential election—with fewer than eighteen thousand votes—ended his political career. Right after the election, Lamartine complained of the ingratitude of "the bourgeoisie, the nobility which I covered with my body for three long months."[34] He

32. See Jean Pommier, *Les Écrivains devant la révolution de 1848: Lamartine, Hugo, Lamennais, George Sand, Michelet, Béranger* (Paris, 1948), p. 35.

33. Marx, *The Class Struggles in France*, p. 39.

34. To Valentine de Cessiat, 11 Dec. 1848, *Lamartine et ses nièces. Correspondance inédite (1842–1854)* (Paris, 1928). Lamartine entitled an article that appeared in *Le Conseiller de peuple* "Ingratitude des riches."

is not entirely wrong if "body" is replaced with "speech." The embittered poet retired from the political scene and decided to devote himself to the education of the people. If the "child people" did not accept a father, perhaps it would accept an advisor.

Politics as Poetry or Poetry as Politics?

In this manner Lamartinian discourse joins poetry and politics. For him the two are the object of an improvised speech. In his first article of "advice" written for the newspaper *Le Conseiller du peuple,* which he founded early in 1849, Lamartine explains the "instinctive" nature of his speeches during the revolution: "Murmuring, agitation, complaints, accusations, some want to protest, but it is useless. It is too late, the word has been spoken. Revolutions are God's great improvisations through the mouths of men. I who have been one of the first to pronounce this work, I swear to you that one hour before I did not know what I was going to say" (*CP,* 1:17). This theme of improvisation provides the common ground for both of Lamartine's discourses, since Lamartine also conceived of poetry as a divine improvisation.

The success of the events on 24 and 25 February nevertheless reveals a fatal contradiction. If Lamartine came to power because he was a poet, this same linguistic trump card soon turned against him since he was never able to separate the poet from the politician in the eyes of the people. Where the people could have accepted the calming words of a poet, this is no longer the case when that poet starts signing decrees that turn into "acts." If he had given up his position as a poet, Lamartine ought to have been able to move into action and become a politician full time. He was asked to choose, and he refused. It is therefore difficult to know if politics were a poetry for Lamartine or if, on the contrary, his poetry was all his politics. The two are intrinsically tied in the Lamartinian discourse on revolution; they cannot be separated. Lamartine knew that this unifying sentiment between poetry and politics posed an insoluble problem at the outset. The poet, retired from the world and looking at society from above, finds it difficult to come down to earth once he has taken off in a burst of lyric inspiration. Charles Baudelaire's image of the poet as "albatross" is a response to a new reality for the poet. At once sublime in his poetic flight and awkward in earthly politics, the poet must choose his world.

In Lamartine's case the genius of the poet-politician lasted hardly more than three months. In the case of the Revolution of 1848 ideas once again yielded before events, and Lamartine tried to revive this idea through mass education. At the end of his sixth article of "advice" to the people, Lamartine appends publicity for the recently published *Histoire de la Révolution de 1848:* "The scenes of the eight days in February, and those of March 17th, April 16th, and May 15th are highly emotional. It is a fact unique in the annals of literature and politics that the actor and the author of such events joined in one man. Monsieur de Lamartine was the first to act, speak and write at one and the same time" (*CP*, 1:263). Here, once again, is the universal man. His work, now an integral part of the history of the Revolution of 1848, is itself one last attempt at improvisation: "It is a two-volume improvisation on the firing line" (*CP*, 1:263). Lamartine could not resign himself to failure. He remained a poet in his actions, his actions bespeak poetry. Thus, his seventh "advice" to the people compares the literary success of *L'Histoire de la Révolution de 1848* to the success of his poetry, *Raphaël* and *Les Confidences*. There is, in a very significant sense, a single Lamartinian text.

In a "talk with the reader," at the end of the tenth "advice," Lamartine offers as a "literary" text a letter he had written 4 October 1849 and comments accordingly: "Upon reflection I had to write a talk for tomorrow to explain 'harmonies' to my readers. I am going to copy this letter, leaving out what is too personal; nothing can better explain what a 'harmony' is: youth that awakes, love that dreams, the eye that contemplates, the soul that arises" (*CP*, 1:442). But Lamartine cannot keep from adding a postscript: "If our Readers welcome this piece with interest, we think that we can promise them to engage Monsieur de Lamartine from time to time to join such literary talks to his political *Conseils*" (*CP*, 1:443). Thus the confusion between the "literary" and the "political" is established. If the people need geniuses to be educated politically, by the same token Lamartine also ascertained that his rejection by the people in June 1848 had to do with a need by this same people for a literary and poetic education. There lay his new path. He gave up the political education of the masses for their literary education, and embarked on the enormous project of *Cours familier de littérature*, twenty-eight volumes published from 1856 until his death in 1869.

Lamartine spent his whole life in song. The romantic revolution and the Revolution of 1848 let him place his voice in the service of the people, the ultimate object of poetic and political desire. After the Revolution, when he was asked why he no longer sang as before, Lamartine gave a long explanation:

> And today I continually receive letters from strangers who ask, 'Why don't you sing any more? We are still listening.' Have these invisible friends of my poetry never realized the nature of my weak talent and the nature of poetry itself? They apparently believe that the human heart is a lyre always readied and tuned, to be strummed at every hour, on which no string gives way or mutes or breaks over the years and under the vicissitudes of the soul? This may be true for the sovereign poets, indefatigable, immortal, ever rejuvenated by their genius, poets like Homer, Virgil, Racine,

Voltaire, Dante, Petrarch, Byron and others I could name if they were not my rivals and contemporaries. As for me, I was not so gifted. Poetry never possessed all of me. In my soul and in my life I gave it only the place that man gives to song in his day: a few moments in the morning, a few more in the evening. . . . The man who would sing forever would not be a man, but a voice. [*CP*, 1:578–79]

Louis Blanc was right to speak of the theatrical role of Lamartine during February 1848. The pictorial representations of the revolution invariably show the poet at the podium or on a chair, declaiming sentences as if they were lines of poetry. One of his contemporaries left this marvelous image of the poet: "There is Lamartine. . . . He sings when he meditates . . . , he sings when he sings, he sings all the time."[35] Lamartine's song during the Revolution of 1848 mixed poetry and politics, a sublime moment when the poet thought he was a universal man and a genius, at one and the same time poet and politician. But soon, having sung too much, Lamartine became no more than one voice among many, one voice that fell silent as rapidly, as spontaneously as it had made itself heard. Poetry turned against the man. The idea of revolution, sung by Lamartine, once again came up short against events.

---

35. The deputy Timon Cormenin, quoted in Harris, *Lamartine et le peuple*, p. 128.

Flaubert's Point of View

Pierre Bourdieu

Translated by Priscilla Parkhurst Ferguson

The break necessary to establish a rigorous science of cultural works is something more and something else than a simple methodological reversal.[1] It implies a true *conversion* of the ordinary way of thinking and living the intellectual enterprise. It is a matter of breaking the narcissistic relationship inscribed in the representation of intellectual work as a "creation" and which excludes as the expression par excellence of "reductionist sociology" the effort to subject the artist and the work of art to a way of thinking that is doubly objectionable since it is both genetic and generic.

It would be easy to show what the most different kinds of analysis of the work of art owe to the norms that require treating works in and for themselves, with no reference to the social conditions of their production. Thus in the now-classic *Theory of Literature*, René Wellek and Austin Warren seem to advocate "an explanation in terms of the personality and the life of the writer." In fact, because they (no doubt along with most of their readers) accept the ideology of the "man of genius" they are committed, in their own terms, to "one of the oldest and best-established

This article is a much-abridged section of a forthcoming book. For reasons of space many of the supporting examples were omitted.

1. See Pierre Bourdieu, "Intellectual Field and Creative Project," trans. Sian France, *Social Science Information* 8 (Apr. 1969): 89–119; originally published as "Champ intellectuel et projet créateur," *Les Temps modernes* no. 246 (Nov. 1966): 865–906. See also Bourdieu, "Champ du pouvoir, champ intellectuel et habitus de classe," *Scolies* 1 (1971): 7–26, and Bourdieu, "The Genesis of the Concepts of *Habitus* and *Field*," trans. Channa Newman, *Sociocriticism* no. 2 (Dec. 1985): 11–24.

methods of literary study"—which seeks the explanatory principle of a work in the author taken in isolation (the uniqueness of a work being considered a characteristic of the "creator").[2] In fact, this explanatory principle resides in the relationship between the "space" of works in which each particular work is taken and the "space" of authors in which each cultural enterprise is constituted. Similarly, when Sartre takes on the project of specifying the mediations through which society determined Flaubert, the individual, he attributes to those factors that can be perceived from\that point of view—that is, to social class as refracted through a family structure—what are instead the effects of generic factors influencing every writer in an artistic field that is itself in a subordinate position in the field of power and also the effects specific to all writers who occupy the same position as Flaubert within the artistic field.

But it is by the theory of the *"projet originel"* that Sartre, following his logic as far as it will go, brings out one of the basic assumptions of every form of literary analysis: that which is inscribed in the expressions of everyday life, and in particular in the many "already," "from then on," "from his early years on," scattered through biographies. These ordinary expressions assume that each life is a whole, a coherent ensemble oriented in a given direction, and that it cannot be understood except as the unitary expression of a subjective and objective intention, visible in the subject's every experience, even and especially the earliest ones. Both the retrospective illusion, which establishes final events as the ends of initial experiences or behavior, and the ideology of predestination, which credits exceptional individuals with divine foresight, tacitly assume that life is organized like a story, that it moves from an origin, understood as a point of departure and also as a first cause, or better yet, as a generative principle, and that the term of a life is also its goal. It is this philosophy that Sartre's *"projet originel"* makes explicit by posing the explicit consciousness of determinants implied in a social position as a principle of all existence.

Analyzing the essentialist philosophy exemplified for him by Leibnitzian monadology, Sartre observed in *Being and Nothingness* that this philosophical position abolished chronology by reducing it to logic. Paradoxically, Sartre's own philosophy of biography produces the same kind of effect but starting from an absolute beginning—in this case, the "dis-

---

2. René Wellek and Austin Warren, *Theory of Literature* (New York, 1956) p. 69.

Pierre Bourdieu holds the chair of sociology at the Collège de France and is director of the Centre de Sociologie européenne at the École des Hautes Études en Sciences Sociales. Among his most recent works are *Distinction* (1984), *Homo Academicus* (1984), and *Choses Dites* (1987).

covery" established by an act of originating consciousness.[3] Sartre is among those who, in Martin Luther's terms, "sin bravely": we can be grateful to him for bringing out so clearly the philosophy that supports methodologies as diverse as the "man and his work" monographs that followed the lead of Gustave Lanson, textual analyses applied to a single fragment of a given work (that is, Jakobson and Lévi-Strauss' analysis of Baudelaire's "Les Chats"), or even the various enterprises of social history of art or literature which, in trying to account for a work starting from psychological or social variables for a single author, are doomed to pass over the essential. A genetic sociology alone can grasp the essential, that is, the genesis and the structure of the specific social space in which the "creative project" was formed.

1. The Theory of the Field within the Space of Possible Theoretic Projects

But first, this genetic sociology must be situated within the universe of approaches to literary phenomena. Indeed, one of the most significant properties of the fields of cultural production is that they propose to those who work within them a *space of possibilities* or, if you like, a problematic (objectively given in the form of an ensemble of real or possible positions) which tends to orient their research, even without their being aware of it, by defining the universe of possible questions. This problematic both fixes their enterprise in time and space and makes it relatively independent with respect to direct social and economic determinants. Product of the history of the field itself, this space is marked by the ensemble of intellectual bench marks, often incarnated in intellectual "stars" or various "isms." These must be mastered, at least in practice, in order to participate in the game. Above and beyond individual agents, this space functions as a sort of common reference system that situates contemporaries, even when they do not consciously refer to each other, by virtue of their common situation within the same intellectual system.

This logic obtains for literary research too, and, if only for purposes of self-analysis, it is worthwhile filling in the space of the possible forms of cultural analysis and making explicit their theoretical assumptions. A first division places internal readings (in the sense that Saussure talks about "internal linguistics"), formal or formalist readings, against external readings, which call on interpretative principles outside the work, like social and economic factors.

The first tradition, in its most widespread form, is rooted in the ethos of professional commentators on texts, that is, professors everywhere,

3. Jean-Paul Sartre, "La Conscience de classe chez Flaubert," *Les Temps modernes* no. 240 (May 1966): 1922–51.

which mediaeval taxonomy opposed, under the name of *lectores,* to the producers of texts, called *auctores.* Sustained by all the authority of the academy, and by the facilities that the academy procures for the fulfillment of its tasks (the famous "explication de textes" of professors in the French educational system), this tradition does not need to set itself up as a doctrine. With a few exceptions (like New Criticism), it can remain a *doxa,* able to perpetuate itself surreptitiously, through and beyond the apparent refurbishing of the academic liturgy like "structuralist" or "deconstructionist" readings of isolated texts. Or again this tradition finds sustenance in the commentary on canons of "pure" reading as in *The Sacred Wood* of T. S. Eliot or by writers of the *Nouvelle Revue française,* notably Paul Valéry.

To give this tradition a theoretical foundation requires us to look in two directions: on the one hand, to the neo-Kantian philosophy of symbolic forms and, more generally, the traditions that affirm the existence of universal anthropological structures, as in the comparative mythology of Mircea Eliade or Jungian (in France, Bachelardian) psychoanalysis; and on the other hand, to structuralism. In the first case, through an internal, formal reading that seeks the explanatory principle in the works themselves, the idea is to grasp universal forms of literary reason, or "literarity," in its different guises, notably poetic, and to apprehend ahistorical structuring structures that are the principle of the literary or poetic construction of the world. This position, perhaps because it appears virtually untenable, is scarcely ever presented as such, even though it haunts all research concerned with an "essence" of "the literary," "the poetic," or metaphor.

Intellectually and socially, the structuralist solution is by far the stronger. Socially, it often takes up the internalist *doxa* and confers a scientific aura on professional commentary as a formal dismantling of atemporal texts. Breaking with universalism, structuralist hermeneutics treats cultural works (languages and myth, that is, structures that have been structured without a structuring subject, and, by extension, works of art) as historical products whose analysis ought to bring to light the specific structure. But this analysis makes no reference to the economic or social conditions of either the production or the producer of the work. (And never even poses the problem of defining the body of work analyzed—do we take a single sonnet of Baudelaire, all of his work, all the contemporary work within which that work is located?)

Michel Foucault undoubtedly made the most rigorous formulation of the bases of structuralist analysis of cultural works. Retaining from Saussure the primacy accorded relationships and well aware that no work exists by itself, that is, outside the relationships of interdependence that connect it to other works, Foucault proposed the term "field of strategic possibilities" for the "system of regulated differences and dispersions" within which each particular work is defined. But, close to the use that semiologists make of a notion like semantic field, he explicitly refused to seek elsewhere than in the field of discourse the explanatory principle of each discourse in the field. Faithful to the Saussurian tradition and to its division between internal and external linguistics, Foucault affirmed the absolute autonomy of this "field of strategic possibilities," of this episteme. He dismissed as "a doxological illusion" (why not just say sociological?) the claim to discover what he calls "the polemical field" and in "the divergence of interests or mental habits of individuals" (which is to say, everything that I was covering at about the same time with the ideas of *field* and *habitus*) the explanatory principle for everything that takes place in "the field of strategic possibilities," the only reality with which, according to him, a scientific approach to works has to contend.[4]

This manoeuver allowed Foucault to transfer into the heaven of ideas the oppositions and antagonisms rooted in the relationships between the producers and the users of cultural works. Obviously, there is no denying the specific determinant exerted by the space of possibilities. Indeed, one function of the concept of a relatively autonomous *field*, endowed with its own history, is to account for such determinants. However, it is not possible to consider the cultural order as a system totally independent of the actors and institutions that put it into practice and bring it into existence: if only because there does not seem any way to account for changes in this arbitrarily isolated and thereby dehistoricized universe unless we endow it with an immanent propensity for autotransformation through a mysterious form of *Selbstbewegung*.

The same criticism can be directed against the Russian formalists. Like Foucault, who drew on the same sources, they considered only the system of works, the network of relationships between texts, their "intertextuality." Hence, again like Foucault, they were obliged to locate the dynamic principle of this system in the textual system itself. Yuri Tynianov, for example, explicitly affirmed that everything that is literary can be determined only by prior conditions of the literary system. And so they were led to devise a natural law of poetic change out of the process of "automatization" and "deautomatization."[5]

As for external analysis, whether it takes the relationships between the social world and cultural works according to the logic of the reflection model or as "symbolic expression," to use Engels' term for law, it ties works directly to the social characteristics of authors or to the avowed or presumed public. Thus we have Marxist-inspired research for which Lucien Goldmann supplied the paradigm and from which, despite his

4. Michel Foucault, "Réponse au cercle d'épistémologie," *Cahiers pour l'analyse* 9 (Summer 1968): 9–40.
5. Victor Shklovsky's well-known terms have been translated variously as "habitualization," "automatism," "disautomatization," "defamiliarization," and "bestrangement." Shklovsky's term in Russian is *ostraneniye*, "making strange." See *Russian Formalist Criticism: Four Essays*, trans. Lee T. Lemon and Marion Reis (Lincoln, Nebr., 1965), and Victor Erlich, *Russian Formalism: History-Doctrine* (Paris, 1969).

every effort to multiply mediations and to break with deterministic philosophy, Sartre is not so distant. This approach ties works directly to the world vision or to the interests of the social group which are supposedly expressed through the artist acting like some sort of medium.

The notion of *field* (artistic, scientific, juridical, and so on) was elaborated against this form of reductionism and against the *short-circuit effect* that it produces. Exclusive attention to *functions* (which the internalist tradition, and notably structuralism, was undoubtedly wrong to neglect) inclines us to overlook the internal logic of cultural objects, in other words, their linguistic structure. Even more important, concentration on function leads us to forget that these objects are produced by actors and institutions, by priests, judges, or artists. The functions fulfilled by these actors are defined essentially within the producers' universe. The social microcosm that I call the *literary field* is a space of *objective* relations between positions—between that of the celebrated artist and that of the avant-garde artist, for example. One cannot understand what is going on without reconstructing the laws specific to this particular universe, which, with its lines of force tied to a particular distribution of specific kinds of capital (economic, symbolic, cultural, and so on), provides the principle for the strategies adopted by different producers, the alliances they make, the schools they found, and the art they defend.

To speak of the field, moreover, reminds us that external factors—economic crises, technological change, political revolutions, or simply the demand of a given group—exercise an effect only through transformations in the structure of the field where these factors obtain. The field *refracts*. Only by exposing the specific logic of this refraction can we understand what it is all about, although it is certainly tempting to tie this logic directly to the forces of power in the social world.

Where are the works in all this? Haven't we lost what the most subtle advocates of internal reading brought to the interpretive enterprise? On the contrary, by analyzing the literary field as a space of positions corresponding to a space of homologous aesthetic positions we are able to transcend the opposition, as strong as it is pernicious, between internal readings and external analysis and at the same time preserve the benefits and requirements of two approaches traditionally considered irreconcilable. If we retain from the notion of intertextuality the fact that the space of works always appears as a field of positions that must be understood as interrelations, we can posit a homology (which empirical analysis will confirm) between the space of positions within the field of production and the space of works defined in terms of their strictly symbolic content, notably their *form,* but considered as positions within the space of works and therefore of forms.

In this way we can resolve several basic problems, beginning with change. We can move beyond the opposition often presented as insuperable, between synchrony and history. We will not find the impetus of the properly literary process of automatization and deautomatization described by the formalists in the works themselves but rather in the constitutive opposition of all fields of cultural production between orthodoxy and heresy. The process that gives works momentum is produced by the struggle between the "orthodox" and the "heretics": between on the one hand, actors who tend to conservatism, to defend routine and routinization, in a word, the established symbolic order and the academic institutions that reproduce that order, and on the other hand, those who incline to heretical breaks, to criticism of established forms, to the subversion of current models, and to a return to original purity.

Knowledge of structure alone can yield a true knowledge of the processes which lead to a new state of that structure and which also comprise the conditions for understanding that structure. It is certain that the direction of change depends on the system of stylistic possibilities that define what is thinkable and what is not, what can be done at a given moment in a particular field and what cannot. It is no less certain that the direction of change depends as well on the interests that direct the actors to one or another of the possibilities proposed, or more exactly, to an area within the space of possibilities homologous to the place that these actors occupy within the space of artistic positions.

In brief, the strategies of actors and institutions involved in literary or artistic struggles depend on the position that they occupy in the structure of the field, that is, within the structure of distribution of capital of the prestige (institutionalized or not) accorded them by their peers and by the public at large, and by their interest in preserving or transforming this structure, in maintaining the rules of the game or subverting them. Conversely, the stakes of the struggle between those in control and the claimants to control, the questions that set them against each other, the theses and even the antitheses contested by both sides, depend on the state of the accepted problematic, that is, on the space of possibilities inherited from preceding struggles, because this space orients the search for solutions and, hence, present and future production.

2. The Literary Field in Flaubert's Time

This method centers around three elements as necessary and as necessarily tied to each other as the three levels of social reality that they grasp: first, analysis of the position occupied by the artistic or literary field within the political field ("champ du pouvoir") and the evolution of that position over time;[6] second, the structure of the literary field,

---

6. "Political field" refers to specifically political institutions and actors ("champ politique") and also to the whole field of power relations in politics and society ("champ du pouvoir"). The latter, broader sense is intended here.

that is, the structure of the objective relations between the positions occupied by actors or groups competing for literary legitimacy at a given point in time; and finally, genesis of the different producers' *habitus*.[7]

The Literary Field and the Political Field

The relationships that tie the literary field to the political field raise the question of the autonomy of the literary field with respect to those who hold political or economic power and, more specifically, the particular form of this dependence. In Flaubert's time the relationship between the producers of culture and dominant social groups is nothing like what it was in previous centuries, whether we consider direct dependence on an individual who commissions a work or loyalty to an official or unofficial patron of the arts. Henceforth we are dealing with a sort of *structural subordination* that obtained very unequally and very differently for different authors according to their position in the field. This subordination was primarily established through two intermediaries. On the one hand, the market worked either directly, through sales, and so on, or indirectly, through the new jobs produced by journalism, publishing, and all the forms of what Sainte-Beuve called "industrial literature." On the other hand, the enduring connections, founded on affinities of life-style and values, through the salons in particular, tied at least some kinds of writers to certain segments of high society and served to guide state subventions of the arts. This subtly hierarchical world of the salon helped structure the literary field and ensure exchange between those in power and the most conformist or the most prestigious writers.

A circular causal relationship tied the development of the market to the influx of a significant population of impecunious young men from the lower-class Parisian milieux and especially from the provinces, who came to Paris hoping for careers as writers or artists—careers that until then had been reserved for the aristocracy or the Parisian bourgeoisie. Despite the many new positions created by economic development, neither manufacturing nor the civil service could absorb all those with degrees from secondary education.[8] Versed in the humanities and rhetoric but

7. "The structures constitutive of a particular type of environment . . . produce *habitus*, systems of durable, transposable *dispositions*, structured structures predisposed to function as structuring structures, that is, as principles of the generation and structuring of practices and representations. . . . [T]he practices produced by the habitus [are] the strategy-generating principle enabling agents to cope with unforeseen and ever-changing situations." Bourdieu, *Outline of a Theory of Practice*, trans. Richard Nice (Cambridge, 1977), p. 72.

8. Their number increased significantly during the first half of the nineteenth century all over Europe and again in France during the Second Empire (1852–70). See Lenore O'Boyle, "The Problem of Excess of Educated Men in Western Europe, 1800–1850," *Journal of Modern History* 42 (Dec. 1970): 471–95, and O'Boyle, "The Democratic Left in Germany, 1848," *Journal of Modern History* 33 (Dec. 1961): 374–83.

devoid of the financial means or the social influence needed to make the most of these claims, the newcomers found themselves pushed back toward various literary professions and, for the artists among them, toward the artistic professions glorified by the salon. Endowed with all the prestige of romanticism, these professions had the added advantage of requiring no academic qualification.

These structural changes were undoubtedly a major determinant of the growing independence of the artistic and literary fields and the corresponding transformation of the relationship between the world of art and literature and the world of political power. However, we ought to guard against reducing this fundamentally ambiguous process to its alienating effects as did Raymond Williams who in analyzing the English romantics simply forgot that this process had liberating effects as well. This new freedom, moreover, provided the very principle of the new dependence—in, for example, the possibility for what Max Weber called the "proletarian intelligentsia" to make a living, however precarious, from all the minor jobs tied to "industrial literature" and journalism.

From this unprecedented gathering of so many young men hoping to live off art and separated from the rest of society by the life-style that they were in the process of inventing, there arose a veritable society within society. Even if, as Robert Darnton has shown, this society within a society can be traced to the eighteenth century, in the mid-nineteenth century this new social reality appeared absolutely extraordinary and without precedent. Not surprisingly, it raised all sorts of questions, even and indeed especially among its members. An ambiguous reality, "bohemia" prompted ambivalent feelings among its most ardent advocates. In the first place, it defied classification. Close to the "people" whose poverty it often shared, bohemia was separated from the poor by the life-style in which it found social definition and which, however ostentatiously opposed to bourgeois norms and conventions, situated bohemia closer to the aristocracy or to the upper bourgeoisie than to the petty bourgeoisie or the "people." All this is no less true for the most destitute members of bohemia, who, secure in their cultural capital and in their authority as tastemakers, could get at discount the outrageous sartorial splendors, the gastronomic indulgences, the affairs and liaisons—everything for which the "bourgeois" had to pay full price.

Bohemia never ceased changing as its numbers increased and its celebrity attracted these impoverished young men who around 1848 made up the "second bohemia." In contrast to the romantic dandies of "golden bohemia" in the 1830s incarnated by Gérard de Nerval, this bohemia of Henry Murger (*Scenes of Bohemian Life*, 1848) and Champfleury, the self-proclaimed head of the realists, constituted a veritable reserve intellectual army, directly subject to the laws of the market and often constrained to take a second job that frequently had no literary connections at all. In fact the two bohemias coexisted, but with different social weight.

The true "proletarian intellectuals" were often so impoverished that they took themselves as their subject and ended up inventing what was called "realism." This bohemia coexisted, not without an occasional scuffle, with the dissolute or debased bourgeois who possessed all the qualifications of the dominant social groups save one—money. Poor relations of the great bourgeois dynasties, aristocrats already ruined or on the way down, foreigners or members of stigmatized minorities like the Jews—these were "bourgeois without a penny," as Pissarro called them, or who bet what money they had on this enterprise knowing they were sure to lose in the short term but ever hopeful of glory in the long term. In their divided or double *habitus*, these aspiring writers had already adapted to the position of being the dominated fraction of the dominant social group. This contradictory position destined them to a sort of objective, and therefore subjective indeterminacy, which was never more visible than in the simultaneous or successive fluctuations of their relationships with the authorities.

The relationships that these writers and artists maintained with the market no doubt contributed to their ambivalent representation of the "general public," at once fascinating and despised, in which they mixed up the "bourgeois" enslaved to the vulgar cares of commerce and the "people" stultified by labor. This double ambivalence induced an ambiguous image of their own position in society and of their social function: whence their conspicuous oscillation in politics and their tendency to slide toward the pole of the field momentarily in the stronger position. Thus when the center of gravity of the field moved to the Left during the last years of the July Monarchy, and in the midst of a general slide toward "social art" and socialist ideas, Baudelaire talked about the "puerile utopia of art for art's sake" and protested violently against pure art. Under the Second Empire, without adhering openly to the regime and sometimes, like Flaubert, even broadcasting their disdain for the man whom Hugo dubbed "Napoleon the Little," a good many of the most prominent writers assiduously frequented one or another of the salons held by the important members of the Imperial court.

In the absence of true credentialling institutions specifically designed for the validation of prestige (the University, for example, carried virtually no weight in the literary field), the political world and the emperor's family exercised direct control over the literary and artistic field through sanctions on publishing (indictment, censorship, and so on) and also through material or symbolic benefits (pensions, positions, honorific distinctions). Salons were not only places where like-minded writers and artists could meet those in power. They were also credentialling institutions through which those in power exerted their control over the intellectual world. The salon guests for their part acted as veritable lobbies to control the disbursement of various symbolic or material rewards.

But an analysis that has emphasized the dependence of the literary world must simultaneously stress one of the major effects of the operation of the literary world as a field, namely, the fact that all those who claimed full membership in this world, and especially those who claimed excellence, had to demonstrate their independence vis-à-vis economic and political power. The indifference with respect to government authorities and the rewards they dispensed, the distance from those in power and their values, tended to be asserted as the practical principle of legitimate behavior. Most of the time these obligations did not even have to be explicit. Negative sanctions, beginning with the worst—falling into disrepute (the functional equivalent to bankruptcy)—were produced automatically by the competition that set the most prestigious authors against each other.

But the effectiveness of these calls to order or injunctions, which were in some sense inscribed in the logic of the field itself, were never more obvious than in the fact that those authors apparently the most directly subject to external exigencies, in their work as in their behavior, felt obliged to manifest a certain distance from dominant values. And we discover, to our surprise if we know them only through the sarcastic comments of Flaubert or Baudelaire, that the most typical representatives of the bourgeois theater go beyond unequivocal praise of bourgeois life and values to satirize the very bases of bourgeois existence as well as the "decline in morals" imputed to the court and the upper bourgeoisie. These concessions to antibourgeois values on the part of these model bourgeois authors confirm the patent impossibility of overlooking the fundamental law of the field since writers apparently the farthest removed from art for art's sake acknowledged that law, if only in the somewhat shamefaced or ostentatiously aggressive mode of their transgressions. Condemned for this substandard success, these writers have purely and simply been written out of literary history. But they were full members of the nineteenth-century art world, not only because they themselves were marked by their participation in the literary field but also because their very existence modified the functioning of that field.

The analyst who endorses these vetoes without even being aware of it, since he knows only those authors from the past recognized by literary history as worthy of recognition, is destined to an intrinsically vicious circular form of explanation and understanding. He can only register, unawares, the effects of these authors he does not know on the authors that he claims to analyze and whose refusals he takes up on his own account. He thus precludes any grasp of what, in their very works, is the indirect product of these refusals. This is never clearer than in the case of a writer like Flaubert who was defined by a whole series of refusals or, more precisely, by an ensemble of double negations that opposed antagonistic doubles of styles or authors: thus his refusal of romanticism and realism, of Lamartine no less than Champfleury.

The Position of Art for Art's Sake within the Literary Field

A preliminary mapping of the field that was gradually fixed between 1840 and 1860 distinguishes three leading positions, namely, to use contemporary labels, "social art," "art for art's sake," and "bourgeois art." These categories are of course highly debatable, given the status of the intellectual field as a major battlefield over taxonomy. They nevertheless have the incontestable virtue of recalling that, in a field still in the process of institution, the internal positions must first be understood as so many specifications of the generic position of writers (or of the literary field within the political field). Or, if one prefers, as so many forms of the objective relationship to temporal power. Although writers as such belonged within the dominated fraction of the dominant social group, there was considerable tension among writers, between those who tended toward the dominant pole of the literary field, those located at the dominated pole, and those in between.

At the dominated pole of the literary field, the advocates of social art had their hour of glory just before and after February 1848. Republicans, Democrats, or Socialists, like Proudhon and also, though less markedly, George Sand, or again liberal Catholics like Lamennais, all denounced the "egotistical" art of art for art's sake, and demanded that literature fulfill a social or political function. These writers were structurally very close to the "second bohemia" of Murger and company, or at least close to the "realist" tendency that began to characterize that part of bohemia in the 1850s for which Champfleury became the theoretician. Other writers can be tied to this position, like the "worker-poets" sponsored by George Sand. Their inferior position in the field fostered a relationship of circular causality with their solidarity with respect to the dominant social milieux. In effect, this attitude can be linked to their provincial and/or working-class background, not only directly, as they themselves wanted to believe and have everyone else believe, through the solidarity and fidelity of the group, but also indirectly, through their dominated position within the field of production to which they were assigned by their background.

At the opposite pole of the literary field, the representatives of "bourgeois art," who wrote in the main for the theater, were closely and directly tied to the dominant social milieux as much by their background as by their life-style and values. This affinity was the very principle of their success in a genre that presupposed immediate communication between author and public and assured these writers not only significant material benefits (the theater was by far the most remunerative literary activity), but also all the tokens of success in the bourgeois world, and notably, the Académie française. These writers presented their bourgeois public a bowdlerized form of romanticism, a revival of "healthy and honest" art which subordinated the zany aspects of romanticism to bourgeois norms and tastes, glorified marriage, careful management of property, and establishment of children. Moralizing became more emphatic with Dumas fils, who claimed to help transform the world by a realistic depiction of the problems of the bourgeoisie (money, marriage, prostitution, and so on). Against Baudelaire's proclamation of the separation of art and morality, Dumas insisted in the preface of his play, *Le Fils naturel* (1858), that "all literature that does not have in mind perfectability, moralizing, the ideal, in a word, the useful, is an aborted, unhealthy literature that is born dead."[9]

The writers located outside these two opposing positions gradually invented what was called "art for art's sake." Rather than a position ready for the taking, it was a *position to make*. Although it existed potentially within the space of the existing positions, its occupants had to invent, against the established positions and against their occupants, everything that distinguished this position from all the others. They had to invent that social personage without precedent—the modern artist, full-time professional, dedicated to his work, indifferent to the exigencies of politics as to the injunctions of morality, and recognizing no jurisdiction other than the specific norm of art. Through this they invented too-pure aesthetics, a point of view with universal applicability, with no other justification than that which it finds in itself. The occupants of this central yet contradictory position were destined to oppose the established positions and thereby to attempt to reconcile the irreconcilable. Against bourgeois art, they wanted ethical freedom, even transgression, and above all distance from every institution, the state, the Académie, journalism. But this desire for freedom did not mean that they accepted either the careless abandon of the bohemians who invoked this same freedom in order to legitimate transgressions devoid of properly aesthetic consequences or simple regression into what they denounced as "vulgar." In their concern to situate themselves above ordinary alternatives, these advocates of pure art deliberately imposed on themselves an extraordinary discipline that opposed the easy way out taken by all their adversaries. Their independence consisted in the freely chosen but total obedience to the new laws which they invented and to which they proposed to subject the Republic of Letters.

Baudelaire's own aesthetic principle resided in the double breach on which he based his position but at the price of an extraordinary strain, manifest notably in the paradoxical display of singularity in his daily life. His hatred of debased forms of romanticism had a lot to do with his denunciation of improvisation and lyricism in favor of work and study. At the same time, Baudelaire's refusal of facile breaches of decorum was behind his determination to be both contentious and methodical even

9. Alexandre Dumas, preface to *Le Fils naturel* (Paris, 1894), p. 31.

in the mastery of freedom contained in the "cult of the multiplied sensation."

Flaubert was also situated in this geometric locus of contraries, along with a number of others who were all different from each other and who never formed a real group: Théophile Gautier, Leconte de Lisle, Barbey d'Aurevilly, to name the best known. I shall cite only one exemplary expression of these double refusals, which, in their general form, could be formulated as follows: "I loathe X (writer, style, theory, school), but I loathe just as much the opposite of X." Whence the discord among all those who rejected romanticism that Flaubert put so succinctly: "Everyone thinks that I am in love with realism, whereas I execrate it. For I started on this novel [*Madame Bovary*] out of hatred of realism. But I loathe just as much false idealism, which has us hoaxed these days."[10]

The key formula, which simply translates the contradictory properties of the position in the field, allows us to comprehend the principle behind divers particularities in the behavior of those who occupy this position. First of all, their political neutrality, associated with the refusal of any kind of commitment or any kind of preaching, whether glorifying bourgeois values or instructing the masses in republican or socialist principles: their horror of "the bourgeois," in which they included, according to Flaubert, "the bourgeois in overalls and the bourgeois in a frock coat"[11] was sustained, within the field, by the execration of the "bourgeois artist," who secured/ guaranteed his own short-term success and bourgeois honors by denying himself as a writer. "There is one thing a thousand times more dangerous than the bourgeois," Baudelaire noted in *Les Curiosités esthétiques*, "and that is the bourgeois artist, who was created to come between the artists and the genius, who hides each from the other." But their scorn as professionals for the literary proletariat prompted by their very exacting conception of artistic work no doubt lay at the heart of the representation they made of the "populace."

This concern to keep distant from all social sites implied the refusal to be guided by the public's expectations. Thus Flaubert, who pushed this indifference further than anyone else, reproached Edmond de Goncourt for having addressed the public directly in the preface to his novel, *Les Frères Zemganno,* to explain the aesthetic intentions of the work: "Why do you need to talk directly to the public? It is not worthy of our secrets" (*CC,* 8:263). And he wrote to Ernest Renan about his *Prière sur l'Acropole:* "I don't know if there exists in French a more beautiful page of prose. . . . It's splendid and I'm sure that the bourgeois won't understand a word

---

10. Flaubert, *Correspondance,* ed. Jean Bruneau, 2 vols. (Paris, 1980), 2: 643–44; further references to this work, abbreviated *CP,* will be included in the text.

11. *Oeuvres complètes de Gustave Flaubert: Correspondance, nouvelle edition augmentée,* 14 vols. (Paris, 1926–54), 5:300; further references to this work, abbreviated *CC,* will be included in the text.

of it. . . . So much the better!" (*CC*, 7:368). The more the artist asserted himself as an artist by asserting his autonomy, the more he turned "the bourgeois" into the "bourgeois," the philistine. This symbolic revolution, whereby artists emancipated themselves from bourgeois standards by refusing to acknowledge any master other than their art, had the effect of making the market disappear. The very moment that they defeated the "bourgeois" in their struggle to master the sense and the function of artistic activity, they eliminated the bourgeois as a potential customer. And this antinomy of modern art as a pure art showed up clearly in the fact that, as the autonomy of cultural production increased, the interval of time necessary for works to impose their norms also increased.

This temporal gap between supply and demand tended to become a structural characteristic of the field of limited production. In this anti-economic economy fixed at the pole that was economically dominated but symbolically dominant—with Baudelaire and the Parnassians for poetry, with Flaubert for the novel—producers could end up, at least in the short term, with only their competitors for customers. "Bourgeois artists" were assured of an immediate clientele. The producers of commercial literature who worked on commission, like the authors of vaudeville entertainments or popular novels, could live well off their earnings and at the same time earn a secure reputation as socially concerned or even as socialists (like Eugène Sue). Quite to the contrary, the tenants of pure art were destined to deferred gratification. Some, like Leconte de Lisle, went so far as to see in immediate success "the mark of intellectual inferiority" while the Christly mystique of the "accursed artist" ("l'artiste maudit"), sacrificed in this world and consecrated in the next, was undoubtedly the idealized or professionalized retranscription of the specific contradiction of the mode of production that the pure artist aimed to establish. It was in effect an upside-down economy where the artist could win in the symbolical arena only by losing in the economic one (at least in the short term) and vice versa.

In a very paradoxical manner this paradoxical economy gave full weight to inherited economic properties and in particular to private income. In more general terms, the state of the field of production determined the probable effects of the properties of individual actors, either objectively, as with economic capital and private income, or subjectively, as in the *habitus*. In other words, the same predispositions engender very different, even antagonistic, positions, according to the state of the field. In brief, it was still (inherited) money that assured freedom from money. A private fortune also conferred objective freedom with respect to the authorities and those in power, which was often the condition of subjective freedom, thereby enabling "pure" writers to avoid the compromises to which they were particularly exposed.

Thus only after characterizing the different positions within the literary field is the analyst to confront the individual actors and the personal properties predisposing them more or less to realize the potential inscribed in their positions. It is striking that on the whole the adherents of "art for art's sake," who were objectively very close to each other by virtue of their political and aesthetic attitudes, and who, though not really a group, were tied by bonds of mutual esteem and sometimes friendship, followed similar social trajectories. Thus Flaubert was the son of a well-known provincial doctor; Baudelaire was the son of an office manager in the House of Lords who had ambitions of becoming a painter, and he was the step-son of a general; Barbey d'Aurevilly and the Goncourt brothers came from the provincial nobility.

To account more fully for the particular affinity that tied writers from this background of "men of talent" ("capacités") as they used to say in Flaubert's time, to pure art, we can invoke the fact that the occupants of these central positions within the political field who, endowed with just about equal amounts of economic and cultural capital, wavered (like Frédéric in *Sentimental Education*) between the two poles of business and art and were therefore predisposed to occupy a homologous position in the literary field. Thus the dual orientation of Flaubert's father, who invested in the education of his children and in real estate, corresponded to the indetermination of the young Flaubert, faced with various equally probable futures.

But this is not all. At the risk of seeming to push the search for an explanation a bit far, it is possible, starting from Sartre's analysis, to point out the homology between the objective relationship that tied the artist as "poor relation" to the "bourgeois" or "bourgeois artist" and the relationship that tied Flaubert, as the "family idiot," to his older brother, and through him—the clear objectification of the most probable career for their category—to his class of origin and to the objective future implied by that class. We would therefore have an extraordinary super-position of redundant determinations. Everything happened as if his position in his family and the position of this family in the political field predisposed Flaubert to experience at their strongest the force of the contradictions inscribed in the position of the writer and in the position of the pure artist where these contradictions attained their highest degree of intensity.

3. Flaubert's Point of View

So far, having grasped very partially the specificity of Flaubert, the analysis has remained generic. It has not engaged the logic specific to the work. We can almost hear Flaubert object: "Where do you know a critic who worries about the work *in itself*? There are all kinds of analyses of the milieu where the work was produced and the causes that brought it about; but *unknowing* poetics [poétique *insciente*]? where does it come from? its composition, its style? the author's point of view? Never!" (*CC*, 6:8). To accept the challenge, one must take Flaubert literally and re-construct the artistic *point of view* from which the "unknowing poetic" was defined and which, as a *view taken from a given point* within an artistic space, characterized that point of view. More precisely, it is necessary to reconstruct the space of the actual and potential artistic *positions adopted* in relationship to which Flaubert constructed his artistic project. This space, it may be supposed, is homologous with the space of positions within the field of production outlined above.

When Flaubert undertook to write *Madame Bovary* or *Sentimental Education,* he situated himself actively within the space of possibilities offered by the field. To understand these choices is to understand the differential significance that characterized them within the universe of possible choices. In choosing to write these novels, Flaubert risked the inferior status associated with a minor genre. Above all, he condemned himself to take a place within a space that was already staked out with names of authors, names of subgenres (the historical novel, the serial, and so on), and names of movements or schools (realism). Despite Balzac's prestige, the novel was indeed perceived as an inferior genre. The Académie française was so suspicious of the novel that it waited until 1863 to welcome a novelist as such, and when it finally did so, it chose Octave Feuillet, the author of novels full of aristocratic characters and elevated sentiments. In the manifesto of realism that was their preface to *Germinie Lacerteux* (1865), the Goncourts felt obliged to claim for "the Novel" (a necessary capital letter) the status of a "great, serious form."[12] But the genre already had its history and its founding fathers. There were those claimed by Flaubert himself, like Cervantes, and also those in every educated mind, like Balzac, Musset, or Lamartine. When Flaubert started to write *Madame Bovary* there was no novelist "in view," and one found in the same grab bag Feuillet, Murger, Barbey d'Aurevilly, Champfleury, and a good many others, second-raters who are completely forgotten today but who were best-sellers at the time. In this mixed-up world Flaubert knew how to recognize his own. He reacted vehemently to everything that could be termed "genre literature"—his own analogy with genre painting —that is, vaudeville, Dumas-type historical novels, comic opera, and other works that flattered the public by tossing back its own image in the form of a hero psychologically rooted in the daily life of the petty bourgeoisie (*CP*, 2:358). He reacted just as fiercely to the idealistic platitudes and sentimental effusions in novels like those of the eminently successful Feuillet.

But these reactions did not put Flaubert in the realist camp, who like him contested the first group but who defined themselves against

12. Edmond and Jules de Goncourt, preface to *Germinie Lacerteux* (Naples, 1968), p. 2.

all the important professional writers, among whom Flaubert counted himself. His designation as leader of the realist school after *Madame Bovary*'s success, which coincided with the decline of the first realist movement, made Flaubert indignant: "Everyone thinks that I am enamoured with realism, whereas I execrate it. . . . But I loathe just as much false idealism." This crucial formula once again reveals the principle of the totally paradoxical, almost "impossible," position that Flaubert was about to create for himself and thereby present himself as unclassifiable.

The space of positions adopted by the writer that the analyst must reconstitute does not appear as such to the writer himself. Otherwise these choices would have to be interpreted as conscious strategies of distinction. The space appears from time to time, and in a fragmentary state, in the moments of doubt concerning the reality of the difference that the writer claims, in his work, and beyond any explicit search for originality. But the threat to artistic identity is never as strong as when alterity assumes the guise of an encounter with an author who occupies an apparently nearby position in the field. This indeed happened when Flaubert's good friend Louis Bouilhet drew his attention to a novel by Champfleury then appearing as a serial and whose subject—adultery in the provinces—was very close to that of *Madame Bovary* (*CP*, 2:562–63). There Flaubert undoubtedly found an opportunity to assert his difference and to become aware of the principle of that difference, that is, the style, or more exactly, in his tone a certain inimitable relationship between the refinement of the style and the extreme platitude of the subject, which he shared with the realists or with the romantics or with the authors of vaudeville entertainments, or, in certain cases, with all three at once.

"Write well about *mediocrity*" (*CP*, 2:429). This oxymoron condenses Flaubert's whole aesthetic program and tells a good deal about the impossible situation in which he put himself in trying to reconcile opposites, that is, exigencies and experiences that were ordinarily associated with opposite areas of social space and of the literary field, hence socio-logically incompatible. In fact, on the lowest and most trivial forms of a genre held to be inferior Flaubert imposed the most exacting demands that had ever been advanced for the noblest genre—poetry. The very enterprise challenged the established mode of thought that set prose against poetry, lyricism against vulgarity, and it did so by banning that sacrilege represented by the mixture of genres. At the time the enterprise seemed like folly:

> To want to give to prose the rhythm of verse (but keeping it very much prose), and to want to write about ordinary life as one writes history or the epic (without denaturing the subject) is perhaps an absurdity. That's what I wonder sometimes. But perhaps it's also a grand undertaking and very original! [*CP*, 2:287]

He was indeed putting himself in an impossible situation, and in fact, the whole time he was working on *Madame Bovary*, Flaubert never stopped talking about his suffering, even his despair. He felt like a clown performing a real tour de force compelled to "desperate gymnastics." He reproached his "fetid" and "foul" material for keeping him from "bawling out" lyric themes. He waited impatiently for the time when he could once again drink his fill of stylistic beauty. But above all, he repeated over and over again that he did not, strictly speaking, know what he was doing and that it would be the product of an unnatural effort, unnatural for him in any case. The only possible assurance when confronting the unthinkable was the feeling of a tour de force implied by sensing the immense effort involved. "I will have written the real, and that is rare" (*CC*, 3:268). The questioning of forms of thought by the symbolic revolution, along with the absolute originality of what that questioning engendered, had as its counterpart the absolute solitude implied by the transgression of the limits of the thinkable for a mode of thought that had become its own measure.

In fact, this mode of thinking cannot expect that minds which are structured according to those very categories that it questions, think the unthinkable. It is striking how the judgments of critics, applying to works the principles of division that those works have demolished, invariably undid the inconceivable combination of opposites by reducing it to one or the other of the opposite terms: thus, the critic of *Madame Bovary* who deduced the vulgarity of the style from the vulgarity of the objects. Others stressed content, related *Madame Bovary* to Champfleury's novel on the same subject, and put Flaubert and Dumas fils in the same boat. Then there were those who, more attentive to tone and style, placed Flaubert in the line of formalist poets.

What made Flaubert so radically original, and what confers on his work an incomparable *value*, is his relationship, at least negative, with the whole literary world in which he acted and whose contradictions and problems he assumed absolutely. So that the only chance of grasping and accounting for the singularity of his creative project is to proceed in exactly the reverse direction of those who sing the litany of Uniqueness. By historicizing him we can understand how he tore himself away from the strict historicity of less heroic fates. The originality of the enterprise only emerges if, instead of annexing him consciously or unconsciously to one or another prestigious position in today's literary field (like the *nouveau roman*) and to make him an inspired (if unfinished) precursor, this project is reinserted as completely as possible in the historically constituted space within which it was constructed. In other words, taking the point of view of a Flaubert who had not become Flaubert, we try to discover what he had to do and wanted to do in a world that was not yet transformed by what he in fact did, which is to say, the world to which we refer him by treating him as a "precursor." In effect, the familiar world keeps us from understanding, among other things, the extraordinary effort that he had to make, the exceptional resistances that he had to surmount, beginning within himself, in order to produce and impose that which, largely because of him, we now take for granted.

Flaubert is really there, in this world of relationships that should be explored one by one, in their symbolic and social dimension. At the same time, he is unquestionably beyond that world, if only because the active integration of all these partial relationships implies going beyond the given. By locating himself in the geographical locus of all perspectives, which is also the point of highest tension, Flaubert put himself so to speak in the position of pushing to their highest intensity all the questions posed by and in the field. He was able to act fully on all the resources inscribed in the space of possibilities offered by the field.

Sentimental Education undoubtedly offers the best example of this confrontation with all the relevant positions. The subject situates the novel at the intersection of the romantic and realist traditions: on the one hand, Musset's *Confession of a Child of the Century* and Alfred Vigny's *Chatterton,* but also the so-called intimate novel that anticipated the realist novel and the thesis novel; on the other hand, the second bohemia, whose romantic intimate diary eventually turned into the realist novel, especially when, with the novels of Murger and Champfleury, it recorded the often sordid reality of these artists' existence. By taking on this subject, Flaubert confronted not only Murger and Champfleury, but also Balzac, and not only *A Great Man of the Provinces in Paris* or *A Prince of Bohemia,* but also *The Lily of the Valley.* The great ancestor is explicitly present in Deslaurier's advice to Frédéric: "Remember Rastignac in *The Human Comedy.*" By giving the reference to Deslauriers, the petty bourgeois par excellence, Flaubert authorizes us to see in Frédéric what is clear from everything else in the novel, namely, that he is the "counterpart" of Rastignac— not a failed Rastignac, or an anti-Rastignac—but the equivalent of Rastignac in another world. In fact, Frédéric opposes Rastignac within the universe of another possible world, which really exists, at least for the critics, but also for any writer worthy of the name who masters the space of possibles well enough to foresee how what he is doing risks putting him in relationship with other creative projects which are liable to divert his intentions. Take as proof this note of Flaubert's: "Watch out for *The Lily of the Valley.*" Nor could he avoid thinking about Eugène Fromentin's *Dominique,* and especially about Sainte-Beuve's *Volupté.* "I wrote *Sentimental Education* for Sainte-Beuve, and he died without reading a line of it" (*CC,* 6:82).

Moreover, by assuming the impassivity of the paleontologist and the refinement of the Parnassian poet in order to write the novel of the *modern* world, and without pushing aside any of the events that passionately divided literature and politics, Flaubert broke up a whole series of obligatory associations—which tied the "realist" novel with "literary riff-raff" or "democracy," or "vulgar" subjects and a "low" style. He thereby broke the solidarities founded on the adherence to one or another of the constitutive terms of these opposites. Thus Flaubert sentenced himself to disappoint, even more than with *Madame Bovary*, those who expected literature to demonstrate something, the partisans of the moral novel as much as the defenders of the social novel.

This series of ruptures explains better than the conjuncture the cold reception that the book received. It took place at the deepest level of "unknowing poetics." The work on form was undoubtedly the instrument of anamnesis, which was both favored and limited by the denegation implied by formalization. The work is not the effusions of the subject— there is a vast difference between Flaubert's objectification and the projection of Frédéric that critics have seen. Nor is the work a pure document, as some of his supposed disciples seemed to think. As Flaubert complained to George Sand, "Goncourt is happy when he picks up in the street a word that he can stick in a book and I am content when I have written a page without assonance or repetition" (*CC*, 7:281). And if the work can reveal the deep structures of the social world and the mental worlds in which those structures were reflected, it is because the work of formalization gave the writer the opportunity to work on himself and thereby allowed him to objectify not only the positions in the field and their occupants that he opposed, but also, through the space that included him, his own position.

It is not by chance that this project was realized with *Sentimental Education*, this *Bildungsroman* in the literal sense of the term, in an unequaled effort by the writer to objectify his own intellectual experience and the determinants that weighed on those experiences, beginning with those tied to the contradictory position of the writer in the political field. In the obsessive chiasmic structure (dual characters, crossed trajectories, and so on) and in the very structure of the relationships between Frédéric and the other main characters of *Sentimental Education*, Flaubert objectified the structure of the relationship that tied him, as a writer, to the political field: or, which comes down to the same thing, to the positions in the literary field homologous to those in the political field.

There is therefore a relationship of circular causality between his social position and his exceptionally lucid consciousness of that position. If his work as a writer could take him beyond the incompatibilities established in things—in groups, schools, and so on, and also in minds— as principles of vision and division, perhaps it was because, in contrast to Frédéric's passive indeterminancy, the active refusal of all the determinants associated with a given position in the intellectual field, to which he was inclined by his social trajectory and the contradictory properties that were the principle of that trajectory, predisposed him to a broader view of the space of possibles and, hence, to a more complete use of the freedom inherent in its constraints.

4. The Invention of "Pure" Aesthetics

The logic of the double refusal, and the break that the primacy given to form implied with the half-break effected by realism, provides the principle for the invention of pure aesthetics accomplished by Flaubert in an art, which like the novel (and in about the same degree as in painting where Manet achieved a comparable revolution), seemed predestined for a simple, naive search for the illusion of reality. Realism in effect was a partial, and failed, revolution. It did not really question the tendency to mix aesthetic value and moral (or social) value, which continued to guide critical judgments. If realism questioned the existence of an objective hierarchy of subjects, it was only to reverse that hierarchy, out of a desire for rehabilitation or revenge, not to do away with it. For this reason realism was recognized by the social milieux that it represented rather than by the more or less "low" or "vulgar" way of representing them. Murger himself was perceived as a realist because he represented "common subjects," heroes who dressed poorly, spoke disrespectfully about everything, and were utterly ignorant of proper behavior.

By breaking this privileged tie with a specific category of objects, Flaubert generalized and radicalized the partial revolution of realism. Like Manet confronted with a similar dilemma, he painted both bohemia and high society. If the pure gaze ("le regard pur") might accord special interest to objects socially designated as hateful or despicable (like Baudelaire's carrion) because of the challenge that they represented, it remained totally unaware of all the nonaesthetic differences between objects, and it could find in bourgeois worlds, by virtue of their privileged tie to bourgeois art, a particular opportunity to assert its irreduceability.

An aesthetic revolution could only occur aesthetically. It was not enough to establish as beautiful whatever official aesthetics excluded or to rehabilitate modern, "low," or "mediocre" subjects. It was necessary to assert through form ("write well about mediocrity") the power of art to constitute everything aesthetically, to transmute everything into literary beauty, through writing itself. "For this reason there are neither beautiful nor ugly subjects and one could almost establish as an axiom, taking the point of view of pure Art, that there are no subjects, style by itself being an absolute manner of seeing things" (*CP*, 2:31). The alternative between formalism and realism to which critics tried to restrict Flaubert (and Manet as well) was patently absurd. Because he mastered the highest demands of form, he could assert almost without limitation the power of form to establish aesthetically any reality whatsoever.

The revolution of the gaze, and the rupture of the bond between ethics and aesthetics implied by that revolution, effected a total conversion of life-style. This revolution, which led to the aestheticization of the artistic life-style, could only be half-accomplished by the realists of the second bohemia, enclosed within their petty bourgeois ethos, partly because they did not accept the ethical implications of that revolution. The advocates of social art saw very clearly the ethical foundations of the new aesthetics. They denounced the ethical perversion of a literature that was "venereal and close to an aphrodisiac"; they attacked the "singers of ugliness and filth," who united "moral ignominy" and "physical decadence"; and they were especially indignant about the method and the artifice in this "cold, reasoned, thoroughly researched depravation."[13] This literature was deemed scandalous because of its perverse complacency but also because of cynical indifference to infamy and to scandal itself. Thus an article on *Madame Bovary* and the "physiological novel" reproached Flaubert's pictorial imagination for "enclosing itself in the material world as if in a vast studio peopled with models who in his eyes all have the same value."[14]

It is certain that the pure gaze that had to be invented (and not, as is the case today, simply put into action), at the price of breaking the ties between art and morality, required an attitude of impassivity, indifference, aloofness, and even cynical extravagance. Although it never excluded a good deal of posturing (namely, Baudelaire), this attitude presupposed very particular dispositions, associated with positions and trajectories that favored distance with respect to the social world. This distance was the opposite of the double ambivalence, based in horror and in fascination, of the petty bourgeois toward the "bourgeois" and the "people": thus for example Flaubert's violent anarchistic temperament, his sense of transgression and jokes, along with the distance that let him get the most beautiful aesthetic effects out of the simple description of human misery. Here we can mention the letter to Ernest Feydeau, at the bedside of his dying wife, in which Flaubert encouraged his friend to make artistic use of the experience: "You have seen and will see more beautiful scenes, and you can make good studies of them. It's paying them dear. Bourgeois do not even suspect that we serve them our hearts. The race of gladiators has not died: every artist is one. He amuses the public with his afflictions" (*CC*, 4:340). This aestheticism pushed to its limits tended toward a kind of neutralism, even ethical nihilism.

This freedom with respect to the moral and humanitarian conformity that constrained "proper" people was no doubt responsible for the profound unity of the habitués of Magny's restaurant: Flaubert, Turgenev, Sainte-Beuve, and Taine. Between literary anecdotes and obscene stories, they affirmed the separation of art and morality. This was also the foundation of the affinity with Baudelaire, which Flaubert invoked in a letter when he was writing *Salammbô:* "I'm getting to the dark tones. We're starting to walk around in the intestines and burn the dead. Baudelaire

13. Luc Badesco, *La Génération poétique de 1860—La Jeunesse des deux rives,* 2 vols. (Paris, 1971), 1:304–6.

14. Gustave Merlet, "Un Réaliste imaginaire: M. Henry Murger," *Revue européenne* 8 (1 March 1860): 35; cited by Bernard Weinberg, *French Realism: The Critical Reaction, 1830–1870* (New York, 1937), p. 133.

will be satisfied" (*CC*, pp. 454–55). The aristocratic aestheticism stressed here in the provocative mode was revealed more discreetly and no doubt more authentically in a judgment of Hugo: "why does he display such a silly morality which diminishes him so much? why the Académie? the clichés! the imitation, etc." (*CP*, 2:330).

This distance from all social positions favored by formal elaboration was inscribed by that elaboration in the literary work itself: whence the merciless elimination of all received ideas, of all clichés, and of all the other stylistic features that could mark or reveal adherence to one or another position; whence also the methodical use of free indirect discourse which leaves indeterminate, or as indeterminate as possible, the relationship of the narrator to the facts or characters in the narrative. But nothing is more revelatory of *Flaubert's point of view* than the characteristic *composition* of his works, and in particular of *Sentimental Education,* a novel criticized from the beginning for not being structured or for being poorly organized. Like Manet somewhat later, Flaubert abandoned the unifying perspective, taken from a fixed, central point of view, which he replaced with what could be called, following Erwin Panofsky, an "aggregated space," if we take this to mean a space made of juxtaposed pieces without a preferred point of view. In a letter to Huysmans about his recently published novel, Flaubert wrote that "Missing from *The Vatard Sisters,* as from *Sentimental Education* the falseness of a perspective! There is no progression of effect" (*CC*, 8:224). Thus his declaration to Henry Céard about *Sentimental Education:* "It's a condemned book, my good friend, because it doesn't go like that: and joining his long, elegant yet robust hands, he made a pyramid."[15]

In itself the refusal of the pyramid construction, that is, an ascending convergence toward an idea, a conviction, a conclusion, contains a message, and no doubt the most important one: a vision, not to say a philosophy, of history in the double sense of the word. As a bourgeois who was vehemently antibourgeois and completely devoid of any illusions about the "people" (though Dussardier, sincere and disinterested plebeian, is the only shining figure in *Sentimental Education*), Flaubert preserves in his absolute disenchantment an absolute conviction, which concerns the work of the writer. Against preachers of every sort, he asserted, in the only consistent way possible, without *phrases* and by the very structure of his discourse, his refusal to give the reader the deceptive satisfactions offered by the false philistine humanism of the sellers of illusion. It is here, in this narrative with no beyond, in this narrative that recounts itself, in the irreconcilable diversity of its perspectives, in the universe from which the author has deleted himself but remains, like Spinoza's god, immanent and coextensive with his creation—it is here that we find Flaubert's point of view.

15. Quoted in René Descharmes and René Dumesnil, *Autour de Flaubert,* 2 vols. (Paris, 1912), 2:48.

Kafka's Place in the Literary Field

Régine Robin

Translated by Amy Reiter-McIntosh

If the studies of cultural context, discursive context and "co-text," and social discourse about the "Jewish question" are indispensable, they do not suffice to explain Franz Kafka's place in the literature of his era or his position in a literary field that was simultaneously Praguian, Austro-Viennese, and primarily German. This literary milieu implies a multiform totality with hierarchies on the scale of legitimacy, variants and specificities beyond narrow affiliations and ties, because Prague is neither Leipzig, Munich, Vienna, nor Berlin. Nonetheless, language remains the directing and unifying thread, as does the fact that these cities share the same zeitgeist—a particular conception of the "superiority" of German culture, and at the core of this German culture, the ambivalent and conflicting place of Jewish authors confronted by the rise of anti-Semitism and, especially in Prague, by the rise of nationalism.

The sociological perception of the structured ensemble formed by the literary institution and its numerous ramifications is an obligatory meditation for anyone who wants to attempt to understand Kafka and his work or, at least, to understand the historicity of his writings. However, Kafka resists sociology while from all sides we feel the necessity to depart once again from the text (which has already been commented on again and again) in order to attempt to glean a certain number of determinations

This text is an excerpt that has been reworked from *Kafka*, a book in press at Éditions Belfond in Paris; the colloquium on the Sociology of Literature held in Rome in 1987, whose proceedings are also in press; and my article, "De la sociologie de la littérature à la sociologie de l'écriture: le projet sociocritique," which appeared in the May 1988 issue of *Littérature*.

This article owes much to Jill Robbins, "Kafka's Parables," in *Midrash and Literature*, ed. Geoffrey H. Hartman and Sanford Budick (New Haven, Conn., 1986), pp. 265–84.

from it. The biographical isn't enough; neurosis isn't an adequate explanation. Neurosis does not enable us to understand some fundamental choices, themes, and literary positions. It cannot account for an evolution. We have to accept the fact that it is to some extent socially determined.

If we do not want to attempt to rewrite Kafka from the perspective of Jean-Paul Sartre's *Questions de méthode* or *L'Idiot de la famille,* we will stop here, not without having insisted on the necessary sociological perception of the work. François Héran pleasantly notes that

> everything occurs as if the relatively hermetic and strongly decontextualized character of the work (the words "Prague," "Jewish," and "insurance company" never appear) had favored the emergence of an international corps of exegetes particularly interested in practicing a hermeneutic tenacity (which translates into an enormous bibliography exceeding ten thousand titles). As a result of the outbidding between professionals, the sacred line separating the work of art from the social sphere never ceases to be displaced, one moment bound to the saint of saints, the next moment stretched to the far-off annexes of the temple.[1]

Nonetheless, insofar as Viennese culture is concerned, Carl E. Schorske, Michael Pollak, and William M. Johnston have attempted this great crossing of determinations of the literary field in diverse approaches. Joachim Unseld, too, has recently devoted an important book to Kafka and his relations with the literary institution.[2]

The first mediation is what Max Brod calls the "Prague circle." There are those who consider Prague to be a veritable imprisonment on an intellectual plane. Franz Werfel, one of the leaders of expressionism who

---

1. François Héran, "Analyse interne et analyse externe en sociologie de la littérature: le cas de Kafka," in *Sociologie de l'art: Colloque internationale, Marseille, 13–14 juin 1985,* ed. Raymonde Moulin (Paris, 1986), p. 318; hereafter abbreviated "A."

2. See Carl E. Schorske, *Fin-de-Siècle Vienna: Politics and Culture* (New York, 1981); Michael Pollak, *Vienne 1900: une identité blessée* (Paris, 1984); and William M. Johnston, *The Austrian Mind: An Intellectual and Social History, 1848–1938* (Berkeley and Los Angeles, 1972). See also Joachim Unseld, *Franz Kafka: Ein Schriftstellerleben, Die Geschichte seiner veröffenlichunger Mit einer Bibliographie sämtlicher Drucke und Ausgaben der Dichtungen Franz Kafkas 1908–1924* (Munich, 1982); translated into French by Éliane Kaufholz, under the title *Franz Kafka, une vie d'écrivain* (Paris, 1984).

Régine Robin is professor of sociology at the Université de Québec à Montréal. The author of *Le Réalisme socialiste: une esthétique impossible* (1986), among other works, she is currently completing a book on Kafka. She is also the author of two novels. **Amy Reiter-McIntosh**'s translation of Yve-Alain Bois' "Piet Mondrian, *New York City*" appeared in the Winter 1988 issue of *Critical Inquiry.*

left Prague for Leipzig in 1912, accounts for this imprisonment in many writings. There are those who think of Prague as a national, ethnic, and linguistic ghetto and those who, like Brod, contend that it was nothing of the sort, that Prague was open to the entire German cultural arena and that the literary milieu was very fluid and permeable, that everything was circulating in this vast space: magazines, newspapers, literary publications and awards, conferences, fashionable ideas, and so on. Undoubtedly Brod was correct, but almost all of Prague's German authors felt an uneasiness at being cut off from a real public and felt provincial in the face of real centers of decision, in the face of Berlin, which was growing stronger and stronger.

The group of Prague authors who were writing in German is impressive (almost all were Jewish, with some notable exceptions): Brod, Werfel (until 1912), Kafka, Oskar Baum, Leo Perutz, Ernst Weiss, Paul Kornfeld, Rudolf Fuchs, Ludwig Winder, Hermann Ungar, Otto Pick, Egon Erwin Kisch, Paul Leppin, Gustav Meyrink, Oskar Wiener, Franz Blei, not to mention the poet of the "old guard," Hugo Salus. (Rainer Maria Rilke left Prague in 1890.) Angelo Neumann, the soul of the Neues Deutsches Theater, and Heinrich Teweles, the editor-in-chief of the powerful liberal newspaper, the *Prager Tagblatt,* must also be added to this heterogeneous group.

In Prague, German culture formed and maintained itself first at the university. Students were grouped into corporate bodies and fraternities, which jealously defended their ideologies and forbade entry to undesirables. Jewish students met in the Lese- und Redehalle der deutschen Studenten as a reading and discussion group; some of them, in the "Bar Khochba" group, were of Zionist persuasion. They also met in the city's literary cafés. The avant-garde intelligentsia were prominent at the Arco Café, where all the new ideas on aesthetics were brewing. Karl Kraus, with habitual zest, criticized those who frequented the café, calling them the "Arconauts." There was also the Café Louvre, a café of a higher echelon, where Franz Brentano's disciples reigned. According to Klaus Wagenbach, Kafka's ideas were strongly influenced by Brentano's philosophy of language.[3] It was also at the Café Louvre that people were given to spiritualism, under Berta Fanta's influence. Theater was a local passion, and the largest daily papers, the *Bohemia* and the *Prager Tagblatt,* were the chosen spots for serial writers and others who were trying to control these literary newspapers. Even Kafka was published in the *Bohemia.* Other groups and coteries made cultural life in German Prague both lively and varied, at least on the surface. The entire network was publishing in short-lived local journals, and writers regularly read their works in the various conferences and public lectures that characterized the sociability of Germanic

3. See Klaus Wagenbach, *Franz Kafka; eine Biographie seiner Jugend, 1883–1912* (Bern, 1958), esp. pp. 106–9.

environments at the turn of the century. They continued to do so until World War I.

The Prague authors writing in German, lacking "community" behind them, were producing work in a neoromantic decadence, in an eroticism full of cadavers, in a dream state, or in the realm of the fantastic; their style was often bombastic, overdone, affected, full of autumnal nostalgia and mystical examinations. The Jewish theme was present as decor or legend, or was directly inscribed in the narrator's *diegesis* and commentary. (We need only recall Brod's novels in particular to support this claim: *Schloss Nornepygge* [1908], *Jüdinnen* [1911], and *Arnold Beer* [1912].) Thus Kafka was left to find his place with respect to the surrounding neo-decadentism and the entry of the Jewish theme directly into the work.

Prague was not this ghetto that writers have in their minds; it was a city in communication with the rest of the literary cluster and with Germanic culture in its strong ties with Munich, Leipzig, and Berlin. Through Werfel, we have the entry of "pathos" into the German world and into the expressionist avant-garde. Through Robert Musil and Otto Pick, there was a possibility of making a name for oneself in Berlin, where it "really counted."

During the period from 1910–20, Leipzig was a great publishing center. The Rowohlt firm was established and was taken over in 1912 by Karl Wolff, whose role in the publication of Kafka's works was to be a decisive one. Leipzig also saw the launching of the avant-garde collection "Der Jüngste Tag," which was to witness the abundance of literary expressionism. Thus Kafka was not isolated; far from it. He was part of the group of writers distinguished by Werfel and Wolff. He was a friend of Brod's, a person who was received everywhere, and Musil tried to have his work published at Samuel Fischer's in Berlin. He had some success, which culminated in 1915 in an incredible affair concerning the Fontane literary prize: Karl Sternheim received the prize, but Kafka received the prize money.

After World War I, Berlin became the center of literary life, and Kafka tried to have his work published in *Die Schmiede,* which served to gather the legacy of the expressionist movement and which published authors as diverse as Rudolf Leonhard, Kurt Heynicke, Max Hermann, Otto Flaka, Ivan Goll, Alfred Wolfenstein, Rudolf Kayser, and even Heinrich Mann.

As for Vienna, Kafka hated it, as he hated anything or anyone that appeared to come from there, whether it was Arthur Schnitzler or others. Yet the Viennese metropolis had its moment of glory, namely with the group of artists, painters, architects, and authors who, at the turn of the century, attempted to shake the traditions of grandiloquence and respectability with their stylistic revolt. Like all the authors of his generation, Kafka had read Hugo von Hofmannsthal, who influenced him enormously. But it was no longer Vienna that was in the sights of the great networks that make reputations (and unravel them) in the literary world and that mark the rise and fall of the symbolic "capital" on the scale of "legitimacy"; it was Berlin. This is a sign, among other signs, of the decadence of the Hapsburg Empire.

Thus Kafka published in the small Prague journals as well as in the Berlin reviews and the journals from those publishing firms that were making names for themselves in Leipzig and Berlin: from *Hyperion* to *Die Schmiede*, from *Arkadia* to *Marsyas*, from *Selbstwehr* to *Der Jude*, from *Neue Rundschau* to *Die Weissen Blätter,* and so on. As Unseld aptly observes in his study of Kafka as an author plunged into the publishing world, there is nothing more untrue than the image of Kafka fleeing publication to take refuge alone in the desolate spheres of metaphysics. Kafka fought tenaciously to have his work published, although that battle was a contradictory one.[4] We will discuss here only the example of his *Metamorphosis*.

Kafka wrote *The Metamorphosis* on the heels of *The Judgment* and his meeting with Felice, in the middle of the revision of "The Stoker," in December 1912. It was at the same time that his first volume of new *Meditations* appeared, published by Rowohlt. *The Judgment* came out in *Arkadia,* a journal under Brod's guidance.

Karl Wolff solicited "The Stoker" (the first chapter of what would be known as *Amerika* after his death) from Kafka. Kafka emphasized in his letter to Wolff that this fragment, along with *The Judgment* and *The Metamorphosis* (which he promised to send soon), would constitute a book that meant a great deal to him and could be called *Sons*.[5] In the absence of Wolff, Werfel had "The Stoker" published as the third volume of the collection known as "Der Jüngste Tag." In May 1913, Kafka received his copies without any mention having been made of the upcoming publication of his *Metamorphosis*. In February 1914, Kafka received a letter from Musil requesting a submission for the *Neue Rundschau* in Berlin. It was for a literary supplement edited by Fischer, who had called on Musil in order to prevent Wolff's power. Wolff had been wise enough to have asked Werfel to be in charge. Kafka accepted, but after a long silence that followed the reception of his manuscript, Musil proposed a number of considerable cuts for editorial purposes. Infuriated, Kafka responded:

> And now that months have passed after this acceptance I am being asked to shorten the story by one-third. This is undignified conduct. To tell the truth, dear Herr Doktor, for I know you will admit that I am completely right, if this request had been made to me at the beginning, before the acceptance, you and I would have been spared the present embarrassment. But I would not have shortened

---

4. See Unseld, *Franz Kafka, une vie d'écrivain.*
5. Franz Kafka, quoted in ibid., p. 99.

the story then any more than I would today. I am sure you will also approve of this stand—there is no other possible course.[6]

Kafka tried again to have his *Metamorphosis* published in the *Weissen Blätter*, an avant-garde journal under the directorship of René Schickele (who had just replaced Franz Blei), which was, along with *Der Sturm* and *Die Aktion*, one of the leaders of expressionism.

In April 1915, Kafka received the same comments from the editor of the journal and, once again, *The Metamorphosis* had to wait until the end of October of that same year to be published in the journal and until November to appear in book form from Wolff in Leipzig. It took three years of struggle—from the end of 1912, when Kafka wrote *The Metamorphosis*, to the end of 1915—to get this text published, a text that has since become a great classic of modern literature.

Such an example makes it clear that Kafka did not remain outside the world of writers and the network of literary relations. His entry into this world was facilitated by the enormous social power of Max Brod. Kafka wanted to be published, and his many moments of discouragement can be explained as much by his temperament and his relationship with Felice as by his difficulties with the publishing world. However, we can also see that it was difficult for Kafka to manage to acquire symbolic capital sufficient to allow him to publish what he wanted when he wanted; he remained an outsider, within the literary institution without being altogether there—hoping to make a place for himself, but not ready to pay the price for that place. This was undoubtedly due to the niche he unconsciously tried to carve out for himself, that of the displacement of the great ancient, classical, and contemporary intertexts by searching for an original form that gave an account of this displacement. It was also due to his concept of writing, which did not altogether conform with a classical writer's career.

In attempting to account for the particular place that Kafka tried to create for himself in the literary field of Germanic letters and modernity, Héran discusses three strategies: retention, outbidding, and reversal. The technique of retention consists of playing the ascetic in life in order to throw the work into relief more effectively.

> Kafka's strategy, according to his own formula, consisted of "economizing everywhere," of "reducing on all sides" as if to better enlarge his work. In imitation of an objet d'art, this enclave where the ordinary laws of the social world seem to be suspended, Kafka's life was meant to be in the world without being part of that world. By retreating from the world, he constructed his biography like a

---

6. Kafka, letter of July 1914, *Letters to Friends, Family, and Editors*, ed. Max Brod, trans. Richard and Clara Winston (New York, 1977), p. 109; hereafter abbreviated *FFE* with date of letter.

work of art, he put *life into the work,* so to speak. At the same time, he created the optical effect that was to set a trap for the commentators who saw in him only the genius-writer misunderstood by his contemporaries. ["A," p. 328]

The outbidding of disinterest allowed Kafka to consider himself outside, while simultaneously criticizing Brod, Kraus, and Werfel. He alone would approach writing without making a career of it. In concluding his novel study, Héran presents the problem of a sociology of literature that would take as its object the very limit between what arises from "art" and the remainder. "Rather than seeing itself confused with an external analysis which still respects 'the opposition between the inside and the outside of the work,' a veritable 'epistemological obstacle' to the progress of the sociological analysis, it might take as its object that very opposition, examining *the work of the institution of the limit* between external and internal" ("A," p. 329). In fact, this outbidding of disinterest is present everywhere in Kafka's journals and correspondence.

Kafka did not write in order to become a famous author or to defend a cause (as Brod did) or to be a leader of a literary school (like Werfel). His need to write was vital, existential; he literally wrote to keep himself from dying. Writing is ascetic, a fundamental, painful choice that obliges the author to sacrifice everything. Kafka repeatedly explained that he was remaining single because he wanted to be able to write.

Kafka had a sacrificial concept of writing. He sacrificed everything for it, particularly the foundation of family, but this was no guarantee. Inspiration could leave him forever. It was similar to Pascal's wager, Jansenism without being Jansenism. There is something poignant in this endless asceticism. This is even more true because Kafka dreamed of a particular type of writing that would secularize him; he dreamed of writing without lacunae.

Not only did Kafka fantasize about biographies and dream of writing an autobiography, he aspired to plenitude, in the sense of writing fully, and to a desire for totality and totalization. He wanted to stop up the leaks once and for all; he wanted to avoid the fragmentary. He dreamed of a text where all parts would hold together. It is a surprising proposal for anyone who knows him from his journal and his correspondence as well as from his literary works.

The disordered sentences of this story with holes into which one could stick both hands; one sentence sounds high, one sentence sounds low. . . . it is only disconnected starts that always make an appearance, disconnected starts, for instance, all through the automobile story. If I were ever able to write something large and whole, well shaped from beginning to end, then in the end the story would never be able to detach itself from me and it would be possible for me calmly and with open eyes, as a blood relation of a healthy story, to hear it read, but as it is, every little piece of the story runs around homeless and drives me away from it in the opposite direction.[7]

My repugnance for antitheses is certain. They are unexpected, but do not surprise, for they have always been there; if they were unconscious, it was at the very edge of consciousness. They make for thoroughness, fulness, completeness, but only like a figure on the "wheel of life." They curl up, cannot be straightened out, are mere clues, are holes in wood, are immobile assaults.[8]

The need for plenitude is evident in Kafka's manner of inundating his friends, particularly Felice, with his correspondence. Later it would be the same thing with Milena: an attempt to furnish the void, the lack, to make the most of words. He was never to renounce his desire for amalgamation, for bonds, for union with the universe of the maternal, the mother's voice, for the spoken word of communication in opposition to solitary writing, the stigma of isolation. Nor would he renounce the primitive happiness that was, for him, the world of the stability of words, of an ancient community structure, the gemeinschaft that was totally ruined and destroyed and toward which Kafka confusedly strained. It was undoubtedly an unconscious strategy that consisted of privileging a type of writing that is miles away from the one produced, a strategy that perpetually devalued fragmentary writing—the short text that is so precisely characteristic of Kafka's work.

The questions posed by the sociologists of literature, particularly those put forth by Héran, are quite legitimate regarding a text and its boundaries: between what is and is not writing, between the spiritual and the ordinary worlds, between the interior world and the exterior one, between life and literature, and so on. What causes the difficulty in this path (which has been inspired by Pierre Bourdieu's work) is first the incredibly reductive character of the three strategies or techniques that Kafka is supposed to have unconsciously put to work in order to create a place in the market of symbolic goods. If such an unconscious strategy exists, it is a question of what touches life and death, what allows breathing, survival, or death—problems that go far beyond the search for a "place" in the literary institution. The sociology of literature also tends not to be concerned with the text.

Earlier we referred to the necessity of sociological mediation and the urgent need to do this work in the area of Kafka studies. That means that apart from the study of conditions of production and reception, apart from the literary networks and circles, we also need to consider

7. Kafka, letter of 5 Nov. 1911, *The Diaries of Franz Kafka 1910–1913*, ed. Brod, trans. Joseph Kresh (New York, 1948), pp. 133–34.
8. Kafka, letter of 20 Nov. 1911, ibid., p. 157.

and analyze what is new about Kafka's text and how it reverberates into the literary milieux. This sociological mediation implies a "return to the text" that is neither the formalist counterpart of a reductive sociologism nor the supplement of a contextual and "co-textual" approach.

In fact, the approach to Kafka's work has its own history. This approach was first extratextual—that is to say, questions of biography or erudition about the life of Kafka and what was necessary to know of it in order to interpret a work that seemed, at first sight, to escape interpretation. Later on, specialists (who were, for the most part, German) approached the text differently, paying more attention to its uniqueness: its wordplay, its peculiar narrative perspective, its system of characters, its underestimation and the unstable equilibrium of its argumentation, its coherence and cohesion within the text. Then, in a cyclical movement, as is often the case in cultural junctures, there dawned a tiring of formalism and a need for new sociological approaches arose, a need for an approach that would not be a return to the exterior of the text, which allowed the critic to say almost anything.

The sociology of literature excels at taking into account everything that surrounds the text. In its analysis of ideologies and representations, the sociology of literature has sought to bring together the ensemble of aesthetic transformations and artistic practices with social contexts and to pull symbolic and social forms toward one another. In this domain, great strides and advances have been made in the last twenty-odd years. Large sectors of knowledge have been conquered concerning everything relating to the surroundings of the text [*l'entour du texte*]: the study of its public, the sociology of reception, of the book, of the reader, and of reading as an autonomous socialized activity; the study of literature as an institution, as a field, a space in which its creators attempt to find a position or a niche, with regard to their symbolic capital and the expectations of the public that they cut out for themselves within a narrow (avant-garde) circle or a wide-ranging sector (the public at large). It is a space where the struggle for legitimation engenders symbolic hierarchies and legitimacies while at the same time reinforcing the dominant values of society as a whole.

By this time, the reader will have recognized Bourdieu's problematic, which remains an irreplaceable contribution to the field. Bourdieu defined the conditions in which literature in Europe was to become autonomous. He studied very precisely the determinations of literary production, the field of mass production destined to a broad public and that of limited production destined to the educated few, and he listed those authorities that decree what is acceptable and legitimate in terms of literary production. It can be said that Bourdieu not only heralded a true sociology of the literary institution, but that he also laid the foundations toward a possibly new apprehension of the text, one that is yet to be developed. Yet, fruitful though it may be, Bourdieu's approach does present some problems.

The structural mechanism may be transformed by internal plays of positioning within various fields, but we must also contend with the impact of historical conditions, ideological changes in society, and, in the literary text, the inscription of a social discourse always on the lookout for something new. In short, what is lacking in Bourdieu's system is a sense of historicity. Let us mention here another field where the sociology of literature has recently shone: career moves, prosopographies of writers, and changing genres in order to find a more suitable niche. From Rémy Ponton to Anne-Marie Thiesse, this branch of the sociology of literature has shown both the heavy and subtle determinations that can lead to the creation of a literary text.

If these frameworks surrounding the text are studied closely, things often become confused when it is necessary (for the sociologist as for the historian) to understand the text as a social object having a social life within the text and to apprehend the text as a unique object at the same time encompassing a questioning of dominant ideology, a problematization of disciplines.

More heuristic are the approaches that do not surround the text, that do not seek a nontextual transparent referent in the text or confuse the order of the real and the order of language. These approaches encompass multiple mediations between social determinations and writing. However, they do not make allowances for the specificity of the literary text, thus erasing its singularity.

Beyond the frameworks of the text, the here and there of the text, its inner and outer facets, there is the textless text [*le text sans texte*], if you will. All of the studies that have been done on literary fields with Bourdieu's conceptualization have been akin to the attempts to displace genres, writing, and aesthetics by relating the marginalization of producers newly arrived on the market of symbolic goods to the vehemence of their aesthetic plans or to their desire to distinguish themselves from the dominant norms. Based as they are on legitimacy and distinction, these methods do not take into account a number of shifts and impresses between popular culture and learned culture, ironic and parodic reuses, but also something of a transverse that knocks over and about the fine layout of the legitimate order. All of this research views the transformations of genre and stylistic and aesthetic modifications as institutional effects. The studies are not concerned with the problem of how the process of textualization functions, how the effects of specific texts are constituted, or what the aesthetic and ideological effects of this process (the *mise en texte*) are. Furthermore, these steps do not distinguish the conscious ideological and aesthetic project of the creator or what he or she in fact produces. As important as it may be today, this research in the field of the sociology of literature is concerned only with the literary text in terms of what it is not, or in terms of what is not text within the text.

The same problem exists concerning approaches founded on the notion of *social discourse*. It is a matter of taking into account the totality of what is written or printed in a given society at a given moment in time, as Marc Angenot has shown with printed material in France in 1889.[9] It is a matter of looking at the recurring ideologemes that cross all the zones of social discourse: medical discourse, legal discourse, the discourse of literary criticism and literary production, and so on. Thus we are aware of great constellations of images taking shape, syntagms asserting themselves, locutions and ensembles that literally cross all institutions and genres. These basic ideologemes will show up again in fiction and novelistic production, but they will be thematized, caught in a story, a system of characters, or a plot. Nevertheless, what is interesting in the framework of such a problematic is not the specific way in which thematization occurs but discovering in the literary text the inscription of social discourse. The processes of textualization are only seen in relation to the stereotypes circulating in the whole of social discourse without the possibility of the text transforming the stereotypes, or displacing them, or even speaking of them ironically. In the problematic of social discourse, the literary text is certainly present, but it is stripped of all literariness, flattened. It becomes a simple discourse among all other types of discourse.

For us, the large problem with many of the sociologies of literature resides in their inability to take into account the specific forms of textualization that are the very material of the social imaginary, the cultural memory, and the phantasmic love of language. What do we remember long after reading a novel? Not whether it sprang from a circle consisting of the avant-garde or the general public. Not whether the novel inscribed such and such a syntagm then in fashion or a particular argument of social discourse. All of this is very important, but the sociology interested in symbolic forms must also pay attention to the history of the social imaginary. This underpinning of individual and collective phantasms, this first memorial matter is textualization in its formal organization. It is a particular treatment of language.

When the Russian formalists asserted that poetic language was not to be confused with ordinary language and that the metaphors of poetic language were to defamiliarize the reader, to take from him or her the automatisms of perception and comprehension, they were undoubtedly seeking a niche within the narrow circle of letters and Russian criticism, a niche of modernity distinct both from all the forms of decadentism that had oversaturated the market of Russian modernity before the revolution and from the various sociological schools and the realistic aesthetics that were regaining the upper hand. Indeed, all of this is true and is of

9. See Marc Angenot and Régine Robin, "L'Inscription du discours social dans le texte littéraire," *Sociocriticism* 1 (July 1985): 53–82.

primary interest to the sociology of literature. But, to my mind, the formalists were also declaring something else: a sort of "universal" of aesthetics, a use value of the practices of writing and *mise en texte* beyond their exchange value. All of this re-presents the infamous problem of the eternal charm of the Greek statue, the problem that intrigued Marx.

From the sociology of literature to the sociology of writing, from the interrogation on the exchange value of aesthetic productions to a questioning of their use value, from the search for writers' positions in the literary field and the modification of genres entailed in such a search or the multiple inscriptions of social discourse in fiction to the analysis of specific processes of textualization and the study of these forms as an object of the history of the social imaginary: this is the displacement we must undertake today in approaching Kafka's text.

What specificity exists in this text that can explain why Wolff, for example, was interested in Kafka from beginning to end? If an unconscious strategy exists, it must be related to the literary domain, to writing, to the decisions on form and the *mise en texte*. It must be related to work on intertext and interdiscourse. A sociology of literature unable to evaluate the production of works in the marketplace without taking into account the processes of their textualization, that could see only responses to social demands and diversified inscriptions of ideological figurative fragments in those works without seeking to account for the specificity of figuralization in the text itself, would completely miss its mark. For if writers have a place to conquer in a market that implacably functions as a jungle, it is as writers that they must conquer it, in terms of the themes being discussed in the society and in cultural discourse, in terms of modes of expression and genres, in terms of what will constitute a mark of originality or novelty, and in terms of what their contemporaries consider to be "real literature." It is in this way that we must confront Kafka's work at present. We must see what exact place it occupies by its aesthetic work as such, by the work of writing.

There have been so many commentaries on Kafka's text, so many interpretations have been produced, that sometimes we ask why it has been so easy to miss the essential. Since his death in 1924, and after his friend Max Brod revealed to the literary world the unfinished novels that Kafka had ordered burned, especially *The Trial* and *The Castle,* for more than fifty years the text has resisted and the end is not in sight. Luckily, in the late fifties, we began to examine what the text was composed of, how it was arranged, and finally we began to question the deluge of commentaries and interpretations.

Imagine Kafka caught between his admiration for the classics, Goethe, Dickens, or Dostoyevski, even his passion for Flaubert (whose work he read aloud to his sisters and to Brod), caught between this admiration and his expressionist contemporaries or those close to the expressionist wave. Kafka's particularity is that he created a type of text in which strangeness plays a role, but so, too, does a real undecidability. Whether he inscribes autobiographical elements, traces of his immediate readings, or the influence of a particular author or philosopher in his fiction, whether he presents the whole arsenal of legal discourse or whether he crosses through the great intertexts of culture, parodying, displacing, or pulverizing them, Kafka is always writing the same text in an identical structure that renders it impossible to interpret or determine. In fact, his text is indeterminable at every level: in its way of obscuring the referent, of playing on the untrustworthiness of messages, on the interpretation and the argumentation in the text, in the way it puts instability itself to work as well as genre and the alteration of legends, in a word, in its manner of saying it is impossible to take this course into account, by means of word and image, in the outline for a veritable *mise en procés* of language. Or, if you will, it is a matter of the impossibility of distinguishing fact from hypothesis, and from there, of distinguishing turmoil from the coherence, consistency, and cohesiveness of the world. This lack of cohesion engenders a certain fragility of what is being brought from the world, when one wants to write its story or account for its past. It follows that all writing, that all fiction, can have only one illusory character insofar as it uses adequate words and images in its attempt at figuration, representation, or translation.

Kafka's texts confuse mimesis, the universe of the probable and of representation, in more ways than one. This is especially true in the texts written before 1917, the date of a fundamental turning point in his life and in his writings: *Description of a Struggle, The Judgment, Amerika, The Metamorphosis, The Trial,* and even *In the Penal Colony.* It is a matter of a world said to be real, of the exterior world, often an urban world, which some have even recognized as Prague, as in *The Trial,* for example. It is a world of offices, halls, and stairways, a world of streets and vague terrain, but it is also a social world with families, hierarchical superiors, traveling salesmen, petit bourgeois stiffly ensconced in their daily routines. Their world of technique, machines, and technological modernity is also very much present, and it is not a minor note that Kafka was one of the first authors in German literature to speak of planes and aviation after the aerial meeting he and Brod witnessed in Brescia in 1909. Also very much in evidence is another aspect of modernity: bureaucracy cut off in its buildings, the tentacular offices—the regulatory truth of our daily lives is omnipresent.

Despite this figurative reality, however, the troublesome strangeness quickly settles in by way of bizarre or improbable details, which immediately counterbalance the proliferating details of decor and social or day-to-day life. It occurs in *Amerika:* in the arrival in New York with the Statue of Liberty brandishing her sword; in the strange, gigantic environment of the Oklahoma theater. In *The Judgment,* Georg's old father, half-dead, is transformed into a giant, and his son rushes to execute the death sentence his father has just uttered. It also occurs in the transformation that poor Gregor Samsa undergoes in *The Metamorphosis*. Gregor insists (at least in the beginning) on continuing the habits of a traveling salesman who is about to miss his train. Then there are the settings, people, and strange situations Joseph K. encounters in his quest, without saying anything of Kafka's works that, while not pure allegories, abandon their moorings in reality (such as *The Country Doctor* or *The Castle*). It has been said time and time again that the referent is affected because beyond the real world (or its figuration in referential illusion) Kafka indicates another indecipherable, invisible reality that nonetheless invades the rather banal life of the protagonists and transforms them, distresses them, radically changes their existence without their ever being capable of understanding what has actually happened to them, without their ever holding the key to decipher it, and without the narrator being able to let us, the readers, know what has actually occurred regarding them. Between these two worlds, the material world and the "other" world, there is no division. On the contrary, a porous border worms its way into the real world, akin to an intermediate space in which beings, objects, hybrids, bonds, and relays travel. It is a border that belongs to a logic other than the logic of noncontradiction that presides in the universe of mimesis and that takes on the aspect of the dream and the riddle.

For Kafka, the material world, with its little streets, its offices and apartments, its street traffic, and so on, is the world of illusion, fallacy, and lies. That which can be seen is false or blurred, a bit like Plato's cave. It is a world of appearances further amplified in its illusions the moment we attempt to explain it.

Argumentation, in Kafka's work, is one of the fundamental elements that makes the text, in the strongest sense of the term, indeterminable. We recall this scene from *The Castle:* the mayor of the village in which K. has just arrived claims that he has been named on the orders of the castle land surveyor, and there is a strange exchange with K.:

> "Allow me, Mr. Mayor, to interrupt you with a question," said K. "Did you not mention once before a Control Authority? From your description the whole economy is one that would rouse one's apprehensions if one could imagine the Control failing."
> "You're very strict," said the Mayor, "but multiply your strictness a thousand times and it would still be nothing compared with the strictness that the Authority imposes on itself. Only a total stranger could ask a question like yours. Is there a Control Authority? There are only Control authorities. Frankly, it isn't their function to hunt out errors in the vulgar sense, for errors don't happen, and even when once in a while an error does happen, as in your case, who can say finally that it's an error?"[10]

10. Kafka, *The Castle*, trans. Willa and Edwin Muir (New York, 1966), p. 84.

True, if as Ch. Perelman and L. Olbrechts-Tyteca suggest, "The domain of argumentation is that of the credible, the plausible, the probable, to the degree that the latter eludes the certainty of calculations."[11] Or if, again, it is a question of convincing an audience, by means of the validity of one's assertions and arguments, to believe the authentic good of what is being suggested, the least that can be said is that the mayor, in this example from *The Castle*, follows a peculiar logic.

First, in this administration, no errors occur. It is too controlled for such an occurrence, and, besides, the control procedures are not geared to reveal errors, since there are none.

Second, there may still be an error.

Third, K., in this instance, is completely exceptional.

Fourth, this may not be an error, since errors do not occur.

In other (more amusing) words:

A. There is never an error.
B. If there were to be one,
C. As in your case,
D. Then, it would undoubtedly not be an error,
E. Because there is no error possible.

This is the same logic that Freud brings to light in *Jokes and Their Relation to the Unconscious*. It is a logic of noncontradiction, or, in another direction, a logic of sophism, that is, the masking of false reasoning. The emblematic joke of this logic, for Freud, is the following: "A. borrowed a copper kettle from B. and after he had returned it was sued by B. because the kettle now had a big hole in it which made it unusable. His defence was: 'First, I never borrowed a kettle from B. at all; secondly, the kettle had a hole in it already when I got it from him; and thirdly, I gave him back the kettle undamaged.'"[12] As Freud emphasizes, each explanation, in and of itself, is entirely cohesive and satisfactory. What causes the problem is the juxtaposition of the three arguments without a liaison, taken in a logic of noncontradiction, therefore a logic of non-credibility, except in the case where we might presume a reading that is purely oneiric or fantastic.

Such a logic, which causes the proliferation of sophism and paralogism, arises from the paradigm of parataxis, that is, from a movement that lays out two propositions side by side without distinguishing the relationship of dependence that would unify them, and this for a very good reason:

11. Ch. Perelman and L. Olbrechts-Tyteca, *La Nouvelle Rhétorique: Traité de l'argumentation*, 2 vols. (Paris, 1958); trans. John Wilkinson and Purcell Weaver, under the title *The New Rhetoric: A Treatise on Argumentation* (Notre Dame, Ind., 1969), p. 1.

12. Sigmund Freud, *Jokes and Their Relation to the Unconscious, The Standard Edition of the Complete Psychological Works of Sigmund Freud,* ed. and trans. James Strachey, 24 vols. (London, 1953–74), 8:62.

that is to say that Kafka's text is more metaphoric than metonymic and that a logical, rigorous structure is missing from it, particularly given the ensemble of what might be called conjunctions (simultaneously temporal and argumentative conjunctions). But it is the opposite that occurs in Kafka's work.

Horst Steinmetz has aptly demonstrated the importance of conjunctions in Kafka's work: *aber, freilich, allerdings, vielmehr, trotzdem, übringens, vielleicht,* and so on. The conjunctions, adverbial modifiers, and the ensemble of modals are infinitely more frequent in Kafka's work than in that of any other author in the German language.[13] In the concordance to *The Trial,* Walter Spiedel brings to light the importance of the connecting argumentation in the novel. Richard Thieberger has also shown the leitmotif of the dubitive phrase "as if" ["*als ob*"] in Kafka's work.[14]

Everything in the text is constructed to mark its undecidable character. We take off from the factual, a set of givens we have no reason to doubt in the beginning. From these givens, from the factual, we construct a whole universe of hypotheses, chains of assertions in all possible directions. Little by little, in the complex chain of reasoning, facts turn into hypotheses and hypotheses into fact, which in turn becomes a new reliable subject, which serves itself to a new rigorous interrogation, so much so that finally it is impossible to know what is really true, what is probable, and what is completely impossible.

The parataxical logic of the mayor is entirely caught up in a rhetoric and a discourse that are, on the contrary, hypotaxical, that is, they are caught in argumentative chains that are rigorously connected. It is in this contrast, this difference between logic and rhetoric, that the strange humor of this fiction resides. Kafka has his own argumentative system that is integrated (as I have already stated at the beginning of this essay) into an ensemble of signs that target the dissolution of all that is certain and credible in every domain.

His writing is eminently metonymic, playing on association by contiguity, the part for the whole. In *The Trial,* it is clearly stated that everything—the characters, the objects, the plots, the meetings, the vocabulary—belongs to the court of justice. The same is true in *The Castle:* association by contiguity, but also the interchangeability of words, forms, universes, and characters. Just to remind the reader, I would recall the surveyor's two assistants, the two policemen who arrest and follow Joseph K., or the phonic proximity of Sortini and Sordini, the castle's two servants. In any case, however, Kafka uses a great deal of

---

13. See Horst Steinmetz, *Suspensive Interpretation: Am Beispiel Franz Kafkas* (Göttingen, 1977).

14. See Walter Spiedel, *A Complete Contextual Concordance to Franz Kafka: "Der Prozess"* (Leeds, 1978). See also Richard Thieberger, "Sprache," *Das Werk und seine Wirkung,* vol. 2 of *Kafka—Hambuch,* ed. Hartmut Binder (Stuttgart, 1979).

metaphor, and it is undoubtedly this that has evoked such a deluge of commentary. In the paradigm of metaphor, in fact, we are seeking above all else to determine the meaning, a sense beneath the meaning, a derivative meaning next to the literal one. In this search for meaning, argumentation will play a major role since it exists as the support of the interpretation for the exegete. If the mayor says that there is no error in the administration of the castle, we are, much as Brod stated, in the realms of divine transcendence and grace. If errors do exist, it is in the sense that the ways of God are impenetrable and that only God may decree whether there is or is not an error. In the paradigm of metaphor, everything is for the sake of meaning, whether that meaning is open or closed, in terms of basic hypotheses and the intertextual culture of the reader. We can thus construct a coherence around a nodal point: the Jew and his rank of pariah; the homosexual and his rejection from society; the author cut off from life's pleasures, an ascetic of writing; the sick person who, like the author, is someone alone, in quarantine; the condemned, the guilty, or the innocent person already destined to die before the story even begins; the pariah, the stranger, and the other in all their forms. All of these interpretations are correct, unassailable, valid, and partial, abandoning the essential of Kafka's text, that is, the impossibility of interpreting it in all its dimensions, not because it would be the bearer of the ineffable, but because of its own arrangements, argumentation being among them.

As Theodor Adorno very aptly observes,

> Walter Benjamin rightly defined it [Kafka's prose] as parable. It expresses itself not through expression but by its repudiation, by breaking off. It is a parabolic system the key to which has been stolen; yet any effort to make this fact itself the key is bound to go astray by confounding the abstract thesis of Kafka's work, the obscurity of the existent, with its substance. Each sentence says 'interpret me', and none will permit it.[15]

In return, if we imagine the metonymic paradigm, the search for meaning is secondary. It is the arrangement that causes meaning. It is no longer a question of the mediating or immediate relationship of the images to the referent but of the allusive character of the images or *Andeutung*, the play on images, the destruction of metaphors more than their reformulation, the play of paradoxical and chiasmatic figures, the place that has fallen to silence and gesture in a new interrogation of the powers of language, a questioning of the stability of words, of the referent and of communication.

In the metadiscourse of his reasoning characters, Kafka himself established the untrustworthiness of messages and the impossibility of

15. Theodor Adorno, "Notes on Kafka," *Prisms*, trans. Samuel and Shierry Weber (Cambridge, Mass., 1981), p. 246.

interpretation. He repeatedly explains his text or stops those who would like to ascribe a figurative, realistic, expressionistic, or allegorical representation to it.

When *The Metamorphosis* was in press, Kafka learned that Ottomar Starke was in the process of drawing an illustration for its cover. He immediately wrote, on 25 October 1915:

> It struck me that Starke, as an illustrator, might want to draw the insect itself. Not that, please not that! I do not want to restrict him, but only to make this plea out of my deeper knowledge of the story. The insect itself cannot be depicted. It cannot even be shown from a distance. Perhaps there is no such intention and my plea can be dismissed with a smile—so much the better. But I would be very grateful if you would pass along my request and make it more emphatic. If I were to offer suggestions for an illustration, I would choose such scenes as the following: the parents and the head clerk in front of the locked door, or even better, the parents and the sister in the lighted room, with the door open upon the adjoining room that lies in darkness. [*FFE*, pp. 114–15]

We can see clearly what lies at the root of Kafka's outburst. It is impossible to represent Gregor Samsa because he is the personification of a polysemic problem: of otherness and the rejection by the sphere of this other's so-called normal life, the father's chastising because of a fault for which the son is not responsible, the son-transformed-into-vermin's unfortunate love for his mother and his sister, but, also, an ambiguous liberation of the daily alienation of the traveling salesman, the condition of interiority, even at the price of universal rejection of death. It is also impossible to represent this figure from *The Metamorphosis* because, like all true fiction, its overall scheme relies greatly on autobiography.

When Kafka gave Martin Buber two texts ("Jackals and Arabs" and "A Report to an Academy") for his journal *Der Jude* in 1917, Buber proposed "Two Parables" as a general title. Kafka reacted by stating that his texts were not really parables and that it would be more appropriate to call them simply "Two Animal Stories" (12 May 1917; *FFE*, p. 132). Kafka refused the term "parable" as he refused "allegory."

Kafka criticized a manuscript entitled "Legend," written by Grete Bloch's brother, which Kafka thought was spoiled by its recourse to allegory: "I can't get over the dryness of the entire allegory, which is nothing but an allegory, which says all there is to say without ever delving deeper or drawing one deeper into it."[16] Allegory does not allow us to project beyond the text. Without seeking a hidden meaning, a double background in the text, Kafka demands an unfolding of the text, an

16. Kafka, letter of 6 June 1914 to Grete Bloch, *Letters to Felice*, ed. Erich Heller and Jürgen Born, trans. James Stern and Elisabeth Duckworth (New York, 1973), p. 421.

overflowing of meaning that would point toward this imperceptible spiritual sphere, but from which would emanate an eternal light, however feeble that light might be.

Neither parable, nor allegory, nor metaphor! These caused him to despair of literature. Kafka used the German word *Gleichnis,* which could call to mind a symbolic or parabolic story as well as an image, or better still, a figure. We cannot do without symbols or figures, yet "all these parables really set out to say merely that the incomprehensible is incomprehensible, and we know that already."[17] The incomprehensible is beyond our grasp in the same manner that legend cannot be explained. Regarding Prometheus, Kafka quotes four legends, four versions of the myth, but nothing that really permits him to approach a "truth": "There remained the inexplicable mass of rock. The legend tried to explain the inexplicable. As it came out of a substratum of truth it had in turn to end in the inexplicable."[18]

Kafka was to use the two logics, parataxis and hypotaxis, the two forms of reasoning, and play them one against the other, in their very incompatibility, in order to destroy one by the other. Parable, allegory, symbols and figures, legend: these are just so many words that define a paradigm of texts that plays with ancestral forms and the wisdom of midrash and the Talmud. In Kafka's texts, even before the period of aphorisms of Zürau, there is a familiar atmosphere in the writing, in the form, and in the thematics, like a common thread that passes through the great unfinished novels as well as through the fragments and short stories. Kafka alters legends, Hasidic stories, and the myths of antiquity in the same way as he endlessly varies the play on kabbalistic letters or the indeterminable character of the unpronounceable Name.

In view of the untrustworthiness of messages (which are perpetually misunderstood) and their transmission and the impossibility of going "beyond," there is no exit for Kafka's hero. To return to the argumentation, nothing better demonstrates the absence of escape than the scene in which Joseph K. meets the painter Titorelli, the official painter of those gentlemen of the court, who is supposed to finally be able to get poor Joseph K. (who is done in) off the hook.

The discussion begins with the following question from Titorelli: " 'Are you innocent?' "[19] But, as we have known from the outset of the novel, either K. is innocent and everything that ensues afterwards is a real nightmare or he is not innocent, but at any rate, given the second hypothesis, he doesn't know and will not know until the end why he is

---

17. Kafka, "On Parables," trans. Muir, *The Complete Stories,* ed. Nahum N. Glatzer, (New York, 1971), p. 457.

18. Kafka, "Prometheus," trans. Muir, *The Complete Stories,* p. 432.

19. Kafka, *The Trial,* ed. Brod, trans. Muir (New York, 1968), p. 149; hereafter abbreviated *T.*

guilty and what he is guilty of. K. answers: " 'I am completely innocent.' " Thus K. is afforded the great astonishment of hearing this from
a so-called professional, one who is supposed to know all the meanderings
and labyrinths of the court: " 'If you are innocent, then the matter is
quite simple' " (*T,* p. 149).

The black humor and the author's logic are obvious here. Everything
first occurs in the conversation as if we were in a normal world where
the guilty person is punished and where the innocent person comes forth
to prove his or her innocence before a court that acts in good faith and
passes judgment depending on the law. As soon as the dialogue continues,
however, the reader sees a complete reversal of such fine logic and then
enters into oneiric reasoning that is improbable and implacable. I will
summarize the dialogue.

In reality, the court is completely inaccessible to proof and has never
acquitted an innocent person as far as anyone can remember. This is
the basic known fact of the argument. Thus no one can officially do
anything, but anything may be tried in the hallways, and this is just what
Titorelli proposes to do for Joseph K. What can he obtain quietly, behind
the scenes? There are two possibilities: definite acquittal or unlimited
parole (known in some translations as *indefinite postponement*).

In order to obtain definite acquittal, it is necessary to win the maximum
of subordinate judges (highly ranked judges are inaccessible at any rate),
by all means, whether legal or not, in such a way that they might sign a
declaration of innocence, and the accused would find himself acquitted
after having accomplished a few formalities. The problem is that it is a
question of influential intervention. In order for the acquittal to be definitive, the supreme court must render the verdict. However, the supreme
court is inaccessible; thus, by definition, the verdict cannot be rendered.
Only the lower court declares the accused acquitted. Titorelli explains
to Joseph K. in great detail the consequences of this half-liberty:

> "That is to say, when you are acquitted in this fashion the charge
> is lifted from your shoulders for the time being, but it continues
> to hover above you and can, as soon as an order comes from on
> high, be laid upon you again. . . . One day—quite unexpected-
> ly—some Judge will take up the documents and look at them
> attentively, recognize that in this case the charge is still valid, and
> order an immediate arrest." [*T,* pp. 158–59]

" 'And the case begins all over again?' asked K. almost incredulously.
'Certainly,' said the painter" (*T,* p. 159).

This type of acquittal, which hardly seems to suit Joseph K., demands
an intense but interrupted effort because there is peace between the
moment of acquittal and the moment when a superior court judge will
once again pick up the file. But since the files are never lost and since

the path toward definite acquittal is blocked, we never know when things might fall on us again or whether that will ever even occur. This situation resembles that of Damocles' sword, or perhaps is itself a metaphor for sickness and death.

Indefinite postponement is another matter. This demands a bit more effort than the first possibility, but a constant effort nonetheless. The trial must be maintained at its lowest level and prevented from climbing into the higher levels of the system. It is necessary to know the judges quite well in order to do this. One must establish a solid network of relations, come before the court from time to time, play the game with unswerving attention, and maintain the trial at its initial stage.

We can see which alternative Titorelli's reasoning demands of Joseph K. Everything is reducible to chains of syllogisms or pseudosyllogisms that leave no escape for the accused.

1. An innocent person has nothing to fear.
   A. You are innocent.
   B. Thus, you have nothing to fear.
2. However, the court has never acquitted an innocent person.
   A. You are innocent.
   B. Thus, you cannot be acquitted.
3. Therefore, you only have a choice between two forms of non-liberty.
   A. The lower-court judges can declare you free. This is a specious acquittal.
   B. Otherwise it would be necessary that it be ratified by the supreme court.
   C. But the supreme court is inaccessible, and it might have you arrested again.
   D. Therefore, specious acquittal is obviously specious, and so on.

Kafka's despair, like that of his heroes, resides entirely in this absence of escape, in the impossible, in the lack, in the obsessed person's argumentation without any form, which leaves no argument to chance and where reasoning cannot come to any certainty or any place to moor itself.

It is this effect of indeterminacy that explains the amazing reception of the text, and the porosity of its trademark leaves to every generation the task of interpreting it according to its own obsessions.

Prismatic Effects

Alain Viala

Translated by Paula Wissing

Literary history and criticism have always made great use of visual metaphors—Lucien Goldmann's worldview, Hans Robert Jauss' horizon of expectations, and Jean Starobinski's lively eye, to name a few. Although the title of this essay places it within the same tradition, my purpose is not to enlarge the collection of metaphors. Instead I would like to set aside one that I suspect to be unsound and replace it with another that will prove more solid. In other words, and metaphor for metaphor, I believe that we should be suspicious of "reflection" and all "theories of reflection," and take *prismatic effects* under advisement. By prisms I mean those mediations, those realities, at once translucent and deformative that are formed by the literary codes, institutions, and fields interposed between the social referent and the text as well as between the work and its readers—those realities that determine meaning. The sociology of literature takes on the task of describing these prisms and accounting for their effects.

A number of traditional visual metaphors refer to the relationships between literature and society, long a concern of students of literature. At the very beginning of the twentieth century, the influential literary historian Gustave Lanson acknowledged that literature is indeed the expression of society but that the "incontestable truth had nonetheless spawned many errors."[1] Today one is tempted to revive this statement

---

1. Gustave Lanson, "La Méthode de l'histoire littéraire," *Revue du mois* (10 Oct. 1910), rpt. in *Essais de méthode, de critique et d'histoire littéraire*, ed. Henri Peyre (Paris, 1965), p. 46. The phrase in full—"Literature is the expression of society as language is the expression

word for word, so true it is that the analysis of relationships between literature and society, or the different attempts to practice a "sociology of literature," have produced dubious interpretations and sometimes even obviously untenable positions. "Back to Lanson" is a rallying cry heard now and then; it is hardly new. Lucien Febvre was already saying it nearly fifty years ago, and he was neither the first nor the last.[2] It seems that ever since the programmatic texts of the founding father of literary history appeared in France, Lanson's disciples and epigones have been betraying the program and wasting the patrimony by misappropriations or abdications.

Things are perhaps more simple and clear-cut. It is indisputable that Lanson was able to pose the question of the relationship between literary history and sociology and thereby open the field.[3] But Lanson's literary history is a child of positivism involving a deterministic conception of society and an instrumental view of literature.[4] A statement such as "literature is the expression of society" establishes a mechanistic-causal relationship: social phenomena are produced; works express them. With the idea of "reflection" in place, the machine is set in motion. Naive in the work of some critics, such as Henri Peyre's division of literary generations, the idea can assume more complex forms and the machinery can become more complicated and sophisticated, as in the analyses of Goldmann. However elaborate the metaphor, in the end the determinism is still there.

Generally speaking, literary scholars have no training in the disciplines of history and sociology and so, with the excessive and dogmatic

---

of man"—comes from Louis Gabriel Ambroise de Bonald, *Législation primitive, considérée dans les derniers temps par les seules lumières de la raison*, 2 vols. (Paris, 1802), 2:207.

2. See Lucien Febvre, "Littérature et vie sociale; de Lanson à Daniel Mornet, un renoncement?" *Annales d'histoire sociale* 3 (1941), rpt. in Febvre, *Combats pour l'histoire* (Paris, 1953), pp. 263–68; for a more recent study, see Antoine Compagnon, *La Troisième République des lettres, de Flaubert à Proust* (Paris, 1983).

3. See Lanson, "Programme d'études sur l'histoire provinciale de la vie littéraire en France" and "L'Histoire littéraire et la sociologie," *Essais de méthode, de critique et d'histoire littéraire*, pp. 81–87 and 61–80.

4. See Compagnon, *La Troisième République des lettres*, pp. 19–212. Compagnon emphasizes Lanson's debt to Durkheim but also notes the influence of Langlois and Seignobos, standard-bearers of historical positivism, and the ineluctable return of the reference to Taine.

Alain Viala is a professor at the Université de Paris III—Sorbonne Nouvelle. Author of *Naissance de l'écrivain: Sociologie de la littérature à l'âge classique* (1985) and *Les Institutions de la vie littéraire en France au XVIIe siècle* (1985), he is currently working on studies of the sociology of literature, Racine, and literary strategies. **Paula Wissing** is a free-lance translator and editor.

zeal of neophytes, they resolve issues that continue to puzzle historians and sociologists (Goldmann's discussion of Jansenism being a case in point) in order to fit each literary work with the appropriate explanation. The idea of reflection and its corresponding theories, whether implicit or explicitly developed, are polymorphous, and their history would take a whole book. They have become ingrained in habits of critical and historical writing (whatever scientific front they may adopt) because the initial postulate is not as "incontestable" as it seems.

In recent years the sociology of literature has developed on the basis of another formula: literature is part of the larger social order. It is not the "expression of society" but an integral part of it. The idea is simple, the implications are great. Literature as part of the social order goes beyond a study of the external social manifestations of literature, beyond the sociology of the book, author, and reader practiced, for example, by Robert Escarpit—a sociology which leads inevitably to a positivist outlook.[5] Nor can we be satisfied with a wholesale borrowing of sociological concepts that does no more than provide the tools for arguments in favor of one or another theory of literature.[6] Whatever the interest of these theories (and sometimes it is very great), a sociology of literature becomes possible only when it includes the sociology of the theories elaborated on the subject itself. (So far my purpose has led me gradually to substitute the term "sociology of literature" for "literature and society." Philosophical or political theories can be propounded on the relations between literature and society, but these relations can be studied scientifically only in sociological terms.)

Thus the questions should be: how is literature, this social element, related to other social components, and what specific forms do these relationships take? In all respects, literature constitutes a social discourse: a discourse *addressed to* society, for it exists, socially speaking, only from the moment that it is read; a discourse *about* society, for even when it does not speak of them directly, literature engages values, cultural schemes, and modes of representation; and finally, a discourse *within* society, for it always functions there, at least as a discriminant. At the same time this discourse is unique, since it both partakes of the common linguistic background and is distinguished from other verbal actualizations by the series of markers that define it, or deny its definition, as "literature." It is doubly unique since unlike other modes of social signification (for example, money, clothing, housing, and interior design) it belongs entirely to the symbolic order. The sociology of literature must include a literary pragmatics; it must analyze the interaction between works and their audiences.

---

5. See Robert Escarpit, *Sociologie de la littérature* (Paris, 1958). See also Escarpit et al., *Le Littéraire et le social: Éléments pour une sociologie de la littérature* (Paris, 1970).

6. Pierre V. Zima's presentations of the sociology of literature seem to be taking him toward this failing. See Zima, *Pour une sociologie du texte littéraire* (Paris, 1978).

Thus we locate the object of the sociology of literature in the *mediations* that make up the systems of relations between literature and other social praxes, that is, in prismatic effects.

The most basic mediation is the literary field, provided that, as Pierre Bourdieu has emphasized, we define the term in the strict sense and strictly limit the concept, reducing neither the term nor the concept to the traditional ideas of "social context" or "literary milieu."[7] The term should be understood to refer to the relatively autonomous social space formed by the group of actors, works, and phenomena comprising literary praxis, a space whose structures are defined by the system of forces active within it and by the conflicts among these forces. Bourdieu defines the literary field as "a field of forces acting on all those who enter this space and differently according to the position that they occupy there, at the same time as a field of struggle aiming to transform this field of forces" ("CL," p. 5). This analytic model should be utilized only for the periods and situations for which it is relevant; thus in France one can speak of the literary field only since the classical period.[8] Finally, the concept should be used only with the awareness that mediation does not work in a single direction. The field is not only the mediation through which the social determinations acting upon literature pass but is also the space where literature takes form according to the logic of the mediations belonging to this space. If needed, literature acts on the other spheres of social practice in accordance with the same mediation.[9]

Whoever analyzes the literary field finds two series of givens functioning in a narrow and permanent dialectical relationship. On the one hand, literary space can be understood only through analysis of its situation with respect to other social fields. Specifically, it is essential to situate the literary field at the various moments of its history within the intellectual

7. See Pierre Bourdieu, "Le Champ littéraire. Préalabes critiques et principes de méthode," *Lendemains* 9, no. 36 (1984): 5; further references to this article, abbreviated "CL," will be included in the text. For Bourdieu's first statement, see his "Champ intellectuel et projet créateur," *Temps modernes* 22, no. 246 (Nov. 1966): 865–906.

8. See Viala, *Naissance de l'écrivain: Sociologie de la littérature à l'âge classique* (Paris, 1985).

9. In this respect, Bourdieu's description of a "specific mediation . . . through which external determinations are exercised upon cultural productions" risks giving the impression that determinism and causal explanation have again entered the discussion ("CL," p. 5). However, in his analysis, Bourdieu takes care to modulate the expression in his analysis of the relations between the field of positions and the field of positions taken. Yet here, and once again in his important critique of Michel Foucault's symbolic structuralism ("CL," pp. 6, 7), the ambiguity is not entirely absent; it appears that at this stage in his analysis there is still no accounting for the fact that the field is its own mediation, that the literary field is one of those in which internal relationships exist only in mediated form, and thus that the analysis must always deal with mediations of mediations. I treat this matter here so as not to deviate from my main intent, which is to clarify a move toward a limited theoretical debate necessary to the overall undertaking. The search for prismatic devices taken up below attempts to account for these mediations of mediations.

field and among the powers it shares as the locus of a fraction of symbolic power. The effect of the transformations that the literary field induces correlates with its degree of autonomy and its position in the hierarchy of cultural values.

On the other hand, mediations are also linked to the structures of the field, which are the "cumulative product of its own history" ("CL," p. 5)—hierarchies and internal rules, its division (in the nineteenth and twentieth centuries) into two distinct spheres, the accepted or contested hegemony of a particular school or movement, the greater or lesser prestige accorded each genre, the authority and limits of an institution. The analysis of literary works in terms of positions taken (a narrow construction of the sociology of texts that some critics propound) must be linked to an analysis of the objective positions held by the actors taking part in the literary event (authors, readers, publishers). Phenomena that traditional literary history ascribes to individual talent (for example, the everlasting parallel between Corneille and Racine) then appear for what they are: effects of the field.

These effects of the field are nothing less than prismatic effects. The situation looks promising; in fact, the past twenty years, under the stimulus of Bourdieu, the sociology of literature as the analysis of the literary field has begun to take shape, and its theoretical and historical statements have indeed made some progress. This promising situation, however, has little if any bearing on specifically literary phenomena. By remaining in abstract and general terms, a theoretical formulation of this sort is in danger of becoming an expandable container for whatever is dictated by the need of the moment or the ease or difficulty of the discussion.

Until now, my main issue has been to account for the attainments and output of the sociological study of literature. Now it is time for another phase and a project as modest as it is essential: we need to see how a sociology that uses the notions of field and mediation, pragmatics and prisms, can change the traditional objects and methods of literary studies. First we must inventory these prisms. Anyone who makes an inventory runs the risk of unwittingly leaving out something or someone. With that caveat in mind, let us take the risk, for without it any analysis based on a model originating in the sociological field could well be suspected forever of being an import, or even contraband, inappropriate to literature and hence not taken up by those who study it. Given the present state of research, the points listed below are only the main headings that can be seen at work in the logic of prismatic analysis. They are the prime indicators of a properly literary character that a social pragmatics can and should consider.

1. Institutions of Literary Life. These institutions constitute the best linkages between the structures of the literary field and those of the social sphere in which the field is located.[10] Moreover, they are the *objects* to which literary history has never given much thought, objects that are relatively new to a science of literature. These institutions are authorities, groups, or laws (written or implicit) that are entirely or primarily devoted to the social regulation of literary life: academies and circles, schools, patronage, censorship, the legislation of publishing and authors' rights, prizes, and rituals. Their role is crucial, for they serve as spaces for potential dialogues and conflicts between the literary space and political, financial, and religious power (under what conditions does one attain the status of patron? does a writer or a cardinal have a better chance of entering one of the academies? and so on). The existence of these institutions as well as their existence within a network, their vitality or their absence, are good indicators of the degree of autonomy of the literary field. Such institutions also play an essential role in the processes of consecration (election to the French Academy, acceptance by an influential group, like Maupassant at the soirées in Médan hosted by Zola) carried out and reinforced by general social institutions (through education). And their respective influences, as well as the tendencies that each promotes or defends, reveal the lines of force of the field's structure in the course of its history.

Finally, institutions and readers alike perceive works in terms of their distance from the political, theoretical, and aesthetic positions represented by the various institutions according to their state and function at different times in history. Censorship offers a good example: either authors respect the norms of censorship and its laws, side with conformity, and, if need be, censor themselves, or else they defy the authorities and are labeled nonconformists, which might attract attention to their work but might just as easily exact a high price (sanctions, even the death sentence, a reputation for extremism, and so on).

This is the first set of prisms: the institutions of literary life that act as mediators between literature and other social activities and function within the literary field and for the discourse about literary works. Their obvious social character (group structures, collective practices, laws) has made them a favorite target of the sociological approach to literature, and some critics believe that they have found the last word in the "institutional analysis" of the literary world. This is going too fast and falling a bit short of the mark. These institutions are indeed a prismatic group but they are not alone.

---

10. See Viala, *Les Institutions de la vie littéraire en France au XVIIe siècle* (Lille, 1985). The basic sociological indicators (age, sex, education, profession, residence, religion, social origin) are the usual tools; although an inventory is not required here, their value should not be understated.

2. Sociopoetics. "Literarity" alone defines literature—such was the position of formalist criticism not so long ago. A sociology that does not account for questions of form (genres, style) would be justifiably accused of bypassing an essential element of literature. Simply naming the genres, tones, and forms of "literary" institutions distinguishes them from the institutions of literary life discussed above and emphasizes that the aesthetic genres and codes belong to history and the realm of social fact. Poetics, a discipline essential for examining the definitions and classifications of these codes, could never keep up with their fluctuations if they were viewed as absolutes. But when well done, poetics can demonstrate how the same formal properties produce divergent effects "according to pragmatic contexts and situations," as Gérard Genette puts it.[11]

It is true that the terminology and the conceptual tools used by poetics are extremely complex and not firmly fixed. But it is also true that genres constitute social codes, that styles in the classical sense of the term (levels of expression measured according to the cultural norm of the day) correlate with linguistic norms and thus to a social fact. It is also true that types of style are not equally distributed among periods or social strata.[12] Each of these headings must be envisioned not solely from a formal viewpoint (which would be as absurd as divorcing the background from the form) but also from the perspective of the interactions between the framework established by formal conventions and the contents and themes it accepts or questions according to the period or current. The same (but here more latitude is possible) is the case for what can be called *writings* (following Roland Barthes) until a better definition of the notion is possible. And it is obvious that stylistic choices are not only personal choices, like "signatures" that authors use to stamp their works with individuality, but are also positions taken vis-à-vis society. Burlesque, for example, shows how a stylistic practice indicates both a cultural referent and a code shared by a writer and a reader who both know perfectly well what such language means.[13]

The pact implied in the act of reading, the key to the formal readability of the literary work, is also a pact of sociability. And doubtless one day we will be better able to analyze how in this mediating relationship (since it occurs by means of a formal convention) writing means anticipating or calculating the effects of reading. The study of literary audiences, as yet a new discipline, offers particularly rich possibilities to the sociology

11. Gérard Genette, *Palimpsestes: La Littérature au second degré* (Paris, 1982), p. 95. Note that Genette includes the category of the "literary field" (p. 4).

12. On the difference between these notions, see Viala and M. P. Schmitt, *Savoir-lire* (Paris, 1982), pp. 210–12.

13. See Genette, *Palimpsestes,* pp. 64–79.

of literature. The orientation suggested by Jauss concerning the notion of the horizon of expectations, although only a limited outline, has already proved its interest. The social valuation of forms and aesthetics, seen as both codes and discriminants, justifies this enterprise of analyzing formal prisms which I propose to call sociopoetics.[14]

3. Theme, Fashion, and Tradition. Here we find the richest harvest of all, for if there is any one thing definitely expected of a sociology of literature, it is an account of the "contents" of a work—the "subject," the "ideas," or the "author in his time"—or in simple and precise terms, what a text speaks of—its referents—and what it says about them—its discourse. This is where we find ourselves in the midst of interpretive debates that have been raised by approaches based on causal explanation.

It falls to philology to establish a correct and reliable version of a text. It is the task of semantics to denote its literal meaning and that of poetics and semiology to construct meaningful isotopies. A specifically sociological analysis does not come afterward but at the same time, in other words, at the very moment that questions of meanings, of the connotations actualized by the work's actual and potential readers, enter into play. Connotation does not exist outside of intertextuality. But we are not dealing with intertextuality for its own sake, a practice which will confine us to hunting down sources. A properly sociological approach requires detecting which aspects of the work's potential meaning have been activated at various moments in its history by its readability and its readers. Intertextuality thus functions as an indicator of positions taken over time and across audiences.

The analysis of the thematic network in a given text calls for the analysis of thematic networks found in other texts as well as in the social discourses related to the primary text. Therefore a dual evaluation becomes possible: first, evaluation of the objective social position of the intertextual themes of which the work "speaks" (and which can be defined by the position of referents in social hierarchies whenever there are at issue referents directly pertaining to the description of social structure: persons, types, groups, classes); and second, evaluation of the relative position occupied by the text considered within these intertextual themes.

The categories of *fashion* and *tradition* work as operative concepts. To place oneself within or outside of fashion or tradition is to take a position. And positions stated in the text, whether explicit (the author's political, philosophical, or theoretical statements in the work) or implicit

14. This is the term that seemed to me (certainly without claiming to have coined it) the most satisfactory one I could propose for this discipline. See Viala, *Les Institutions de la vie littéraire en France au XVIIe siècle*, p. 67.

(the selection of certain motifs, the way of qualifying them), are meaningful in proportion to their conformity to the effects of fashion and tradition and the conflicts they represent. In particular, one cannot speak of a worldview without having carefully analyzed these seemingly trivial but crucial problems: the role of the effects of fashion, legacies, and customs of the literary world, all the meaningful expression of a body of traditions. Of course the audience (assumed if not reached by every work) must be made a key indicator: what is fashionable for some is for others already passé, or even part of tradition, or, conversely, still unknown. The analysis must not be reduced to the "subject" but must focus on aesthetic codes (forms and thematics). Furthermore, it is crucial, when dealing with fashion and tradition, to know where and how they arose, what institutions have maintained them and how. Specifically, the unequal distribution of cultural capital, which creates unequal access to innovation, is a powerful determinant. Likewise, authors' access to this capital (from reading, educational baggage, personal experience, systematic research, whatever) characterizes the types of relationships they have with the effects of fashion and tradition. The choice of subjects and ways of treating them appears not as the result of chance or the pure freedom of the writer but represents a relative freedom with a margin to maneuver equal to whatever is permitted by the prism of the field of possible positions.

4. Trajectories. Literary studies tend to focus either on works, even fragments, viewed in isolation or on texts of a global nature. They are also likely to accord an essential place to the biography of the author. This is necessary. Writers are the principal actors in the literary field. But there is a great risk of falling into an interpretation based on projection of the sort that ascribes *L'Ecole des femmes* to Molière's unhappy marriage. The danger vanishes as soon as anecdotes are dropped and biography is conceived as a *trajectory,* that is, when biography accounts for the series of objective positions that the author occupied in the literary field and their relations with his social positions and, if need be, the modifications of those positions. This is one of the cases in which literature acts on the system of social positions (just as literary positions can act on the system of positions taken in society as a whole). Thus, in seventeenth-century France, the rapid success visible in some writers' trajectories means that literature acted as a catalyst to change the channels of social promotion.

The moment a writer is recognized as such in society by publications, the capital so constituted weighs on each subsequent creation; to redo or continue what has already been done or else to break this trend amounts to being judged on the basis of and through the image of the writer and other preexisting images. Thus, even when unconscious, the choices of forms, referents, manners, and possible explicit statements acquire meaning only in relationship to the range of images that can be examined, just as each text can be understood in relation to this series of representations.

5. *The Psychology of the Author and* 6. *Language.* These are two other obvious mediations—important ones at that. If the first seems to belong solely to the domain of psychology (or psychoanalysis) and the other to linguistics, being and language and their possible unity nonetheless remain the material of social analysis. Language is the most social fact there is. "Legitimate" literature provides models of acceptable, "legitimate" language via dictionaries and formal education, in this way influencing the totality of social practices. Conversely, the code constituted in this manner serves as an evaluative norm in literary productions (a typical case where the field is its own mediation). And the writer's imagination, kneaded by the work of language, bounded by the limits of his linguistic competence, is made manifest in a text by linguistic performances. The image the writer builds of himself in the midst of the literary field and society is displayed in his work and his trajectory. The psychic givens mobilized in literary creation are largely internalized social representations, the shaping of personal predispositions into specific habits of representation, work, and reading, in which formal education, long dominated by the humanities (in France at least), plays a major part. The analysis of these predispositions in terms of habits, and the analysis of linguistic discriminants (including individual "style") in terms of performance with respect to a norm, should make the social stakes of the effects of these two prisms apparent.

The end of this inventory brings to mind three remarks. The first is a logical theoretical complement to the foregoing but one that we do well to emphasize. Prismatic effects can only be envisioned as an arrangement of prisms. No single prism can provide the foundation for a correct statement about the social significance of a work. The play of their interactions creates the play of meaning. The analysis of these arrangements makes it possible to sort out the mediations belonging to literature from all the other mediations. But this does not mean that anything can be arranged in any manner. Couching the analysis in terms of a relatively autonomous field and of *strategies* supplies the material needed for the construction of the objects to be studied.

The second remark may serve as a stylistic justification. Is it necessary to use the metaphor "prismatic effects"? The image of the prism suggests an object with several sides, one which selects and changes the rays that pass through it but whose principle, luminosity, is itself modified by the impact of these rays. Just as the network of mediations is not stable and does not suggest the same arrangement of prisms for every time and every text, so too not every mediation, not every prism, is indefinitely identical to itself. Even scientific practices do well to look to the imagination. The imagination that finds expression in literary studies in France is accustomed to visual metaphors. To change the network of mediations from within, one may as well utilize this metaphorical network instead of one taken from acoustics or magnetism (therefore the use, itself metaphorical, of the term "field").

These comments lead us to the third and final remark. The sociology of literature does not create objects different from those studied by criticism or philology, but it changes the way we look at those objects, the angle of attack, the means used, and the stakes. The goal of the inventory proposed here was to provide both a practical recapitulation and a verification of validity. But a sociology with this orientation, which takes literary pragmatics fully into account, also disrupts certain habits. What is postulated as an absolute value (the originality or the style or the rank of the author) in the normal view of a normative criticism is presented here as a relative value. What elsewhere is a desperate search or the positivist illusion of a definite, definitive, eternal, and definable "meaning" of a work (hence an explainable meaning, which justifies interpretive criticism) here is the relativity of meaning, open but contingent—all within the intrinsic limits of the scientific approach. It is not a matter of replacing the dialogue among readers (including critics) but of accounting for it. The price (to be paid, but to be gained as well) is that instead of assigning and stamping each work with an explanation-response, the work appears as a question posed to history and the social sciences. It is an open question made even more so because in this singular realm the way things are said matters as much as what is said. Sociologically, literature is not society's last word but a praxis whose distinctive property is indeed that there is no last word.

Publishing History: A Hole at the Centre of Literary Sociology

John Sutherland

For most literary sociologists serious modern work starts with Robert Escarpit's *Sociologie de la Littérature* (1958), a book which proposes that sociology (or a sociological perspective) can usefully explain how literature operates as a social institution. Subsequent Escarpit-inspired work on the literary enterprise covers topics such as the profession of authorship; the stratified "circuits" (Escarpit's hallmark concept) of production, distribution, and consumption; and the commodity aspect of literature. Critics have objected that Escarpit's increasingly macroquantitative and statistics-bound procedures bleach out literary and ideological texture. And his model of literature as discrete social system encourages the abstract model making which Raymond Williams despises.[1] But, whatever its shortcomings, Escarpit's definition of literary product and practice as social *faits* (not facts, but things made) forms an essential starting point for the sociologist intending to investigate the apparatuses of literature.

In what follows, I shall mainly fix on a problem currently disabling constructive research on the literary-sociological lines projected by Escarpit: namely, scholarly ignorance about book trade and publishing history technicalities. This sets up, I shall suggest, a large and troubling hole at the centre of the subject, and there is little indication, at this stage, how or when the hole is to be filled.

1. See Raymond Williams, "Literature and Sociology," *Problems in Materialism and Culture: Selected Essays* (London, 1980), pp. 11–30.

There is, one must add, no superficial complacency about this state of affairs. Any number of scholars piously urge (usually in passing) the need for more information about the machineries and the material processes by which books ("literature") are produced, reproduced, distributed, marketed, merchandised, and consumed. But vagueness on these matters, if not total, remains surprisingly extensive. For instance, Robert Darnton's *The Literary Underground of the Old Regime* is probably the most lavishly praised work of literary sociology (broadly defined) of the last few years. Yet Darnton concludes what is essentially an investigation of the eighteenth-century French book trade with the admission that "we need to know more about the world behind the books" and presents "a new set of questions" (as yet unanswered), relevant not just for the eighteenth century, but "almost any period of history":

> How did writers pursue careers in the Republic of Letters? Did their economic and social condition have much effect on their writing? How did publishers and booksellers operate? Did their ways of doing business influence the literary fare that reached their customers? What was that literature? Who were its readers? And how did they read?[2]

This questionnaire tacitly admits to vast areas of academic incompetence. And it is a tribute to Darnton's ingenuity that he can write authoritatively about the literary underground ("Grub Street hacks, pirate publishers, and under-the-cloak peddlers of forbidden books") in confessed ignorance of how publishers, authors, and booksellers of the period actually did their business. It is not a situation flattering to scholarship. But at least Darnton is candid about what he does not know. Many of the new-Marxist critics finesse the problem by invoking sub-Brechtian concepts of "production" in which (magically) the text is conceived to make itself.[3] Or, alternatively, the "local mode of production" (as Terry Eagleton has

2. Robert Darnton, *The Literary Underground of the Old Regime* (Cambridge, Mass., 1982), pp. viii–ix; further references to this work, abbreviated *LU*, will be included in the text.

3. A good example can be found in chap. 6 ("Towards a Productive Literary Practice") of Catherine Belsey's *Critical Practice*, New Accents (London, 1980), where the "production" of automobiles in factories is assimilated to Machereyan notions of the production of literary meaning in texts.

John Sutherland is professor of literature at the California Institute of Technology. His books include *Fiction and the Fiction Industry* (1978), *Bestsellers* (1980), and *Offensive Literature* (1982). He is currently completing an encyclopedia of Victorian fiction.

called it) is parenthesized as something sufficiently dealt with at the level of summary description not to impede engagement with more urgent issues.

The sociologist of literature probably expects eventual answers to Darnton's set of questions from the newly defined subject area known provisionally as publishing history (in Britain) or history of the book (in America), and sometimes as nouvelle bibliographie matérielle (in France). The emergence and expansion of this specialism over the last twenty years has been phenomenal. Its physical manifestations have been in new journals, numerous conferences, the establishment of "centres of the book," and a massive stockpiling of publishers' and book-trade archives in academic repositories.

But as Darnton has elsewhere observed, publishing history, though it flourishes with extraordinary juvenile vigour, lacks binding theoretical coherence. Territorially, its status is Balkan, opportunistically annexed when convenient by history, bibliography, economics, sociology, literary criticism, library science. Publishing history operates in what Darnton aptly calls a "riot" of "interdisciplinarity."[4] And before its insights can be methodically used, its material must be "disciplined." As things now look, the necessary ordering of publishing history is expected by collaboration with two firmly entrenched and separate academic departments. One is history, especially as redirected by the French "l'histoire des mentalités" school. The other is Anglo-American bibliography—not, one should add, in its traditional "analytic" form, but as regenerated by the current crisis taking place within its ranks.

It is pleasant enough to move subject pieces around the academic board in attractively new formations. But for the engaged scholar, the issues present themselves as knotty problems of how best to advance his or her research. It gives a useful close-up on what these problems are to survey the work in progress of currently active scholars. I have chosen a representative trio—Darnton, Jerome McGann, and D. F. McKenzie—whose recent publications stake out the more significant new lines of history, publishing history, literary criticism, and literary sociology. If this were a different form of discourse (say refereeing, prize nomination, book reviewing) one might tout these three as "the outstanding scholars of their generation." In fact they would, in my opinion, merit the description more than most. But the intention here is to consider their work (more particularly their field of work) diagnostically. Darnton, McGann, and McKenzie each mounts a critique of current disciplinary orthodoxies and proposes a future "great work" of comprehensive publishing history. In so doing, they indicate very precisely what can be done and what, given the present organization of literary and historical studies, probably cannot be done. Put another way, the "great work" which they project raises

4. Darnton, "What Is the History of Books?" *Daedalus* 3 (Summer 1982): 67.

structural and theoretical issues which call into question the competence of their disciplines to handle the task of publishing history.

Robert Darnton

Primarily a historian of the French eighteenth century, Robert Darnton has made brilliant use of publishing history materials in two applauded books, *The Business of Enlightenment: A Publishing History of the Encyclopédie 1775–1800* and *The Literary Underground of the Old Regime.*

Two intimately connected ideas inform Darnton's research: that of underground (in the guerrilla, or resistance sense) and that of underworld (in the sense of Grub Street). So infused is his thinking with these ideas, that he even sees publishing historians (to most observers a rather dusty crew) as a dynamic maquis within the academic establishment.[5]

In the largest sense, Darnton opposes what he calls "the summit view of history." His intention is "to strike out in a new direction, to try to get to the bottom of the Enlightenment, and even to penetrate into its underworld, where the Enlightenment may be examined as the Revolution has been studied recently—from below" (*LU*, p. 1). This tiering of over- and underworld (with their respective culture and counterculture) is accompanied by another dominant symmetry in Darnton's analysis: namely, his sense that the world of the book divides evenly between the "legal" (which does not excite him) and the "clandestine" (which fascinates him). Darnton is particularly drawn to "forbidden literature," with its symptomatic contests between state authority and political dissidence.

One of the features which makes Darnton's work so readable is its infectious sense of excitement and his habitual glamourizing of academic drudgery as adventure, struggle, discovery. The description of his initiation into the Aladdin's cave of publishing history is typically dramatic:

> I was able to uncover [the literary underground] because seventeen years ago I walked into a historian's dream: an enormous cache of untouched archives, the papers of the Société typographique de Neuchâtel in the municipal library of Neuchâtel, Switzerland. The Société typographique was one of the largest of the many publishing houses that grew up around France's borders in order to supply the demand for pirated and prohibited books within the kingdom. Its papers contain the richest vein of information about an eighteenth-century publisher anywhere in existence. [*LU*, p. vi]

Darnton's main asset as a historian is his extraordinarily vivifying imagination (an imagination, incidentally, which often recalls Carlyle

---

5. See ibid., p. 65. This essay also gives a brief but fairly comprehensive account of the growth of the new subject with a superb bibliography.

rather than the Annales school to whom he formally genuflects as his main intellectual influence). It seems an effortless reflex with him to breathe life into documents: "It is an extraordinary sensation to open a dossier of fifty or a hundred letters that have lain unread since the eighteenth century. Will they come from a Parisian garret, where a young author is scribbling away, his vision suspended between Parnassus and the threats rising from the landlady on the ground floor?" (*LU*, p. vii). And so on. While surrendering to the pleasure of Darnton's animations, a certain uneasiness forms as to his method. His modus operandi is self-confessedly opportunistic. Hence his disarming confession in the preface to *Literary Underground* that "having explored as much of the literary underground as possible, I realized that it could be pictured more effectively by a set of sketches than by a grand tableau. Sketching in history provides a way of catching men in motion, of holding subjects up to unfamiliar light and examining their complexities from different angles" (*LU*, pp. vi–vii). Raiding the Neuchâtel archive for sketchbook material, Darnton consciously postpones "systematic study for a later work" (*LU*, p. viii).

The decision to publish before undertaking "systematic study" of his materials allows full play for Darnton's novelistic imagination. But it leads to an excessive reliance on what he calls the "cas typique." His studies invariably begin with a a highly schematic historical mise-en-scène, followed by a single example which is made to bear an inordinate load of general significance. Thus a chapter such as the fourth in *The Literary Underground* opens by briefly indicting the utter failure of previous scholarship to penetrate the activities of clandestine booksellers and confidently promises that "by exploring the world of one of them, we can see how the underground operated and what material it conveyed to ordinary readers in an ordinary town" (*LU*, p. 122). Perhaps. But what intellectual controls are there in this procedure? How do we know that Darnton's single "cas" is "typique" or whether it is as eccentric as single cases are prone to be? There is often a surprising disparity between the titles of Darnton's works and their actual content. Thus *The Business of the Enlightenment: A History of the Encyclopédie, 1775–1800* turns out to be a history of one reprint edition of Diderot's work. "Readers Respond to Rousseau: The Fabrication of Romantic Sensitivity" turns out to be (essentially) one reader's response.[6] This stopping down of focus to the individual instance is not the outcome of idleness. It witnesses to Darnton's dedicated quest for living textures. Book history, for him, is best conducted by studying in extenso the "life cycle" of a single book or the exemplary careers of single-book people.

6. See Darnton, *The Great Cat Massacre and Other Episodes in French Cultural History* (New York, 1984), pp. 215–50.

In its total effect, Darnton's historiography introduces its readers to a vivid dramatis personae. It includes Joseph Duplain ("one of the scrappiest book dealers in one of the toughest towns of the book trade"); Charles-Joseph Panckoucke ("the aggressive publisher from Lille," who came to dominate the Parisian trade); Jean Ranson (the merchant from La Rochelle who read Rousseau); Jacques-Pierre Brissot (the "spy in Grub Street"); Le Senne ("pamphleteer on the run"); Mauvelain (the "clandestine bookseller in the provinces"). We come to know this troupe intimately; as well almost as we might know characters in Balzac. But, unlike the population of Balzac's fiction, their number remains few, nor do they by any stretch make up a statistically adequate sample from which to examine the "base" of the book world. Everything is made to hang on their being preternaturally "representative."

In itself and as far as it goes, Darnton's work is dazzling. But as a guide to the direction that publishing history should take it has clear risks. He has, for instance, a pronounced distaste for the quantitative dimension of book history and its habit of "freezing human beings out of history." In fact, he is downright sceptical about its effectiveness. "The historical sociology of literature," he contends, "has failed to develop a coherent discipline of its own, and . . . its commitment to quantification has not yet produced answers to the basic questions about reading and writing in the past" (*LU*, p. 182). The "yet" is mere politeness; Darnton clearly doubts that quantification ever will produce the desired answers. But given the massified nature of the modern book world, organization by category, statistics, and large unit is inevitable. What form, one wonders, will Darnton's eventual "systematic study" of the Neuchâtel archive take? Surely not a fifty-thousandfold multiplication of individual case histories? Most future publishing history will be drudging, unexciting labour. The main task will be classification and the patient (and in itself very boring) uncovering of business routines. And this will take place in the relatively unexciting domain of the "legal" book trade, usually at periods of undramatic historical event.

In fact, one suspects that the systematic labour at Neuchâtel will not be done, at least not by Darnton. He has, as the French say, more interesting cats to whip. His latest book indicates that his current affiliation is now firmly to interpretive anthropology as defined by Clifford Geertz. And situated as he is on the terrain of the "blurred genre" between history and social science, Darnton's natural scholarly activity is the brilliant essay rather than the accumulating of neutral (and in itself unpublishable) data for others to use. In retrospect, his advocacy of the cause of publishing history will be seen as a justified career manoeuvre by which he has arrived at where he really wanted to be. Its "riot of interdisciplinarity" was, transitionally, a useful liberation. Nevertheless, Darnton's contribution to the future of publishing history has been profound; if only in the PR sense of glamourizing what was previously unglamourous. And if he has failed to discipline the subject, he has gone a long way towards deprovincializing it for those who remain more centrally within its affairs.

Jerome McGann

Jerome McGann's scholarly energies over the last decade have been mainly directed towards editing the complete works of Byron. It is an undertaking most would conceive a life's work. McGann has all but completed it in less time than others spend on Ph.D. dissertations. In addition to this formidable editorial task, McGann's immersion in Byron has inspired two connected theoretical preoccupations which he has found time to elaborate at monograph length. The first (which does not concern me here) is with Romantic "ideology." The other is with the nature of the literary "text."

From a position strategically on the edge of the American bibliography establishment, McGann strikes a radically nonconformist stance on the issue of modern textual criticism. Very simply, he maintains that the discipline has taken a wrong turning over the last twenty-five years. In this period, under the generalship of Fredson Bowers and the less doctrinaire adjutancy of G. Thomas Tanselle (McGann's main theoretic opponents), American bibliography's self-imposed mission has been to establish "authoritative" editions of American (and other) classic works. Thousands of man-hours have been spent and millions of dollars invested in this project. And largely wasted, McGann implies.

His critique[7] of the dominant orthodoxy of American bibliography can be summed up in a number of interlocking theses. The first is that current editorial practice pursues a chimera, in its attempt to reproduce the pure text "intended" by the author. Notoriously, the fetishization of final authorial intention has led to a doctrinal preference for the manuscript as copytext. This stage alone finds the author quarantined from subsequent contaminating processes of material production and transmission. (Publishers and printers are suspiciously regarded as inveterate corruptors.) Ideally, the Bowersonian editor should be a clairvoyant, since only by penetrating to the pre-scriptive level of thought process can "intention" be satisfactorily located. But if the laws of physics prevent him being a mind reader, the editor, *faute de mieux*, must be a manuscript reader.

McGann's opposition to this is radical. In his view, the text is not the product of lonely authorial intention (thought). It is a "social product." The publisher (particularly), the merchandiser, and the reader, as much as the author, can beget the literary work. And they achieve this not by

---

7. McGann's arguments are most concisely expressed in *A Critique of Modern Textual Criticism* (Chicago, 1983).

thought but, precisely, by work or "collaboration" (a keyword in McGann's *Critique of Modern Textual Criticism*). For McGann, the literary text is correctly located not in some primal idea of itself but in its collaborative production and its material existence(s).

Three ideological systems are tacitly invoked by McGann in making this large and controversial assertion. The first, clearly enough signaled by his repeated stress on "materialism," is Marxist. Although he has not (as far as I know) made a declaration on the subject, it is clear that McGann aligns himself with the pro-Marxist critical interventions of the 1970s.[8] And his central contention is an unattributed gloss of Pierre Macherey's edict: "the work is not *created* by an intention (objective or subjective); it is *produced* under determinate conditions."[9]

The second ideological system is religious. For McGann, Bowersonian quests for the pure "soul" of the text are quixotic. The literary work is unredeemably fallen, mired in the materialities of production and consumption. It is, to use his specifically theological imagery, flesh, not spirit: "Human beings are not angels. Part of what it means to be human is to have a body, to occupy physical space and to move in real time. In the same way, the products of literature, which are in all cases human products, are not disembodied processes."[10]

The third ideological system McGann invokes is the legal. He implicitly contradicts the notion (on which the law of copyright is based) that there is a single immaterial form of the work, which inalienably belongs as property to the author, or "creator." For McGann, the work can belong impartially to a series of collaborators and participants who are thus released from merely passive roles as transmitters and consumers.

McGann's critique goes beyond theoretical disagreement on what constitutes textual objects to a specific *j'accuse* directed at his profession: "It is [my] assumption . . . that literary study surrendered some of its most powerful interpretive tools when it allowed textual criticism and bibliography to be regarded as 'preliminary' rather than integral to the study of literary work."[11] McGann alludes here to the pontifical utterances of Bowers, notably "Some Principles for Scholarly Editions of Nineteenth-Century Authors." Bowers there proclaims it the duty of bibliography to establish a set of monolithic authoritative texts "that will stand the test

---

8. Notably influential seems to have been Terry Eagleton's *Criticism and Ideology: A Study in Marxist Literary Theory* (London, 1976).

9. Pierre Macherey, *A Theory of Literary Production*, trans. Geoffrey Wall (London, 1978), p. 78.

10. McGann, "Shall These Bones Live?" *Text* 1 (1981): 25–26; further references to this work, abbreviated "SBL," will be included in the text.

11. See McGann, "The Monks and the Giants: Textual and Bibliographical Studies and the Interpretation of Literary Works," in *Textual Criticism and Literary Interpretation*, ed. McGann (Chicago, 1985), p. 182.

of time and, heaven willing, need never be edited again from the ground up."[12] This task achieved, the literary work is ready, like a prepped patient, for the separate operations of the literary critic.

McGann's contention is that the bibliographer should not subordinate himself as merely an editor, a server up to the critic. He should impertinently meddle with the act of criticism. More particularly, the bibliographer should play the role of "memory," recalling the material facts of the work's existences or "histories" in the moment of critical engagement. "Textual scholars," McGann asserts, "must labor to elucidate the histories of a work's production, reproduction, and reception, and all aspects of these labors bear intimately and directly on 'the critical interpretation of a work.'"[13] Conventionally, as McGann puts it, criticism proceeds in a state of "anamnesis," professorial absentmindedness, in which the material circumstances are quite deliberately forgotten. And this is abetted by a textual theory which programmatically "desocializ[es] our historical view of the literary work."[14]

McGann provides a sample illustration of his ideally concatenated textual and critical operation in an extended discussion of "The Charge of the Light Brigade."[15] But more interesting to me (as a Trollopian) is an example he throws off in passing: "The aesthetic field of literary productions is neither an unheard melody nor a linguistic event, as one can (literally) *see* by merely glancing at Trollope's *The Way We Live Now* either in its first printing, or in some subsequent edition, like Robert Tracy's recent critical text" ("SBL," p. 26). A footnote adds, "That is to say, the printed numbers of Trollope's novel—their size, their format, their schedule of appearance—are all relevant matters, as are the physical characteristics of any edition" ("SBL," p. 39).

Although he does not himself pursue the idea, a brief summary of *The Way We Live Now*'s "histories" indicates the strenuous exercise in material recollection that McGann proposes. (It requires, one must chide, rather more than "merely glancing.") Trollope's novel was published in twenty monthly parts by Chapman and Hall, 1874–75. The issue was eccentric, given the fact that novels in numbers were a thing of the long past. Trollope was on the board of his publisher, and his reason for choosing the anachronistic form is mysterious. The work (execrably illustrated) was poorly reviewed and (probably) sold poorly. Before the

12. See Fredson Bowers, "Some Principles for Scholarly Editions of Nineteenth-Century Authors," *Studies in Bibliography* 17 (1964): 223–28.
13. McGann, "The Monks and the Giants," p. 189. It is not clear whether McGann means reception during the author's lifetime, or in subsequent historical time. I assume the latter.
14. McGann, *Critique of Modern Textual Criticism*, p. 121.
15. See McGann, "Tennyson and the Histories of Criticism," *Review* 4 (1982): 219–53.

end of its serial run, Frederick Chapman sold the copyright (at a tenth of what he had paid for it) to Chatto and Windus. This second publisher brought out a 6s one-volume edition in November 1875 (with twelve of the original twenty illustrations cut down to smaller page size). This reprint was designed primarily to appeal to the circulating libraries as part of Chatto's campaign against the three-decker. The 6s edition was not successful (selling only 3,700 copies in seven years) and was remaindered at 3s 6d in 1882. The work continued to be reprinted by Chatto in 3s 6d and 2s reprint forms: ugly, cramped books, aimed at the downmarket railway reader. Chatto kept the work in print until 1928, the stereotype plates having been destroyed in 1907. The novel never did well for Chatto, and it passed through a notable deep trough during 1914–18, when some seven hundred copies were pulped for the war effort. Altogether, some fifteen thousand copies were sold by Chatto and Windus in fifty-three years. Things looked up (critically, at least) for *The Way We Live Now* in 1927, with the publication of Michael Sadleir's *Trollope: A Commentary.* As part of a wholesale critical reassessment, Sadleir proclaimed the work Trollope's masterpiece. This led directly to publication in Oxford University Press' World's Classics as one of their oversize "double" volumes, in 1941. Publication in this prestigious series, devised by E. V. Rieu at the turn of the century, marked a rite of honorific canonization. *The Way We Live Now*'s critical reputation gathered in subsequent years, culminating in Tracy's annotated critical edition (1974) which McGann mentions. But *The Way We Live Now* stubbornly declined to be generally popular. As late as 1969, Penguin turned it down for their English Library, on the grounds that it was too long and unlikely to sell profitably. This changed in 1970, with a BBC TV miniseries of the novel (dramatized by Simon Raven). Since this mass-media treatment, the novel has seen publication in a number of paperback forms—notably in the revamped World's Classics (very different from Rieu's original series), where it now sells year in, year out an unprecedented two thousand copies annually. Critical esteem and reader popularity have at last converged, some hundred years after the novel's first publication.

This is only the most skeletal outline of the histories of the novel's productions and reputations. But it will give some idea of the Funes-like burden of memory which McGann would impose on the critic. All these facts and more must, he insists, be "borne in mind," not merely appended, footnoted, or, perish the thought, ignored in the misbegotten quest for what Trollope originally intended. McGann has been profoundly influenced in his thinking and practice by the computer and he seems to demand of his ideal critic a huge random access memory which can effortlessly load and hold all the data of "production, reproduction and reception." More worryingly, McGann prescribes this taxing intellectual effort while at the same time vigorously wanting to dismantle the disciplines that normally organize, dignify, and materially reward such labour.

McGann stands at an interesting point of his intellectual career. As a textual critic, he has had what effectively amounts to a service of excommunication performed on him by Tanselle and Bowers.[16] Increasingly, any reforms he brings about will have to be battled for. They will not be easily legitimized by an institutional establishment which at present displays the same enthusiasm for his "socialized concept of authorship and textual authority" as does the AMA for socialized medicine. This casts McGann in the adversarial role where he probably feels most comfortable. But it may limit his future interventions to those of the provocateur.

One cannot, I think, look to McGann personally (or as a research director) to supply the factual data which his program of resocializing the text demands. The value of his intervention lies principally in his exposure of the nature of American institutional power to mobilize and regiment scholarly orthodoxies even where those orthodoxies rest on contentious foundations. Intellectually, like Darnton's, McGann's affiliation to publishing history seems to have been tactical: that is to say, it represented a transitional stage in his career. But as with Darnton's, McGann's contribution has been valuable to the cause of publishing history. Particularly valuable is his eloquent insistence that the material facts of literature's making are neither contextual nor subtextual but, in a primary and inherent sense, textual.

D. F. McKenzie

Donald McKenzie, having spent most of his academic life working at Wellington in New Zealand, was in 1986 appointed to the Readership in Textual Bibliography at Oxford. (Despite its modest-sounding rank, this is a post of seniority and prestige.) McKenzie's qualifications for this post are by any standards solid. His first major undertaking in bibliography was the taxonomic listing of Stationers' Company Apprentices, published serially from 1960 to 1978 (mainly under the auspices of the Oxford Bibliographical Society). For those, certainly few, students of literature who have any call to consult it, McKenzie's compilation must seem a labour of quite staggering diligence and Sisyphean inconsequence. Effectively, it is a census of all the registered guild personnel employed in the seventeenth- and eighteenth-century printing industry. The number of entries runs into the thousands, listing name, county of origin, social status (by profession of father), and other recordable items (such as money advanced to and from the company). The effort of accurate tran-

16. Tanselle in his article "Historicism and Critical Editing," in *Studies in Bibliography* 39 (1986): 20–27, and Bowers in his presidential address to the Society for Textual Scholarship in New York, April 1984.

scription involved must have been heroic. But exactly what the utility of the exercise was I, for one, have never understood.

In 1966 McKenzie produced the second major work of his career with the completion of the massively documented study, *The Cambridge University Press, 1696–1712*. As a history of the oldest press in the English-speaking world, McKenzie's account is strange. Cambridge University Press began 250 years earlier and is today the largest publishing house (in terms of titles) in Britain. McKenzie's selection of fourteen years from the press's five hundred is justified on two grounds: first, that this is the crucial juncture when the character of the press was formed (which is questionable), and, second, that it is only for this period that the "records" remain. It is, one may think, a relief that more records do not remain, since if they did, and if McKenzie transcribed them as assiduously as he does those for 1696–1712, his history of the press would run to 120 quarto volumes. As it is, this "study in depth" offers 170 pages of general history and 641 pages of transcribed minute books, stock books, and vouchers (business receipts).

Again, after admiring the sheer secretarial labour involved, one is driven to ask, what is the point? Rather halfheartedly, McKenzie suggests in his preface that his data (drawn from an elite university publishing house in the provinces) gives a valid picture of the whole publishing industry of the period which was, of course, nonacademic and London-based.

Whatever else, these early works of McKenzie's witnessed to his fanatic reverence for precise notation of the publishing historical fact. He evolved from this phase of his career (in which his highest ambition seemed to be to punish himself by compiling ever more complex lists) in the mid-1970s. In terms of classical developmental sociology, McKenzie graduated from Comtean positivism to a Weberian interest in ideologically formed institutions. His influential Sandars lectures at Oxford in 1976 were widely circulated in typescript (an unusual form of scholarly communication in the West) and took as their subject the London book trade in the later seventeeth century. In them, McKenzie proclaimed (in implicit self-criticism), "one needs an historical understanding of the trade and its practices before the facts of physical bibliography and textual criticism can be seen in perspective." And as part of this new responsibility McKenzie discarded the term "historical bibliography" in favour of "what we might agree to call the sociology of the text."[17]

Arising out of an increasingly theorized involvement with publishing history, McKenzie went on to proselytize for his "sociology of the text" (to the consternation of some of his fellow bibliographers). In a paper given at a German conference on book-trade history in 1977, he elaborated on the theorem with precise reference to the printing of Congreve's

17. D. F. McKenzie, unpublished manuscript, pp. 1, 16.

drama. As McKenzie argued, the different typography and page layout of the play's successive printings (in which Congreve actively participated up to 1710) are the outcome of subtle shifts of sensibility, part authorial, part social. The modulation from Restoration libertinism embodied in the early quartos to the decorum of the three-volume octavo *Works* cannot be recorded by a single, modern-format, eclectic, "critical" text, however scrupulously it is composed. Nor, if one follows McKenzie, would it be intellectually honest to attempt any such homogenization. The traditional procedures of bibliography inevitably sever (while they hope to transcend) the subtle links which bind a literary work to its time. As McKenzie was at pains to show, these typically inhere in "accidental" as much as in "substantive" variants. He goes on to quote approvingly from the Germanist J. P. Stern: "Every story, poem and play was written in time, belongs to time and *shows* its time." Bibliography has traditionally been unconcerned with the fine detail of that "showing" and McKenzie concludes, aggressively: "Current theories of textual criticism, indifferent as they are to the history of the book, its architecture, and the visual language of typography, are quite inadequate to deal with such problems. Only a new and comprehensive sociology of the text can embrace them."[18]

The force of McKenzie's critique, like McGann's, is that it specifically controverts the faith of modern bibliography in the reproducibility of the "essential" text, if only institutionally approved procedures are followed. There is, for McKenzie and McGann, no ahistorically essential text to reproduce. The task of McKenzie's "sociology," as he sees it, is in any case not reproduction but the reinsertion of the text into the critical moments of its historical and political existence. The work, this is to say, must be put back into time and contingency. And this calls less for "editing" than commentary, or a bibliographically informed criticism. It also broadens the textual critic's horizons beyond the merely literary object. McKenzie has recently demonstrated the appropriateness of the nonliterary text in an essay entitled "The Sociology of a Text: Orality, Literacy and Print in Early New Zealand." This article begins with the round assertion that "bibliography must expand."[19] He goes on to analyze the conception, mediation, and reception of the most important text in New Zealand history, the Treaty of Waitangi, 1840. This "agreement" effectively alienated the colonial territory from the Maoris, and McKenzie, with great precision (and no cultural condescension), elaborates the different understandings of a legal document in the colonial and native minds. And at the end of what is a powerful performance (originally a presidential address to the Bibliographical Society), McKenzie grandiosely steps forward as the in-

18. McKenzie, "Typography and Meaning: The Case of William Congreve," *Wolfenbütteler Schriften zur Geschichte des Buchwesens,* vol. 4 (Hamburg, 1981), p. 125.

19. McKenzie, "The Sociology of the Text: Orality, Literacy and Print in Early New Zealand," *The Library* 6 (Dec. 1984): 334.

carnation of bibliography become sociology: "I myself cannot help but see texts, their distinct versions, their different physical modes, and their comprehension in social contexts—in a word, the sociology of texts—as the substance of bibliography."[20]

As a bibliographer, McKenzie proposes new and transmuting liaisons with sociology. But significantly he has also retained his early reverence for the primacy of the narrowly defined publishing historical fact. And in his role of publishing historian, he has recently proposed a vast gathering of factual knowledge, in the form of a collaborative history of the English book, from A.D. 400 to the present day. Taking the long historical perspectives afforded by Oxford (where time has never been a problem), McKenzie tables a fifteen-year schedule for this team-written venture.

A main problem facing McKenzie's twin empirical/theoretical projects ("a sociology of the text"; "a history of the English book") would seem to be logistical. Can his theory of the "sociology of the text" be contained within the cramping structures of departmental bibliography as it is institutionally administered? Second, can the necessary team effort be mobilized, organized, and sustained for the proposed history (effectively an encyclopaedia) of the English book? Oxford history is littered with the wrecks of similar long-term collaborative efforts.

The isolated work of three scholars has obvious limitations for general diagnosis. But there are indicative points of convergence between McGann's "socialized concept of authorship," Darnton's "life cycle of a book," and McKenzie's "sociology of the text." Each stresses the sociomaterial instance rather than the essence of the literary work. Each takes an adversarial stance against traditional "discipline." And, more important, each sees his current scholarship as preliminary to a great concerted task—writing (or in McGann's case "remembering") the comprehensive history of the book and the processes of its production, reproduction, and consumption.

It is this large writing project which seems to me the more urgent and problematic. And the soundness of much future literary sociology will, I believe, depend on how the task is carried out. This is not to presume that once publishing history is comprehensively "written" the discourse of literary sociology will be that much easier to write. The opposite is more likely. If the evolution of sociology proper has proved anything it is the truth of Theodor Adorno's rule that "empiricism and theory cannot be accommodated in a single continuum."[21] In Adorno's view, the best that can be expected are "fruitful tensions" between the two domains. But as things now are, such tensions in literary sociology

20. Ibid., p. 365.
21. Theodor W. Adorno, "Sociology and Empirical Research," in *Critical Sociology: Selected Readings*, ed. Paul Connerton (Harmondsworth, 1976), p. 239.

are denied by the sheer unavailability of necessary empirical knowledge. Put another way, one of the things that makes literary sociology so easy to do at the moment is that we don't know enough to make it difficult.

At its crudest, writing publishing history will be a daunting physical undertaking. Literary criticism (at the moment, publishing history's main sponsor) has not, in the past, distinguished itself in the fulfilment of such large tasks. One reason, Eagleton has suggested, is that the character of the profession (trade? occupation?) is essentially "artisanal" and petit bourgeois in its mentality. That is, it breaks its scholarly work force down into single-unit operatives, engaged (often in conditions of jealously guarded privacy) on their "own" projects or "my research." Eagleton implicitly holds out the saving prospect of co-ideological unity on party lines which seems quixotic given the politically conservative (but generally unpoliticized) nature of the academic profession. Nevertheless, his analysis of the present state of affairs is shrewd if somewhat spiteful.

It is conceivable that publishing history might be approached in the same way that some other large projects recently have been: the Toronto Press Erasmus edition, for instance, or the Cambridge University Press collective edition of D. H. Lawrence's works and private papers. But there is a large difference. These other cooperative ventures effectively link a number of straightforward and in themselves manageably small tasks (typically single-volume commissions) into a composite whole. They are unambitious theoretically, drawing as they do on the established expertise of the English or history departments.

Publishing history, by contrast, would seem less in need of antlike collaboration than a new theoretical base from which to proceed. That base is alien to the inherited text-centric and canonically exclusive theories on which academic English, for instance, founds itself. And without theoretic formulation, the publishing history enterprise very quickly founders on intractable hard cases. Put in the form of a blunt example: it is difficult to see either history or English as disciplines happily sponsoring a comprehensive account of sheet-music publishing in the nineteenth century, of prime importance though the topic is in strict publishing history terms.

Publishing history will also need funding on a large scale. Again, put crudely, it is more expensive to maintain than, say, deconstruction (which is one reason why so much more disposable money can currently be used in the form of sky-high salaries to attract luminous "critics"; publishing history, by contrast, is likely to subsist in genteel poverty, its finances drained off into resource management and research backup). Traditionally, the sources of funding for publishing history have been self-interested. Narcissistic "house histories" by firms wanting to celebrate anniversaries in their existence have been the major form of publishing history in Britain and America. In the case of businesses such as Longman's which have operated for 250 years (and whose commissioned history is just now being undertaken by Asa Briggs), the house history can subsume a large slice of general book-trade activity. But such ventures are, ultimately, mercenary, uncritical, and self-serving. Less nakedly, but arguably more insidiously, this is also the case with the national publishing histories currently subsidized by the French and German governments through their state cultural agencies.

The way forward lies, initially at least, in the formation and support of semiautonomous "Centres of the Book," as they have been established at National Libraries in Washington and (with any luck) in the new British Library Euston site. Domiciled here, as a self-reflexive department within major book collections, publishing history will necessarily regard itself as primarily a resource: an accumulation of raw and neutrally databased material, accessible indifferently to all comers. This, of course, sidesteps theoretical problems by concentrating on logistical priorities. But logistics have always been an initial issue with publishing history: whether as a matter of preservation (incredibly, for instance, the British Museum simply threw away book jackets for most of the twentieth century); storage (publishers have traditionally found it difficult to persuade libraries to accept their archives, even as gifts); or accessioning (Darnton's systematic work on the Neuchâtel papers presumes discreet but extensive servicing of the material by its institutional custodians). For the moment, publishing history should probably decline to write itself, concentrating instead on the preliminary business of gathering itself.

A possible small-scale model for the future of the enterprise is the Gabler-Garland Joyce project. This began some twenty years ago with the acquisition and eventually the transcription and reproduction of primary materials. Only latterly, and as a conscious superstructure, did the heavily theorized (and highly controversial) composite text of *Ulysses* emerge. Success depends on a number of uncertain factors: money, manpower, institutional will. But it is as the outcome of a similar double-step process (the first of which has barely as yet been taken) that I expect an adequate publishing history eventually to be written.

Response to John Sutherland

G. Thomas Tanselle

John Sutherland's remarks on "publishing history" ("Publishing History: A Hole at the Centre of Literary Sociology," pp. 267–82) focus on the work of three scholars, and I ought therefore perhaps to begin with what he says about them, although it remains curiously disconnected from the central issues presented by his ostensible subject. The three scholars he has chosen—Robert Darnton, Jerome McGann, and D. F. McKenzie— are indeed prominent exemplars of a view of literary history that stresses the social nature of the production and dissemination of verbal works, and I have no wish to question his selection of them as a way of approaching his topic. But I do wonder how he can say that they deserve "more than most" to be called " 'the outstanding scholars of their generation' " (p. 269) when he proceeds to sum up their achievements as follows: (1) Darnton's "advocacy of the cause of publishing history will be seen as a justified career manoeuvre by which he has arrived at where he really wanted to be," and his "contribution to the future of publishing history has been profound" if only "in the PR sense of glamourizing what was previously unglamourous" (p. 272); (2) McGann's "affiliation to publishing history seems to have been tactical," and the value of his work "lies principally in his exposure of the nature of American institutional power to mobilize and regiment scholarly orthodoxies" (p. 277); (3) McKenzie's later work (the earlier having been "sheer secretarial labour" of "Sisyphean inconsequence" [pp. 278, 277]) shows him "grandiosely" stepping forward "as the incarnation of bibliography become sociology" and proposing projects the "main problem" of which "would seem to be logistical" (pp. 279, 280). Whether or not these assessments are just is irrelevant to the purpose at hand, which presumably is an evaluation of the essential soundness of the ideas set forth by these scholars, not the effect of their arguments on their careers or the practical difficulties their positions may entail.

Let me suggest a different way of commenting on these scholars. Whereas Sutherland finds Darnton's individual case studies "dazzling" but is troubled by the thought that they may not be representative (p. 272), I would take a nearly opposite view. Case studies, whether typical or not, are part of the total picture and must be taken into account in responsible generalizations; how those studies are pursued is the crucial matter, and Darnton's are weakened by a tendency to neglect the physical evidence present in books, a failure to recognize that the clues preserved within books constitute the primary evidence of their production history and that details found in external manuscript records can only be secondary evidence. He does not, in other words, show a grasp of what has come to be called analytical bibliography. As for McGann, Sutherland takes his concept of literary works as collaborative products to be "a radically nonconformist stance on the issue of modern textual criticism" (p. 273) and locates Marxist, religious, and legal implications in it. By contrast, I am not concerned with whether or not McGann's position can be considered "nonconformist" but with the quality of the argument supporting it; and on that score McGann cannot be praised, for in *A Critique of Modern Textual Criticism* he wavers regarding the place of authorial intention in editorial thinking and thus fails to offer a coherent case for the social approach to literature—which is in fact an important and fruitful approach. As with McGann's position, the "force" of McKenzie's " 'sociology of the text,' " according to Sutherland, is that "it specifically controverts the faith of modern bibliography," in this case by emphasizing the importance of contemporary typography and layout as "subtle links which bind a literary work to its time," links that are claimed to be severed by scholarly critical editions (p. 279). I would instead think about whether graphic design is always an integral element in the conception of verbal works and whether one cannot have a legitimate interest in the minds of individual authors as well as in the collaborative physical products of printers and publishers.

Sutherland's political approach to these scholars' work trivializes the fields of publishing history and textual criticism by treating them as

---

G. Thomas Tanselle is vice president of the John Simon Guggenheim Memorial Foundation and adjunct professor of English and comparative literature at Columbia University. The author of many essays on bibliographical and textual matters, he has most recently published *Textual Criticism Since Greg: A Chronicle, 1950–1985* (1987) and *A Rationale of Textual Criticism* (1989).

academic games in which one gains publicity by attacking orthodoxies. Any field can benefit, of course, from vigorous debate and challenges to entrenched positions, if the debates are intellectually serious and the established positions ill-founded and stifling. But if the discussions are motivated by "career manoeuvres" and the nature of the "establishment" is misunderstood, the results are not likely to be a gain for the cause of scholarship. Sutherland seems to envisage a surprisingly powerful bibliographical establishment displaying all the shortcomings that he finds attributed to it by these three scholars. It is unfortunate that he did not look into the substantive issues more independently. When he comments on McKenzie's position, for instance, he reports—without raising any objection—that it "controverts the faith of modern bibliography in the reproducibility of the 'essential' text, if only institutionally approved procedures are followed" (p. 279). The last clause is presumably a reference, at least in part, to the Center for Editions of American Authors and its successor, the Center for (or Committee on) Scholarly Editions, of the Modern Language Association of America, with its program of awarding an emblem of approval to editions that meet its standards. Although that program may in some ways have been a mistake, it did not spring from an intolerant narrowmindedness. The emblem reads "An Approved Edition," not "The Approved Edition," and those who devised it, as well as many of those connected with the Center in other ways, have made a point of insisting that more than one responsible approach exists and that no critical edition is ever "definitive." (The CSE's official statement in 1977 said explicitly that the emblem carries "no implication that the texts involved are the only responsible or valuable ones that can be prepared.")[1] The bulk of the discussion stimulated by the Center has emphasized authorial intention on the assumption that a concern with texts as the collaborative products that reached the public could best be served by facsimile, not critical, editions. Editors focusing on authorial intention have never, as far as I am aware, thought they were producing what Sutherland calls (in a variation on his earlier phrase) an "ahistorically essential text" (p. 279); they were attempting the historical task of reconstructing the text intended by the author at a particular time. And using the work of W. W. Greg as a general guide regarding intention has given full rein to individual editorial judgment, as the diversity of the published CEAA/CSA editions attests. It is ironic that some of those who favor a social approach to literature attack the CEAA/CSE as a doctrinaire institution, when their own effort to discredit other approaches is a far more doctrinaire way of proceeding.

An example is offered by Sutherland's summary of McGann's views. In the course of it he says, "Ideally, the Bowersonian editor should be a clairvoyant, since only by penetrating to the pre-scriptive level of thought

---

1. *The Center for Scholarly Editions: An Introductory Statement* (New York, 1977), p. 4.

process can 'intention' be satisfactorily located," but "the laws of physics prevent him being a mind reader" (p. 273). By couching this statement in sarcastic terms and offering no criticism of its implications, Sutherland is apparently willing to be understood as believing that a concern with authorial intention is too subjective to be worthy of historical scholarship. But all reconstructions of the past are subjective, being inferences drawn from what we believe to be the relevant surviving evidence; the search for intentions is no different in this respect from the effort to understand the sociology of literary production. Furthermore, everything that happened in the past is of interest (if, that is, we are interested in history at all) and worth the effort of attempting to reconstruct it—including the intentions, motivations, and other thoughts that particular minds have had at given times. Because the texts we encounter in printed or manuscript documents can only be instructions for re-creating works, not the works themselves (the medium of literature being language, not paper and ink), we are presented with two coordinate classes of historical pursuits: one looks at the texts surviving in documents, each of which is the collaborative result of the efforts of all the people involved in its production and preserves the wording actually read by an audience; the other attempts to assess the accuracy with which the texts of documents reflect the intended texts of works and then to reconstruct those intended texts, focusing on the intentions of the authors alone or of the authors in conjunction with certain other individuals. Anyone who feels that an undue emphasis has previously been placed on one of these historical goals is not making the best case for the other by claiming that the supposedly dominant one is inappropriate, instead of accepting it as one of the alternative possibilities and concentrating on the merits of the neglected one. When Sutherland introduces an example from Anthony Trollope to illustrate what McGann's approach entails, he refers to the "facts" that would be "ignored in the misbegotten quest for what Trollope originally intended" (p. 276). No one should ignore relevant evidence, obviously, but relevance is determined by the goal; and to regard a quest that one is not personally drawn to as misbegotten seems the antithesis of the frame of mind underlying scholarly endeavor.

Sutherland's principal substantive point is that there is a "large and troubling hole at the centre" of literary sociology, formed by "scholarly ignorance about book trade and publishing history technicalities" (p. 267). A great amount of research has in fact been accomplished on printing and publishing history, but much more remains to be done, as in all other fields; and it is of course true that some literary historians are neglectful of what already exists. The main obstacle to progress in the field, Sutherland argues (echoing Darnton), is the lack of "binding theoretical coherence" (p. 269)—which for him seems to mean the lack of likely sponsorship by an academic department. He asserts that "without theoretic formulation, the publishing history enterprise very quickly founders on intractable hard cases" and immediately adds: "Put in the form of a blunt example: it is difficult to see either history or English as disciplines happily sponsoring a comprehensive account of sheet-music publishing in the nineteenth century" (p. 281). Why should they sponsor it, rather than musicology? More important, why do not the interconnections among social, cultural, textual, printing, and publishing history provide sufficient "theoretic formulation" or "binding theoretical coherence" on which to proceed? Textual study is central to these interconnections: first, because (looking backward from the moment of publication) the wording and punctuation of texts are affected by the physical processes of printing and the business negotiations of publishing that brought them to the public; second, because (looking forward from the moment of publication) the precise makeup of the text of every edition of a work influences the way in which that work will be understood by those who read and comment on it and in turn determines the impact that the work will have on society.

All forms of research in these fields—from the analysis of compositors' stints to the examination of bookstore inventories and library circulation records—thus fall into place as contributory elements in a single great enterprise. Sutherland's idea that bibliographical studies have now been "regenerated" from their "traditional 'analytic' form" (p. 269) suggests a lack of openness to the full range of bibliographical work; in the urge to elevate the study of typography and format for their social implications, he undervalues another way of reading physical evidence: for what it can reveal about printing-shop procedures and textual history. It should be no cause for concern that those who are interested in pursuing one or another specialty within this encompassing design will inevitably come from a variety of disciplinary backgrounds—nor that their work is unlikely to be coordinated in an orderly fashion. Sutherland is being unrealistic when he recommends, "For the moment, publishing history should probably decline to write itself, concentrating instead on the preliminary business of gathering itself" (p. 282). Scholarship does not progress in this way. There is never a time when all the evidence has been gathered, nor a time when the last word of synthesis has been uttered. We need both approaches at all times, continually revising our synthetic accounts as new evidence requires, but having such accounts available as a context for the new evidence. It is clear, as these comments show, that I would approach Sutherland's topic very differently; but it is equally clear, I think, that we both believe in the importance of publishing history and consider it integral to textual criticism and literary history.

Index

———